LITERATURE AND THE ARTS IN THE REIGN OF FRANCIS I

ESSAYS PRESENTED TO C.A. MAYER

EDITED BY

PAULINE M. SMITH

AND

I.D. McFARLANE

FRENCH FORUM, PUBLISHERS
LEXINGTON, KENTUCKY

co

301846

Library of Congress Catalog Card Number 84-81850

ISBN 0-917058-56-9

Printed in the United States of America

CONTENTS

ACKNOWLEDGEMENTS

Acknowledgement is made to the following institutions and agencies for permission to reproduce illustrations: Fig. I, VIII, IX, XI, XV, XVI, XVIII (Bibliothèque Nationale, Paris, Cabinet des Estampes); fig. XVII (Bibliothèque Nationale, Paris, Réserve); fig. II (Musée de la Société de l'Histoire du protestantisme français, Paris. Photo Bulloz); fig. III (Musée du Louvre, Paris. Photo Agraci); fig. X (Musée de Cluny, Paris); fig. XII (Bibliothèque municipale, Arras. Photo Giraudon); fig. V, VII (Musée historique de la Réformation, Geneva); fig. IV (Museo Civico, Piacenza); fig. VI (Museum Slaskie, Wroclaw).

Unless otherwise stated, all references to Marot's works are to the critical edition in 6 volumes by C.A. Mayer (1958-1980). The following abbreviations are used for the separate volumes: *Ep.* (*Les Epîtres*); *OS, Oeuvres satiriques*; *OL, Oeuvres lyriques*; *OD, Oeuvres diverses*; *E, Les Epigrammes*; *T, Les Traductions*.

PREFACE

C.A. MAYER

Klaus Mayer was born in Mainz on 16 November 1918; but the emergence of Nazism in Germany resulted in his family moving to France and, after a few years, to England. All these interruptions in the normal tenor of his adolescence must have had a most disrupting effect, but there was at the same time a silver lining to that cloud, in that he grew up under the sign of three major cultures, an experience that was to be of immense benefit in his professional career. The War, during which he served in the British army, brought further delays and he was nearly thirty years old when he took a First in French at University College, London. His Ph.D. was completed within two years, all the more remarkable for its dealing with a wide-ranging subject: satire in French literature from 1525 to 1560, with particular reference to sources and technique. An interesting aspect of this monograph was the attention paid to Lucian, and though in recent years a number of scholars have followed the same trail, Klaus' pioneer work has not yet been superseded.

Posts and security of tenure were not easy to find after the War, but Klaus was appointed Assistant at University College for the year 1948-1949; he subsequently held posts at Hull, Southampton and Bedford College, London, where he was promoted to a Readership in 1959. By then he had already built up an impressive number of publications and it came as no surprise that he was offered the Chair of French at Liverpool University in 1965, a post he was to occupy for the next thirteen years.

Above all, Klaus has made his name as the editor and biographer of Clément Marot. One may be rather surprised that, until he worked on the poet, no reliable edition of his poetry was available, and that in spite of the fact that until recently Marot was considered a major link in the traditional view of French poetry. Marot had been unlucky enough to attract scholars whose career was cut short prematurely, Charles Guiffrey and Pierre Villey; I am not sure whether that pioneer in Marot studies, Philipp-August Becker, ever got round to planning a critical edition of his works.

Of course, Marot is a particularly difficult author to edit: many poems have been attributed to him on grounds that do not stand up to close scrutiny, and there remain doubts about the authenticity of certain texts. Religious considerations have compounded the problems, not all editions published in Marot's lifetime have equal value and quite a number of poems were published after his death, sometimes a long time later. Klaus brought to his edition an unrivalled knowledge of the period, a sound bibliographical training, a critical sense able to cope with the problems posed by the texts and a very high standard of accuracy. The basic *instrument de travail* appeared early on, the *Bibliographie des Oeuvres de Clément Marot* (1954), building on and going beyond Villey's pioneer work in the field. Then over the years the volumes gradually saw the light of day, beginning with the *Epîtres* in 1958 and ending with the *Traductions* in 1980. At last we had an edition on which scholars could rely and which should remain the standard one for a very long time to come. During the appearance of the series, other substantial works were also coming out, including the life of Clément Marot in 1972: anyone who has tackled the life of a Renaissance humanist or author knows the difficulties that surround the task: the loss of correspondence, the years for which no evidence has survived, the silence of friends and colleagues, the disappearance of key documents over the centuries, the reticences of the poet himself in a period when silence could be the better part of valor. At the same time, a steady stream of articles appeared, sometimes on points of more detailed relevance to Marot, but equally often on other topics pertinent to the first half of the century.

Klaus' boundless energy has not confined itself to scholarly matters within his chosen field. He was for many years a prominent member of the Society for French Studies of which he was successively Secretary (in which capacity he served generously from 1962-1969), Vice-President (1969-1970), President (1970-1972) and retiring Vice-President (1972-1973). Other concerns have continued to take up his time and vitality. There is his deep and abiding interest in opera, on which he can talk endlessly, well-informed and entertaining; better known probably is his enthusiasm for the theater, both as actor and as producer. He has put on a series of plays, especially at London University, by Sartre, Anouilh, Ionesco, Cocteau, productions characterized by thoroughness, polish and satisfying tempo. We all know just how time-consuming such undertakings can be, and the frustration and deficiencies that always seem to beset their preparation until, by some splendid magic, it comes right on the night. And there is Klaus' passion for gastronomy: he is a superb cook—is there any secret link between acting and cooking? It is remarkable how some of the finest restaurants in the land are run by former actors, all the better it seems for not going through the traditional hoops of cookery schools. At all events, Klaus' talents would put to shame many with professional claims; I remember, fifteen years on, a memorable Renaissance banquet (on which, naturally, there figured a coq-à-l'âne) at which Henri and Catherine Weber, the greatly lamented Franco Simone and myself were fortunate enough to be present. Coming away from a hard-working but rewarding colloquium, we were only too ready for such mouth-watering *divertissement*.

Publishing scholarly contributions is no doubt very satisfying, but it is equally, if not more, gratifying to see one's interests prolonged through the research students one has helped to train and who will go on to make a name for themselves in the profession. Over the years, Klaus has produced a series of young scholars whose theses, more often than not, have been deemed worthy of publication. These works range from thematic studies to sound editions of authors whose writings had long been crying out for modern scholarship to take an interest in them. Moreover, almost all these works have been published abroad, in Switzerland and in Germany.

Of course, it is not only Klaus' students who have made themselves known abroad; he himself has long had a wide and learned following among his colleagues in Europe and in America; he has often been invited to lecture, especially in France, and he has enjoyed the distinction of having an honorary doctorate bestowed on him by the University of Montpellier; and this *Festschrift*, by the range and quality of its foreign contributions, shows the regard in which he is held in the world of scholarship; indeed, the list of contributors might have been rather longer, had illness or heavy commitments not prevented friends from meeting the deadline. In all this activity, Klaus has been fortunate in having the dedicated support and collaboration of his wife, who has herself published in the same field and with her special interests brings her own contribution to Marot studies. May Klaus see in this *Festschrift* a token of the esteem in which his work is held in the British Isles and beyond.

Ian McFarlane

D. Bentley-Cranch

A LIST OF THE PUBLICATIONS OF C.A. MAYER

Bibliographie des Oeuvres de Clément Marot. I. *Manuscrits.* II. *Editions.*
Travaux d'Humanisme et Renaissance, 10 and 13. Geneva: Droz,
1954; t. II, revised and reprinted, Paris: Nizet, 1975.
Clément Marot, *Oeuvres complètes.* Edition critique. 6 vols. 1958-1980.
      I. *Les Epîtres.* London: The Athlone Press, 1958; rpt. 1964;
          rpt. with revised introduction, Paris: Nizet, 1977.
      II. *Oeuvres satiriques.* London: The Athlone Press, 1962.
      III. *Oeuvres lyriques.* London: The Athlone Press, 1964.
      IV. *Oeuvres diverses.* London: The Athlone Press, 1966.
      V. *Les Epigrammes.* London: The Athlone Press, 1970.
      VI. *Les Traductions.* Geneva: Slatkine, 1980.
La Religion de Marot. Travaux d'Humanisme et Renaissance, 39. Geneva:
Droz, 1960; rpt. Paris: Nizet, 1973.
Anthologie de Clément Marot. Ecrivains d'hier et d'aujourd'hui, 16. Paris:
Seghers, 1964; rpt. 1969.
Clément Marot. Paris: Nizet, 1972.
Clément Marot. L'Enfer, les Coq-à-l'âne, les Elégies. Edition Critique. Paris:
Champion, 1977.
Lucien de Samosate et la Renaissance française. La Renaissance française,
3. Geneva: Slatkine, 1984.

ARTICLES

"The Lucianism of Des Périers." *Bibliothèque d'Humanisme et Renaissance,* 12 (1950), 190-207.

"Pierre Tolet and the *Paradoxe de la faculté du vinaigre.*" *Bibliothèque d'Humanisme et Renaissance*, 13 (1951), 83-88.

"L'Honnête Homme: Molière and Philibert de Vienne's *Philosophe de Court.*" *Modern Language Review*, 46 (1951), 196-217.

"*Satyre* as a Dramatic Genre." *Bibliothèque d'Humanisme et Renaissance*, 13 (1951), 327-33.

"The Genesis of a Rabelaisian Character:Menippus and Frère Jean." *French Studies*, 6 (1952), 219-29.

"Le Texte de Marot." *Bibliothèque d'Humanisme et Renaissance*, 14 (1952), 314-28; 15 (1953), 71-91.

"Une Edition inconnue de Clément Marot." *Bulletin du Bibliophile* (1953), pp. 151-66.

"Rabelais's Satirical Eulogy: The Praise of Borrowing." In *François Rabelais, 1553-1953.* Geneva: Droz, 1953, pp. 147-55.

"Réalisme et fantaisie dans l'œuvre de Rabelais" (paper read at the 5th Congress of the Association Guillaume Budé, Tours, September 1953). *L'Information Littéraire* (October, 1953), pp. 127-31.

"Une Epigramme inédite de Clément Marot." *Bibliothèque d'Humanisme et Renaissance*, 16 (1954), 209-11.

"Une Plaquette contenant une ode de J. Du Bellay." *Bibliothèque d'Humanisme et Renaissance*, 17 (1955), 284-85.

"The Problem of Dolet's Evangelical Publications." *Bibliothèque d'Humanisme et Renaissance*, 17 (1955), 405-14.

"Le Départ de Marot de Ferrare." *Bibliothèque d'Humanisme et Renaissance*, 18 (1956), 197-221.

"Clément Marot et le grand Minos." *Bibliothèque d'Humanisme et Renaissance*, 19 (1957), 482-84.

"Clément Marot et le général de Caen." *Bibliothèque d'Humanisme et Renaissance*, 20 (1958), 277-95.

"Clément Marot et le docteur Bouchart." *Bibliothèque d'Humanisme et Renaissance*, 21 (1959), 98-102.

"La Fantaisie dans l'œuvre de Marot." *Annales de l'Institut d'Etudes Occitanes* (1960), pp. 82-87.

"*Rabelais poète*" (with C.M. Douglas). *Bibliothèque d'Humanisme et Renaissance*, 14 (1962), 42-46.

"Coq-à-l'âne, définition, invention, attribution." *French Studies*, 16 (1962), 1-13.

"Notes sur la réputation de Marot au XVIIe et XVIIIe siècles." *Bibliothèque d'Humanisme et Renaissance*, 25 (1963), 404-407.

"Ronsard et Molinet." *Bibliothèque d'Humanisme et Renaissance*, 26 (1964), 121-22.

"Le Premier Pétrarquiste français, Jean Marot" (with D. Bentley-Cranch). *Bibliothèque d'Humanisme et Renaissance,* 27 (1965), 183-85.

"Le *Sermon du bon pasteur*: un problème d'attribution." *Bibliothèque d'Humanisme et Renaissance,* 27 (1965), 286-303.

"Encore une édition inconnue de Clément Marot." *Bibliothèque d'Humanisme et Renaissance,* 27 (1965), 669-71.

"Clément Marot, poète pétrarquiste" (with D. Bentley-Cranch). *Bibliothèque d'Humanisme et Renaissance,* 28 (1966), 32-51.

"Marot et 'Celle qui fut s'amye.'" *Bibliothèque d'Humanisme et Renaissance,* 28 (1966), 369-76.

"Un Manuscrit important pour le texte de Marot." *Bibliothèque d'Humanisme et Renaissance,* 28 (1966), 419-26.

"Marot et l'archaïsme" (paper read at the 18th Congress of the Association Internationale des Etudes Françaises, Paris, July 1966). *Cahiers de l'Association Internationale des Etudes Françaises,* 19 (1967), 27-37.

"Le Premier Sonnet français: Marot, Mellin de Saint-Gelais et Jean Bouchet." *Revue d'Histoire Littéraire de la France,* 67, No. 3 (1967), 481-93.

"Les Oeuvres de Clément Marot: l'économie de l'édition critique." *Bibliothèque d'Humanisme et Renaissance,* 29 (1967), 357-72.

"Clément Marot and Literary History." In *Studies in French Literature Presented to H.W. Lawton.* Manchester: Manchester Univ. Press, 1968, pp. 247-60.

"Bonaventure des Périers," "Marguerite de Navarre," "Clément Marot." Entries in *The Penguin Companion to Literature. II. European.* Harmondsworth: Penguin Books, 1969, pp. 224, 510, 513-14.

"La Première Epigramme française: Clément Marot, Jean Bouchet et Michel d'Amboise. Définition, sources, antériorité" (with P.M. Smith). *Bibliothèque d'Humanisme et Renaissance,* 32 (1970), 579-602.

"*La Tierce Epistre de l'Amant Verd* de Jean Lemaire de Belges." In *Mélanges d'histoire et de critique littéraire offerts à Pierre Jourda, doyen honoraire de la Faculté des Lettres et des Sciences Humaines de Montpellier par ses collègues, ses élèves et ses amis.* Paris: Nizet, 1970, pp. 27-36.

"Le Texte des *Psaumes* de Marot." *Studi Francesi,* 43 (1971), 1-28.

"Prolégomènes à l'édition critique des *Psaumes* de Clément Marot." *Bibliothèque d'Humanisme et Renaissance,* 35 (1973), 55-71.

"Lucien et la Renaissance." *Revue de Littérature Comparée,* 47 (1973), 5-22.

"Clément Marot." Entry in *Dizionario critico della letteratura francese.* Turin: UTET, 1973, pp. 750-53.

"Gabriele Simeoni et le premier sonnet français." *Studi Francesi*, 53 (1974), 213-23.

"Le Personnage du pédant chez Molière." *Studi Francesi*, 57 (1975), 411-27.

"Du nouveau sur le sonnet français: Marot, Du Bellay et Castiglione." *Studi Francesi*, 60 (1976), 422-29.

"Clément Marot et ses protecteurs." In *Culture et pouvoir au temps de l'Humanisme et de la Renaissance* (Actes du Congrès Marguerite de Savoie. Annecy-Chambéry-Turin, avril 1974). Geneva: Slatkine; Paris: Champion, 1978, pp. 259-70.

"Monologue ou récit-aveu comme technique satirique." *Studi Francesi*, 65-66 (1978), 373-79.

"Stoïcisme et purification du concept chez Montaigne." *Studi Francesi*, 72 (1980), 487-93.

"Florimond Robertet: Italianisme et Renaissance française" (with D. Bentley-Cranch). In *Mélanges en l'honneur de Franco Simone*. Vol. IV. Geneva: Slatkine, 1983, pp. 135-49.

"La Date de *L'Enfer* de Clément Marot." In *Mélanges en l'honneur d'Henri Weber* (in preparation).

"Evangélisme et protestantisme." *Studi Francesi* (in preparation).

D. Bentley-Cranch

The Iconography of Clément Marot

The iconography of Clément Marot deserves study, not only because it satisfies our natural curiosity about the appearance of an eminent sixteenth-century poet, but also because it covers an important period in the history of portrait painting.

Clément Marot was born at Cahors in the province of Quercy, probably in 1496.[1] The son of the *Rhétoriqueur* Jean Marot, Clément spent most of his life in various Courts; in 1506 he was with his father at the court of Anne de Bretagne; from 1519 to 1526 he was in the service of Marguerite d'Angoulême, future Queen of Navarre, and in 1527 he fulfilled his ambition of becoming *valet de chambre* of François Ier, a post which he occupied for nearly all the rest of his life. Suspected of favoring Lutheranism and forced to flee from France in October 1534 after the *Affaire des Placards*, he took refuge at the court of Renée, the French duchess of Ferrara, sister-in-law and cousin of François Ier. He remained in Ferrara until he fled to Venice in June 1536;[2] at the end of that year he travelled back to France, reaching the French court in March 1537. Five years later Marot was again forced to flee and this time he never returned to France. By way of Geneva and Savoy he reached Piedmont, and died at Turin in September 1544.

Although his life was troubled and relatively short, Clément Marot nonetheless managed to leave for posterity a considerable and everlasting poetical *œuvre*. Marot was an innovator in the truest sense of the word. Without posing as a revolutionary, he transformed wherever possible the poetry of the *Rhétoriqueurs*, discarding what could not be transformed, and replacing it by poetry modelled on Greek and Latin sources. By so doing, by imitating in an intelligent manner the poets of Antiquity as well as Petrarch, he well deserves to be called a Renaissance poet.

Marot was writing at a time when literature and art were closely linked and when intimate relations existed between writers and artists, not only because they were all members of the same Court circles but also because they all drew their ideas from a common source—Antiquity—and came under the influence of "Italianism" and the new ideas which were to result in Humanism.

In spite of these close links, poets were ahead of artists in assimilating the new ideas and transforming foreign influences into a native product. A striking example can be found in the translation, or rather, adaptation, of the *Trionfi* of Petrarch by Jean Robertet (a contemporary of the father of Clément Marot and who probably died about 1502), in which he reduced Petrarch's very lengthy work into six nine-lined verses.[3] In these poems Jean Robertet introduces both the beginning of the "Italianism" which was to spread throughout France, and one of the themes characteristic of the Renaissance, the conception of man's immortality due to his virtuous life, an immortality conferred by the poet who is himself endowed with divine inspiration. And yet the method which Robertet chose to disseminate his ideas is completely out of sympathy with those ideas; his poems were woven on the borders of tapestries depicting the Triumphs in a style so completely medieval—lack of perspective, a confused mingling of background and foreground, a mass of bizarre details, crowds of people all labelled with their names, and so on—as to be called "style Rhétoriqueur," and which demonstrates the artist's inability to understand the poet.[4]

Later, artists were to achieve parity with writers, and that in the sphere of portrait painting. The portrait, in the Middle Ages an object, in the physical sense, almost interchangeable with the person it represented—carried on pilgrimages in place of the supplicant, sent to royal suitors during marriage negotiations, placed near the statues of saints in churches to afford the givers saintly protection, etc.—the portrait had become, with a few exceptions, an effigy, and an effigy which established its identity not by a likeness but by an entourage of identifying objects and attributes. Three painters, Jean Clouet (c. 1485-1541), his son François Clouet (c. 1510-1572)—both immaterially and confusingly called "Janet" by their contemporaries—and Corneille de Lyon (?—c. 1574) succeeded in transforming the portrait in France, by a technique probably modelled on that of Florentine artists and especially on that of Leonardo da Vinci, allied to a masterly capacity of observation in all that concerns the human face. All their work shows clearly that they conceived the portrait as having to be able to represent, at one and the same time, a sharply defined moment in the sitter's life, and a link for all eternity between the sitter, the painter, and the spectator. By so doing, they joined the poets in assimilating in the portrait the Renaissance ideals of the glorification and immortality of man culminating in Humanism.

When considering the iconography of Clément Marot, several different factors have to be taken into account: the physical possibility of meetings between the poet and his real or supposed painters, the question of who ordered the portraits and for what purpose, and the problem of the "lost originals" which served as models for later reproductions. The latter two factors may be put aside for consideration with the portraits in question. The first raises a problem which has been endlessly discussed and for which there is no satisfactory answer: where did the writers and artists who held the post of *valet de chambre du roi* spend most of their time? Did they follow the Court about in all its wanderings throughout France, or did they have permanent lodgings in Paris or in the provinces? As regards Clément Marot, his presence near the king does not appear to have been obligatory, and he seems to have divided his time between the Court and Paris.[5] In his poetry he implies that he has a lodging in Paris.[6] It was in Paris that Marot, suspected of Lutheran tendencies, was arrested in 1526 during the absence from that city of his protector Marguerite de Navarre; it was again in Paris that he was threatened with arrest in 1532 during the absence of François Ier,[7] and when that monarch presented Marot with a house in 1539, it was in Paris that this house was situated.[8]

Of the three portrait painters already mentioned, Jean Clouet, a foreigner who was never naturalized, seems to have resided in Tours between 1521 and 1526. After that date documents indicate that he lived in Paris until his death in 1541.[9] His son François, who certainly worked with his father, probably spent most of his time in Paris.[10] Corneille de Lyon, a native of The Hague (and also known as Corneille de La Haye), arrived in France at an unknown date; he was certainly established in Lyons by 1533,[11] and the Lyons Archives mention his name from 1544 until 1574.[12] It is possible, therefore, that he spent almost all his life in Lyons.

The first portrait of Clément Marot to be discussed falls into the category of "lost originals." It concerns a picture, supposedly painted by Holbein, known today only through 18th- and 19th-century prints. (Fig. I). Holbein (born at Augsburg in 1497-98, died in London in 1543) visited France during the year 1524.[13] Little is known of his activities during this visit, although the theory that he used his time to learn, from Jean Clouet, both the method of drawing with colored chalks[14] and the art of miniature painting,[15] is an interesting one. In 1538 and 1539, Holbein, then in the service of King Henry VIII of England, was sent abroad several times to draw the portraits of possible wives for his master; on March 12, 1538 he portrayed Christine, Duchess of Milan,[16] in Brussels, in June Louise de Guise at Le Havre,[17] in August in Joinville he looked in vain for Renée de Guise, but managed in the same month to draw Anne de Lorraine at Nancy.[18] In July 1539 he visited the Duchy of Cleves to portray Anne of Cleves.[19] If the lost portrait of Marot was Holbein's work, the question arises as to when they met. Was it during Holbein's first visit when Marot's career was just beginning, or was it during Holbein's flying visits during 1538 and 1539 when Marot's fame was at its height? And if Holbein did paint Marot, was it because he was attracted by the poet's humanism? Unanswerable questions. It is well known, however, that Holbein, a friend and protégé of Erasmus, felt at home in humanist circles in Basle and later in London. It was in London that he drew the portrait of another French humanist poet, Nicolas Bourbon,[20] who had fled from France to seek refuge at the English Court. Bourbon was to immortalize the artist both by using the portrait as the frontispiece for his books,[21] and by praising Holbein in his well-known verses.[22] There can be no doubt that Nicolas Bourbon was Marot's friend, contributing a liminary poem to the latter's *Adolescence Clementine* in 1532[23] and repeating this friendly gesture in the *Suite de l'Adolescence Clementine* published in 1533.[24] If in reality Holbein painted Marot—and the absence of the slightest word of thanks or praise for Holbein in all Marot's work must be noted[25]—then Holbein's pictures of French subjects would consist, apart from those of the "prospective brides" of Henry VIII already described, and those of three French ambassadors posted to England,[26] only of those of the two humanist poets. It should be added, however, that all Holbein's work is not known to us.

Another factor in this problem is the confusion between "Janet" (see p. 18) and Holbein in the 18th and 19th centuries, when works were attributed at random to either of these artists.[27] The possibility arises, therefore, that Jean or François Clouet could be the painter of this "lost original." It is certain that Marot knew the Clouets and admired their work, even going so far as to compare "Janet" with Michelangelo:

> Christ y verrez par David figuré,
> Et ce qu'il a pour noz maulx enduré,
> Voyre mieulx painct mille ans ains sa venue
> Qu'apres la chose escripte & advenue
> Ne le paindroient (qui est cas bien estrange)
> Le tien Janet ne le grand Miquel l'ange.
> (*T*, XV, I, *Clem. Marot, Au Roy Treschres-*
> *tien Françoys, premier du nom. S.*, vv. 83-88)

but in the absence of the slightest proof in favor of this hypothesis, the problem admits of no solution.

In the prints derived from this "lost original," Marot is dressed in a tunic buttoned up to the throat, a coat and a little cap. He has a moustache, and a beard which is fairly long and divided into two points. He has a somber look and rather piercing eyes. These details are constant, but variations occur: in some versions Marot is turned three-quarters to the right,[28] in others three-quarters to the left;[29] some versions have the oval frame of the picture decorated with flowers, musical instruments and the fool's cap and bells;[30] others add J.-B. Rousseau's laudatory verses on Marot;[31] one version, by emphasizing the somber look, succeeds in turning Marot into a fanatical and romantic visionary.[32] All versions mention Holbein ("Holbein pinx," "D'après le tableau d'Holbein," etc.) and in those versions where the date of Marot's death is included, this date is always incorrect (1554).

For the next portrait, the problem is different. There is no question of a "lost original" since the portrait is in existence; the question is rather to establish the identity both of the painter and the subject. In this picture (Fig. II), now in the Musée de la Société de l'histoire du protestantisme français,[33] the subject is turned three-quarters to the left and looks directly at the spectator. He has a thin moustache and a short beard, and is wearing a black tunic with a turned-down white collar and a black cap. Everything in this beautiful picture—the sideways turn of the body, the position of the head, the feeling that the subject with his half-defiant, half-ironic expression is forcing himself to look at the spectator—indicates an attribution to the painter Moroni, and recently the picture was exhibited as the work of this master.[34] But, if the painter is Moroni—and it cannot be denied that the attribution is very likely—is it possible that the subject could be Clément Marot? Moroni was born about 1520-25 in Albino near Bergamo, and passed almost all his life, until his death in 1578, in Brescia, where he worked with Moretto, and in Bergamo. It is not known definitely whether he ever visited Venice, although in that town his works were known and admired, especially by Titian. Clément Marot journeyed twice through Italy during his two exiles; on his first visit, he arrived at the court of Ferrara about May 1535 and stayed there until the following year. In June 1536 he had to flee to Venice, where he wrote several of his most beautiful poems.[35] Having received permission to return to France, he arrived in Lyons, via Geneva, towards November or December 1536. During his second exile, he remained in Geneva probably from December 1542 until the end of 1543. He then went via Annecy, Bellegarde and Chambéry to reach Piedmont during the summer of 1544, dying suddenly in Turin in September 1544.[36] Taking these itineraries into account, it is hardly feasible to imagine that Moroni would be precocious enough to produce such a portrait in 1536. The only other possible time for a meeting between the painter and the poet, therefore, would appear to be the few weeks or months during the summer and autumn of 1544 when Marot's exact whereabouts are not definitely known. It must be admitted, in defence of the identification of the subject as Marot, that the portrait shows an extraordinary resemblance to the poet as revealed by his iconography. In the absence of any real documentary evidence, however, the problem remains insoluble.

Returning from his first exile, Marot arrived in Lyons in November or December 1536. His presence in that town is mentioned in a letter from the Cardinal de Tournon, Governor of Lyons, to Anne de Montmorency, dated December 14.[37] At Lyons, between that date and January 1, 1537, Marot fulfilled the necessary condition for his return to France, that is to say, he underwent the ceremony of recantation. Eustorg de Beaulieu, in a poem which he addressed to Marot by way of a New Year's greeting, made a clear allusion to this ceremony,[38] as did Marot himself in his light-hearted cantique, Les Adieux de Marot à la ville de Lyon (OL, LXXVII, Cantique II), written when he left Lyons. The date of his departure is uncertain, but by the end of February Marot was in Paris.[39] The painter Corneille de Lyon was settled in Lyons by 1533 (see p. 19); it is possible that he took advantage of Marot's stay in Lyons during the winter of 1536-37[40] to take the portrait of a poet whose religious ideas appear to have tallied with his own.[41] Now in the Louvre,[42] this portrait (Fig. III), of which there is a copy at Piacenza[43] (Fig. IV), shows the poet wearing a black cap and a black tunic with a white collar; his beard and hair are black and his eyes are brown. Turned almost three-quarters to the left, he is looking directly at the spectator. The beautiful workmanship of this picture—which by its tiny dimensions could be classified as a miniature—places it among the best works of a painter whose portraits, to judge by contemporary opinion, were very lifelike. Thus, Eustorg de Beaulieu enthuses:

> Pour bien tirer ung personnage au vif
> Ung Painctre dict Cornylle est aloué
> Et de plusieurs extimé & loué
> N'avoir en France aulcung comparatif.
>
> Car veu son œuvre, on dict de cueur hastif
> C'est tel, c'est telle! O l'homme bien doué
>   Pour bien tirer.
> Bref, ce qu'il painct monstre ung Incarnatif
> Qu'on diroit Chair, dont il est advoué

N'avoir eu per puis le temps de Noé
Non Apelles, jadis superlatif
Pour bien tirer.[44]

Of all the portraits of Marot perhaps this picture is the only authentic one.[45]

Geneva was visited twice by Marot (see p. 21); in that town, at the Musée historique de la Réformation, are two portraits of the poet which are noteworthy, not so much from the artistic point of view, since neither reaches the standard of Corneille de Lyon's work, but rather because of their close links with other representations of Marot. The first of these portraits[46] (Fig. V) shows the poet turned almost three-quarters to the left, looking directly at the spectator with a gloomy expression; the black beard, hair and dress—lightened only by a scrap of white ruffle—melt into the somber background. This portrait, of mediocre craftsmanship, appears to have been the model for a picture of Marot in the possession of one of the most outstanding art collectors in the second half of the 16th century, Thomas Rhediger. Rhediger, born in 1540 at Striesa near Wroclaw (formerly Breslau) into a rich family, spent his short life in studying (notably at Wittenberg under Melanchthon), in travelling, in associating with scholars and intellectuals—Henri Estienne was one of the writers whom he protected—and in being a patron of the arts. At his death, due to an accident, in 1576, his library of more than 6,000 books and 300 manuscripts[47] and his collections of pictures, medals and other works of art, were bequeathed to his family with instructions to display them in suitable surroundings at Breslau, and this was done. In 1865 his books and manuscripts were removed to the Town Library in Breslau, and the pictures were placed in the Kunstgewerbe Museum, from which they were transferred to the Museum Slaskie, again in Wroclaw, in 1956. Rhediger's collections, therefore, were never dispersed, and the provenance of his pictures can be traced with certainty. The portrait of Marot[48] (Fig. VI) is one of a collection of nineteen pictures, of which eighteeen are single portraits while the last shows a group of scholars including Guillaume Budé. The subjects of the portraits are those which appear constantly in 16th-century collections, being French kings, queens and Court personalities.[49] Clément Marot, whether present in his role as a humanist poet or as a religious martyr, is the exception in this company. The unknown artist who painted this portrait has cleverly succeeded, while basing himself entirely on the above mentioned model and retaining the same pose and facial features, in dispersing the gloomy broodiness of the original and showing us a Marot, perhaps idealized but nevertheless serious, high-minded and intelligent.

The second portrait of Marot (Fig. VII) in the Musée historique de la

Réformation in Geneva was probably the model not only for another representation of Marot in Thomas Rhediger's collections, in this case a wax medallion (see p. 25), but also for a large number of posthumous prints of the poet (see p. 25), and owing to its close links with Théodore de Bèze it may well be authentic. There is no documentary proof that Théodore de Bèze, scholar, poet, reformer and Calvin's disciple, met Marot when the latter stayed in Geneva from December 1542 until the end of 1543, but it would be surprising if he had not done so. It is well known that during Marot's visit Calvin tried unsuccessfully to obtain a pension for the poet from the Conseil de la Ville de Genève[50] to enable him to complete his translation of the Psalms, and that in the end Bèze undertook this work. In his book, of which the Latin edition, *Icones id est verae imagines virorum* . . . was published by Jean de Laon in Geneva, 1580, and the French edition in 1581,[51] Bèze praised Marot for the services he had rendered to the Church by his Psalm translations,[52] adding in homage the well-known lines:

> J'admire ton esprit en mille inventions,
> Qui ton nom graveront au temple de Memoire,
> Mais des Pseaumes saincts, tes riches versions
> Te couronnent, Marot, d'une eternelle gloire.

Was Bèze the first owner of the portrait in question? It seems almost possible to trace it back to him. Bèze's adopted granddaughter, Mlle de Bèze, married his godson and disciple, Théodore Tronchin (born in 1582) who by this marriage became Bèze's heir; and it was one of Tronchin's descendants, Jacqueline Tronchin, marquise de Hillerin, who gave this portrait of Marot to the Musée historique de la Réformation. In this picture,[53] Marot is shown in profile, a required pose at the time for frontispiece pictures.[54] It is obvious, given the provenance, that this portrait was the model for the woodcut of Marot with which Bèze illustrated his book[55] (Fig. VIII), and it is very probable that it was also the source for a whole series of posthumous representations of Marot, from the woodcut used as a frontispiece in the editions of Marot's *Oeuvres* published by Jean de Tournes,[56] and including the famous print by René Boivin (see p. 25). Several features of the portrait—the serious look, the slightly bent head, the thin arched eyebrow, the arrangement of the hair to show the high forehead, the drooping moustache, the full beard covering the chest, the sober garments[57]—are always to be found in the copies. Variations among the copies are due to the exaggeration of one or more of these features, by the addition of wrinkles on the forehead, by changing the black hair to white, by attempts to age the poet, to produce finally the venerable, romanticized Marot of the 19th-century print[58] (Fig. IX), where the poet, sitting at his worktable, surrounded by his books, wearing a big fur robe, holds his feathered pen while gazing in a distracted and melancholy fashion at his manuscript. However, the unknown artist who prepared the wax medallion of Marot for Thomas Rhediger (see p. 24)—of which the present whereabouts are unknown but of which there is a replica at the Musée de Cluny[59] (Fig. X)—while using as his source the same original portrait, succeeded, by simply slightly tilting up the downbent head and thus lifting the chin and beard off the chest, in producing a younger- and certainly happier-looking Marot. In Rhediger's collection of twenty wax medallions —unfortunately lost, but documented[60]—Marot is present either as the only poet, or else as a humanist and reformer in company with Luther and Melanchthon, in a collection consisting for the most part of French Court personages, just as he is the only poet in the similar, although incomplete, Cluny collections of wax medallions.[61]

When René Boivin (1525-?1580), one of the most important engravers of the period whose known work comprises more than 226 prints,[62] produced his engraving of Marot[63] (Fig. XI) in a series of portraits of outstanding Reformers, he probably also made use of the same portrait as a model and copied the principal features. The slight alterations which he made consisted of curling the poet's hair, drawing forward a curl on the forehead, exposing the lower lip and marking the forehead with three deep wrinkles. Boivin's print cannot be precisely dated. It was published in 1558 by Hieronymus Cock (1507-1570), himself a celebrated painter and engraver whose workshop at Antwerp became a meeting-place for humanists, in a book commemorating the victories of Charles V.[64] From the 16th century onwards Boivin's print was copied many times. One of the most interesting imitations (Fig. XII)—in reality an exact copy of the print —can be found in an album, now in the Bibliothèque Municipale in Arras,[65] which contains 280 portraits of noble families of France, Spain and the Low Countries. The artist who made the copy was probably Jacques Le Boucq (?-1573) of Valenciennes, historian, genealogist and collector, who, in his will, listed among his books, his "libvres a patrons de princes et pourtraictures servant a paintres et a orphebvres."[66] Passing next into the hands of Alexandre Le Blancq,[67] the album was at the Abbaye de Saint-Vaast in the 18th century, and finally reached the Bibliothèque Municipale in Arras. The inscriptions under the portrait of Marot, in four different hands (probably those of Jacques Le Boucq, Alexandre Le Blancq, his secretary and a monk of the Abbaye de Saint-Vaast[68]) provide extra interest: Marot, at first simply "Clément Marot poète français," becomes "l'un des premiers Huguenots du Royaume," to be described finally as the man who "a versifié les 50 premiers pseaumes en stile de derision et de Calvinisme." The history of this curious album throws a light on a common practice in 16th-century portrait painting: the compilation of books of "patrons" which could be copied and recopied, leading to the widespread dissemination of a particular representation which finally became, as it were, the official "effigy" of the subject.

The influence of Boivin's print of Marot has endured to the present day, serving as the model for two representations of the poet in his birthplace, Cahors: a monument erected in the town center[69] (Fig. XIII) and a bust in the Musée de Cahors[70] (Fig. XIV).

René Boivin followed up the success of his print of Marot with a second one (Fig. XV) in 1576,[71] which, in respect of the features, closely resembles the first. But, by replacing the sober clothes with a toga, by arranging the hair in a classical style, by placing a laurel wreath on the head, and especially by raising the pupil of the eye to gaze dreamily up to heaven, Boivin gave his public a Marot crowned with glory, a classical poet seeking his Muse. Boivin's second print was as popular as his first, being copied and recopied until the 19th century. One of these copies engraved by G.F.L. Debrie in 1729[72] (Fig. XVI) deserves mention; the bust of Marot is placed within an oval frame, decorated with garlands, on the top of which two cherubs hold Apollo's emblems. Beneath the frame a little scene is depicted, the subject of which appears to be the arrest of Marot; in a street crowded with horsemen and passersby, the poet, rather strangely clad in his toga and laurel wreath, is being seized by two men; in the right foreground a man hidden behind a wall is watching this, and in the left foreground a man points to the poet in a theatrical gesture addressed to the spectator.[73]

In 1553 Guillaume Roville published the *Première Partie* of his picture book, the *Promptuarium Iconum* or *Promptuaire des médailles* containing portraits and biographies of famous people from Adam to Quintilius;[74] he followed this with the *Seconde Partie*, from Jesus Christ to Henri II, at a date unknown but before the death of the latter in 1559.[75] From 1577 onwards he published a second enlarged edition "en laquelle sont adjoustez les personnages plus insignes, depuis survenuz." A portrait of Marot (Fig. XVII), which did not appear in the first edition, was published in the second. The pictures, all in the form of medallions (3.5 cm in diameter), were not, in respect of the 16th-century personages, original works but were all copied from existing portraits. For example, the picture of Queen Eléonore in widow's weeds was copied from the drawing by François Clouet, and the picture of Marguerite, daughter of François Ier, from the oil painting by Corneille de Lyon.[76] From what picture was the portrait of Marot copied? It appears to have been yet another "lost original." The little medallion shows the poet turned three-quarters to the right, with curly hair and a small beard, dressed in a toga, crowned with a laurel wreath, and having the jolly and slightly befuddled look of one of the followers of Bacchus, a view of Marot as disconcerting as the malicious and fanciful biography which accompanies the picture.[77] This medallion, in itself not particularly interesting, may have been the model for a 17th-century print[78] (Fig. XVIII) where Marot, transformed into an old and venerable "Jupiter-figure," gazes at the spectator with an austere yet kindly look—another example of the "glorification" of the poet by a posthumous "effigy."

How can the iconography of a 16th-century personage be evaluated? Shortly after having enjoyed enormous popularity, 16th-century portraits sank into an oblivion which has lasted almost to the present time. This lack of interest, together with the ravages of time and neglect, caused the irremediable loss of many works and thus renders impossible the task of assembling a complete "portrait gallery" of any personage of that period: such an iconography must always have many gaps. In the case of Clément Marot, the few portraits gathered together here—which, after all, represent only isolated moments, or phases of his life—do not disclose to us (to paraphrase Jean Pommier) "beaucoup de secrets que nous n'aurions pu découvrir par la consultation des documents écrits"[79] and, it must be added, by studying the works of the poet himself. The iconography of a 16th-century personage, therefore, while only partially satisfying our natural curiosity about the appearance of such a person, serves rather to shed light on the history of portrait painting. It draws attention to painters' methods, to the practice of compiling books of "patrons," to the multiple copies taken from a single model, to the changes effected in these copies with the subsequent weakening of the original features resulting either in "effigies" or romanticized versions, and above all it draws attention to the attitude of the 16th-century public. It may be observed that Jean Robertet, one of the first poets to try to give expression to Renaissance ideals (see p. 18), was somewhat revolutionary in advocating a development in the art of painting based on an understanding of the laws of perspective and the ability to achieve a likeness when, to satirize a bad painter, he wrote: "En perspective est ung peu inutile / Pareillement à faire ung doulx visaige."[80] Although, as has been shown (see pp. 18-19), the Renaissance portrait painters succeeded in transforming the portrait, this transformation was never really appreciated by their contemporaries; the artists saw their attempts to express Renaissance and humanistic ideals in a lasting medium undermined by their imitators and misunderstood by their public, who, in its simple admiration of a likeness, hardly got beyond the criterion: "faire ung doulx visaige."

Fig. I   Portrait of Clément Marot, from a lost original attributed to Holbein. (BN, Paris, Cabinet des Estampes)

Fig. II   Portrait of Clément Marot. (Musée de la Société de l'Histoire du protestantisme français, Paris. Photo: Bulloz)

Fig. III   Portrait of Clément Marot by Corneille de Lyon. (Musée du Louvre, Paris. Photo: Agraci)

Fig. IV   A copy of Fig. III. (Museo Civico, Piacenza)

Fig. V   Portrait of Clément Marot, provenance and artist unknown. (Musée
historique de la Réformation, Geneva)

Fig. VI   Portrait of Clément Marot in the Thomas Rhediger collection. (Museum
Slaskie, Wroclaw)

Fig. VII   Portrait of Clément Marot, artist unknown. (Tronchin Bequest, Musée historique de la Réformation, Geneva)

CLEMENS MAROTVS.

Fig. VIII   Portrait of Clément Marot, a woodcut published in Théodore de Bèze, *Icones* (1580). (BN, Paris, Cabinet des Estampes)

Fig. IX   Clément Marot, a 19th-c. print. (BN, Paris, Cabinet des Estampes)

Fig. X   Wax medallion of Clément Marot, artist unknown. (Musée de Cluny, Paris)

CLEMENS MAROTIVS PRIMVS:
SVI TEMPORIS POETA GALLICVS
La mort uy mord:

Fig. XI   Clément Marot, an engraving by René Boivin published in Antwerp by
Hieronymus Cock, 1558. (BN, Paris, Cabinet des Estampes)

Fig. XII   Clément Marot, an exact copy of Boivin's print, probably by Jacques Le Boucq. (Bibliothèque municipale, Arras. *Recueil d'Arras*, MS. 266. Photo: Giraudon)

Fig. XIII   Monument to Clément Marot, Cahors. (Author's photo)

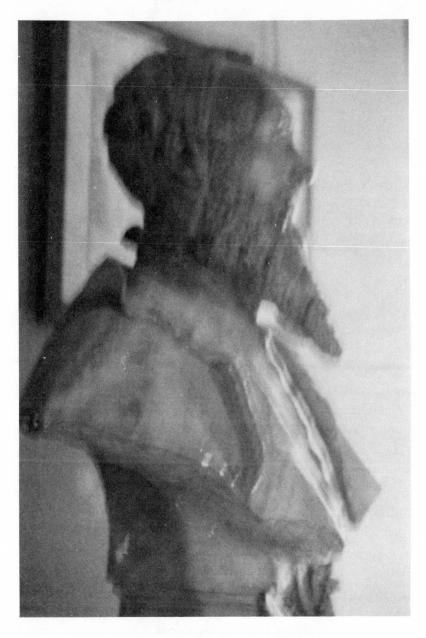

Fig. XIV   Plaster bust of Clément Marot, Musée de Cahors, a copy of a bronze
by J. Turcan. (Author's photo)

· LA · MORT   NY · MORD ·

CLEMENS · MAROTIVS ·
POETA · GALLICVS ·
· B · 1576 ·

Fig. XV   Clément Marot, a second print by René Boivin (1576). (BN, Paris, Cabinet des Estampes)

Fig. XVI   Clément Marot, a copy of Boivin's second print engraved by G.F.L. Debrie in 1729 and published as a frontispiece in *Les Oeuvres de Clément Marot* (The Hague, P. Gosse and J. Neaulme, 1731). (BN, Paris, Cabinet des Estampes)

Fig. XVII   Clément Marot, a portrait in the form of a medallion from a lost original published from 1577 onward in the second, enlarged edition of
G. Roville's *Promptuaire des Médailles*. (BN, Paris, Réserve)

Ante rudis, per te, calamos, inflante Thaleia,
Edidicit dulces Gallica lingua modos.

Fig. XVIII   Clément Marot, a 17th-c. print in J. Boissard, *Bibliocaliographie*, 1650.
(BN, Paris, Cabinet des Estampes)

NOTES

1. For a detailed biography of Marot, see C.A. Mayer, *Clément Marot* (Paris: Nizet, 1972). For his works, see the critical edition in 6 volumes by C.A. Mayer.

2. See C.A. Mayer, "Le Départ de Marot de Ferrare," *Bibliothèque d'Humanisme et Renaissance*, 18 (1956), 197-221.

3. See Jean Robertet, *Oeuvres*, ed. C.M. Zsuppán, Textes Littéraires Français, 159 (Geneva: Droz, 1970), XX.

4. See C.A. Mayer and D. Bentley-Cranch, "Florimond Robertet: Italianisme et Renaissance française," in *Mélanges Franco Simone*, IV, 135-49.

5. See C.A. Mayer, *Clément Marot*, pp. 41-42, p. 446.

6. Cf. *L'Epistre au Roy, du temps de son exil à Ferrare* (*Ep.*, XXXVI, vv. 124-31).

7. See C.A. Mayer, *Clément Marot*, pp. 83-110.

8. *Archives Nationales*, Trésor des Chartes, JJ 254, no. 301, fo. 57ᵛ; see C.A. Mayer, *Clément Marot*, pp. 448-49. Marot thanked the king for this gift in his *Eglogue de Marot au Roy, soubz les noms de Pan & Robin* (*OL*, LXXXIX).

9. In March 1529 one Loys du Moulin went from Blois to Paris to fetch "plusieurs portraicts et effigies au vif" made by Jean Clouet and take them back to Blois (*Archives Nationales*, KK 100, fo. 49ᵛ); and, in 1537, Jeanne Boucault, wife of Jean Clouet, travelled from Paris to Fontainebleau "pour aporter et monstrer audict Seigneur [François Ier] aucuns ouvrages dudict Jehannet . . ." (*Archives Nationales*, J 961 [11], no. 58). Cf. P. Mellen, *Jean Clouet* (London: Phaidon, 1971), pp. 80-89.

10. In an act dated November 1541, François Ier conveyed all the property of Jean Clouet to his son, François, since Jean, as a foreigner, had not been allowed to make a will (*Archives Nationales*, Trésor des Chartes, JJ 254, no. 466, fo. 86ᵛ). The king instructed the Parisian *Prévôt* to carry out this conveyance, proof that François lived in Paris as his father had done. In bestowing on François Clouet the title of *valet de chambre*, the king noted that he had already "très bien imyté" his father, adding "et esperons qu'il fera et continuera encores de bien en mieulx cy-apres" (ibid.).

11. Jean Second describes in his travel journal his visit to Lyons in June 1533 where all the inns were full as the Court was in residence. The poet was glad to be offered a night's lodging by his friend Corneille de Lyon (*Ioannis Nicolaii Secundi Opera Omnia*, ed. Bosscha [Leyden, 1821], II, 258-59, *Itineraria Tria, Iter Hispanicum, Bruxella in Arragoniam*). Cf. D. Bentley-Cranch, "A Portrait of Clément Marot by Corneille de Lyon," *Bibliothèque d'Humanisme et Renaissance*, 25 (1963), 174-77.

12. See D. Bentley-Cranch, ibid., and N. Rondot, *Les Peintres de Lyon du XIVᵉ au XVIᵉ siècles* (Paris, 1887), pp. 99-103.

13. See Erasmus' letter to Willibald Pirckheimer, June 3, 1524 in P.S. and H.M. Allen, *Opus epistolarum D. Erasmi Roterodami* (Oxford, 1906-1958), V, 468-71.

14. See J. Pope-Hennessy, *The Portrait in the Renaissance* (London: Phaidon, 1966), p. 195, and R. Strong, *Holbein. The Complete Paintings* (London: Granada, 1980), p. 10.

15. The miniature of François Ier in *Les Commentaires de la Guerre Gallique* (first part of the manuscript, 1518, British Museum, MS. Harley, 6205) is generally attributed to Jean Clouet, as are the seven miniatures of his generals, *Les Preux de Marignan* (second part of the manuscript, 1519, Bibliothèque Nationale, MS. fr. 13429). These miniatures are circular, about 5 cm in diameter and with a blue background; the same shape and color are found in Holbein's miniatures. On Jean Clouet's miniatures, see A. Blunt, *Art and Architecture in France 1500-1700* (1953; rpt. London: Penguin Books, 1957), p. 34; and P. Mellen, *Jean Clouet*, pp. 232-34.

16. National Gallery, London; oil and tempera on wood, 179 cm x 82.5 cm; R. Strong, *Holbein. The Complete Paintings*, no. 112 and pp. 7-8.

17. Cf. *Letters and Papers, Foreign and Domestic of the Reign of Henry VIII, 1509-1547*, ed. J.S. Brewer, J. Gairdner and R.H. Brodie, 21 vols. (London, 1862-1910), XIII, Part 1, 1135. See also J.J. Scarisbrick, *Henry VIII* (London: Penguin Books, 1971), pp. 465-67, and A.B. Chamberlain, *Hans Holbein the Younger*, 2 vols. (London: George Allen, 1913), II, 138-55.

18. See A.B. Chamberlain, ibid.

19. Musée du Louvre; oil and tempera on paper mounted on canvas, 55 cm x 48 cm; R. Strong, *Holbein. The Complete Paintings*, no. 115. See *Letters and Papers*, XIV, Part II, 33, 117.

20. In the collection of Her Majesty the Queen; drawing on pink primed paper with black and colored chalks, reinforced with pen and ink; 30.7 cm x 25.7 cm, left profile. See K.T. Parker, *The Drawings of Hans Holbein in the Collection of His Majesty the King at Windsor Castle* (London: Phaidon, 1945), no. 37; and catalogue of the exhibition *Holbein and the Court of Henry VIII*, The Queen's Gallery, Buckingham Palace, 1978-1979, no. 18.

21. The woodcut taken from Holbein's drawing and bearing the date "1535" appeared for the first time in the *Paidagogeion* (Lyons, 1536); Bourbon is shown in right profile and his hand, which is lightly sketched in on the original drawing, is replaced by the poet's two hands holding a sheet of paper and a pen. The edition of the *Nugarum libri octo* . . . (Lyons: S. Gryphius, 1538), contains not only this woodcut, but in addition, on p. 17, a variant of it showing Bourbon crowned with a laurel wreath. See J.P. Oddos, *Catalogue de la Bibliothèque Municipale de Troyes: poètes et versificateurs champenois de la Renaissance* (Troyes, 1980), pp. 10-11; and A.S. Det, "Hans Holbein et Nicolas Bourbon de Vendeuvre," *Mémoires de la Société Académique de l'Aube*, 73 (46, 3e série) (1909). These portraits are mentioned in the famous literary quarrel between Bourbon and Jean Visagier; see R. Copley Christie, *Etienne Dolet, the Martyr of the Renaissance* (London, 1880), pp. 309-10.

22. Bourbon, *Nugarum libri octo* (Lyons: S. Gryphius, 1538). *De Hanso Ulbio et Georgio Reperdio pictoribus*. "Videre qui uult Parrhasium cum Zeuzide, / Accersat a Britannia / Hansum Ulbium & Georgium Reperdium / Lugduno ab urbe Galliae" (libro III, viii). *In Hansum Ulbium pictorem incomparabilem*. "Dum divina meos vultus mens exprimit, Hansi, / Per tabulam docta praecipitante manu, / Ipsum & ego interea sic uno carmine pinxi / Hansus me pingens maior Apelle fuit" (libro VI, xii). *De Morte pincta a Hanso pictore nobili*. "Dum mortis Hansus pictor imaginem exprimit / Tanta arte mortem rettulit, ut mors vivere / Videatur ipsa; & ipse se immortalibus / Parem Diis fecerit, operis huius gloria" (libro VII, clviii). *In picturam Hansi regii apud Britannos pictoris & amici*. "Sopitum in tabula puerum meus Hansus eburna / Pinxerat & specie qua requiescit Amor. / Ut vidi, obstupui, Chaerintumque; esse putavi / Quo mihi res non est pectore chara magis. / Accesi propius, mox saevis

ignibus arsi: / Osculaque: ut coepi figere, nemo sui" (libro VIII, xxxvi). In the second edition of the *Historiarum veteris Testamenti Icones* (Lyons: Frellon, 1539), Bourbon, in a foreword in Latin verse, named Holbein as the artist and added at the end a couplet in Greek and Latin which has become famous: "Cernere vis, hospes, Simulacra simillima vivis? / Hoc opus Holbineae nobile cerne manus."

23. See C.A. Mayer, *Bibliographie des éditions de Clément Marot publiées au XVIe siècle* (Paris: Nizet, 1975), no. 9.

24. C.A. Mayer, ibid., no. 15. On Nicolas Bourbon see C.A. Mayer, *Clément Marot*, pp. 167-68 and 240-43. Bourbon's Latin poem in the first edition of the *Suite*: *Nic. Borbonius Vandoperanus ad Lectorem.* Hic liber ignaro Domino volitare per orbem / Inque tuas, lector, gaudet abire manus. / Ex his conjicito quae sint et quanta futura / Caetera quae authoris lima seuera premit" is followed, from the second edition (*Bibliographie*, no. 17) by a French translation by Antoine Macault: "Lecteur, ce livre s'esjouyt de venir / Entre tes mains sans le sceu de son maistre, / Par qui peux veoir que sera ce du mettre / Lequel repose soubz plus meur souvenir." (On the literary convention of a supposed "theft," see C.A. Mayer, *Clément Marot*, pp. 243-44.) Marot later addressed a charming epigram to Bourbon: "L'Enfant Amour n'est pas si petit Dieu / Qu'un Paradis il n'ayt soubz sa puissance, / Ung Purgatoire aussi pour son milieu, / Et ung Enfer plein d'horrible nuisance. / Son Paradis, c'est quand la jouyssance / Aux Poursuyvans par grace il abandonne. / Son Purgatoire est alors qu'il ordonne / Paistre noz Cueurs d'ung espoir incertain; / Et son Enfer, c'est à l'heure qu'il donne / Le voller bas et le vouloir haultain" (*E*, CXXXV, *Au Poete Borbonius*).

25. Contrary to Nicolas Bourbon's work, Marot's poetry does not contain many references to painters and their works of art. Besides one mention of "Janet" only two *rondeaux* take artists as subjects (*OD*, *Rondeau* XXVII, *Aux amys & seurs de feu Claude Perreal, Lyonnoys* and *Rondeau* LIV, *A la fille d'ung Painctre d'Orleans belle entre les autres*). Furthermore, this latter *rondeau*, instead of praising a specific painter, is rather a vehicle for the platitudes of Petrarchist poetry associated with the "real and painted image" (see D. Bentley-Cranch, "La Réputation de Clément Marot en Angleterre," *Studi Francesi*, 50 [1973], 201-21), an image invoked several times by Marot, for example in his epigram *Une Dame à ung qui luy donna sa Pourtraicture* (*E*, XXVIII: "Tu m'as donné au vif ta Face paincte").

26. The portrait of Jean de Dinteville and Georges de Selve, *The Ambassadors*, is in the National Gallery, London; oil and tempera on wood, 207 cm x 209 cm, 1533 (R. Strong, *Holbein. The Complete Paintings*, no. 86). The portrait of Charles du Solier, sieur de Morette, is in the Gemaldegalerie Alte Meister, Dresden; oil and tempera on wood, 43.5 cm x 43.5 cm, 1534-1535 (R. Strong, ibid., no. 95).

27. On this problem, see R. Strong, ibid., p. 10.

28. Bibliothèque Nationale, Cabinet des Estampes, folio N. 2, no. 26 (Landon Direx.), nos. 28, 28a (D. Sornique sculp.); J. Calmon, *Catalogue dactylographié de l'exposition "Clément Marot" à la Bibliothèque Municipale de Cahors, juin-juillet 1948* (copies deposited at the Bibliothèque Nationale and at the Bibliothèque Municipale in Cahors), no. 31, 32 (Landon direx.), nos. 33, 34, 35, no. 36 (Hersent del.), nos. 37-42 (D. Sornique sculp.).

29. Bibliothèque Nationale, Cabinet des Estampes, fo. N.2, nos. 18, 18a (N. de Launay sculp.), nos. 22, 22a, 22b (C.S. Gaucher inc. 1777), no. 23 (Hersent et Chretien del.), no. 25 (gravé par Hopwood); J. Calmon, cat. cit., no. 16 (gravé par Hopwood), no. 17, no. 18, no. 19 (C.S. Gaucher inc.), no. 20, no. 21 (Hersent et Chretien del.).

30. Bibliothèque Nationale, Cabinet des Estampes, fo. N.2, nos. 18, 18a.

31. (1671-1741). "Par vous en France Epîtres, Triolets, / Rondeaux, Chansons, Ballades, Virelais, / Gente Epigramme et plaisantes Satires / Ont pris naissance." Bibliothèque Nationale, Cabinet des Estampes, fo. N.2, no. 18a; J. Calmon, cat. cit., no. 18.

32. Bibliothèque Nationale, Cabinet des Estampes, fo. N.2, no. 23; J. Calmon, ibid., nos. 21, 36.

33. The picture was given to the Musée in March 1892 by Baron Fernand de Schikler, who had acquired it at the Sale of the Collection of Docteur Louis Girou de Buzareingues, February 28, 1892 (no. 57, *Portrait de Clément Marot*, Ecole vénitienne, peint sur toile, 53 cm x 43 cm, au verso un cachet de trois étoiles couronnant un lion). In the *Catalogue du Musée de la Société de l'histoire du protestantisme français* by J. Pannier (1927), the picture, no. 28, *Portrait présumé de Marot*, is attributed to Dosso Dossi; see also J. Pannier, "Les Portraits de Clément Marot," *Bibliothèque d'Humanisme et Renaissance*, 4 (1944), 144-70.

34. See Catalogue of the Exhibition *Le Seizième Siècle européen: peintures et dessins dans les collections publiques françaises* (Paris, Petit Palais, October 1965-January 1966), no. 205, *Portrait d'un docteur*. For an analysis of Moroni's work, see the Catalogue by A. Braham for the Exhibition *Moroni, 400th Anniversary Exhibition*, National Gallery, London, 1978.

35. See C.A. Mayer, *Clément Marot*, pp. 336-66.

36. Ibid., pp. 477-516.

37. Ibid., pp. 369-70.

38. E. de Beaulieu, *Les Divers Rapportz* (Lyons: P. de Saincte Lucie, 1537), fo. XLVIII^v: *Douzain envoyé de par l'Aucteur (ung premier jour de l'An) à Treseloquent & docte Poete maistre Clement Marot, pour lors estant à Lyon*; see also C.A. Mayer, *Clément Marot*, pp. 370-74.

39. C.A. Mayer, ibid., p. 373.

40. Although Marot could have visited Lyons before this date, either alone or with the court (according to the *Itinéraires, Catalogue des Actes de François Ier*, ed. P. Marichal [Paris, 1887], vol. VIII, the Court was at Lyons in May, June and December 1533, in January, April and July 1538, in September 1541 and in August 1542), his visit there during the winter of 1536-1537 is the only one confirmed by documents. However, it should be added that Marot was certainly in Lyons in July 1538 for the publication of his *Oeuvres* by Etienne Dolet (*Bibliographie*, no. 70). See C.A. Mayer, *Clément Marot*, pp. 420-23.

41. "Corneille de Laye painctre et sa femme et sa fille et serviteurs" are mentioned in a list, dated December 2, 1569, of "Huguenots Reduictz et qui ont fait confession de foy et qui ont vescu despuis et tousjours vivent catholicquement et frequentent les esglises" (*Archives de Lyon*, série GG, non classée). See N. Rondot, *Les Protestants à Lyon au XVIIe siècle* (Lyons, 1891), p. 13.

42. 12 cm x 10 cm; oil on wood, green background. The portrait was in the collections of the Comtesse de Montbrison and M. Schloss, and was given to the Louvre in 1949 by the latter's heirs. See *Catalogue de l'Exposition de portraits peints et dessinés du XIIIe au XVIIIe siècles* (Paris, Bibliothèque Nationale, 1907), no. 522; D. Bentley-Cranch, "A Portrait of Clément Marot by Corneille de Lyon," art. cit., and C. Sterling and H. Adhémar, *Catalogue des Peintures, Ecole française, XIVe, XVe, XVIe siècles, Musée National du Louvre* (Paris, 1965), no. 78, pl. 187.

43. Museo Civico, 12 cm x 8.5 cm; oil on wood; green background; in a bad state of preservation; attributed to Corneille de Lyon and dated "d'environ 1550."

See F. Arisi, *Il Museo Civico di Piacenza* (1960), no. 335, pl. 142.

44. See also the testimony of the nephew of Giovanno Cappello, Venetian ambassador to France from 1551 to 1555, who, passing through Lyons when accompanying his uncle from Venice to Paris, noted in his travel journal: "Nous allâmes faire visite à un peintre excellent, qui . . . . nous fit voir toute la cour de France, tant gentilshommes que demoiselles, représentée sur beaucoup de petits tableaux, avec tout le naturel imaginable" (E. Moreau-Nélaton, *Les Clouet et leurs émules* (Paris, 1924), I, 92; and that of Brantôme, describing a visit to the painter's studio in Lyons by Catherine de Médicis and the Court in July 1564: "Sur quoy il me souvint qu'elle estant allée un jour voir à Lyon un peintre qui s'appelloit Corneille, qui avoit peint en une grand'chambre, tous les grands Seigneurs, Princes, Cavalliers et grandes Reynes, Princesses, Dames, filles de la court de France; estant donc en ladite chambre de ces peintures, nous y vismes cette Reyne parestre painte tres-bien en sa beauté, et en sa perfection, habillée à la francèze d'un chapperon avec ses grosses perles, et une robe à grandes manches de toille d'argent fourrées de loups cerviers; le tout si bien representé au vif avec son beau visage qu'il n'y falloit rien plus que la parolle . . ." *Oeuvres complètes*, ed. L. Lalanne (Paris: Renouard, 1864-82), VII, 343-44.

45. The portrait of Clément Marot by Corneille de Lyon was apparently the model for a picture by the German 19th-century painter, Alexander Bruckmann (1806-1852), where the poet is represented in the romantic style, almost full-length, holding a book in his hand and looking young and handsome. This picture—its present whereabouts are unknown—was exhibited in 1904 at Dusseldorf, and in the following year at Munich; at these exhibitions Bruckmann's source was stated to be a picture of Marot by Titian in the Collection of Neuwied, Fürst zu Wied. See J. Calmon, no. 4.

46. 45.5 cm x 35 cm; oil on canvas; at the top: *Clem. Marot*; provenance and artist unknown. See *Nos Anciens et leurs œuvres, Recueil genevois d'art* (Geneva, 1908), p. 75; and *Catalogue de la collection de portraits, bustes, miniatures et médaillons de la Bibliothèque de Genève* by A. Bouvier, I (Geneva, 1932), II (Geneva, 1935); II, 2, no. 150.

47. See A. Wachler, *Thomas Rhediger und seine Büchersammlung in Breslau* (Breslau, 1828), and *Catalogus Codicum Latinorum Classicorum qui in Bibliotheca urbica Wratislaviensi adservantur* (Breslau, 1915).

48. Museum Slaskie, Wroclaw; 46.4 cm x 32.7 cm; oil on wood; at the right top; *Clement Marot*; the original white ruffle is replaced by a white collar. See D. Bentley-Cranch, "Further Additions to the Iconography of Clément Marot," *Bibliothèque d'Humanisme et Renaissance*, 26 (1964), 419-23.

49. The list is as follows: 1, François Ier, 2. Eléonore, wife of François Ier, 3. Henri II, 4. Charles IX, 5. Elizabeth, wife of Charles IX, 6. Le connétable de Bourbon, 7. François, duc de Guise, 8. Le Cardinal de Lorraine, 9. Le duc d'Aumale, 10. Le Prince de Condé, 11. Coligny l'amiral, 12. D'Andelot, 13. Le Cardinal de Chatillon, 14. Poltrot de Méré (*qui tua mons de Guise*), 15. Emmanuel Philibert, duc de Savoie, 16. Le Cardinal Farnèse, 17. Elizabeth, daughter of Henri II, Queen of Spain, 18. Clément Marot, 19. A group of scholars.

50. C.A. Mayer, *Clément Marot*, pp. 503-05.

51. *Les Vrais Pourtraits des hommes illustres en pieté et doctrine, du travail desquels Dieu s'est servi en ces derniers temps, pour remettre sus la vraye Religion en divers pays de la Chrestienté. Avec les descriptions de leur vie & de leurs faits plus memorables* . . . (Geneva: Jean de Laon, 1581).

52. "J'ay voulu adjouster aux illustres personnages sus mentionnez cestui ci, lequel par une admirable félicité d'esprit, sans aucune cognoissance des langues, ni des sciences, surpassa tous les poètes qui l'avoyent devancé: pource qu'estant sorti par deux fois hors du Royaume à cause de la Religion, il fit un notable service aux Eglises, & dont il fera memoire à jamais, traduisant en vers français un tiers des Pseaumes de David." Ibid., p. 162. See also C.A. Mayer, *La Religion de Marot* (Paris: Nizet, 1973), p. 94.

53. 30 cm x 20 cm; oil on wood; green background; at the top: *Clemens Marotus Francus Poeta Prim.*; unknown artist. See H. Bouchot, *Catalogue de l'Exposition des Primitifs français* (Paris, 1904), p. 142, no. 377; and F. Aubert, article in *Les Musées de Genève* (June 1951).

54. Cf. the portrait of Nicolas Bourbon by Holbein. See above, p. 20.

55. *Icones* (1580), fo. y iii^v; *Les Vrais Pourtraits* (1581), p. 161, x i.

56. *Oeuvres* (Lyons: Jean de Tournes, 1558) (*Bibliographie*, no. 210; the frontispiece is illustrated on p. 71); the same frontispiece appeared in the edition of the *Oeuvres* published by Jean de Tournes in 1585 (*Bibliographie*, no. 229).

57. Note the incident at Geneva when Marot, dicing in an inn with his friend François Bonivard, was mistaken for "un ministre de la parole de Dieu" because of his clothes. See C.A. Mayer, *Clément Marot*, pp. 504-05.

58. Bibliothèque Nationale, Cabinet des Estampes, N.2 supp.; J. Calmon, no. 61.

59. Musée de Cluny, no. 1322; 10.5 cm in diameter; the dress, beard and hair are black and the ruff is white.

60. See L. Courajod, "La Collection des médaillons de cire du Musée des antiquités silésiennes à Breslau," *Gazette des Beaux-Arts*, 29 (1884), 236-41; H. Bouchot, *Les Portraits aux crayons des XVIe et XVIIe siècles conservés à la Bibliothèque Nationale (1525-1646)* (Paris, 1884), pp. 385-86; L. Dimier, *Histoire de la peinture de portrait en France au XVIe siècle* (Paris, 1924-1926), III, 264-69; D. Bentley-Cranch, "Further Additions to the Iconography of Clément Marot," art. cit. The medallions, in colored wax on a blue background, were in little leather circular boxes.

61. The medallion of Marot and four others (Catherine de Médicis, Charles IX, Henri III and Jean-Philippe, comte du Rhin) were bought from M. Evans by the Musée de Cluny in 1851 after the Delonge Sale. Eleven other medallions, from the same sale, were acquired by the Musée. All the medallions are in circular boxes of decorated leather; the subjects, in colored wax, stand out in relief against the blue background.

62. A.P.F. Robert-Dumesnil, *Le Peintre-Graveur français ou catalogue raisonné des estampes gravées par les peintres et les dessinateurs de l'école française*, 11 vols. (1842), VIII, 11.

63. Ibid., VIII, 62, no. 113; Bibliothèque Nationale, Cabinet des Estampes, N.2, no. 13; Catalogue of the Exhibition *L'Europe humaniste*, Brussels, Palais des Beaux-Arts, 1954-1955, no. 186.

64. *Divi Caroli V Imp. Opt. Max. Victoriae, ex multis praecipuae. Magno Philippo, Divi Caroli V.F., Regi Hispan. Angl. Franc. &c. Patri patriae, Principi nostro indulgentissimo, has, ex plurimis quidem praecipuas, paternarum victoriarum imagines, ad immortalem Sacrosanctae illius Maiestatis gloriam, immortalibus chartis commissas, Hieronymus Coccius, typographus, pictor, quanto potest humilitatis ac reverentiae adfectu, ultro adfert, dicatque* (Imprimé en Anvers aupres la bourse neuve au Quatre vens, en la maison de Hieronymus Cock, 1558), fo. 62^r, "Clementius

Marotus, primus sui temporis poeta gallicus. La mort ny mord.''

65. MS. 266.

66. See L. Campbell, "The Authorship of the *Recueil d'Arras*," *Journal of the Warburg and Courtauld Institutes*, 40 (1977), 301-13; 305.

67. See R. Aulotte, "Alexandre Le Blancq et sa collection de manuscrits au XVIe siècle," *Revue du Nord*, 1 (1968), 301-16; 316, n. 114.

68. L. Campbell, art. cit., pp. 303-04 and p. 313.

69. The inauguration of the Clément Marot monument took place in Cahors on May 7, 1888 (see *Bulletin de la Société des Etudes du Lot*, 1892, pp. 119-26). The monument consists of a Renaissance-style fountain with the bronze bust of Marot by J. Turcan placed in a niche against a sky-blue background decorated with foliage. Below is a panel in low relief by M. Puech with a man and a woman, holding laurel branches and garlands of flowers, representing the rivers Seine and Lot.

70. A copy in plaster of the bronze bust by J. Turcan.

71. A.P.F. Robert-Dumesnil, *Le Peintre-Graveur*, VIII, 62, no. 112; Bibliothèque Nationale, Cabinet des Estampes, N.2, no. 14.

72. Published as frontispiece in *Les Oeuvres de Clément Marot* (The Hague: P. Gosse and J. Neaulme, 1731).

73. Marot was arrested twice, in spring 1526 for breaking the Lenten Fast (see C.A. Mayer, *Clément Marot*, pp. 83-112), and in October 1527 for having rescued a prisoner from the Watch (ibid., pp. 143-46); in March 1532 a warrant for his arrest was issued but was not proceded with (ibid., pp. 103-04). To which incident does this little picture refer? Marot described his two arrests in a very picturesque fashion, the 1526 one in the *ballade Contre celle qui fut s'Amye* (*OD*, LXXX, Ballade XIV, vv. 9-16) and the 1527 arrest in the epistle *Marot, prisonnier, escript au Roy pour sa delivrance* (*Ep.*, XI, vv. 8-12, 27-31).

74. *Prima Pars Promptuarii Iconum Insigniorum a seculo hominum, subiectis eorum vitis, per compendium ex probatissimis autoribus desumptis* (Lyons, 1553).

75. *Promptuarii Iconum Pars Secunda incipit a Christo nato; perpetuam ducens, seriem ad usque Christianissium Francorum Regem Henricus hoc nomine secundum, hodie feliciter regnantem*, n.d. (before 1559).

76. See D. Bentley-Cranch, "L'Iconographie de Marguerite de Savoie (1523-1574)," in *Culture et pouvoir au temps de l'Humanisme et de la Renaissance, Actes du Congrès Marguerite de Savoie* (Annecy, Chambéry, Turin, 1974) (Geneva: Slatkine-Champion, 1978), pp. 243-56; p. 248 and plate XII. Among many other examples four medallions may be noted: those of two sons of François Ier, the Dauphin François and Charles, duc d'Orléans, copied from their portraits by Corneille de Lyon, the medallion of Marguerite de Navarre copied from the drawing by François Clouet, and that of King Henry VIII of England copied from the celebrated portrait by Holbein.

77. "Clement Marot François natif de Cahors en Quercy, a acquis une grande louange, des le temps que la Poesie Françoise a commencé d'estre en prix & estime. Aujourd'huy les vers de iceluy, quoy qu'ils soyent purs & gais, sembleroient peu de chose, à la comparaison de ceux qu'aujourd'huy escrivent les Poetes modernes, desquels le nombre est bien grand, & seroit difficile les nombrer tous par le menu: toutesfois je feray bien tost mention du Prince d'iceux. Il a traduit en carmes François, quelques Psaumes: il a traduit la Metamorphose d'Ovide, les Eglogues de Virgile, le jugement de Minos, la louange de Beralde, & plusieurs autres choses de plaisir, il estoit du temps de ce grand Roy François premier, lequel le favorisa fort à cause de

la gaillardise de sa Poesie, mais depuis qu'il print le parti ou pour le moins qu'il fut soupçonné de la nouvelle religion, il ne fut plus si bien veu & s'absenta de France et s'en alla en Piedmont & à Ferrare là où il mourut."

78. *Bibliocaliographie* de J. Boissard, 1650; J. Calmon, cat. cit., no. 30; Bibliothèque Nationale, Cabinet des Estampes, N.2, no. 12. Beneath the frame decorated with grapes and birds is a Latin couplet: "Ante rudis, per te, calamos inflante Thaleia, / Edidicit dulces Gallica lingua modos."

79. J. Pommier, *Michelet interprète de la figure humaine* (The Cassal Bequest Lecture 1959), University of London, 1961.

80. Jean Robertet, *Oeuvres*, ed. cit., *Soubz une meschante paincture faicte de mauvaises couleurs et du plus meschant peintre du monde, par maniere d'yronnie par maistre Jehan Robertet*, XXI, vv. 7-8. See also C.A. Mayer and D. Bentley-Cranch, "Florimond Robertet: Italianisme et Renaissance française," art. cit.

Robert Griffin

La Concorde des deux langages: Discordia concors

Jean Lemaire de Belges has been the beneficiary and victim of partial treatment in the overall study of Renaissance poetry. Although his name usually figures in generalizations and bibliographies of consulted works, only recently has an ambitious overview been managed.[1] Urged on by his obvious verbal skill, yet dissuaded by the dubious company of poets we think he kept, literary historians have not known whether one should rank him as the finest of a verbose "school" of rhyming pyrotechnicians or speak of how his distilled learning lays the way for the midcentury florescence of verse. In the process, we have found for him the ultimately useless label of *Janus bifrons*, meaning that Lemaire draws from the past and portends the future—as if every other mortal does not. Accordingly, some of his finest work has suffered from partial reading and idle questions. The issue of past-versus-present has, perhaps understandably, plagued *La Concorde des deux langages* through our continued compulsion to weigh and compare the earlier French and Italian authors mentioned in the prologue. The names are opaque and uninteresting as they are marshalled there, although the question of the impact of Italian culture remains fascinating. On the other hand, the title of the work has moved us to seek a comparison with or establish an evolution toward the *Deffence et Illustration* and later manifestos of writing. Yet why doesn't Lemaire help us out more by resolving the question of primacy (we do suspect that he prefers the French side of things) more forthrightly?

This and allied questions can be answered productively only within a context of *Discordia concors* that motivates nearly every aspect of *La Concorde* and which, in turn, is made apprehensible entirely by the seemingly random details that constitute the work. Accentuating the reciprocity of idea and illustration may at first seem a critical truism but it has a special pertinence for the way Lemaire delineates the persona of the poet and for the *Discordia concors* motif. In a nutshell, the concept may be summarized as a reconciliation of opposites that points to the harmony of the Cosmos in which the reconciliation takes place. Yet an appreciation of the finer contours of this proposition is exceptionally involved since it is one of the oldest organizing principles of systematic mythologies the world over, is at the heart of the most ancient works of literature known to man, but, so far as I know, its full sweep has never been the subject of scholarly inquiry.[2] Moreover, the theme's affinity for paradox and for constantly regenerated and refashioned mental coordinates makes summary definitions unsatisfying at best. When taken to its metaphysical and most paradoxical extremes, the opposites to be harmonized include such mutually exclusive predicates as the ineffable and the Logos, time and eternity, the many and the One. Since the concept of a self-transcending principle by which reconciliation is effected—and generative of other principles—lies beyond all human understanding, it must be dramatized as it is in *La Concorde* by numberless splintered images. These images are endowed with all yet none of their traditional semantic values, each image is as expressive of the main idea as many other constituents of the poem, and yet each depends for its full appreciation on the aggregate meaning of all others. Finally, such imagery must illustrate the intellectual and affective dynamic of a world of scattered and fragmented things and creatures yearning to rediscover, beyond all pairs of opposites, the original source of unity which, by its essence, cannot remain confined within itself. As an erstwhile student of astrology and other arcane sciences, as an adept of neo-Platonism, and as one thoroughly conversant with medieval theological commonplaces, Lemaire was culturally well placed to wrestle in a syncretic text with a question that, in other forms, would obsess the entire 16th century: to what extent can a credal theology, one that assigns itself the task of delimiting the proper *relationship* of fallen creature with Creator, of prodigal son with Father, also accommodate an aspiration to ultimate *identity*?[3]

The prologue of *La Concorde* gives no indication that such an ambitious program might be on its agenda or even vaguely on the horizon. Much like a continuing chapter of *Gli Asolani* or *Il Cortegiano*, the story begins offhandedly *in medias res* with two speakers who engage in "diverses entremeslées" on the relative worth and potentialities of French and Italian. As we note the opinions of the faceless speakers and follow their conversation, it soon becomes clear that our eye is meant to follow less their exchange of views (we rarely know who says what to whom) than the verbal axes, symmetries and expanding configurations of the narrator's description. The speakers are of "noble et gaillarde" nature in the "art et estude mercurial et palladien." As their exchange moves by turns through "amoureuse concordance," "gracieuse jalousie," and "tumulte amoureux," they debate the merits of a French group headed by Jean de Meung and Alanus de Insulis and an Italian list headed naturally by Dante, Petrarch and Boccaccio, with Serafino Aquilano bringing up the rear.[4] Finally, one voice champions the French cause in terms so odd and cryptic, "d'un hault cueur virille et masculin pronunçoit maintz nobles termes amoureux et prudentz, par elegance feminine," that Jean Stecher felt obliged to identify biographical referents, while Jean Frappier tagged them as moral *or* esthetic terms.[5] Then the speakers disappear for good, preempted by the narrator who purports to imitate through his poetry the appearance of their union.

The narrator is actually the second mediating agent on the scene. The first is the image of the tree trunk and root, which enters at the end of the opening paragraph and which, due to the vast flux of symbolic associations that have always attended it, one should avoid classifying as "inanimate" merely for a facile contrast with the animate narrator. We will have to scrutinize both mediations at length in order to grasp something of the basic operation by which Lemaire draws imagery from the living past so as to alter our understanding of the future. The tree image is incorporated into the context of *La Concorde* for the way its shape visually expresses the two languages that grow out of, without outgrowing, the Latin mother tongue. But a metaphor of convenience is immediately transformed into the portentous Tree of Knowledge by the added simile which likens derivation to streams proceeding from a fountain and leading ultimately to "amoureuse concordance." Furthermore, the tree is the work's nuclear image, generating and organizing its most expressive associations. For this reason, it calls for a few words about its great watershed of symbolism, as the inclusive *Discordia concors* dictates, and about the way it embraces Christian and proto-Christian alike in mutual illumination.

In many of the world's creation myths, as in the pathology of dreams and in primitive puberty rites, the tree functions as a "threshold"[6] symbol laden with affective meanings that ease the mind's passage beyond Angst. The opening chapters of Genesis tell the story of Unity become duality and then multiplicity, of how the First Adam fell by the Tree of Knowledge. In so doing, he introduced both the world of time and death but also reproduction and awareness of the eternal Virtues that allow for redemption on Holy Rood. The Hebrew editors of Genesis drew on a wealth of

Sumero-Babylonian myth from nearly two millennia before, radically modifying scenes from paradise that depict godhead incarnated in a pair of (often winged) serpents intertwined around an *axis mundi*, the tree of the world; for it was around the time when men began congregating in the cities of ancient Sumer that the idea of opposites in coincidence found its first recorded visual expression in the tree of the world adorned with the immortal serpents. It was only natural that over many centuries this caduceus should become the prime symbol of office of Hermes ("Mediator"); that the Romans should take Mercury's beautiful yet terrible serpent staff as the symbol of moral equilibrium and good conduct; that to him should be ascribed the invention of the harp and other emblems of salvation; and that his ability to see beyond the limitation of paired opposites should make him the patron of medieval alchemy and hermetic learning. Since Homer was Lemaire's prime source book for the *Illustrations de Gaule*, he would have found Hermes there as the mediator of heaven and earth, patron of rebirth and lord of the knowledge beyond death, which may be known to his initiates even in life; and he figures as the androgynous god traditionally associated with the triads of the Graces and those goddesses of destiny—Aphrodite, Hera and Athene—who, in the great legend, caused the Trojan War (I, 230). Throughout his symbolic transmigrations from archaic times to the late Middle Ages Hermes-Mercury retained his age-old ties with life reconciled or regenerated through the living tree;[7] this symbolism has a substantial impact on the development of *Discordia concors* in the 16th century and beyond. Just as for the syncretist Raymond Lull two centuries earlier, the trunk of the *Arbor elementalis* brings together the constituents of matter that flower into the nine "accidents" of its branches (thus creating the universal "limit" number of ten), so too the caduceus integrates earth with its wand, air with its wings, and fire and water from the undulations of the serpents. For the alchemist bent on transmuting spirit and matter from the vagaries of lower forms into the elevations of unity and stability, the serpents came to represent the instincts, while the wings betokened the spiritual. Like the divine messenger, the tree is taken as the axis linking heaven and earth by Rabanus Maurus, who in the 8th-century *Allegoria in Sacram Scripturam* posited it as the symbol of human nature for the way it seems to reflect micro- and macrocosm. And four centuries before that Macrobius established the connection in all its essential aspects between caduceus and Genesis (*Saturnalia*, I, 19).

These random examples are meant only to suggest the depth and solidity of the vibrant tradition of symbols of reconciliation inherited by the "waning" Middle Ages. Especially in the 14th and 15th centuries one runs

across dozens of allegorical paintings and manuscripts where the four virtues surround a castle as its battlements, or support a Tower of Wisdom, or
where Justice mediates between Trees of Life and Knowledge, since the
virtues emanate from the fountain at the foot of the Tree of Knowledge in
Genesis 3. Inasmuch as symbols are largely interchangeable in both arcane
and sanctioned traditions, one encounters debates between Jesse's green
tree and Adam's dry tree, against a background of zodiacal signs (e.g.,
Guillaume de Digulleville's *Pèlerinage de l'âme*, ca. 1355); one also finds
complementary green and dry trees symbolizing androgyny at the center
of the zodiac wheel in alchemical tracts (e.g., Bartholomaeus Anglicus' *De
proprietatibus rerum*, published in Lyons in 1485).[8]

The tree has thus been taken as the primordial emblem of division and
reconciliation and, in the modern era, as the hope of overcoming the serpent's power. But the doctrine of balanced opposites was not discursively
formulated as an ontological and metaphysical principle until Pythagoras,
Heraclitus and Empedocles. It was the latter who focused on the tree's
opposing lines of force and likened the spreading roots to the four elements
that are separated from their source by Discord and united in Concord.
Among the many purveyors of the idea and symbol to the Renaissance,
Plato, Cicero, Plotinus and St. Augustine stand out for the way they place
man within schemes of opposites, and all four resort to some form of
Pythagorean arboreal or musical harmony image to convey a judgment
about man's moral circumstances. Among emblematists, mythographers,
mystagogues, theologians and political theorists of the Renaissance, the
world trees of cross and caduceus inspire countless variations on the
mutually reinforced theme of reconciled universal opposites. Hence, we
should not cite Lemaire's conjuring up of Peace born from Prudence under
the sign of the caduceus (III, 65) as a source for, let us say, D'Aubigné's
character Prudent in his "Caducée ou l'ange de Paix," even though both
texts resolve "tout discord en bonne concordance." The essential fact to
retain is that D'Aubigné's text should be situated in the spectrum of
irenism which stressed the affinity of Christ and Hermes as in Postel's
eschatological *concordia mundi*, and which uniformly saw falling away
from the Cross as the fundamental cause of Discord.[9] Nor should D'Aubigné be adduced as more than an analogue of Spenser's great *Faerie
Queene* IV, notwithstanding obvious parallels: at the center of the garden
of Venus's Temple we find the goddess Concord who assures elemental
balance and maintains the celestial bodies on course; as the embodiment
of the universal life-principle and mother of Peace, she stands for friendship beyond sexual differences ("Both male and female, both under one
name," IV, x, 41); and inside the temple we find the statue of Venus

entwined by a serpent. The point is that despite the myriad interpretations that are attached to and borrowed from its various parts, the function of the *axis mundi* in organizing the human microcosm, the estates of society and the spheres of the cosmos have remained remarkably consistent since its origin. In *La Concorde* it provides the surest key for deciphering the couplings of masculine and feminine, of "amoureux et prudentz," immediately before the narrator intervenes midway in the prologue to give the "apparence par mon escripture" of the speaker's resolved differences.

The narrator complements the first mediating agent by deflecting our attention from the moot question broached by the speakers over French or Italian superiority; he will soon shift our interest from a moralizing opposition of Venus against Minerva in order to probe the more vital matter of the interchange and relationship between them. Of the two real reasons that have moved him to write, "concurrentes, et non discrepantes," the first is the contemporary cultural interchange between the two countries. With unerring intuition, Frappier's note (12) speculates that the terms used to describe the appeal of French to the Italian ear, "gentillesse et courtoisie humaine," may be redolent of *qualités morales, noblesse, grâce*, and *valeurs de l'humanisme*. In fact, the terms were of great interest to both the French and Italian authors assembled in the prologue, who carefully sort out the interchange among moral virtues, intellectual attributes, and social intercourse.[10]

Following the reference to enlightened tourism, the narrator elevates his discourse to his second motive for writing—a wish for political peace and union of the two countries that have been separated by Nature in word and deed. Here at the end of the prologue he intensifies the pairing of complementary opposites set in motion by the *axis mundi* image. His discussion bears on the dialectic of pleasure and duty, "tant en general comme en particulier," and it extends the "domesticque et privée" setting of the overture to include now "la chose publicque."[11] At the same time, we get an idea of *La Concorde*'s architectural balance by the way the end of the prologue foreshadows the end of the work in manifold ways. The linguistic interchange and the narrator's gift of his work to Minerva are transformed into the political gift of Charlemagne from which stem French "franchise" and Florentine "flourissance";[12] and the derivation of the trinity of prudence, peace and concord from Minerva is reflected in the final image of Minerva's *speculum mundi*.[13] But the most telling instance of balance and imbalance involves the work's principal mythological figures: Minerva, "la belle et vertueuse deësse," emblematizes a ubiquitous Renaissance ideal of conciliation; Venus "trop amoureuse" is censured for an imbalance that Lemaire embroiders throughout the entire following section (e.g., vv. 46-48, 192).

Transition from the prose of the prologue to the fiction of the versified autobiography is established by the poetic transformation of the tree image in the first line and by the accent on imagined appearances, "comme se" the narrator "euz choisie" the familiar path trod by Petrarch. Flight to Lyons from the rumor of war in his native Hainaut, from the Mars of life to the Venus of art, soon ends in parody: he achieves only voluble "clamours" that reach to neighboring towns. This Petrarchan cacophony subtly contrasts with innocuous punning and sustained alliteration that will soon take on far more significant dimensions. Tired of complaining and groaning, he lapses into a dream. Although the expected dream vision may elicit a wince or smile, we ought not to overlook the metaphysical stature of dream in allegory nor the aim of this generic convention. It is intended to embrace a willing suspension of disbelief and to create a greater mood of receptivity. We continue for a while to trace Petrarchan themes from the *Rime*, *De remediis* and *Trionfi* (vv. 34-36) but we soon move deeper into the fantasy from the frustrating search for Venus's temple in the narrator's *biographia literaria* to the perceived need to seek it, "où il est," i.e., in the exempla of art and in the zodiac of his own wit.

The epiphany of Venus with her "doulz attraicts" offers Lemaire the chance to rival his predecessors by trying his hand at the *ekphrasis* of epic mural art (v. 73). But more than that, it allows him to lay the groundwork for the development of the work's major theme. Venus's arrival on the cusp of the old and new zodiac year puts Apollo on the threshold of Aries (vv. 64-66), the sign of creation and transformation by which primordial energy, once fecundated, passes from potential to virtual, from unity to multiplicity and back. Since for Lemaire—and those of his contemporaries who were imbued with astrological lore—the zodiac calendar was an acknowledged ideogram of time and the emblem of the cosmos, it is unlikely that many of the details in the description of Venus's retinue are "innocent" of semantic complications. For example, the brush stroke depicting Flora "qui son tresor deslie" (v. 76) is balanced by the harmonious song of Pan and other minor mythological figures, "Tous d'un accord," with their "doulce noise" (v. 86), which in turn recalls the "guerre et noise" of v. 13 and anticipates the later "doulce noise" and "les clers cieulx leurs beautéz desnuërent" (pp. 12 and 40).[14]

This last line ends the description of the entourage, causing the narrator to apostrophize "o Clio, eslargis moy facunde" (v. 130). Invoking the Muse to describe the "haulx faictz" of Venus combines the vocations of historiographer and the métier of poetry with its "matiere fecunde."

Both come together in the placement of the Temple of Venus "en lieu fort autenticque," suggesting at once the historically particular and the universality of the *locus classicus*.[15] But the architecture of the temple is "realistic" only through its deceptions. For like many other castles one enters in Renaissance allegory and romance—especially those one encounters early in a narrative—reality lies in the symbolized state of mind. The whole of an accretion of seemingly random details turns out far greater than the sum of any of its parts:

> L'ordre du comble, ordonnée en croisant,
> Fait enlasser les beaux piliers ensemble,
> Qui sont d'ivoire et de fin or luisant.
> Tout le dehors ung paradis ressemble;
> Le dedens n'est ne trop cler ne trop brun,
> Mais delectable à veoir, comme il me semble.
> (vv. 154-59)

Frappier is alert to the likelihood of a marvelous dimension in the description of the gothic pillars (p. xxxiv), but the suggestion could be carried much further. In view of our discussion of the caduceus, of the "entremeslées" seen in the opening paragraph and the numerous similar variations yet to come on the theme of opposites reconciled,

> Tous sexes or en concorde se vouent;
> Masle, femelle ont accord reciprocque,
> Jusque aux poissons qui soubz les undes nouent.
> Mutuel meuf, unïon univocque
> Font connexer la machine du monde
> Soubz ung moteur qui à paix les provocque
> (vv. 382-87)

a symbolic reading of the details proves to be more rewarding than the tourist's passing review of anonymous images.[16] Like many another allegorist of his time, Lemaire repeats key details as if to prevent us from missing the point. Verse 157 and its rhyming companion (v. 159) are mutually reflective, since the "delight of the eyes" is the main cause of man's Fall, condemning him to a life of shadows and appearance.[17] A brief review of the paradigms implied by the narrator's list of French and Italian writers in the prologue confirms Lemaire's brilliantly economic variations on the tradition he draws upon here. Beginning with Dante's dark wood and Beatrice's description of the garden of light in the heavenly paradise as nothing but shadowy prefaces (*ombriferi prefazii*) of the ultimate truth, we learn that artistic embodiments of harmonized opposites are at best "masks of god." All the more removed from the source of light,

the pleasant seductions in the garden of earthly delight offer only paro-
distic understandings of harmony, attained more at odds than in concert
with our higher faculties. Serafino's allegorical picture is "pien di luce"
and "tenebre profonde," as is Ariosto's, whose "pareami" underscores the
fallibility of sight when confronting the play of light and shadow at Alci-
na's castle (*Orlando Furioso*, VI, 47 and 69). So also in Spenser, the pic-
torial details of Lucifera's castle draw our attention to their illusoriness
and artifice (*FQ*, I, iv, 4); since we are led to infer the virtues that are
conspicuously lacking or contravened by these pleasances, they become
the mirror reflection of what truly is. We can come geographically and
historically closer to *La Concorde* through the example of the "Minerva"
tapestry made for Guy de Baudreuil (1491). There the goddess is represented standing on the rocky path to wisdom, flanked by an atrophied
Tree of Knowledge and a green Tree of Grace, from which is suspended a
cuirass of virtue and around which is twined the motto "Sub sole sub
umbra virens." Rudolf Wittkower reads this as "the adoption of the medieval scheme: the side of sun and life and the side of shade and spiritual
night are reconciled in the figure of 'Alma Minerva,' the mother of art and
science . . . the faith in eternal life must have as its counterpart the knowledge of human sin."[18] This is akin to the transcendence of the "obscurité
tenebreuse" (v. 469) in *La Concorde*; and it is the perfect anticipation of
the reconciliation of opposites beyond "la nuyt obscure et brune" prior
to the work's closing image of Minerva's mirror "fait par art magique,"
itself the fitting recollection of *La Concorde*'s opening sentence.

Coexistence of shadow and light epitomizes the entire "Venus" section,
where scenes of bounty alternate with scenes of corruption; the alterna-
tion is marked by clear divisions, as in the address to Clio, although the
complete meaning of extremes is made apprehensible only by explicit
reference ("volupté, sans nulle aultre," v. 192) to their partiality. Much
like the models of *La Commedia* and Meung's *Roman de la Rose* it posits
in the prologue, *La Concorde* represents itself as an encyclopedia. The
concept of a *plenum* that synchronizes all of its scattered parts is epitomized, precisely, in each of those parts. We should, therefore, see no
disheveled mixture of metaphors or radical departure from tradition in
Lemaire's reduction of the world to court life or of the Temple of Venus
to the proportions of the human body. In Albertus Magnus and John
Lydgate the Virgin becomes a house with seven columns, a city, temple,
and tower, whereas the rose's enclosure in the *Roman de la Rose* upholds
a long tradition of seeing the garden as a body allegorized. But the most
arresting comparison is again with Alanus. After comparing the cosmos to
a city, Natura deputizes the Heavenly Venus to unite the two sexes for

procreation; but she degenerates into the *Venus monstrosa*, "Venus in Venerem pugnans," by committing adultery and thus becoming a figural projection of an event that really takes place within men: Paradise contains the seeds of its own destruction.[19] Frappier cites a discussion of Sacred Prostitution in the *Illustrations* (I, 244) and ventures the opinion that Lemaire's passage may have come from Boccaccio (vv. 160-80; note 51). His source surely is Boccaccio (cf. II, 101; IV, 147), but Frappier's citation should have included the preceding sentence on the attributes of the heavenly Venus, "gentille et gracieuse, pleine d'urbanité" and the following allusion to "amoureuse concordance." For Sacred Prostitution had more to do with the theme of fertility and regeneration in general than with sensuality. Its setting was the drama of great changes that annually overtake the earth, its personae were the opposing principles of life and death, and its theme was the Sacred Marriage that secured the linchpin between heaven and earth and averted disintegration into chaos.[20]

Lemaire continues to play upon the ebb and flow of degeneration and abundance by introducing the meretricious archpriest of Venus, Genius, who later rejects the narrator's gift freely given and whose attributed speech ("Son tintinable et mener grand tintin; / Qui ne le peut sonner, il n'aura rien," vv. 209-10) conjures up the contemporary and easily translatable ditty of Johann Tetzel "As soon as the coin in the coffer rings, / The soul from purgatory springs" (cf. *Paradiso* XIV, 118). But before Genius begins his long sermon on the brevity of youth, the doors open to reveal the productive affinities and interchange among architecture, science, painting, music and poetry. As in Marot's "Temple de Cupido,"[21] the temple as *plenum* forecasts potential marriage of all things. For Alanus, love is the golden chain that binds all creation, and concord is the knot of peace in the marriage of heaven and earth—"plurality returned to unity, diversity to identity, dissonance to harmony."[22] Invited by such catchphrases as "poésie parlante," commentators have long pointed out the dynamic connection sought by medieval and Renaissance poets between music and poetry, between painting and poetry, and the like.[23] What should be underscored is that this idea developed along countless lines of transmission and that in Plutarch, Pico, Ficino, Leone Ebreo, and in many ancient dicta, civic concord and the arts of painting, music, and writing are all examples of the balancing of contrary principles that structure the spiritual and physical universe. The music of the spheres corresponds to the idea of harmony, order and justice in the little world of man (*La Concorde*, vv. 262-64), but the most immediate analogy of creative conciliation is that of the physical body and sexual generation.[24] This complex of ideas has immense esthetic implications because it lies at the heart of

Renaissance concern for perspective and proportion, and as such marks a special place for *La Concorde des deux langages*.

The symphonic poem to Venus with its "canticque, entrebrisé d'accordz . . . accordant sons discordz"

> Serins, tarins, faisans proportions
> Murmuroiënt par tenson non rebelle.
> Chardonneretz, en diminutïons, . . .
> Leurs versetz dictz alternativement
> Delecterent les oreilles des dieux.
> (vv. 227-29, 233-34)

anticipates Geoffroy Tory's discussion in *Champ fleury* of micro-macro-cosmic proportion, recreates the *cantus firmus* of the period with its incipient counterpoint of tenor and soprano voices, and has a clear relevance to the *De harmonia mundi* of the Franciscan cabalist Francesco Giorgio:

Ideo etiam de cura summi Opificis circa consonantissimam dispositionem, et mensuras membrorum, ex multis pauca percurramus: in quibus omnis concentus, omnisque harmonia consummata vi debitur, caeteris omissis, quibus intermedia tanquam intervalla repleta perficiuntur. Totius enim corporis ad truncum est proportio sesquioctava. A trunco vel thorace ad crura tota usque ad plantas, sesquitertia . . . in quibus tonus diatessaron, diapente, et diapason resultant.[25]

The diapason refers to the precise mathematical ratio (2:1) that must occur between two strings of equal weight and tension to produce two notes exactly an octave apart. The discovery of this ratio has by legend been attributed equally to Pythagoras and to Jubal (like Franchino Gafurio in his *Practica musicae* [Milan, 1496], Lemaire uses *Tubal* and *Jubal* interchangeably; cf. Genesis 4:22). The sound of the striking of a blacksmith's hammer supposedly revealed the relationship between the concordant intervals of the musical scale and the mathematical ratio of the diapason. Prime tonal intervals are dogmatically taken by Pythagoras to equate with the proportions between the component numbers (1 + 2 + 3 + 4; = 2:1, 3:2, 4:3) of the Sumerian decad. Ten is the "limit" number of the physical universe, although the diapason can be repeated like the recurring seasons and extended up and down an expanse of sound from the infinitesimally low to the ineffably high; this scale is sometimes represented iconographically as a universal monochord tuned by a divine hand. That is why, surveying the participants in the paean to Venus, Lemaire gives the obligatory nod of recognition to Apollo and Terpander but then says that for each "Thubal ou Putagore, / Il en est cent, et pour cent en est mille" (vv. 242-43). Since ten is the number of perfection, its squares create extrapolated abstracts of the cosmos, just as the Trinity for Dante explicitly contains the square root of the nine circles; in the Pythagorean number system ten stands for rectitude in faith, one hundred stands for the amplitude of charity and one thousand for the height of hope. And it is why Lemaire's instruments range from *decacordes* to *monocordes* (vv. 250-52). Before the intrusion of Eris at the marriage of Thetis and Peleus, four sirens create the harmony of "diapason, triple, diatesseron" (I, 219), i.e., the sesquitertial proportion (4:3 = 1 1/3; cf. v. 186) which determines the musical interval of a fourth; and of course, 4:3 is the ratio between the rhyming patterns of the Minerva and Venus sections of *La Concorde*. But the most intriguing analogy occurs in a *sirventès* initiated by Jean Molinet and completed by Lemaire (IV, 323-30). It begins with the creation of Terpander's harp of seven strings, invented in conformity with the seven planets. After a comparison of the harp's beautiful form to the Virgin descended from the tree of Jesse, we are told the strings create harmony akin to the four cardinal virtues, notably Prudence, and the three theological virtues. God's reestablished covenant with man is described as "doulx accordz sa corde recorda," leading to the refrain where the harp stands as a surrogate for the Cross: "compas et mesure, / Harpe rendant souveraine armonie." Just before that refrain, we read that Pan never surpassed the "Dyapason au son de ses musettes, / Pytagoras oncques n'organisa / Dyapente de si doulces busettes / Par sept accordz qui sont les sept vertus."

In the midst of the love feast, Venus "s'endort mieulx que au chant des seraines, / Ou que à manger pavotz ou mandragore" (vv. 245-46; cf. v. 102). The detail is more symbolic than mimetic, thus placing her somewhere between Eve's loveliest daughter, Helen of Troy (*Odyssey*, IV, 219-28) and Spenser's Cambina who carries the caduceus of peace in one hand and a cup of nepenthe in the other for inducing forgetfulness and dispelling past enmities (IV, iii, 42-43). Inasmuch as Lemaire's poetic memory at this juncture in *La Concorde* is probably more iconographic than literary, the close connections among details symbolizing cosmic harmony can be best illuminated through the thesaurus of Italian graphic art of the previous generation, both abstract and representational. For instance, the frontispiece of Gafurio's *Practica musicae* depicts a scheme of cosmic harmony of which the axis is a serpent descending like the monochord from the looped tail, symbolic of the sun-door to eternity, down to a tricephalous on earth composed of a dog's, lion's and wolf's head (as in Titian's "Allegory of Prudence"). The serpent bisects eight spheres, each corresponding to a planet, to a note in the Dorian-Phrygian tetrachord (our A-minor scale), and to a muse, beginning with Clio and culminating with Urania in the motionless realm of the stars. Closer inspection would show

that Apollo (*sol* in the diatonic scale) mediates between Mars and Venus
and thus reduces the series to a double triad; the fact of the sun's creation
on the fourth day of the seven (Genesis 1: 14-19) divides equally the time
of the creation, and by analogy the material extension of the cosmos too,
into two pairs of three each (cf. *La Concorde*, vv. 64-66, 79). At the summit is the enthroned Apollo (whose name means "unity") holding a seven-
string lute in one hand and with the other gesturing to the three Graces.[26]
As in Botticelli's "Primavera," the Graces assume a 2:1 configuration, with
Aglaia receiving Apollo's blessing and Evrhosina facing away, to symbolize
that earthly graces emanate from divine grace, while, in turn, the ninth
muse Thalia mediates by balancing the outgoing and returning modes. She
recurs just below the three-headed animal at the bottom of the scale, justifying her twin attributes of abundance and silence. Abundance belongs
to her etymologically and as a member of the triad of Graces; this may
help to explain why the temple of Venus "tant a abundance" (v. 195) and
why the resplendence of "Le tronc d'Amours" coincides with "le nombre
des graces eslargies" (vv. 302-03). The silence of *surda Thalia* recurs time
and again in *La Concorde* since harmony is not possible without pauses of
silent intervals. It was also the requisite posture of Pythagorean initiates,
carried on and expanded by Vives, Alciatus, Pontus de Tyard, and many
others. The notion of Thalia's "silence" was transmitted to the Renaissance through numerous channels (e.g., Plutarch's *De Iside et Osiride*), but
especially through the well-known *Somnium Scipionis* of Cicero and
through Macrobius's commentary on it. There we read about an endlessly
repeatable range of harmonies, about the mystique of numbers, and about
how the earth's silence results from its immobility in the scheme of
spheres. Hence, in the allegory of Gafurio we begin in the midst of the
four elements under the protective nimbus of tricephalous-Prudence, symbolizing an awareness of the three moments of time. One mounts the scale
along the serpent of time to behold the meaning and wisdom of Thalia's
silence only at the Apollonian summit of eternal grace.

Analysis of *La Concorde* against this background is a sollicitation of
neither text, and the present reading of mythic symbols is not farfetched
at all. Petrarch's *Africa* (III, 188-204) combines the lion-wolf-dog icon
with the lyre of Apollo and the serpents, symbolic of his invasion and
victory at Delphi. Lemaire rehearses the three moments of time, under the
aegis of prudence (I, 239), the meaning of silence (I, 245), and the origin
of earthly grace from the divine paradigm (IV, 83). What should be emphasized is not that these meanings were common and shared, so much as
their occurrence in a highly intricate scheme of associations that make
reading at once more demanding and more approximate to the poet's eye.

Above all, we can appreciate that, far from regenerating only vacuous imagery as Huizinga would have it,[27] the elaborate "infolding" through intertextuality of allegorical imagery of this period allows the entire poem to become incomparably greater than the sum of its parts: *De peu assez*. For instance, the magic elixir given to Venus in *La Concorde* for making her more receptive to the advent of Harmonia calls for comparison with the "liqueur prudente et vertueuse" and with the avoidance of "terrienne amour" by gazing into a "miroir de speciosité celeste" (I, 238). This nectar image is found again in "Nostre Eaige," a work assigned to Lemaire's youth. The nectar waters the garden of the heart to produce three flowers, i.e., the three theological virtues which, however, are posed like the Graces of Botticelli, Gafurio, Lemaire of *La Concorde*, and others. We are meant to measure human conduct against these standards of excellence in order to assure universal abundance and concord. The poem begins with the same words that are given as the theme of Genius's sermon (v. 365), interlarded with recollections of the *Imitatio Christi* (I, 19), and, more interestingly, pursue the imagery of interweaving. Reminiscent of the end of *La Concorde*, the narrative culminates in a balance between the handiwork of Flora and the placement of the three flowers on Minerva's aegis of virtue. The narrative extols the symbolic value of silence but bids others to ply this theme for its "sens moral ou aussi [sur] amours." Most relevant to *La Concorde*'s predilection for numerology and fascination with triplicity is what now follows: Prudence gives an awareness of past, present, and future that allows us to recognize evil the way the Tree of Knowledge allows us to recognize virtue. Since we are on the threshold of the deepest Christian mysteries, where the darkness and light separate in St. Paul's mirror, the inherent power is described as a "vray mistere pur." And since the power is there for whoever accepts "dieu trine et ung," it follows that "Nombre de trois est tousjours florissant" (IV, 335-37; cf. *Le Temple d'Honneur*, vv. 731-42).

Just as well known as the musical scheme of Gafurio, Ambrogio Lorenzetti's "Allegoria di buon consiglio" in the Palazzo Publico of Siena would have been required viewing for any foreign tourist, on the eve of that city's cultural eclipse by Florence. In the Fonte Gaia there could be seen the triad and quaternity of virtues combined with Sapientia, and in the Lorenzetti political allegories one could examine Prudence holding a three-flamed torch or the posture of Concordia attended by the three-plus-four virtues in the "Good Counsel" fresco; in fact, good counsel and command of the three modes of time had been equated in pseudo-Platonic sayings since the Silver Age. Analysis of the latter allegory would be interminable, but one should note that the positioning of the two groups of virtues represents

the difference between the actively acquired virtues and those that are
infused by divine intervention, recalling the Florentine neo-Platonists and
Lemaire's

> Les neuf beaux cieulx que Dieu tourne [universe: unus/versus] et tempere
> Rendent tel bruit en leurs spheres diffuses
> Que le son vient jusqu'en nostre hemisphere.
> Et de là sont toutes graces infuses
> Aux clers engins, et le don celestin
> De la liqueur et fontaine des Muses. (vv. 262-67)

And the play of "-corde" throughout La Concorde gains special meaning
from the way Lorenzetti's Concordia is holding the Scales of Justice "con
le corde."[28]

It would be a serious misreading to view this coincidence of sound in
the twilight of the 15th century as a clever conceit whose only aim is the
exercise of wit. The power of musical chords to create concord in the
heart (Lat. cor) was repeated often enough to become an active, real
intellectual construct.[29] The idea of a preternatural cord that bound sky,
state, soul and strings together in harmony enjoyed the great precedents
and prestige of Homer's "golden chain," of Aristotle's doctrine of the
Mean, metaphorically expressed as a perfectly tuned string, and of the
concept of the heavenly harmony of celestial chords that bind the world
together. The latter was gratefully received by Florentine neo-Platonism
for its speculations on love as the vinculum mundi. But again, assignment
of precise sources is risky at best since the idea is found intact in most of
the high literate mythologies of the world.[30] In traditional Christian iconography of the late Middle Ages the Virgin is frequently recast in the
same pose, with an elevated left hand and lowered right, holding a cord
draped across her womb as she holds the fate of mankind; her hands
assume the "boon granting" and "receiving" attitudes of Oriental idols and
of Gafurio's Graces. In order to understand the complete relevance of
these features to the radiated powers of Venus's retinue and to the way
the ambits of Venus and Minerva inevitably interpenetrate, we will have to
say a few more words about the diapason and the magic solvency of
numbers.

The coincidental discovery of mathematics and astronomy by Sumerian
science some forty-seven centuries before La Concorde was aimed partly
at the acquisition of the numerical key to the universe which would enable
man to locate the "navel of the goddess" among the stars, its counterpart
in the "navel of the world," and thus to approach the center of all unity
and continuous generation.[31] Synonymous with the axis mundi, the navel
of the world assumes countless manifestations through the motifs of the

Cosmic Tree, World Mountain, sacred sanctuary or divinely ordained seats of government, to which meditation is directed and by which the social order is fixed. But throughout the variations its central purposes remain remarkably constant: knowledge of the juncture of heaven, earth, and underworld or knowledge of the umbilical point through which eternity breaks into time, symbolized by the apparition of divinity in a transcendent landscape—the central psychic experience of medieval allegory. To appreciate the continuity of this symbolism, one has only to think of the west portal of Chartres with the epiphany of Christ of the Apocalypse in the womb of eternity, surrounded by the evangelists whose symbols are derived from the balanced quadrants of the Sumerian zodiac.[32] The general idea of the *anima mundi* expressed through the harmony of the spheres was probably conveyed to the Renaissance by Plato's *Timaeus* (31B) and Plotinus, but this in turn entails the Pythagorean ternary credo as Plato adapted it. Despite our natural tendency to associate harmony with music and with the *distance* between the opposite strings of an instrument, the term derived from shipbuilding and was first applied to the *connection* between opposing strings, leading to the belief that the connecting point of any other pair of opposites might be found through mathematics. Since unity is split internally into three "moments" of activity, passivity and their resolution, the addition of the mediating term made *three* the cipher most responsible for conservation, reproduction and spiritualization in the cosmos.[33] Hence, the *cantus firmus*, the tri-unity of the heraldic device and the three-part division of the faculties of mind in Genius's sermon (vv. 391, 418-19), from which the vices and virtues are born—seen in the two parts of *La Concorde*—all contain the potentiality to resolve the conflict posed by dualism. The Christian equivalent of the Pythagorean prototype was the Creation in Genesis 1 from undifferentiated unity, the separation of opposing powers to create the World order and the reunification of opposites to generate life. By its unity and priority, One was considered masculine and exalted over Two, which was therefore feminine and— suggestive of the War between the Sexes—a threat to order. They are the constituent elements of the diapason, whose prestige is augmented by the fact that no mathematical mean number can intervene in the 2:1 ratio, that musical harmony is a metaphor for the regularity of the cosmos, and that, taken together as a triad, it stimulates "that fecundity of multiplicity which is in it."[34]

The idea of an ordered generation that interpenetrates all levels of creation competes in the "Venus" section with a threatened entropy (vv. 472-86), in the same way that the theological virtues are always shadowed by the World, the Flesh and the Devil. As the patron of eloquence and thus of *ingenium*, Mercury consecrates the marriage of heaven and earth by translating divine grace into its terrestrial reflections (vv. 262-67, 538-40). We can expect, in turn, for the dance of the Graces to embody the ideas of spiritual regeneration. Lemaire poses them so as to mirror the attraction and diffusion that run through all nature: Pasithée attracts, Egÿalle retains, while *Euphrosyne*—whose prolonged description gives this vignette a 2:1 configuration—radiates the highest social graces: "Eufrosina, gentille et curïalle, / S'adonna toute à ce que sejourner / Long temps les face en amour socïalle" (vv. 355-57).[35] What is remarkable about this scene is the way the exfoliated Graces reveal the properties inhering in the "infolded" Venus; and yet so long as they coalesce as a triad they retain complicated features that shed light on large stretches of, for instance, the "Couronne Margaritique" but can never be explained away since their actions continue to generate new meaning.[36] When the paralysis of old age —likened to the withering of a dying tree—later threatens to seize those who have spurned the charms of Venus, mediation and interchange continue to generate symphonic alliteration: "*F*lastrir, *f*ener / *v*oz *f*leurs / et *v*oz *v*erdures" (v. 435). On the other hand, the "Gent tant courtoise" who —through passive infusion or active acquisition—have been graced with Venus's charms, inhabit a courtly paradise where the elements and humors are held in balance:

> Leur oraison est pure rhetoricque,
> Leur lÿesse est propice et genïalle,
> Et leur attrait amoureux et lubricque.
> Leur façon est humaine, socïalle . . . .
>   (vv. 574-78)

The embodiment of the Graces in the idealized courtiers announces Castiglione and recalls Pico and Ficino.[37]

Following this scene, in which we see the courtliness of the heavenly Graces transformed into the graciousness of earthly courtiers, the sermon of Genius exhorts the reconciliation of the sexes and reaches a crescendo of balanced praise and blame addressed to East and West and to the four parts of the ancient world. Genius closes by inviting parishioners to surrender to the voluptuousness of Venus, "Impossible est que tousjours arc puist tendre," and he cites the example of Mars who succumbs and is disarmed. Far from any closure, the incomplete *terza rima* initiated by the final verse opens onto the next section in the same way the dance of the three Graces unfolds onto the world at court.

The end of the "Venus" section is really an overture to the Minerva section that follows, for Lemaire-Genius has left implicit several details that call for comment. Zumthor has suggested an intersection of erotic strains in this concluding passage.[38] But it should also be borne in mind that as early as Hesiod's *Theogony* the union of Venus and Mars was blessed with the birth of Harmonia. Much has been made of this marriage, and the numerous references throughout *La Concorde* to the controlling influence of the stars and to the components of harmonious government invite further comment. Plutarch, for instance, held that enlightened and unified government issued, like Harmonia, from the marriage of force and graceful behavior. Renaissance astrologers considered that a day on which the two planets conjoined was a favorable occasion for marriage; newly-married noble couples were actually portrayed under the guise of Venus and Mars (e.g., Titian's "Allegory of the Marquis d'Avalos"). The Florentine neo-Platonists were steeped in the mystery of Venus Genetrix and her union with Mars, captured luminously in Botticelli's "Mars and Venus." There we find the peaceful resolution of the strife of all opposites: the spent warrior recumbent upon his discarded cuirass, while Venus's greater proximity to the viewer conforms to the relative position in astrology of her "dominance" when in conjunction with Mars. Thus, it is difficult not to read Lemaire's image of the relaxed bow apart from Heraclitus's dictum that the true connection (ἁρμονία) between opposites is the countermotion detained in countertension, as in the bow and the lyre (frag. B51).[39]

Generation of harmony from the encounter of love and war presumes that extremes are but mirrored reflections of a fleeting unity and thus it gives us the key to understanding the narrator's metaphoric passage from Venus's temple to Minerva's. We are not meant to grasp his pilgrimage as a moralistic rejection of voluptuousness in favor of study—what does that have to do with the concord of French and Italian and how do we justify the exuberant portrayal of Venus?—so much as a progression from incompletion to plenitude that partakes of the attributes shared by the two deities. It is easy enough to understand how the Virgin Mary and the virgin Minerva came to symbolize one another in the Middle Ages and in the Renaissance and how a chaste Venus can be best portrayed in opposition to a *Venus pandemos*, mother of all sensual vices. But it should also be noted that Venus occasionally puts on the armor of Mars, Minerva and Diana to become *Venus armata* and hence, like the Graces, a compound of passive attraction and aggressive transformation (cf. *La Concorde*, vv. 405, 544-46). Edgar Wind has shown that Orphic theology and the Florentine neo-Platonists took the birth of Harmonia as "a sign of mystical glory" and divine proportion, through which *carità* is united with *fortezza*.[40] The observation is interesting for the way it recalls the transformation by Amor of slow virtue into active charity in Poliziano's *Giostra* (II, 44) and for the way it resembles the production of active and passive grace and urbanity as "parts of virtue" derived from Fortitude in "La Couronne Margaritique." In the light of the singular assistance given to Venus in *La Concorde* by Mercury in order to propagate gracefulness among mortals, we should also cite her most spectacular union to produce the androgynous Hermaphrodite; for the Florentine neo-Platonists, the blend of Venus and Mercury symbolized the idealized marriage of *ingenium* and *pulchritudo*, and like the central triadic mediation in Gafurio's scale, Apollo plays the role of Concordia in assuring the union.[41]

Since discord in both Christian and pre-Christian cosmogonies originated with the dissociation of the masculine and feminine principles, it was only logical that the idealized reconstruction of universal, social and individual order should occur through androgyny. This may have something to do with the Renaissance fascination with the virago, and it has everything to do, for instance, with the contrived portrait by Nicolas de Modena (1545) of an androgynous Francis I. The king is outfitted with sword, bow, caduceus, and Medusan breastplate since he is at once "Minerve, Mars, Diane, Amour, Mercure."

In conformity with *La Concorde*'s seesaw rhythm of concord and discord succeeding one another, promise of harmony gives way to the narrator's dismissal from the temple of Venus. His exile is a necessary prelude to the arduous ascent to Minerva's paradise, and its exceptionally rich intertextuality gives Lemaire the chance to demonstrate his own artifice. The narrator's ordeal is fashioned from an elaborate paraphrase of Petrarch's often reformulated "Solo e pensoso" sonnet (32). His wanderings "une fois de ça, aultrefois de là par l'ignorance des sentiers" have deep reverberations in Dante, Boccaccio and Petrarch;[42] and his adventure "sur mer et sur terre" allows Lemaire to quote himself, since this was the theme of the rejected paintings offered to Venus on the previous page.

The details of the narrator's itinerary to the *hortus conclusus* of Minerva scarcely make any literal sense, but by again reading Lemaire on Lemaire we can appreciate how their symbolic values click into place with Mozartian regularity. For instance, learning that "par fortitude" the would-be pilgrim can overcome the guardians at the gate leads us to read this event as the presence in human lower case of the cardinal virtue Fortitude. We have already followed the transformations of the triadic Prudence, and we will shortly encounter Justice in the opposite number of Genius: "Honneur / Qui des biens et vertus est juste guerdonneur" (vv. 107-08; cf. IV, 96).[43] Thus, the "paradis terrestre" of the heart is timeless and "plenier" (vv. 27, 53). Peace, grace, and concord flourish there, dance, music, and "doulces parolles" (Meung's *bels digz*) abound (vv. 36-37, 43-44). Next to the edenic tree and fountain is Minerva's temple, where gifts are bestowed on noble hearts and worshipers can admire the marriage of moral truth and eloquence, after having earlier praised the "haulx faictz" of Venus (v. 131): "Les beaux faitz vertueux en cronicque et histoire, / En sc'ience moralle et en art oratoire" (vv. 71-72).[44] In the following verse French and Italian are joined in silence.

Now that the proper mood of receptivity has been established and moral resolve has displaced physical decay (v. 103), the narrator falls into another dream, which continues the Chinese-box arrangement of a fantasy within a fantasy. His next guide is the venerable prototype of the bearded hermit with whom he discusses the friendly emulation of Meung, Dante, Boccaccio and Petrarch. The hermit cites the heraldic device that links France and Italy in common cause, and in a final sentence of monstrous length (well over two hundred words) he promises the narrator a place in Minerva's temple after his death.

The sentence is exceedingly dense and deceptive. It describes the symbolic attributes of Minerva in intricate detail and the active-passive archangels Guerdon and Repos are introduced: "en ung miroir artificiel, fait part art magicque, il me monstra les vifves ymaiges embrassans l'une l'autre en la presence de la deesse."[45] To appreciate the aptness of this closing triadic image, we should note that the "Haulx esperitz, visaiges angelic-ques" of the Venus section (v. 143) have now jettisoned their physical limitations to become disembodied "Hautz espritz angelins" (v. 88). Readers of *La Concorde* have not failed to comment on the final image because of its conspicuous and sudden appearance, and indeed the speculum tradition of the Middle Ages almost requires some sort of comment. For Christian and non-Christian alike the term *speculum* was applied to any work that epitomized a field of knowledge and prescribed fitting attitudes for accommodating behavior to theory. When illuminated by self-knowledge in the progression from the "ymaginative" of Genius (v. 556) to wisdom's command of universals, the mirror symbolized the soul, the world, and ultimately the universe itself.[46] But merely to say that the mirror reflects living images reconciled by Minerva is almost pointedly to say nothing substantial about it. We too should be circumspect in imposing particular readings when alternate readings are quite as convincing. Like the *Hypnerotomachia*, *La Concorde* can be uniformly read as an alchemical tract, leading up to the *hieros gamos* of Venus and Mars and eventually to the mirror image.[47]

As the incomplete *terza rima* that ends the first part of the work opens onto the second part, the mirror image leaves us with a suggestive structure whose content remains uncommitted and open to newly generated meanings. In *The Waning of the Middle Ages* Johan Huizinga summarily dismissed late medieval allegory because of its supposed rigidity and repeatable forms, like the three figures in the mirror. More recently, Panofsky, Wittkower and other seminal art historians have given form-and-content criticism at the turn of the 16th century a new lease by demonstrating that classical physical postures, made uniform through endlessly repeated *bottega* exercises, lent themselves to intricate artistic statements reflecting altogether divergent ontologies and thus continually synthesized antithetical propositions. At the end of *La Concorde des deux langages* we are laconically informed of the "tresvertueuse concorde" of French and Italian, without ever learning how this comes about. But we do not really need to be told. Like most accomplished Renaissance writers, Jean Lemaire de Belges realized that telling and showing are one. What *La Concorde* mirrors most clearly is the poet at work, drawing on ideas and images from time out of mind, while promising a cultural conciliation that would not be fully realized for half a century.

NOTES

1. Pierre Jodogne, *Jean Lemaire de Belges, écrivain franco-bourguignon* (Brussels, 1972).

2. Thus the notion is variously catalogued as *Concordia discors, Concordia discordantium* or *Discors concordia* by Church Fathers, is labeled *Coincidentia oppositorum* by medieval alchemists, and so on. Malcolm Quainton's fine *Ronsard's Ordered Chaos* (Manchester, 1980) deals with this theme.

3. Cusanus expresses the idea in terms that have a special resonance in *La Concorde*: "For God, being the Absolute Ground of all formal natures, embraceth in Himself all natures . . . . Whence I begin, Lord, to behold Thee in the door of the coincidence of opposites, which the angel guardeth that is set over the entrance into Paradise" (quoted by Joseph Campbell, *The Masks of God: Creative Mythology* [New York, 1978], pp. 296-97). Cf. C.S. Lewis, *A Preface to Paradise Lost* (London and New York, 1942), pp. 72-73.

4. The inclusion of Serafino has always puzzled critics, who have struggled to see a connection between one of his sonnets and the "Conte de Cupido et d'Atropos" (e.g., Marcel Françon, "Note sur Jean Lemaire de Belges et Seraphino dall' Aquila," *Italica*, 28 [1951], 19-22). A more obvious point of comparison with *La Concorde* is his *Rapprezentazione allegorica* (1495) which contrasts chaste virtue and voluptuousness in chiaroscuro scenes that involve *locus amoenus* and temple, attained after a trek down a rough path, amid recollections of Petrarch.

5. Frappier, ed., *La Concorde des deux langages* (Paris, 1947), p. 50. In view of its obvious superiority, this edition will be used in the text, designated by page and/or verse numbers. Otherwise, the Stecher edition (*Oeuvres* [Louvain, 1882-91]) will be cited by roman followed by arabic numbers. For the sake of economy, *La*

Concorde will occasionally be referred to as such.

6. See Philip Wheelwright, *The Burning Fountain* (Bloomington, 1954), p. 261.

7. The olive tree is surely one of the main structuring elements of the *Odyssey*, being the symbol of eternal bounty (VII, 113-20), protection against threats from the underworld (IX, 322-24), and reconciliation in marriage (XXIII, 191-95). But most intriguing for possible relevance to *La Concorde* is that it occurs in paradise settings, accompanied by a perpetual fountain, where the ways of gods and men are distinguished and where Odysseus wakes from the sleep of death (XIII, 79-115). The first occurrence is in Book 5 where Hermes shakes Odysseus from passivity into activity, frees him from the temptress Calypso, and instills in him the knowledge of his own mortality and the idea of life as struggle. Before his escape is completed he buries himself at the foot of an olive tree whose trunk issues in a pair of branches, one wild and the other cultivated (V, 473-80). It is a detail, itself tree-like, that might link Homer and the *Beowulf* poet to a common proto-epic of incalculable antiquity (see Rhys Carpenter, *Folk Tale, Fiction and Saga in the Homeric Epics* [Berkeley and Los Angeles, 1958], chs. 6-8).

8. The iconography is far too complex to summarize adequately. For instance, the 16th-century *Livre des figures hiérographiques* pictures a column flanked by Adam, Eve, and the intertwined serpents, and capped by an androgynous Mercury-Sophia. The six planets that Mercury mediates (3 + 1 + 3) bear attributes that return significantly in *La Concorde*. See *The Collected Works of C.G. Jung* (Princeton, 1970), XII, 229 and 390; XIII, 304; XIV, 70-72 and 225. For the Mercury-Wisdom pairing, see Erich Neumann, *The Great Mother* (Princeton, 1974), Illus. 171.

9. Cf. Andreas Alciatus, *Emblematum libellus* (1542), nos. 18, 27, 77, and esp. 6: "Quem si de medio tollas . . . ," and L.G. Giraldi, *De diis gentium* (1548), 414B. For concord, Minerva and the caduceus, see the court pageantry at Antwerp by Charles G. Smith, *Spenser's Theory of Friendship* (Baltimore, 1935), pp. 16-17. And for heresy, union and discord, see the "Theologie si nouvele et discordente" of D'Aubigné's "Caducée"; *Oeuvres de Gringore* (Liechtenstein, 1972), I, 28, 217 and 330; Jodelle, *Oeuvres*, ed. Marty-Laveaux (Paris, 1868), II, 132.

10. Cf. Dante, *Il Convito*, IV, 17, 19 and 25; Petrarch, son. 205; *Roman de la Rose*, 6852; and Boccaccio's "favilluzza di gentilezza" of *Decameron* I, 8. Henri Estienne comes close to confirming Frappier's conjecture by comparing *Gentilezza* with *Galanterie, gaillardise* with nobility and grace; and again, situating his comments both at court and "en la place du change à Lyon," discusses the popularity of Venus, Mars and especially Mercury among courtier and alchemist alike (*Deux Dialogues du nouveau langage françois italianizé*, ed. P. Ristelhuber [Paris, 1885], pp. 238, 286-87). For courtesy and the Graces from Boccaccio to Spenser, cf. Edgar Wind, *Pagan Mysteries in the Renaissance* (New York, 1968), pp. 29 and 210.

11. Concern for matters "tant privez que publicques" (v. 147) is of course central to Renaissance debates on the links among love (Venus), eloquence (Mercury) and wisdom (Minerva). E.g., Louise Labé, *Débat de la folie et de l'amour*, ed. Jourdan (Paris, 1953), pp. 106-07; Jacques Amyot, *Oeuvres de Plutarque* (Paris, 1784), II, 23, 33-38, 70-72. For Spenser, "publike" and "priuate" are the terms (*FQ* 4, i, 19) that distinguish the virtue of friendship (Book 4) from chastity (Book 3); public love is concord, and its opposite—Ate—reveals ignobility in the knights around her. Cf. Lemaire, III, 233 and 240.

12. Inclusion of what might be termed the "politocosm" (with monarch as king) as the middle term between the Cosmos (with God as king) and man (with

Reason as king) is entirely predictable. But since the appeal from any of these levels to any other is open at will in any direction, it is difficult to ascribe or reject possible sources. For instance, the terminology, rhetoric and function of Lemaire's *concorde* duplicate those of Alanus in *De planctu naturae*. Alanus compared God's kingdom to the kingdom of Reason, not finding it necessary to express the middle term of which both his instances are really metaphors—an indication that the analogues were felt as real, and not simply as metaphors. Cf. the *Entrée royale*, "Par ceste arbre [of virtue], le peuple est entendu; / La fontaine [of grace], c'est le roy nostre sire" (in *Anthologie des grands rhétoriqueurs*, ed. Paul Zumthor [Paris, 1978], p. 132). But for a view totally at odds with mine, cf. Raymond de Lage, "Natura et Genius chez Jean de Meung et chez Jean Lemaire de Belges," *Le Moyen Age*, 58 (1952), 139 and 142. See also Werner Helmich's review of Ulrike Bergweiler's *Die Allegorie im Werk von Jean Lemaire de Belges* (Geneva, 1976). Helmich argues that Lemaire's taste for panegyric allegory divorces him from the "eternal ideas and essences" of medieval allegory (*Bibliothèque d'Humanisme et Renaissance*, 39 [1977], 219-21). My point is that the ancient comparison of a cosmos to a city, commonplace among medieval writers on *Discordia concors* like Alanus, practically mandates political considerations.

13. These are but some of the many tacit points of comparison between the two sections. For instance, the chapter heading of "Le chemin du temple de Minerve" (p. 6) is a disguised 4 + 6 decasyllable in a blanket of prose, just as the signpost "Dedans ce palais est le temple de Minerve" is an alexandrine, situated similarly (p. 43).

14. Cf. the "beautéz desnüerent" (v. 129) and Wind, ch. 8; the knot of the universe explicated by T. Anthony Perry, *Erotic Spirituality* (University, Alabama, 1980), pp. 37-43; and the "knot of concord" in *De planctu naturae*, trans. Douglas Moffat (New York, 1908), p. 33. In the *Enneads* Plotinus took the unequal tones of Pan's flute as emblematic of cosmic balance, and for Pico they stood for the unity of all opposites. Finally, in Jean Bouchet's *Epîtres morales* to Gabrielle de Bourbon (IX), Adam's Fall leads to "guerre, noise, & discorde," whereas the "partial virtues," derived from Thomistic intellectual faculties, lead to charity and civic order.

15. See Frappier, pp. xxx-xxxi and 87.

16. See Rudolf Wittkower, *Architectural Principles in the Age of Humanism* (London, 1949). Of special interest—in view of references later in *La Concorde* to Sacred Prostitution and Sacred Marriage—is the Pillar of Osiris with its eyes that gaze beyond death and its interlacing of cow (♀) and ram (♂) horns, in Joseph Campbell, *The Mythic Image* (Princeton, 1975), p. 22.

17. See Donald Howard, *The Three Temptations* (Princeton, 1966), ch. 2; *Summa Contra Gentiles*, 47; Jean Marot, *Le Voyage de Venise*, vv. 225-30. Leonardo's notebooks are full of speculations on the theological meaning of the coexistence of light and shadows.

18. *Allegory and the Migration of Symbols* (Boulder, Colorado, 1977), p. 135. See also Wind, *Pagan Mysteries*, p. 140. In view of the predominance of triads in *La Concorde*, cf. the "Umbra in lege, imago in evangelio, veritas in coelestibus" cited by Jung in "Transformation Symbolism in the Mass," *Psyche and Symbol* (New York, 1958), p. 155.

19. *De planctu naturae*, pp. 3, 55. See also Robert Hollander, *Boccaccio's Two Venuses* (New York, 1977).

20. Renaissance poets needed no James Frazer to gain access to these ideas.

Cf. the priests of Isis in *FQ* 5, vii, 4 with the "birth" of the moon when Apollo is in Aries (Macrobius, *In Somnium Scipionis* I, vi, 50). And, of course, if one descends from the Stanza della Segnatura directly below to the Borgia apartments one finds ceiling decorations where the Seven Wise Virgins have been prostituted to the descendants of Osiris.

21. *OL*, I, vv. 413-37. Cf. C.S. Lewis, *The Allegory of Love* (London, Oxford and New York, 1971), p. 356.

22. *De planctu naturae*, p. 43. The aura of the *hieros gamos* was invoked, exactly in the same terms, in countless marriage masques, in epithalamia and elsewhere (cf. Du Bartas's "le nœud du sacré mariage / Qui joint les elemens"), and with it related symbols like the double-natured, double-sexed hermaphrodite—from Hermes and Aphrodite.

23. Leo Spitzer has some remarkably insightful comments on this point, in *Classical and Christian Ideas of World Harmony* (Baltimore, 1963), pp. 125-29. See also Paul Zumthor, *Essai de poétique médiévale* (Paris, 1972), pp. 189-243, and *Le Masque et la lumière* (Paris, 1978), pp. 198-99.

24. Cf. Aristotle, *Works*, trans. W.D. Ross (Oxford, 1931), III, 396 b. Details of language are worth attending to here since they show how automatic were the assumptions. Apuleius, for instance, translates the pseudo-Aristotelian *De Mundo* (περι κοσμου) 396 b 12 as "pictura ex discordibus pigmentorum coloribus."

25. *De Harmonia mundi totius cantica tria* (Paris, 1545), f. 101r (cf. also ff. 335v—336r). The translation is as follows: Let us briefly scan a few instances of the great Architect's care to dispose the proportions of the members of the body in the most harmonious manner; in which every concord and every harmony will be seen to have been brought together—omitting others, where the intermediate intervals are, as it were, filled in and completed. For the proportion of the whole body to the trunk is sesquioctaval [9:8]. The trunk or thorax to the whole length of the legs, as far as the soles of the feet is sesquitertial [4:3] . . . the proportions in which the tone, the diatessaron, the diapente, and the diapason resound.

26. Macrobius believed that the seven planets form a heptachord, with a total interval of a diapason (*In Somnium Scipionis*, II, 1-4). Cf. Machaut's *Dit de la harpe* with its harmonization of quaternities and equation of the seventh string with St. Paul's charity.

27. *The Waning of the Middle Ages* (New York, 1954), p. 295.

28. Slightly more than a century after Lorenzetti's fresco, Vasari's *Ragionamenti* (1588) picture Astraea in a Florentine setting holding a pair of scales in a similar pose, while Saturn and Janus sleep the "sweet slumber of the golden age." Cf. Ovid's "concordi pace legavit," *Metamorphoses* I, 25 and François Rigolot, *Poétique et onomastique* (Geneva, 1977), pp. 49-50.

29. Spitzer is again highly informative on the continuity of these associations, from Cicero through Augustine, Alanus and Dante to the advent of *cantus firmus*; and on the relationship between the *Discordia concors* and *cymbalum mundi* motifs on the one hand and, on the other, generating words from *con* and *cordia* etymologies (*Classical and Christian Ideas*, pp. 18-19, 40-43, 70-71, 84-88). Implicit comparison of etymologies is seen in the play of Cretin's refrain, "discord: accordez le / En chant royal" against the line "sapience eslième leurs courages," for the *Sursum corda* in the Mass is an appeal to elevated feelings (in *Anthologie des grands rhétoriqueurs*, p. 190). Cf. the "Levez voz cueurs" of Genius's sermon (v. 523). We should stress that the iconographic components invariably coexist in concert. E.g., Scève sets a personal

reflection against a backdrop in which strings of the terrestrial instrument tap the harmonic mystery of the angelic spheres to reconcile Mars and Venus (*Délie* 196; cf. *La Concorde du genre humain*, v. 264). Similar examples are legion among the Pléiade poets.

30. Mircea Eliade, "The 'God who Binds' and the Symbolism of Knots," *Images and Symbols* (London, 1961), pp. 92-124. In *La Concorde du genre humain*, where the triad and numerology are paramount, "paix fut trouvée et concorde tissue" (v. 145).

31. Cf. Mircea Eliade, *The Sacred and the Profane* (New York, 1959), pp. 73-76. Although the degree of Lemaire's subscription to allegorical belief must remain moot, in the *Illustrations* and elsewhere he evinces a solid and detailed command of alchemy and the way astrology is presumed to exert a controlling influence on the human and terrestrial quaternities, leading to the production of harmony (e.g., I, 271-74). While this is not anomalous for his generation, it should be pointed out that the "meditation ague" granted by the favorable influence of Venus is not far from the "arguzzie" championed later by the Italian commentators of Aristotle as the talent for detecting the hidden connections among all things; cf. esp. Augustine, *De trinitate* IV, ii, 4 and IV, iii, 6. Moreover, Lemaire mentions Berosus (I, 104; II, 266) whose calculations from the Sumerian "King Lists" embrace the creation and dissolution of the world, and can be made to coincide exactly with the mythic numbers in Genesis 6. Undoubtedly, the stories of Apollo's invasion of Delphi and his blind counterpart, the visionary Tiresias, both belong to this family of myth. Their stories intersect in a common tale where the separation of coupling serpents allows the transcendence of sexual partiality and conveys the idea of striking the mystic center where all pairs of opposites are dissolved.

32. Harry Levin reminds us that for Columbus "the newly discovered hemisphere was shaped like a woman's breast, and that the Earthly Paradise was located at a high point corresponding to the nipple," in *The Myth of the Golden Age* (Bloomington, 1969), p. 183. Cf. the description of a mass by Jacobus Obrecht, described as a "musico-mathematical cosmos, a number symphony, a cathedral in tone for Our Lady," in Maren-Sofie Røstvig, *The Hidden Sense* (Oslo, 1963), pp. 21-22. Medieval and Renaissance cartographies tell a fascinating story in this regard, for their symbolic location of center and circumference of the world.

33. Renaissance adherence to the sanctity of the number *three* need not, of course, be traced directly to Pythagoras: cf. *Eclogues* VIII, 75. But regardless of the point of origin, usage is remarkably uniform and tends to conform to the dance of the Graces and elements in *La Concorde*; e.g., "Nombre [trois] chery de Dieu, nombre de qui le centre / Des deux extremitez s'esloigne egalement," *The Works of Guillaume de Salluste, sieur Du Bartas*, ed. Urban T. Holmes, Jr. (Chapel Hill, 1940), III, 175. The "Plato Four" of the Medici Academy never tire of seeing triplicity throughout nature as the ineffable stamp of holy trinities. A fine summary of the divinity and mediation of the "marriage" number three is offered by Christopher Butler, *Number Symbolism* (London, 1970), pp. 38-39. But more fruitful than producing exhaustive lists of similarities would be a comparison of, say, Jean Marot's rondeau to Louise de Savoie in which her nobility derives from the celestial model ("O noble geniture! / Vous estes uni corps, comme une trine essence, / Ung seul cueur en trois corps") with the rhyming triplet that begins Scève's 3,003 verse *Microcosme* ("Dieu, qui trine en fus, triple es, et trois seras . . . A ton image fait et divin, et humain. / Premier en son Rien clos se celoit en son Tout"). Key mathemat-

ical ratios reflect the heavenly proportion in the Creator's divine mind and, in turn, since the Sumerians they have been the sought-for means of linking man's physical world with the spiritual plan of all creation.

34. Johann Reuchlin, *De arte cabalistica*, facsimile ed. (Stuttgart, 1964), p. 170. As distinct from the number *four* which organizes the physical world (elements, humors, etc.), the spiritual "verticality" of a mediating term between divine and fallen nature naturally led Ficino (in *De vita coelitus comparanda*) and many others to identify the Virgin with the *anima mundi*: a mediating point in a trinity composed of extremes. Jean Parmentier especially sees the Virgin as the interstice between "saincte Théologie" and "subtille Astrologie" in a firmament that is proportionate and concordant. Since she is "le cercle où gist, par aliance, / Ordre et Raison en purité parfaicte," and since God created "le Grand Cercle de Vie" of the zodiac and "la grand sphère notée," they are associated by the "maintz haultz secretz de vraye astronomie" (in *Anthologie des grands rhétoriqueurs*, pp. 263, 265, 268). Destrées closes a poem to the mystic saint Catherine of Siena by referring to the "ame Mundi"; Zumthor has shown that the poem is based on an invertible 3-2-1 proportion (in *Le Masque et la lumière*, p. 262; cf. p. 166), where one sees a possible echo of Plutarch's παλίντονος that makes the "harmony of the world like a lyre" (*De Iside et Osiride*, 45).

35. Lemaire's emendation goes far beyond the source in Boccaccio proposed by Frappier (note 114). We might compare his Graces to the voluptuous Venus, contemplative Minerva and active Juno of the *Illustrations*, but Cornelius Agrippa's *De occulta philosophia* (II, 25-26) provides the most intriguing comparison, especially where the harmony, concord and proportion in the microcosm of the bodily temple are at issue: it is music that has the power to *attract* animals, to *hold*, and to *tame* them, thus diffusing joy through the created world. This is expressed through the metaphor of the stringed lyre and diapason (cf. Lemaire, IV, 90). For Pico the division of the unity of Venus into the trinity of Graces is the key to understanding Orphic theology (*Conclusiones*, XXXI, 8). No doubt on the model of I Corinthians 13, grace itself is multiplied by membership in other triads; Ambrose and Augustine assume the mutual illumination of grace, nature, and harmony. In fact, on occasion Venus is accompanied by Faith, Hope and Charity (cf. P. Bersuire, *Metamorphosis Ovidiana Moraliter* [Paris, 1515], f. VIII^v). The name of the third Grace is close to *Sophrosyne*, the Greek ideal of moderation.

36. On the "explication" through the Graces of the "infolded" Venus, see especially Wind, *Pagan Mysteries*, pp. 204-05. In successive tableaux that recall *La Concorde* at many points, Isidore of Seville and Chastelain stress the manifestation—under the signs of Prudence and Temperance—of transcendent Grace in the earthly virtue of *Urbanité*. In addition to the active/passive role of *Urbanité*, they also detail its various aspects: *gentille, courtoise, gaillarde, civile, compagnable*, and its encouragement of friendly eloquence (IV, 82-107).

37. *Laetitia (lÿesse)*, for instance, is the term used by Ficino to translate *Euphrosyne* (*De amore* V, 2). On grace, concord and the interchange of consonants, see Philo, *Quaestiones in Exodum* II, 118. Aspiring swains elbow one another so fiercely at the entrance to Venus's temple that "l'un donnoit empesche à l'autre." The enthusiasm that grips them is described as "fureur amoureuse."

38. *Le Masque et la lumière*, p. 140. He may have "bendant son arc d'ivoyre" (v. 512) in mind. Like the Venusberg music at the close of *Tannhäuser*, mixture of *eros* and *agape* is common currency among the Minnesänger. Cf. Spitzer, *Classical and Christian Ideas*, pp. 91-92.

39. Cf. "Take but degree away, untune the string, / And, hark! what discord follows: each thing meets in mere oppugnancy," *Troilus and Cressida* I, 3. On Heraclitus's part, see Pico's views in *Opere di Girolamo Benivieni* (Venice, 1524), ff. 21ᵛ-22ᵛ. Phonetic resemblance between *life* (Βίος) and *bow* (Βιός) may have helped to strengthen associations.

40. *Pagan Mysteries*, pp. 86-87, 92, 95. Wind demonstrates similar features in the triad of Juno, Minerva and Venus, whose dissension ends when Mercury raises his caduceus. I am indebted to Wind (p. 196) for the discussion of hermaphroditism that will be coming up shortly.

41. Cf. Wind, *Pagan Mysteries*, pp. 39, 129. The arcane traditions are exceptionally fluid with respect to Mercury. In Hermetic learning, Mercury confers on mankind wisdom, moderation, eloquence, and truth. Among Gnostics, for whom the Fall was epitomized by the incarnation of Sophia in nature, the evil Jesus and Mary are foreshadowed respectively by Mercury and Venus.

42. See Robert Durling, *The Figure of the Poet in Renaissance Epic* (Cambridge, Mass., 1965), pp. 258-59. Cf. v. 183 and I, 240-49. The insistent search for "aulcune chose estrange, merveilleuse et anticque . . . anciennes merveilles" anticipates discussion of metaphor later in the century as well as Henri Estienne's *Traité de la conformité des merveilles anciennes avec les modernes*. See also *La Concorde du genre humain*, vv. 393-96; III, 198; and Georges Doutrepont, *Jean Lemaire de Belges et la Renaissance* (Brussels, 1934), pp. 210-11.

43. Lemaire outlines this "concordance" of proper and common nouns, "de merveilleuse antiquité, ce qui le rend plus noble et plus resplendissant" (II, 266). The narrator's pressing need to escape the crushing sun through some "belle liqueur refrigereuse" from an anonymous fountain would probably have been recognized as the *aqua refrigerativa* of Aquarius, the traditional symbol of Temperance. This is what Robert de Grosseteste makes of it (see Siegfried Wenzel, "The Seven Deadly Sins: Some Problems of Research," *Speculum*, 43 [1968], 1-22). For great purveyors of the *Discordia concors* motif, such as Ambrose, Philo and Piero Valeriano's *Hieroglyphica* (recalling John 7: 37), Temperance is symbolized by the Nile since it bathes Egypt, itself symbolic of the enticements of pleasure in Holy Scripture; cf. Lemaire, I, 302.

44. Hermathena was presumed to typify the Florentine Platonic Academy, combining action with steadfastness. Cf. IV, 74; *L'Heptaméron*, 18; and Du Bellay, *Sonnets divers*, 29 and 32. Rosalie Colie points out that Pico's "lordship of concord" was achieved by uniting wisdom and eloquence, *Paradoxia Epidemica* (Princeton, 1966), p. 66.

45. Elsewhere he similarly portrays Minerva in paradise settings where the *etymon* of her name is dissected and the mystic triplicity of the French crest is set forth (*La Concorde du genre humain*, vv. 416-28, 583-93; *Illustrations*, I, 240). Concorde in the former work is characterized as "gaillarde" yet is also an "esprit angelin" (v. 474).

46. Cf. Plotinus, *Enneads* I, iv, 10 and Augustine, "as from one man's face many likenesses are reflected in a mirror, so many truths are reflected from the one divine truth" (quoted by Aquinas, *Summa Contra Gentiles*, 47). St. Paul's I Cor. 13 is, of course, one of the most dominant Scriptural exempla of the late 15th century, but cf. also 2 Cor. 3: 7-8, 17-18; 4: 6, and *Institutio Christianae religionis* I, v, 1. In view of the great frequency of Lemaire's references to Prudentia as the mastery of past, present and future, of which several examples have already been cited, we

should also mention Valeriano's *Hieroglyphica* where three modes are reflected in a mirror.

47. See Jung, XII, 362; XIII, 183. Both Alanus (*Theatrum chemicum*) and Meung (*Le miroir d'alquimie*) are associated with this tradition. A medieval Italian illustration depicts a closural image of Sophia-Sapientia suckling and reconciling two bearded initiates—the "spirit bride" of the Apocalypse; and in an identical 2:1 pose, a 16th-century manuscript of Aquinas's *De alchimia* shows Sapientia sheltering a similar pair beneath a legend from Matt. 12: 42 (illustrated in Neumann, *The Great Mother*, p. 329, and Jung, XII, 362). Cf. Marot, "Leander & Héro," vv. 127-30, 255-56, 268. Long ago Henri Franchet amply demonstrated the abundance of temples of honor and virtue in the 16th century (*Le Poète et son œuvre d'après Ronsard* [Paris, 1923; Geneva: Slatkine, 1969), especially pp. 54, 103).

François Lesure

Musiciens et textes poétiques au XVIe siècle: corrections ou corruptions?

L'une des tâches les plus ingrates des musicologues seiziémistes consiste à identifier les auteurs des poèmes de chansons. Devant les difficultés rencontrées, certains émettent parfois l'hypothèse que les musiciens ont pu écrire eux-mêmes leurs textes. Quelques-uns en étaient sans aucun doute capables: Janequin n'a-t-il pas signé une épître dédicatoire de quelque cinquante vers à Catherine de Médicis, en tête de ses *Octante deux pseaumes*, parus quelques mois après sa mort? Dominique Phinot adresse respectivement un dizain et un huitain aux dédicataires de ses premier et second livres de chansons (1548) et Goudimel place au début de son cinquième livre de psaumes une ode qu'il adresse à son protecteur, le maréchal de Vieilleville (1566). Dans d'autres cas, ces dons nous sont révélés par des hommages poétiques. François Habert en insère deux dans son *Temple de chasteté* (1549): Jean Bastard, maître des enfants de chœur de la Ste-Chapelle de Bourges, "esprit curieux non seulement de ton art de musique, mais des couleurs de phrase poétique"; Jacques Caupain, de Rouen, "poète et musicien," auquel il consacre les vers suivants:

> D'ouyr les sons de ta fluste et fredons
> On ne pourroit ennuyer son aureille,
> Mais tu as bien encores plus beaulx dons
> Que ta Musique exquise et non pareille,
> Car quand ta main d'escrire s'appareille
> Inventions en phrase poétique
> Du stile tien un chascun s'esmerveille
> Plus qu'il ne faict de ta doulce Musique.

La curiosité poétique de beaucoup de musiciens est évidente. Un exemple en est particulièrement frappant. L'épigramme de Marot, *Du beau tétin*, fut écrit, nous disent les biographes du poète, à la fin de 1535: dès avril 1536 paraissait chez Attaingnant à Paris la chanson de Janequin composée sur ce texte![1] Le cas de Marot est d'ailleurs exemplaire: ses chansons, que l'on a parfois présumé conçues pour la musique, n'ont pas toutes intéressé les compositeurs. Observateurs attentifs des courants poétiques de leur temps, ceux-ci préfèrent parfois fabriquer leur propre *poesia per musica* à partir d'épigrammes ou de rondeaux. Cette recherche personnelle d'une série de quelques vers aux thèmes amoureux, convenant à l'esthétique de la chanson parisienne, ressort avec évidence lorsqu'il s'agit de fragments découpés dans de plus longs poèmes.

Jean Guyon, musicien de Chartres, publia, par exemple, en 1550, une chanson sur les vers 159 à 164 d'une poésie qu'il avait trouvée dans *Le Temple de Vertu* de François Habert: "Longtemps y a, innocente pucelle." De même, trois élégies de Marot ont été la source de chansons, non pas dans leur début mais du quinzième au vingtième vers de chacune d'entre elles: "Puisque ton cœur me veulx donc présenter" (*Elégie* V), musique de Jean de Maillard, *Le Parangon* IX (Lyon: J. Moderne, 1541); "Lors tout ravy pour ce que je pensay" (*Elégie* XV), musique de J. Arcadelt, *Vingt-cinquiesme Livre* (Paris: P. Attaingnant, 1547);[2] "Pour ton amour, j'ay souffert tant d'ennuys" (*Elégie* II), musique de D. Phinot (Lyon: Beringen, 1548).

Ces trois musiciens ont donc chacun isolé cinq vers d'une élégie, ayant assez de sens pour constituer une œuvre à part. Il est clair que des recherches systématiques amèneraient d'autres découvertes analogues. Mais, en procédant à de tels découpages, les compositeurs s'exposaient aussi à présenter des textes qui, sur le strict plan littéraire, devenaient fort obscurs, une fois coupés de leur contexte. C'est le cas d'une chanson de D. Phinot: "Pyrrhus le roi de Pire," dont on n'a d'ailleurs pas repéré l'origine.[3]

Pour trouver le support de leur inspiration, les musiciens se procuraient des recueils de poésies, manuscrits ou imprimés, individuels ou collectifs. Si leur choix est par lui-même significatif, le traitement qu'ils faisaient ensuite subir au texte n'est pas sans enseignement.

Une première série de petites modifications ne pose aucun problème: celles qui consistent à dépersonnaliser un vers ou à le simplifier en supprimant une allusion risquant de paraître obscure au chanteur ou à son auditeur. Deux exemples: Jean Maillard dans sa chanson "Ne vous forcez de me cherer" (1559) transforme tout naturellement le troisième vers de l'épigramme de Marot, "*mes vers* vous veulent révérer" en "*seulement* vous veux révérer"; dans le recueil des *Trente Chansons* d'Attaingnant (1529), le musicien anonyme de "D'un nouveau dard" clarifie le second vers de la chanson: "Par Cupido, cruel de soy" devient "Par amour trop cruelle de soy."

Du fait de telles corrections, certains poèmes apparaissent incompréhensibles ou avec un sens aberrant. Il suffit parfois d'une seule coquille pour défigurer le sens d'un texte déjà alambiqué. C'est le cas de la chanson de Pierre Certon sur les vers de Saint-Gelais: "Je ne voy rien si souvent que ses yeux"; le dernier vers "que pour *les* veoir soudain je ne revienne," en devenant "que pour *le* veoir . . ." perd tout son sens. En remplaçant "Delia" par Diane dans un poème de Maurice Scève, Jacques Boyvin ou son éditeur Attaingnant a détruit l'antithèse sur laquelle était bâti le texte.[4] Dans d'autres cas on hésite entre la coquille typographique et la bévue négligente. La chanson de Marot "Une pastourelle gentille" fournit l'occasion au musicien anonyme des *Trente et huyt Chansons* d'Attaingnant (1529) d'une "lecture" particulièrement lourde: "L'autr'hyer, jouant a la bille . . ." . . . . / C'est trop a la ville joué" pour "L'autr'hyer, jouant a la bille . . ."

Lorsque Du Caurroy reprendra ce texte en 1583, il rétablira la version correcte. Il serait d'ailleurs imprudent d'affirmer que ces menus changements étaient l'œuvre du musicien et non celle de l'éditeur ou de son correcteur et il convient dans chaque cas d'examiner le lieu d'impression, les habitudes éditoriales, la date respective des publications, littéraire et musicale, etc. D'un genre plus cocasse mais anecdotique est la métamorphose subie par le rondeau de Marot, "Dedans Paris, ville jolie." Le musicien de Charles-Quint, Thomas Crecquillon, en fit "Dedans Tournai, ville jolie"; ce qui entraîna un peu plus loin un autre changement: "A la plus gente damoyselle / Qui soit d'icy en Italie" laissa la place à "A la plus gente damoyselle / Qu'il soit, je le vous certifie."

Si nous envisageons le point de vue de la forme, beaucoup de musiciens du XVIe siècle semblent avoir perdu le sens des formes fixes anciennes, telles que virelai ou rondeau. Effectivement, la structure de ce dernier apparaît en de nombreux cas tronquée. C'est, par exemple, ce que l'on constate dès 1529 dans les *Trente et cinq Chansons* d'Attaingnant, avec une mise en musique d'un rondeau de François Ier: "L'eureux travail, quant sa fin est plaisante" (Rondeau XXV de l'édition Champollion-Figeac). Le musicien anonyme a fabriqué un texte en ajoutant au premier vers de la première strophe les quatre derniers vers de la seconde! De telles mixtures n'étaient pas rares à l'époque où la mystique de l'union de la poésie et de la musique n'était pas encore établie.

Dans le même recueil déjà cité des *Trente et cinq Chansons* on trouve un quatrain:

Ha hay, estes vous renchérie,
Dieu y ait part, puis devant hier?
Mais venez ça, je vous en prie
Est le cuyr devenu si cher

qui apparaît sous la forme suivante dans un recueil poétique:

Hahay! estes-vous renchérie,
Dieux y ait part, puis devant hier?
Ma dame, c'est pour enrager!
Le faictes-vous par mocquerie?

Mais venez ça, je vous en prie:
Est le cuir devenu si cher?
Hahay! estes-vous renchérie?[5]

Il ne faut pas toujours mettre au compte des corruptions les transformations que certains musiciens font subir au rondeau cinquain. L'exemple de "Mon confesseur m'a dict," mis en chanson par Clément Janequin en 1534 a fait l'objet d'une récente mise au point.[6] L'éditeur Attaingnant paraît responsable d'une présentation quelque peu ambiguë: d'abord les deux cinquains, avec à la fin le retour du vers initial, comme s'il s'agissait d'un refrain; puis le groupe médian de trois vers, se terminant, lui aussi, par le rentrement final. Beaucoup plus tard, en 1570, Guillaume Costeley publie dans son recueil *Musique* un rondeau de Marot (XLV): "Toutes les nuits je ne pense qu'en celle," qui présente la même forme apparemment bâtarde du rondeau, avec ses deux cinquains et, cette fois, sans que les trois vers médians se trouvent mis en musique à la suite ou dans le même recueil.[7] Sur le plan musical, la phrase de chacun des derniers vers des deux cinquains est répétée et la chanson se termine par les trois premiers mots de la chanson: "Toutes les nuits."

Un autre exemple de changement de forme peut être étudié avec le *Chant lyrique d'une damoiselle amoureuse* d'Etienne Forcadel, mis en chanson en 1548 par D. Phinot: "Par un trait d'or trop esmoulu." Le poète avait introduit une alternance dans le dernier vers de chacun des quatrains qui composent son texte, entre "Amour me fait vivre et mourir" et "Je ne puis vivre sans mourir." Le musicien ne conserve pas cette alternance et garde seulement le premier vers, par lequel il termine chaque quatrain. Mais il procède à d'autres corrections et refait presque entièrement le quatrième quatrain:

Hé dieux benins, je ne scay pas
Si venant l'heure du trespas
Je pourray de ce mal guerir
Je ne puis vivre sans mourir.

Phinot   Si mort quand me viendra surprendre
                Mon triste esprit ne peut comprendre
                Me pourra de ce mal guerir
                Amour me fait vivre et mourir.

Il est enfin des problèmes qui laissent supposer des initiatives plus radicales de la part de certains musiciens. Voici le cas d'une chanson dont les deux premiers vers sont semblables à un poème de Saint-Gelais mais dont la suite s'en écarte totalement. Le musicien—Clément Morel, de Nevers— publie en effet en 1543: "Cessez mes yeulx de tant vous tourmenter / Puisque voz pleurs n'y a poinct d'allegence," mais brise ensuite la forme dialoguée adoptée par le poète (cf. Blanchemain, II, 50).

A la question posée en tête de cet article, il semblerait donc que les cas de corruption sont infiniment plus nombreux que ceux qui nous fourniraient une meilleure lecture. Cependant ces derniers se rencontrent également. "Prudemment étudiés," écrit V.L. Saulnier, "les textes des éditions musicales peuvent sur plus d'un point, rendre des services comparables à ceux qu'offrent plus aisément les manuscrits de travail—pièces dont nous manquons toujours, pour le XVIᵉ siècle."[8] Comme beaucoup de chansons sont en réalité des éditions pré-originales de poèmes, les éditeurs de textes seraient bien inspirés en fouillant systématiquement les recueils de chansons.

Prenons comme exemple un dizain de Saint-Gelais, publié par Blanchemain d'après le ms. La Rochetulon:

> De qui plus tost me devrois-je complaindre
> D'Amour, de vous, de moy mesme ou du Temps?
> Amour me veult à le servir contraindre;
> Vous refusez ce qu'a bon droict j'attends;
> Je vy d'espoir et nul bien ne pretends,
> Et par le Temps contraint suis m'absenter.
> Ainsy j'ay cause assez de lamenter,
> Mais plus de vous; car vous estes a mesme
> De me pouvoir promptement contenter
> D'Amour, de vous, du Temps et de moy mesme.

Deux musiciens, Pierre Sandrin en 1549 et Villers vers 1561, l'ont publié, avec seulement quelques variantes orthographiques, sous cette forme:

> De qui plus tost maintenant me doibz plaindre
> D'Amour, de vous, de moy mesme ou du Temps?
> Amour me veult a le servir contraindre;
> Vous reffusez ce que de vous j'atendz;
> Assez congnois qu'en trop hault lieu pretendz,
> Et contrainct suis par le Temps m'absenter.

> Mais je ne doibz de rien me lamenter,
> Sinon de vous, car vous estes a mesme, etc.

Il est certain que dans la seconde moitié du siècle les musiciens, influencés par les idées réformatrices de la Pléiade, deviennent plus respectueux de la lettre des poèmes. Leurs éditeurs sont eux-mêmes conscients de ce nouveau climat. Alors qu'Attaingnant ou Moderne—pour des raisons en partie techniques—n'impriment pratiquement jamais qu'une seule strophe placée sous la musique, leurs successeurs, tels Le Roy et Ballard ou Du Chemin, publient au besoin plusieurs strophes à chanter sur la même musique.[9] Les textes eux-mêmes sont généralement plus soignés.

Quant à établir des lois à partir de l'océan de variantes qui sépare chansons musicales et recueils poétiques, il ne saurait ici en être question. Beaucoup sont purement orthographiques ou n'ont aucune signification. D'autres s'expliquent par des problèmes de prosodie ou de difficultés de prononciation, risquant d'embarrasser les chanteurs. C'est ainsi que l'on a pu relever dans des poèmes de Ronsard mis en musique des variantes tendant à remédier à des assonances ou à des allitérations gênantes.[10]

Mon propos final est double: attirer l'attention des éditeurs de textes poétiques de cette époque sur les recueils musicaux, qui fournissent de précieux éléments de datation et parfois des états antérieurs; souligner le devoir qu'ont les éditeurs de chansons de corriger les leçons les plus fautives de leurs textes, non pas en s'écartant des intentions de la source originale, mais en restituant, s'il y a lieu, le sens correct des poèmes qui ont inspiré les musiciens.

NOTES

1. Pour ne pas surcharger les notes de cet article, nous n'indiquerons pas en détail les références des sources originales. En ce qui concerne les recueils musicaux, celles-ci sont facilement accessibles, grâce aux bibliographies d'Attaingnant (Daniel Heartz, 1969), J. Moderne (S. Pogue, 1969), Du Chemin et Le Roy-Ballard (F. Lesure et G. Thibault, 1953 et 1955), ainsi que par les volumes du *Répertoire international des sources musicales*.

2. Ces deux textes n'avaient pas été identifiés dans mon article "Autour de Marot et de ses musiciens," inséré dans *Musique et musiciens français du XVIe siècle* (Genève, 1976), pp. 37-49.

3. V.L. Saulnier, "D. Phinot et D. Lupi, musiciens de C. Marot et des marotiques," *Revue de Musicologie*, 41 (1959), 75.

4. V.L. Saulnier, "Maurice Scève et la musique," dans *Musique et poésie au XVIe siècle* (Paris: CNRS, 1954), pp. 99-100; "Sur trois dizains de Maurice Scève," *Annales de l'Université de Paris* (1952), pp. 187-91.

5. Attribué à F. Villon par P. Lacroix (éd. 1877), p. 173.

6. J.P. Ouvrard, *"Mon confesseur*, rondeau de C. Janequin," *Revue de Musicologie*, 50 (1978), 203-28.

7. Vingt ans auparavant, Clemens non papa s'était borné à faire une chanson avec seulement le premier cinquain du même rondeau.

8. Saulnier, "Maurice Scève et la musique," art. cit., p. 100.

9. Dans certains cas on observe un choix dans les strophes. Ainsi Tessier dans son *Premier Livre d'airs* (1582), mettant en musique "Amans qui vous plaignés" de Brantôme, ne donne que les strophes 1, 5 et 6 des huit que comporte le poème.

10. R. Lebègue, "Ronsard corrigé par un de ses musiciens," *Revue de Musicologie*, 39 (1957), 71-72.

Claude Longeon

Sur la trace d'une édition perdue d'Etienne Dolet

Des 65 ouvrages condamnés par la Faculté de Théologie de Paris entre le 23 décembre 1542 et le 2 mars 1543, les 4 suivants étaient des presses d'Etienne Dolet: le *Chevalier Chretien* traduit du latin d'Erasme, le *Nouveau Testament*, les *Psalmes de Daniel* [sic] accompagnés du *Sermon du bon et maulvais pasteur*,[1] enfin un "Brief Discours de la Republique Françoise, desirant la lecture des Livres de la sainte Ecriture, et iceux approuvés par les Docteurs de l'Eglise lui être loisible en sa langue vulgaire qui semble de Dolet, à cause qu'il a fait l'épître préliminaire."[2] Pour ce dernier livre, la censure fut rappelée en 1544[3] et en 1551.[4] En 1585 Antoine du Verdier en donnait le titre complet dans sa *Bibliothèque*, à l'article "Estienne Dolet":

Brief discours de la Republique Françoyse desirant la lecture des livres de la Saincte escriture luy estre loisible en sa langue vulgaire. Ledit discours est en Rime. Avec un petit traicté en prose monstrant comme on se doit apprester à la lecture des escritures Sainctes: et ce qu'on y doit chercher. [impr. à Lyon 16°, par luy mesme 1544][5]

La date d'impression est erronée, puisqu'elle est antérieure à l'édit de censure du 2 mars 1543; et comme il n'est pas fait allusion à cet ouvrage dans la liste des œuvres de Dolet "dampnez et reprouvez" par le tribunal inquisitorial de Lyon le 2 octobre 1542,[6] c'est entre ces deux dates qu'il faut placer la naissance de ce livre, dont on n'a retrouvé à ce jour aucun exemplaire et dont on ne connaîtrait pas le contenu exact si Francis Higman n'avait récemment découvert à la Bibliothèque Nationale de Vienne un exemplaire d'une édition de ce texte imprimée ultérieurement à Caen par Martin et Pierre Philippe.

En voici la description:

Brief discours de | la Republique Francoyse, de- | sirant la lecture des Liures de | la saincte Escripture (et iceulx | approuués par les Docteurs de | l'Eglise) luy estre loysible en sa | langue vulgaire. /† * † / [marque des Philippe = Silvestre n° 631] / A CAEN.

16°: a-c⁸ [$ 4 signés; a3 pour a4, b2 pour c2, c3 pour c4]. 24 folios non chiffrés.
car. rom. et ital.
Österreichische Nationalbibliothek Vienne   79.V.56 (3).

a2-a2v: *ESTIENNE | DOLET | au Lecteur Chre- | stien, Sa- | lut.*
a3-a8: *BRIEF DISCOURS | DE LA REPVBLIQVE | Françoyse, desirant la lecture des Li- | ures de la saincte Escripture (& iceulx | approuués par les Docteurs de | l'Eglise) luy estre loysi- | ble en sa langue | vulgaire.*
a8v-b1: *CHANSON CHRE- | stienne sur la Lecture des | Sainctes Lettres.*
b1v-b2: *DIXAIN DE LA | Lecture du Nouueau | Testament.*
b2v-c1: *PETIT TRAICTE | MONSTRANT, | comme on se doibt appre- | ster a la lecture des escri | ptures Sainctes: & | ce qu'on y doibt | chercher.*
c1v: *Rondeau à nostre Sauueur Iesus Christ.*
c2-c5v: *CHANSON SVR LES DIX | commandemens de Dieu, qui se chante | sur le chant Au boys du dueil.*
c6-c7: Preceptes de Philosophie Moral / le, que Aristote enuoya / au Roy Alexandre.
c7: [quatrain signé] Mieulx veult faire / que dire.
c7v-c8: [blancs]
c8v: [marque des Philippe (= Silvestre n° 631), suivie de] De l'imprimerie de Martin / & Pierre Philippe.

Les noms de Martin et Pierre Philippe sont connus des bibliographes de Dolet, puisqu'en juillet 1550 ils imprimèrent pour le compte de Robert Macé, libraire à Caen, la *Maniere de bien traduire d'une langue en autre* et les deux autres traités grammaticaux de l'Orléanais.[8] Il semble que ç'ait été là un des premiers travaux réalisés par les frères imprimeurs: on peut donc penser qu'ils réimprimèrent le *Brief Discours* entre 1550 et 1557, l'année de leur séparation. Quelque temps plus tard, en 1562 précisément, Pierre Philippe affirmera ses opinions protestantes en imprimant l'*Institution de la religion chrestienne* de Calvin.[9] Rien ne nous dit pourquoi ou à la demande de qui les frères Philippe procédèrent à cette réimpression. Et rien ne nous assure qu'ils le firent sans retouches, retraits ou ajouts.[10] Constatons en tout cas qu'ils eurent le courage (ou l'inconscience) de ne pas écarter la préface de Dolet, pourtant remarquée par les censeurs:

f° a2   *ESTIENNE | DOLET | au Lecteur Chre- | stien, Sa- | lut.* Le plaisant Discours de ce petit Traicté a esté cause (lecteur debonnaire) que maintenant tu le vois en lumiere. Dedans lequel tu congnoistras le grand desir (desir certainement Chrestien, et louable) de la Republicque Françoyse envers les livres de son createur et Sauveur. Que pleust a Dieu, que par une bonne ordonnance de ceulx qui ont la charge, et administration de cest affaire, la lecture des Sainctes Lettres fust permise en vulgaire, ainsi que de raison: affin qu'au lieu de plusieurs blasphemes execrables, f° a2v°// propos lascifz, et chansons pleines de lubricité, on n'ouyst en France, que la parolle de Dieu retentir par tout. Par ce moyen nous recongnoistrions plus facilement les faultes, qui sont en nous: et prendrions honte en nous mesmes de noz vices par trop abundants, et excessifz. Voyla ce que tu congnoistras en ce petit Livret: lequel tu prendras en bonne part, rendant graces, et louenges au souverain Autheur de tous biens. Adieu Lecteur.

Imprimant ce discours et les pièces qui suivent, Dolet ne faisait que respecter la décision qu'il avait prise au début de cette année 1542, savoir "produire touts petits traictés delectables et necessaires à l'ame Chrestienne,"[11] "remettre en lumiere tout ce qu['il] voirra [y] estre commode pour l'instruction Chrestienne et edification de nostre Foy."[12] Cette politique délibérée, même si elle fut appliquée à des textes qui ne nous semblent pas pécher d'hétérodoxie, ne laissa pas d'inquiéter certaines autorités. Ces réactions, loin de limiter l'ardeur de l'Orléanais, lui apportèrent la conviction qu'il frappait juste et faisait œuvre saine: "comme on ne peult toucher sus une apostume ou ulcere enchancry, sans causer douleur à celluy qui est infect de telles putrefactions," écrit-il en tête de l'*Exhortation à la lecture des Sainctes Lettres* (Lyon, Dolet, ante oct. 1542), "en semblable sorte ces esprits infects de vice ne peulvent veoir ou recepvoir le contraire et medecine (si bien l'entendoyent) de leur maladie sans mescontentement et infinie complaincte."[13] La préface de ce *Brief Discours*, qui est pour développer les mêmes thèmes que l'*Exhortation* sous une forme moins oratoire, résume centralement quelques pages de cette œuvre où l'auteur anonyme déplore que de son temps "celuy seroit reputé hereticque, qui chanteroit psalmes ou chansons prinses de l'Escripture saincte. Celluy qui chante chansons de paillardise, ou infameté, est estimé vertueux";[14] puis Dolet appelle à la repentance. Rien de pendable dans cette préface, sinon qu'elle est de Dolet. Car depuis 1538 et ses démêlés avec la justice lyonnaise pour avoir commis le *Cato Christianus*, les *Fata Francisci Valesii* et les *Carmina*, l'imprimeur est étroitement surveillé et son nom seul rend suspects des ouvrages en eux-mêmes scrupuleusement orthodoxes. Orthodoxe, le *Brief Discours* l'est, en ce qu'il ne heurte aucun des dogmes de l'Eglise Romaine. Mais on conçoit qu'il ait, comme l'*Exhortation*, irrité les docteurs parisiens puisqu'on y combat pied à pied les arguments de ceux qui proclamaient que lire les Ecritures en français ne pouvait qu'égarer les fidèles, et tout particulièrement les femmes.[15]

f° a3

BRIEF DISCOURS
DE LA REPUBLIQVE
Françoyse, desirant la lecture des Li-
ures de la saincte Escripture (et iceulx
approuvés par les Docteurs de
l'Eglise) luy estre loysible en sa langue
vulgaire.

Non sans raison, et certain jugement
Le Seigneur veult ses sainctes Escriptures
Nommer le vieil, et nouveau Testament.
C'est nostre Pere: et nous ses creatures.
Sçavoir debvons, quelles sont noz droictures,
Quel est le bien, et fruict de l'heritage,
Qu'il nous promist: quel doibt estre l'usage
De sa bonté qu'il veult estre preschée
A tous, par tout, tousjours, en tout langage.

f° a3v   Sa grace doncq' ne doibt estre empeschee.

Son Testament, et volunté derniere
Escripte à tous, de tous doibt estre leue:
Mais je ne sçay la façon, et maniere
De l'accomplir, s'elle n'est entendue.
Si on allegue aux femmes n'estre deue
Par les prescheurs qui ont l'intelligence
Des grands secrets, et certaine science:
Et qu'assez est croire ce qu'ilz ont dict:
Je ne veulx pas blasmer ceste sentence:
Mais je vous dye, que c'est croire a credit:

Car s'il estoit d'adventure advenu
(Ce que, o mon Dieu, ne vueille consentir!)
Que le loup fust pour le pasteur tenu
Du droict chemin il pourroit divertir
Tout le trouppeau: pour lequel convertir
Est descendu du ciel le vray pasteur:
Et de grand maistre, il s'est faict serviteur:
De Dieu, vray homme. O bonté infinie!
Chasse les Loups, et me donne cest heur
Que ta parolle à mon cueur soit unie.

f° a4   Qu'ay je meffaict? suis je excommuniee?
Ne suis je point des membres de l'Eglise?
Pourquoy m'est doncq' la parolle nyee,
Par qui je suis bien instruicte et apprise?
Si j'en abuse il fault que sois reprise:
Car ce n'est pas l'escripture, c'est moy,
Qui a failly, n'ayant la vifve foy,
Qui conduict l'œuvre. Helas je le sens bien.
Ostez l'abus: et ne faictes la Loy,
Qu'un mal privé empesche un commun bien.

Le Sainct Esperit nous appelle, et inspire,
Comme il luy plaist. C'est un poinct arresté.
Et ne sçauroit aucun luy contredire:
Car il faict tout selon sa volunté:
Et n'a jamais nostre sexe excepté,
Que de salut ne l'ayt rendu capable.
Juger ne puis, si c'est hystoire, ou fable,
Ce qu'un Prescheur en la chaire racompte.
Mais qui a veu le texte veritable,
f° a4v   Le reçoipt mieulx, et en faict plus grand compte.

Françoise suis selon ma nation:
Qui n'entends Grec, ny Latin, ny Hebrieu
Femme je suis, qui ay devotion
(Comme je doibs) de congnoistre mon Dieu.
Je vous supply, dictes moy, en quel lieu,
Pour bien apprendre, et sçavoir sa parolle,
Je doibs aller, sinon en son escolle?
Là je ne puis jamais estre deceue:
Là est ma force, et elle me consolle:
Et rien ne sçait celle qui ne l'a sceue.

Si l'homme doncq' ne me la veult permettre,
Il monstre assez, qu'il me veult decepvoir:
Car il congnoist, que par la saincte lettre
Suis attirée à faire mon debvoir:
Et la lumiere en icelle puis veoir:
Qui mon esprit aveugle doibt conduyre
A verité, que chascun veult destruire
f° a5   Par les prisons de sagesse mondaine.

Mais, ò mon Dieu, vueille moy introduyre
A boire l'eau de la vifve fontaine.

Ceste fontaine est l'Escripture saincte,
Qui peult les mortz mesmes resusciter:
Par qui nous est d'Enfer la flamme extaincte:
Et qui par grace au ciel nous faict monter.
Qui pourra doncq' un tel bien nous oster?
La Terre et Ciel, ò mon Dieu, passeront:
Ses saincts escripts à jamais dureront:
Contre peché ilz tiendront la main forte:
Contre la Mort nostre pleige seront:
Et de la vie ilz nous ouvrent la porte.

Quel interest peult le monde pretendre,
Si je m'addonne à la saincte Escripture?
On me dira, que suis fragile, et tendre,
Et que j'en puis commettre forfaicture.
Je le confesse, et congnoys ma nature
Encline à mal, et au bien trop contraire.
Et par ainsi tant plus m'est necessaire
Lire la Bible et de jour, et de nuict:
f° a5v   Cela me peult à IESUCHRIST attraire:
Cela me sert, et aux autres ne nuict.

Que direz vous? Car par texte je preuve,
Que au plus secret mystere, le Seigneur
(Comme en sainct Marc, dernier Chapitre on treuve)
A voulu faire aux femmes cest honneur,
Que devant touts leur monstrer le bonheur,
Ou nous conduict sa resurrection.
Et approuvant nostre devotion,
A Magdaleine, en sa force, et figure
Il s'est monstré apres sa passion.
L'on ne doibt doncq' cacher son escripture.

Là je pourray les choses impossibles:
Là je croiray les choses incroyables:
Là je voirray les choses invisibles:
Là congnoistray les choses inscrutables:
Là gousteray les plaisirs delectables,

Que CHRIST promist aux esleuz de son père:
Là est certain ce qu'il fault, que j'espere:
Là trouveray ce que je doibs chercher.
Lire la veulx doncques sans impropere,
Pour y apprendre, et non pas pour pecher.

Lire la veulx en toute humilité:
Lire la veulx en toute obeissance,
Pour asseurer mon imbecillité:
Lire la veulx pour avoir congnoissance.
Et si on veult dire que la substance
Dedans cachee et sens allegorique
Mal entendu me doibt rendre heretique,
Dieu ne permette (helas) que je la sois.
Mais s'il en est, qui telle erreur implicque,
Il en est plus en Latin qu'en François.

Lire la veux, pour m'instruire à clemence,
A ferme amour et à dilection:
Lire la veux pour trouver patience
En mon ennuy, force en tentation:
Et pour fonder dessus la passion
De IESUCHRIST, et le sainct sacrement

L'espoir certain de nostre sauvement,
M'humilier envers le plus petit,
Le tort souffert prendre modestement:
Et de vengeance oublier l'appetit.

Lire la veulx, pour bien estre informée,
Que c'est de grace, et que c'est de la Loy:
Lire la veulx pour estre reformée,
Et pour unir les œuvres à la Foy:
Et d'elle apprendre obeir à mon Roy
De cueur entier, et d'amour tresloyalle,
Recongnoissant l'authorité Royalle
Venir du ciel, et fondée de Dieu:
Qui est la cause, et raison principalle,
Que nous croyons, qu'il tient icy son lieu,

Si sainct Jerosme admirable docteur
L'a translaté en langue Dalmaticque

Qui nous vouldroit empescher ce grand heur,
Que ne l'ayons en la nostre Gallique?
Si l'une est bien, l'autre n'est pas inique,
Consideré qu'aux femmes escripvoit:
Et d'y vouloir lire les poursuyvoit,
Comme de chose à salut necessaire.

f° a7   O qu'il seroit estonné s'il vivoit,
De veoir aucuns soustenir le contraire!

Le tiltre mis sur la croix Jesuschrist,
(Ou du salut fut attaché le gage)
En Grec, Latin, et Hebrieu fut escript
(Langues qui lors estoient plus en usage)
Pour demonstrer, qu'il veult en tout langage
Estre annoncé, servy, et honoré.
Puis qu'il est doncq' de moy France adoré,
Le François peult s'efforcer de sçavoir,
Veoir en sa langue un thresor preparé,
Qu'aureille ouyr, et qu'œil ne sçauroit veoir.

Aussi Moyse en la Loy de rigueur
A ordonné que par tout soit escripte,
Lyée au bras, à la porte, et au cueur.
Et pour tirer son peuple hors d'Egypte,
Toute maison il vouloit estre instruicte.
Combien est il en ceste Loy de grace
Plus raisonnable, et requis qu'on le face?
L'homme se voit en elle r'achepté:
Et Jesuchrist qui noz pechez efface,
Pour l'enseigner a prins humanité.

f° a7v   Le Sainct Esprit aux Apostres promis,
Et envoyé: quand il fut descendu,
Le don heureux des langues a transmis:
Et n'a aucun langage defendu,
(L'honneur à Dieu en puisse estre rendu)
Et si l'on dict: c'est pour interpreter:
C'est doncq' aussi pour lire sans doubter.
Car c'est erreur, et fureur de deffendre
Lyre en Françoys, ce qu'on doibt escouter,
Et ce, qu'on veult en Françoys faire entendre.

Finablement si je doibs par raison
Selon la Loy, et divin jugement,
Faire de cueur, et de bouche oraison,
Je vous supply apprenez moy comment
Eslever puis à Dieu l'entendement,
Si je n'entends, qu'à luy doibs recourir?
Vray est, qu'il est prompt à me secourir:
Atend aussy que secours luy demande.
Mais qui entend ce, qu'il doibt requerir,
Au cueur en a devotion plus grande.

Si mon Roy doncq' appellé treschrestien
De tiltre, et nom (encores plus d'effect)
f° a8   Et si sçavant qu'en tout n'ignore rien,
De ce que peult sçavoir l'homme parfaict,
Un si grand bien aux siens veult estre faict,
Que leur donner en Françoys l'escripture
(Qui est de l'ame, et de l'Esperit pasture)
Non seulement avecq' triumphe, et gloire
Il regnera sur toute creature:
Mais donnera de Sathan la victoire.

FIN.

Les arguments sont ceux que développe l'auteur anonyme de l'*Exhortation à la lecture des Sainctes Lettres*, la plupart des allusions scripturaires se rencontraient déjà dans ce texte. Ce qui n'implique pas que le prêtre (qui prend soin de proclamer son orthodoxie) auteur de l'*Exhortation* et du traité sur la lecture des Ecritures Saintes soit également l'auteur de ce *Brief Discours*. Rien ne s'oppose a priori à ce que Dolet lui-même l'ait composé: en d'autres lieux il a donné la preuve de son aisance à versifier. Mais plus vraisemblablement on doit penser qu'en cette année 1542 l'Orléanais, tout occupé à faire connaître du plus grand nombre son nom d'imprimeur, n'eut pas le temps d'écrire et se contenta de rassembler pour les publier des textes divers: l'*Enfer* de Marot, les *Psaumes* selon plusieurs traductions, des traductions de Galien, de Guevara, une œuvre de Lefèvre d'Etaples, la *Parfaicte Amye* d'Héroët, un bulletin d'information, le *Chevalier Chrestien* et le *Vray moyen de bien et catholiquement se confesser* d'Erasme, la *Fontaine de Vye*, etc. Parmi ces textes anonymes (le danger est grand) sur la lecture des Ecritures qu'il publie à la suite, avec une belle persévérance que ne modèrent en rien les condamnations. Usant même de récidive puisque le *Petit Traicté monstrant comme on se doibt apprester a la lecture des escriptures Sainctes & ce qu'on y doibt chercher*, qui accompagnait l'*Exhortation*, est repris sans modification à la suite du *Brief Discours*. Visiblement Etienne Dolet agit en homme pressé, rassemblant des textes sans doute de provenances diverses qui puissent composer un ouvrage susceptible d'illustrer son nom et de faire connaître sa capacité à défendre une cause—celle de la langue française—à laquelle il s'était convertie deux ou trois ans plus tôt. C'est ainsi qu'il sépare le *Brief Discours* et le *Petit Traicté* avec une *Chanson chrestienne sur la lecture des Sainctes Lettres* et un *Dixain de la Lecture du Nouveau Testament* suivi de quatre quatrains sur le même sujet:

f° b8v   CHANSON CHRE-
                          stienne sur la Lecture des
                          Sainctes Lettres.

            Vous perdez temps de me vouloir defendre
            D'estudier en la saincte Escripture:
            Plus m'en blasmez, plus m'en voullez reprendre,
            Plus m'esjouist, plus m'en plaist la lecture.
            Ce que Dieu nous commande,
            Fault il qu'on le defende
            Par tourments et menaces?
            Cessez vos grands audaces:
            Que l'Eternel ne bransle sa main dextre,
            Pour vous monstrer que luy seul est le maistre.

            Pouvoir n'avez, si Dieu ne le vous donne,
            De faire mal à ceste chair mortelle.
            Quant à la mort, certes point ne m'estonne,
            Sachant pour vray, que l'ame est immortelle.
f° b1   La mort faict le passage
            Pour sortir de la cage,
            Ou l'ame est enfermee.
            O mort doncq' bien aymée!
            O doulce mort qui de prison delivre
            L'humain Esperit pour mieulx le faire vivre!

            Or vienne doncq' vienne la mort heureuse,
            Quand il plaira au seigneur le permettre.
            Glayve trenchant, ne flamme doloreuse

Ne me fera denier le grand Prebstre.
C'est luy par qui j'espere
Clairement veoir mon pere
Quelque jour face à face:
Helas, mais quand sera ce?
Non pas si tost que mon cueur le soubhaicte.
Mais du Seigneur la volunté soit faicte.

FIN.

f° b1v   *DIXAIN DE LA*
                    Lecture du Nouveau
                    Testament.

Au Lecteur.

Heritier n'est, qui n'ayme la lecture
Du testament, que son pere a laissé.
Encores moins, si de garder n'a cure
Entre ses mains l'escript du trepassé.
Mais pour le vray, le tout bien compassé,
Plus vault un seul parfaict observateur
Du Testament, que cent, et un lecteur.
Si croyons donq', que IESUS nous est Pere,
Lisants, gardons en tout sans vitupere,
Le bon vouloir de nostre testateur.

Au Lecteur mesme.

Grans, et petits, si vous voulez apprendre
    Humilité en Dieu selon l'Esprit,
    Il ne vous fault en tout querir, ne prendre
f° b2   Aultre patron, que le doulx Iesucrist.
Referez vous vers luy à tout propos,
    Et frequentez vouluntiers son escholle:
    En voz Esprits vous trouverez repos,
    En contemplant ses faicts, et sa parolle.
Prenez Iesus pour un singulier don
    De la bonté de Dieu (qui est pleniere)
    Par luy aurez toute grace et pardon.
    Ne cuyder point trouver aultre maniere,

Venez à luy, vous en pourrez jouyr:
Car pour certain il est humble, et facile.
Apprenez doncq' par lire, et par ouyr
Le contenu de sa saincte Evangile.

Cette *Chanson Chrestienne* est bien, comme le soupçonnait Sturel, celle dont Henri Estienne rapporte la première strophe au chapitre XXX de son *Apologie pour Hérodote*:

Sçache donc la postérité qu'il n'y a pas trent'ans qu'il se faloit autant cacher pour lire en une bible traduite en langue vulgaire, comme on se cache pour faire de la fausse monnoye, ou quelqu'autre meschanceté encore plus grande. Car à quiconque estoit surpris y lisant, ou seulement en ayant en sa maison, le proces estoit tout faict: et principalement s'il vouloit responde aux interrogations qu'on luy faisoit, selon ce qu'il avoit leu en ladicte bible. Laquelle rigueur est tesmoignee par plusieurs complaintes mises en lumiere environ ce temps là, mais sans le nom des auteurs. Aussi fut faicte une chanson l'an 1544, sur ce propos laquelle commance ainsi.
Vous perdez temps . . .

Il s'agissait bien évidemment d'une adaptation de la célèbre chanson de Marot, "Vous perdez temps de me dire mal d'elle." Quant au *Rondeau à nostre Sauveur Iesu Christ*, à la *Chanson sur les dix commandemens de Dieu*, aux *Preceptes de Philosophie Morale, que Aristote envoya au Roy Alexandre*, on ne sait s'ils furent imprimés dans l'édition originale de Dolet. Un point cependant mérite d'être noté: la *Chanson sur les dix commandemens* est visiblement inspirée de celle que composa le réformé Antoine Saulnier avant juillet 1533 et qu'on trouve, par exemple, dans le recueil de chansons publié par Mathieu Malingre chez Pierre de Vingle en 1533;[16] mais le remanieur a fait montre de prudence, puisque la strophe 1 est remodelée pour introduire la présence du Saint Esprit et surtout que la strophe 2 de Saulnier ("Tu ne feras aucun pourtraict taillé . . .") n'est pas retenue.

Ne perdons pas espoir de découvrir un jour un exemplaire de l'édition originale du *Brief Discours* (et n'oublions pas dans nos recherches la *Bible* dans la version d'Olivétan, la *Fontaine de Vye*, et les *Heures de la Compaignie des Penitens*, qui sont les trois impressions de Dolet qui restent à trouver). Mais cette réédition nous confirme:

(1) qu'en 1542 Dolet, malgré les menaces de censure ou les censures elles-mêmes, s'appliquait avec la détermination qu'on rencontre chez lui dans les grands moments à faire connaître en sa langue maternelle les principaux ouvrages de l'esprit, et particulièrement les Ecritures Saintes. Encore fallait-il, en ce domaine controversé, apporter la juste contradiction à ceux qui prétendaient qu'elles ne devaient être lues qu'en latin: c'est tout

l'objet de l'*Exhortation à la lecture des Sainctes Lettres* et du *Brief Discours*;

(2) qu'à cette date Dolet n'est pas l'agent secret de Genève qu'on a imaginé parfois: pas plus dans sa préface que dans les textes qu'il imprime on ne relève d'attaques précises contre le dogme romain; une modification d'une chanson réformée connue prouverait au contraire (si elle figure dans l'édition qu'il a lui-même donnée) son souci de ne pas heurter les sensibilités catholiques. Il reste qu'il prenait sciemment des risques en luttant pour l'emploi du français dans la pratique religieuse et qu'il en fut persécuté. Les raisons de cette attitude, souvent provocante, sont à chercher tout ensemble dans la raideur orgueilleuse de ses convictions qui refusent de céder et le désir vaniteux de placer au firmament sa renommée d'imprimeur.

NOTES

1. *Catalogus librorum visitatorum per Facultatem Theologiae Parisiensis a Festo Nativitatis Dominicae, anno 1542, ad secundum diem Martii eiusdem anni*; catalogue non imprimé de son temps mais reproduit par d'Argentré, II, 1, 134-36. Voir F. Higman, *Censorship and the Sorbonne* (Genève: Droz, 1979), no. A 16, A 18, A 8; C. Longeon, *Bibliographie des œuvres d'Etienne Dolet* (Genève: Droz, 1980), no. 215, 214, 155.

2. Higman, A 40; Longeon, no. 225.

3. *Edict faict par le Roy, sur certains articles . . . Avec le Cathalogue des livres censurez . . .* (Paris: Jean André, 1545); Higman, B 53.

4. *Le Catalogue des livres examinez, et censurez par la Faculté de Theologie de l'Université de Paris, depuis l'an mil cinq cens quarante et quatre, jusques à l'an present . . .* (Paris: Jean André, 1551); Higman, D 236.

5. *Bibliothèque* (Lyon: Jean Honorat, 1585), p. 279.

6. C. Longeon, *Documents d'archives sur Etienne Dolet* (Saint-Etienne: Centre de la Renaissance, 1977), p. 27.

7. Je le remercie très vivement de m'avoir spontanément communiqué cette information.

8. C. Longeon, *Bibliographie*, no. 99.

9. Sur les frères Philippe, voir L. Delisle, *Catalogue des livres imprimés ou publiés à Caen avant le milieu du XVIe siècle* (Caen, 1904), II, lxxii sqq.; *Répertoire bibliographique des livres imprimés en France au XVIe siècle* (Baden-Baden: Koerner, s.d.), no. 27.

10. On lit, parmi les 92 livres ou chansons censurés dans le catalogue de Vidal de Bécanis, inquisiteur de Toulouse, postérieur à 1543: "La Françoyse Chrestienne imprimée a Agen ou ailleurs avec une chanson qui est à la fin sur la lecture des sainctes letres qui commence Vous perdez temps" (Art. de Fréville, *Bulletin de la Société de l'Histoire du Protestantisme Français*, 1 et 2.) Mauvaise lecture de A CEAEN pour "AGEN" ou signe de la popularité de ce texte plusieurs fois réédité? Voir R. Sturel, "Notes sur Etienne Dolet d'après des inédits," *Revue du Seizième Siècle*, 1 (1913),

85 sqq.; L. Desgraves, *Etudes sur l'impression dans le Sud-Ouest de la France* . . . (Amsterdam: Erasmus, 1968), p. 59, col. B; *Biblio. Bibliogr. Aureliana*, 2e livr., p. 8.

11. Préface à la traduction des *Psaumes* de C. Marot (Lyon: Dolet, fév. / mai? 1542); voir Dolet, *Préfaces françaises*, éd. Longeon, Textes Littéraires Français, 272 (Genève: Droz, 1979), p. 121.

12. Préface à l'édition des *Epistres et Evangiles des cinquante et deux Dimenches de l'An* (Lyon: Dolet, 1542); voir *Préfaces françaises*, p. 121.

13. *Préfaces françaises*, p. 145.

14. Ibid., p. 30.

15. Par une intuition remarquable René Sturel, qui ne connaissait que le titre de ce *Brief Discours*, l'avait assimilé à une pièce plusieurs fois recopiée dans des manuscrits du XVIe siècle: *Complaincte de la dame françoise qui desire lire la Saincte Escripture, faict l'an VcXLII* (BM Soissons, ms. 203, ff. 96 sqq.), *Brief discours de la dame Françoise qui desire lire la Saincte Escripture* (BN ms. fr. 20025, ff. 163 sqq.), *Une femme françoise à ceulx qui deffendent que le nouveau testament ne soit leu en françois* (BN ms. fr. 12795, ff. 206 sqq.), *De la dame qui desire lire l'escripture* (BN ms. fr. 12489, ff. 2 sqq.). La version choisie par Sturel pour être publiée dans la *Revue du Seizième Siècle*, 1 (1913), 70-79, présente quelques différences notables avec celle de Dolet; c'est pourquoi il nous a paru utile de reproduire le texte proposé par l'édition de Caen.

16. *Sensuyvent plusieurs belles et bonnes chansons que les chrestiens peuvent chanter* . . . (s.l.s.n., 1533); voir Bordier, *Le Chansonnier huguenot du XVIe siècle* (Paris-Lyon, 1870-71), pp. 3 sqq., 421 sqq.

I.D. McFarlane

Clément Marot and the World of Neo-Latin Poetry

Marot's contacts with various Neo-Latin poets are known in some detail: among earlier critics, Becker and Villey were alive to the importance these could have for the poet's evolution.[1] It might however be worthwhile taking a fresh look, partly because some reassessment is timely, partly because we are now more aware of the role played by Neo-Latin poetry in the Renaissance.

I

When Marot enters the scene in the first ten years of Francis I's reign, poetry is at a crossroads: the impetus of the so-called *grands rhétoriqueurs* is fading and the last important representative, Guillaume Crétin, dies in 1525. In the provinces their tradition remains strong (e.g. Jean Bouchet), a late *rhétoriqueur*, François Habert, survives as court poet to Henri II, and genres associated with the tradition persist throughout the century—the *puys* do not exactly die out and Lefèvre de la Boderie will publish *chants royaux* quite late on. Their practices, moreover, may well be prolonged under different labels: an obvious example is their fondness for wordplay which continues under the aegis of the *Greek Anthology* and of Martial. Nonetheless, the broad idiom is losing favor in the 1520s and poets are casting round for new pastures. The change does not occur overnight: for one thing, the new humanism has not sloughed off all medieval attitudes— Erasmus, so forward-looking in many ways, belongs to a late-medieval tradition in his verse, preferring Prudentius to Catullus and the Roman elegists. There is considerable overlap, in theme, genres and style between the *rhétoriqueurs* and the early Neo-Latin poets active in France until the mid-1510s, indeed slightly later, particularly in court and celebratory poetry: the epic or para-epic idiom, the established religious inspiration, the moralizing strain, the wordplay and patterned conceits. Poets of Italian origin, such as Mantuan (Battista Spagnuoli), the writer of eclogues and religious verse or Faustus Andrelinus who settled in France and became *poeta regius* were hardly in the vanguard of poetic progress. By the 1520s authors are going abroad in search of fresh inspiration, looking either to poets in the Petrarchan tradition or to Neo-Latin practitioners, whose thematic and generic range appears wider and more imaginative: these will often acquire popularity in a period when humanism is finding its feet, indeed many will be printed in France.[2] At the same time, contemporaries will look at a broader spectrum of classical authors: they will take more kindly to the Latin love poets, they will pay more attention to the pastoral vein at a time when epic poetry is momentarily on the wane, they will learn something of Greek literature, more often than not through intermediaries, either Latin translations (French versions are rare enough at first) or through poetic adaptations, as say in the works of Pontano or Politian; they will adopt more modern kinds of reading and through Italian models they will see what Latin and Neo-Latin sources can do to revitalize poetry. Marot, who it seems becomes increasingly familiar with the milieux of advanced humanism, cannot but be sensitive to what these sources have to offer, not only for his poetic practice but simply because he thereby becomes more and more aware of the wider issues raised by humanism, linguistic, literary, religious. Critics have however been hampered by the lack of firm evidence about Marot's development in the 1520s, and here we can but try to reduce the areas of uncertainty. I shall first bring together Marot's obvious debts to Neo-Latin literature, then examine his references to humanists and poets in his early years, and also take note of the persons most frequently mentioned in the works of Neo-Latin poets whom he knew particularly well.

Marot's interest in and indebtedness to the classical world and to contemporary Neo-Latins leave considerable traces in his writing. To begin with, there are the familiar translations or imitations: Lucian's dialogue on the judgment of Minos (an early work that leans on a French prose version, *T*, 79-92), Vergil's first eclogue (*T*, 73-79), the *carmen lugubre* of Filippo Beroaldo the elder (*T*, 98-103), a second work by "Lucian" that turns out to be from the pen of Moschos and is rendered by Marot from a Latin translation by an Italian humanist G.B. Marmitta (*T*, 108-12); the first two books of the *Metamorphoses* (I, 112-214), an undeclared translation of an *Ennoea* by Nicolas Barthélemy de Loches (*T*, 92-99), a rendering of the legend of Hero and Leander in the version of Musaeus (*T*, 230-43). *Cantique* IV has seven stanzas that are translated from a poem by Marcantonio Flaminio (*OL*, 288-91), then there are the imitations of Martial (*E*, 217-43) and the Psalm paraphrases (*T*, 309-472); moreover, it seems that Mantuan's fifth eclogue has left clear marks on the Third eclogue (*OL*, 343-53). On a minor scale, there are a number of epigrams that go back to Neo-Latin sources, though these have not all been tracked down: epitaphs on the Connétable de Bourbon, Erasmus, Jean Olivier, and two epitaphs taken from the Greek through modern Latin intermediaries (*T*, 226-29); a version of an epigram by Salmon Macrin (*T*, 225), a *rondeau* "Du Vendredy Sainct" inspired by the commentary in Badius's edition of the Beroaldo poem mentioned above (*OD*, 97); epigrams such as "Des statues de Barbe et de Jacquette" (*E*, 103), "Blason à la louenge du Roy" (*E*, 107), "A Anne" (*E*, 157), "D'un usurier" (*E*, 301), "D'un orgueilleux" (*E*, 304), "A une vieille" (*E*, 305). There are also the translations of three *colloquia* by Erasmus whose authenticity is highly probable, if not proven beyond all doubt (*T*, 247-308). Finally, there are poems that belong to the Neo-Latin world: an epigram answering Latin verse sent by Dr. Akakia (*E*, 125); "De la Venus de marbre . . . ," a topic on which several contemporaries wrote Latin verse (*E*, 117-18); the "Du passereau de Maupas," also treated by Jean Visagier (*E*, 185); the epitaph on the death of Christophe de Longueil, a humanist mourned by many a Neo-Latin poet.[3] No doubt other epigrams will have their Neo-Latin analogues and, perhaps, sources.

In making this list we have gone well beyond Marot's apprentice years, but one cannot but be struck by the consistency with which he pursues translation throughout his life: it forms a vital part of his output, and it takes him into a great variety of poetic paths. What is more difficult to ascertain are the reasons for this continued practice: it is probably not sufficient to allude to the *rhétoriqueurs'* interest in translation, and more generally, translation as a poetic genre does not acquire the intensity it will possess in the second half of the century. Two factors may be in play: on the one hand, he could be doing what his contemporaries were up to in the field of Greek—using translation as a means of mastering the source-tongue. Jacques Toussaint (*Tusanus*) had advised his pupils (among whom was Jean Dorat) to practice translation to this end; Buchanan claims to have been doing the same when he embarked on his translations of Euripides; and nearer our time, James Joyce tackled a play by Gerhardt Hauptmann in the same spirit. It is generally agreed that Marot's knowledge of Latin progresses throughout his career. And on the other hand, translation would be linked with his exploration of fresh poetic paths at a time when home sources had run rather dry; it may also have helped to accelerate his shedding of old-world habits and approaches. The motives behind the Psalm paraphrases may however be in part rather different.

Up to a point, too, these translations reflect contact with the humanist circles Marot appears to have frequented. Here, it is well known, biographical details are hard to come by; and though we can glean some details from the poems, they are not in the profusion we should welcome. Marot would come across many humanists in high places, but these links would not necessarily be confined to those he met in his capacity as a court poet. He certainly knew the tutor to the Royal children, Tagliacarne (Theocrenus) who was in post from 1520 onwards. Tagliacarne was a cultured man who could have introduced Marot to things Italian and was a Latin poet, whose verse however was not published till 1536 and remains of very limited interest.[4] Then there is Etienne Templier (or Du Temple) to whom Marot wrote an early *rondeau* (*OD*, 83):[5] this was a humanist poet from Orleans who published some ceremonial verse, had an interest in Greek literature and was connected with Nicole Bérault, whom we shall meet later as a contributor of liminary verse to the *Adolescence clémentine*.[6] Bérault had a distinguished career, as a scholar, for as early as 1514 he was collaborating with Salmon Macrin on an edition of Suetonius, and as a diplomat, especially in England at the time of the King's Great Matter. He was awake to humanist developments in Italy and was interested in Greek culture—he had indeed edited some texts by Lucian. Moreover, he had, to say the least, Erasmian sympathies and though he seems to have remained more or less within the pale of orthodoxy, his son went over to Geneva. One other name should be mentioned now, that of Geoffroy Tory, known for his passion for Greek literature, his intense cultural patriotism—one might almost say chauvinism—and of course his concern for printing.

Our little list is not only meager, it lacks the names of prominent contemporary Neo-Latin poets of French origin. We hear nothing of Pierre Rosset, known nonetheless to many of Marot's friends. He was a latter-day disciple of Mantuan, apparently a teacher of Greek, a man whose death was commemorated by several members of the Lyons *sodalitium*.[7] He published a number of poems in the 1510s, but his more important compositions came later, the *Paulus* (1522) and the *Christus* published posthumously through the good offices of one of his followers, Hubert Sussannée (1534). We do not hear of Germain de Brie (*Brixius*) either:[8] he had achieved some notoriety after his scholar's brawl with Sir Thomas More who had criticized his *Chordigera navis . . .* , a small epic poem celebrating the sinking of a French vessel against overwhelming British odds. But he was a good Greek scholar, editing St. John Chrysostom, wrote quite a lot of occasional verse and encouraged younger poets; earlier in life he had been a secretary at the court of Queen Anne—where he must have known Jean Lemaire de Belges and Jean Marot. He developed some sympathy for Erasmian attitudes in matters of religion. It is unlikely that Marot knew Salmon Macrin much before the 1530s: though this poet had made something of a mark as a poet and scholar in the reign of Louis XII, he faded out for some twelve years and seems to have been a tutor mainly in the provinces.

Two points should nevertheless be made. In the first place, silence does not prove much: George Buchanan's closest friends, scholars like himself, are never mentioned in his works and it is only through collateral evidence that we can speculate sensibly. Here I am thinking particularly of Nicolas Barthélemy de Loches, not mentioned by Marot but the source of one of his poems.[9] His output was considerable, indeed he was probably the most prominent French Neo-Latin poet during the 1520s, bridging the gap between the reigns of Louis XII and Francis I. His religious verse is certainly more up-to-date than the other models available; and his epigrams reflect attitudes current in humanist circles: he exploits the familiar veins against Church abuses, the professions, composes epitaphs, addresses poems to leading humanists; he also works in the field of the eclogue. He had many friends and patrons among the more enlightened humanists—Germain de Brie, Budé, Danès, Vatable, Toussaint, Jean Robertet, Lascaris, Chancellor Duprat. We find that these names recur in the poems of Marot's Neo-Latin friends, though he does not mention all of them himself, the exceptions being Guillaume Budé,[10] Duprat and the Robertet family. Jacques Lefèvre d'Etaples' name comes less frequently to the fore, but after 1525 he is no longer in Paris, and ends up under Marguerite de Navarre's wing at Nérac.[11] But the fact that most of these names keep on recurring—and this is my second point—does suggest that Marot moved in certain humanist circles rather than in others, and one must remember that ambiance is just as important as direct influence by some particular individual. The *Mécènes* most frequently mentioned—Marguerite de Navarre, Duprat, the Robertets, the Bohiers, Jean du Bellay, Jean de Lorraine—have a similar concern with the prestige of French culture, and in varying degree, show interest in classical literature, both Latin and Greek, and awareness of, sometimes sympathy with, the religious attitudes so often associated with these milieux.

There is reason to believe that Marot was associated with some of these personalities. We have already noted Nicole Bérault and Guillaume Budé; there is also Jan Lascaris, one of whose epitaphs he rendered into French:

this scholar, who did a good deal for Greek studies, held court functions, wrote Greek epigrams, edited an early selection of the *Greek Anthology*. It is also possible that Marot knew Jacques Louis, whose Latin translation from Lascaris' Greek was the intermediary (*T*, 227): a native of Rheims, he taught in Paris and was known to Nicolas Bourbon (*Nugarum libri VIII*, 1538, p. 464). The Robertet connection is common knowledge: Florimond was a man of culture who had known Robert Gaguin, Thomas More and Guillaume Budé; later Jean du Bellay's help was sought to succour Marot in distress.[12] All in all evidence, circumstantial and direct, suggests that Marot's contacts with these milieux were crucial for his development. His interest in the eclogue must be linked to his awareness of classical models, but the genre was already well acclimatized in French Neo-Latin poetry[13] as well as in Italian (Mantuan, Faustus Andrelinus, Arnoullet, Castellus, Barthélemy); there are similarly models for the elegy; and we have seen the flourishing of the epigram, where Martial is already an established model (there are a good number of editions brought out especially at Lyons between ?1502 and 1518, and the Simon de Colines edition started its successful run in 1528). In all this we should not forget the role played by the Low Countries humanist-poets who settled in Paris, the most prolific perhaps being Petrus Caecus de Ponte, whose eclogues and *Epistolae familiares* appear to have enjoyed some success. The important thing to note here is not that this or that Neo-Latin poet may have influenced some text by Marot, but that this steady, cumulative activity in Latin must end in stimulus to production in the vernacular. Finally, one should not forget that both Latin and vernacular poetry are becoming firmly established at Court—as they were in the reigns of Charles VIII and Louis XII. When Louise de Savoie dies in 1531, French and Latin poets join in the chorus of commemoration—and the names have a very familiar ring: Germain de Brie, Salmon Macrin, Geoffroy Tory, Antoine Macault, Alnetus (Delaunay), Theocrenus, and Marot (*OL*, 323-37).[14]

It is against this background that we should read the liminary verse of the *Adolescence clementine*, whose title surely reflects humanist preoccupations. We have already seen that two of the contributors were distinguished humanists, Nicole Bérault and Geoffroy Tory.[15] One must be struck by the fact that Marot secured the collaboration of two such famous figures—and that their offerings were in Latin. One would hardly think that this was sheer opportunism, though heaven knows there are all sorts of reasons for writing liminary verse: friendship, social status, desire for patronage, feelings of solidarity within a group, and so forth. In Marot's case, there were doubtless ties of friendship, but I suspect that Bérault and Tory saw in our poet the vernacular expression of many of their literary ideals and hopes, nor was there any divorce between Latin and vernacular literature provided there was advantage to the country's cultural prestige. I think also—a point to which I shall return—that they felt Marot to be sufficiently learned to earn their praise and company: in a certain sense Marot was one of them.

II

All this emerges yet further on the appearance of the *Suite de l'Adolescence clementine* towards the end of 1533, when three new names are added to the list of liminary contributors: Antoine Macault who appears in the guise of translator of the two others, Salmon Macrin and Nicolas Bourbon (the latter's poem being translated for the second edition).[16] Two points arise from these additions. The first has been dealt with in some detail by Klaus Mayer:[17] the subject of these poems is curious, in that they both suggest that the manuscript of the volume had been stolen and published without the consent of the author. There seems little to support this claim, and one may see it as a sort of joke—though Salmon Macrin was not usually given to such pranks; the theme of the purloined manuscript is almost a Renaissance topos, with the author pretending not to publish on his own initiative. So that the two Neo-Latin poets may have been indulging in a parodic activity. At all events, Marot reprints the poems in the 1538 edition of the *Oeuvres* and Bourbon maintains his in the second, enlarged edition of the *Nugae* in 1538.[18] The second point is that Marot has got the backing of the two most illustrious Neo-Latin poets in France at that time. Salmon Macrin had begun his career in Louis XII's reign, as we saw, but it is his *Carminum libellus* (1528) that puts him on the literary map: in it he had widened the spectrum of amatory inspiration, and though in singing of his wife he was following in the paths of Pontano, he breaks new ground in the context of French poetry. In 1530 he brought out his *Carminum libri IV*, and in 1531 a second edition of the *Carminum libellus*, accompanying the *Lyricorum libri II*. He was becoming established as a court poet and before 1534 had been appointed *cubicularius regius*.[19] In a sense, Macrin and Marot had become a sort of poetic tandem at court, holding the prestige of French poetry high. Nicolas Bourbon, who was a protégé of Marguerite de Navarre and later became tutor to her daughter, had published the first edition of his *Nugae* in 1533;[20] and presumably his contribution to the *Suite* appeared before his incarceration on religious grounds at the end of the year. In his volume he had indeed printed a Latin rendering of Marot's *rondeau* liv (*E*, 122), though he did not acknowledge his source until the second edition:

Olim qui Veneris vultum depinxit Apelles,
    Maximus, & primus fertur in arte sua.
Ecce tamen genitor tuus est praestantior illo,
    Cuius periculo facta puella Dea es.
Illa quidem multos urebat Apellis imago,
    Atque aliquot iuuenes capit amore sui.
Non habuit tamen unde suos restingueret ignes:
    Tu simul inflammas, & medicamen habes.
(*N*, p. 295)

The French text is 15 lines long, and understandably certain metrical and stylistic features associated with the *rondeau* are not taken over; but the theme, with its Apelles topos, fits into the Neo-Latin world and confirms the impression that, even when Marot was using *rhétoriqueur* idiom, he was already writing epigrams of more Renaissance color. So Bourbon gives an abbreviated version that removes its old-world formal character and assimilates it to the conventional Neo-Latin epigram. That Marot should be associated with both Macrin and Bourbon should occasion no surprise: they were working towards similar goals, and one might add that, so far as their religious views were concerned, there was some sympathy, though the degree of their Erasmian involvement may have varied considerably. At a literary level this association of Marot with the Neo-Latins opens the way to a more widespread admiration among the younger humanist poets.

The three poets remain in contact for some time; they had many common friends and they collaborated in the *tombeau du dauphin* organized by Etienne Dolet in 1536.[21] I am inclined to think however that Macrin, in spite of his obligations at court, remained in less close touch with Marot than did Nicolas Bourbon. Marot and Bourbon were both to get into hot water for their religious views and both went into exile for a time. And when the second edition of the *Nugae* came out, it contained a fair number of references to Marot: Bourbon pens a short poem supporting his friend in the Sagon controversy (*N*, p. 465); writes in his praise, likening him, as do others, to Vergil (with the inevitable wordplay *Maro/Marot*) (*N*, p. 294); in a letter to Dr. William Boston, Bourbon informs him that he is sending poems by the two Scèves and Marot that should move the reverent gentleman to laughter (*N*, p. 86). He includes two further translations of Marot poems: the first "De passere Lampadis puellae. ex vulg. Maroti" (*N*, p. 297 = *E*, 183), a poem which may have attracted him because of the *fait divers* underlying it, something which also caught Visagier's eye. The second, so far as I am aware, is a rather risqué affair, of which the original has not come down to us:

Claudebat dominae latus adcumbenti amator,
  Una ex adverso forte maritus erat.
Exarsit iuuenis totusque intentus amori
  Dextra foemineos serpsit ad usque locos.
Illa simul furtim laevam demisit: at ingens
  Mentula per medias ivit utrinque manus.
Tum trepida exsiliit mulier, subitoque sinistram
  Dum reuocat, coniux, vir male cautus ait:
Ah uxor, cultri ne acies te laesit: at illa
  Non, non respondit, nam capulo tenui.

(N, p. 465)

There were other signs of Bourbon's continued interest: he contributed liminary verse to Marot's *Oeuvres* in 1538 to which Marot printed a sort of reply (*E*, 202), in which he saw both poets striking out along fresh paths of love poetry. And in 1539, Bourbon sent poems by his friend to an unknown correspondent.[22] After that date, nothing more is heard: this is partly explained by Bourbon's silence in print until the death of Francis I and partly, I suspect, by his moving away from Paris humanist circles and settling in the Southwest, under the protection of Marguerite de Navarre.

I am less sure about Macrin's response, after the initial contribution to the *Suite*; and yet they were colleagues at court—though this does not mean that they were in permanent residence, rather on permanent call; they were both protected by Marguerite de Navarre; they obviously had religious affinities, and literary ones as well, for they wrote court poetry, amatory verse, psalm paraphrases, religious verse. Admittedly Macrin is less interested in the epigram, especially of the satiric type; he does not exploit the eclogue, and his religious verse soon follows orthodox paths. After 1533, so far as I am aware, there is but one overt reference to Marot, when he reproaches the latter for not sending a copy of his latest volume;[23] and there is an unpublished translation of an epigram.[24] Macrin takes no part in the Marot-Sagon quarrel, he makes no reference to Marot's exile or to his return, he writes no poems interceding on his behalf. He himself publishes little between 1531 and 1537: the only volume of verse to appear during that period is the very rare *Elegiae, epigrammata et odae*, which Antoine Augereau brought out in 1534. Shortly afterwards, Augereau was burned as a heretic and presumably as many copies of his stock as could be seized were destroyed; I know of only two copies of Macrin's volume in public libraries.[25] I suspect that Macrin, even though he tended to play the part of the elder statesman and did not write an excessive amount of liminary verse,[26] may have felt threatened, both by the Augereau incident and the *Affaire des Placards*; though he probably remained within the pale of orthodoxy—but how often can one be sure of the religious attitudes of these humanists? there persisted an impression in some quarters that he was not absolutely "sound," and he doubtless felt that, with a numerous and growing family to support, discretion was the better part of valor.

There remains one point in this period: when Marot is in exile in Ferrara, he must have picked up an early volume of verse by Marcantonio Flaminio, out of which he found a poem that nurtured the first seven stanzas of *Cantique* iv (*OL*, 288-91). He may of course have read further Neo-Latin authors during his stay there, but it is a pity perhaps that he did not live long enough to see Flaminio's excursions into verse psalm paraphrases which appeared for the first time two years after his death.

III

By the time he returned to France, Marot was becoming a significant figure even among Neo-Latin poets. The point at which Neo-Latin and vernacular verse converge in spectacular fashion was during the years 1536-1538, when for a variety of reasons several Neo-Latin poets formed what came to be known as the *sodalitium lugdunense*. They found themselves in Lyons at a time when the Court was in residence: some of them were teaching in the region, others became involved in the printing world, yet others were passing through. All established fruitful links with the humanist and literary centers in Lyons itself: the names associated with this rather loose group are: Dolet, Bourbon, Visagier, Sussannée, Antoine de Gouvea, Jean de Boyssonné and Gilbert Ducher; other writers remain in touch such as Jacques Delaunay (Alnetus), the two Scèves, Jean Raynier. In differing degrees members of the *sodalitium* were connected with humanist foci in nearby regions, such as the Orleans group whose main member Jean Dampierre is mentioned time after time in contemporary epigram collections; and there were kindred spirits in Carpentras and Tarascon.[27] It is during these few years that a high proportion of their verse comes out, often in Lyons, but not exclusively so. Up to a point, they come under the umbrella of Etienne Dolet, a man whose energy and attempts at leadership were frustrated by inability to get on with people— and many echoes of these quarrels are found in the poems published by members of the *sodalitium*. Two other poets of stature are associated: Salmon Macrin as something of a figurehead, and Clément Marot. A strong feature of the *sodalitium* was its cultural patriotism, its belief that French literature should now be able to steal a march on the Italians. A majority of these poets worked in Latin, but they did not always neglect the vernacular: Macrin was said to have deposited some French verse with a Poitiers bookseller;[28] Nicolas Bourbon was writing in French as early as 1529;[29] Jean de Boyssonné completed an interesting love-cycle (*Centuries*) which however cannot be dated with accuracy and was not published till this century.[30] There was no real rivalry between Latin and the vernacular, so long as the literary output was of high quality—though Latin had an advantage as an international language. When Dolet organized the *tombeau du dauphin*, he did not exclude offerings in the vernacular; and it is significant that Marot should have been asked to participate in the undertaking.[31]

The Neo-Latin poet on whom critics have tended to concentrate, so far as Marot is concerned, is Etienne Dolet.[32] Now Dolet is indeed important as one of Marot's publishers, but I am not considering that side of his activity here. He is sometimes seen as an interesting intermediary for Marot's exploitation of the epigram and also because of his leading role in organizing the *sodalitium*. There is indeed a short, intense period in which the two men get on very well; and it will be remembered that Marot was one of the friends invited to the banquet celebrating Dolet's acquittal on a charge of murdering a painter: the party included Macrin, Guillaume Budé, Rabelais, Nicole Bérault, Pierre Danès, Jacques Toussaint, Nicolas Bourbon, Jean Dampierre and Jean Visagier. In his *Carmina* (1538) Dolet pointed to affinities between himself and Marot, both in their writings and in their fortunes (*C*, 32-33); in fact ten poems concern Marot directly and there are others in which he receives a *mention honorable*. Dolet hopes that Marot will soon regain the permanent favor of the King (*C*, 81) and expresses joy at the way in which Francis welcomes him on his return from exile (*C*, 82). He speaks in flattering terms of Marot as a love-poet, comparing Anne to Bourbon's Rabella (*C*, 57) and he includes a most complimentary passage in the *Commentarii*.[33] He naturally contributes liminary verse to the 1538 edition of the *Oeuvres* published by himself, as did Marot (one poem and a letter). Soon after Dolet had brought out the *Oeuvres*, the two men quarrelled for reasons that are not clear; and so in the Gryphius edition of the *Oeuvres* (also 1538), Dolet's Latin tributes disappear as does Marot's letter; later in the 1542 edition of *L'Enfer*, Dolet will retain Marot's piece to himself but cut out his own poems to his erstwhile friend. After the quarrel the French poet unleashed two satiric poems at Dolet's expense (*E*, 239-40 and, in all probability, *E*, 265) and switched a poem, originally addressed to Dolet, to Germain Colin Bucher (*E*, 176). In all this, I fail to detect in Dolet a major influence on Marot's evolution, indeed one may well be more sensitive to the differences between the two poets. Dolet is a vigorous Ciceronian, unlike most of the poets associated with the *sodalitium*;[34] he is rather purist in his poetic outlook; he does not indulge much in the epigram; he virtually excludes amatory verse from his *carmina* (apart from some passing references to episodes in Venice), he does not, with the odd exception, compose religious verse. I do not see great affinities of sensibility between Dolet and Marot, or for that matter most members of the *sodalitium*; nor would one imagine that they had all that in common on the religious front. My impression is that we should look elsewhere for fruitful links between Marot and the Neo-Latins, and two names in particular spring to mind.

The first one is Gilbert Ducher: admittedly little is known about him, but he was probably rather older than most members of the group. He had collaborated with Pierre Danès as early as 1522 in an edition of Caesar's *Commentaries*; and in 1526 he published a poem of the death of Queen Claude. What interests us is that he edited Martial in 1526 (*chez* Girault), an edition that may have been re-issued in the mid-1530s, since Nicolas Bourbon has a poem on this event (*N*, pp. 364-65). In 1538 Ducher published his two books of *Epigrammata* (Lyons, Gryphius): they show him to be connected with the humanists we have already come across—German de Brie, Bérault, Lascaris (two of whose epigrams he renders into Latin, pp. 6 and 18), Toussaint, Erasmus, Melanchthon. He may have been affected by Erasmian evangelism and he published one psalm paraphrase. His *Epigrammata* contain several "imitations" of Martial (pp. 8, 63 and 128), he addresses a poem to Marot (p. 103) and translates two of his poems: "De Lycore & Aegone iocus" (p. 58) and "De Lycida & Chlori iocus: ex rhythmo *mei* (my italics) Maroti" (p. 140). Ducher spent only eight months near Lyons in 1537 and after the appearance of the *Epigrammata* all trace of him vanishes. There is a remote possibility that Marot could have met him in Parisian humanist circles in the 1520s, but Ducher's importance lies for us in the interest he takes in Marot and Martial; but he is only one of the group.

Our second Martialian contact—and one on which we are rather better informed—is Jean Visagier (*Vulteius*). Incidentally, there should be no doubt about his real name, though fanciful gallicisations have enjoyed currency (Faciot, Voulté). The poet took the trouble of revealing his name in an acrostich poem;[35] in the first edition of the *Nugae* (1533, No. 555) Bourbon wrote him a poem "Ad Ioannem Visagerium"; and in Gaullieur's monography on the Collège de Guyenne there is a facsimile of the signatures of various persons who taught there, including Visagier.[36] Originally from Vandy-sur-Aisne, although he styles himself *Remensis*, Visagier studied at the Collège de Sainte-Barbe, found his way to Bordeaux where he taught for a spell, and eventually turned up in Lyons. He died young, killed in 1540 by a man who had lost a lawsuit against him.[37] He seems at one time to have harbored Erasmian sympathies, but by the time of his death his friend Denys Faucher de Lérins assured a correspondent that he had died in the odor of sanctity.[38] His poetic output is concentrated into three intense years (1536-1538) and the references to Marot are pretty frequent; one can also detect certain thematic parallels here and there.[39] His *Epigrammata* follow the Neo-Latin pattern with a broad range of theme: the traditional satiric targets (the professions, the abuses of the church, monks, women, etc.), some religious verse, the lineaments of a love-cycle. Visagier is one of the first to express sympathy for Marot in exile: the first edition (1536) contains five poems on the subject, to which we can add an epigram on poets who write *blasons du corps féminin*. The first poem to Renée of Ferrara is a short piece lamenting the poet's exile (p. 115), but the second, addressed to Jean du Bellay seen as a possible ally, is very attractive in a literary sense (p. 120): written in the form of a prosopopoeia, it rather resembles a Marotic epistle in the plangent mode ("Hei mihi quam varios peperit fortuna dolores . . ."). Visagier, through Marot's voice, points out how various court figures and the King himself describe his poetry as "docta carmina, docta manu" and take note of his literary talents. The poem ends on a plea that Du Bellay intercede on his behalf. The poem to Francis I (p. 122) reiterates the belief that the poet has been falsely accused and that his absence is all the more regrettable as he has neglected his poetic activity during his exile. A shorter piece, also in the form of a prosopopoiea (p. 125), is addressed to the King, but is much less substantial, as is the "De eodem" on the same page.

These very decent intercessions on Marot's behalf were amplified in the 1537 edition of the *Epigrammata*, which also contains some alterations. In part, these changes come about as a result of the souring of relations between Visagier and Bourbon, so that some poems originally addressed to Bourbon (who, it will be remembered, had gone into exile in England) were now transferred to Marot. Only a few variants were necessary, since *Borbonius* and *Marotus* are metrically interchangeable where a spondee is not *de rigueur* and since few biographical details were explicitly stated. There was considerable thematic overlap in the work of Marot and Bourbon, and the question of French or Latin was of no consequence (cf. pp. 11, 15, 24, 57 in the 1536 edition). One or two other references to Bourbon were switched to Dolet. But there were additions, because Marot had returned from Italy while Visagier was at work on the second edition (1537 edition: pp. 60, 182, 191-92 [2 poems], 230, 240 [4 poems], 244 [2 poems], 248, 249). There is talk of innocence being vindicated, but more important is the theme that Marot's return will revitalize the Muses. One poem elevates Clément well above his father. Visagier also includes versions of Marot's poems: the first is an epigram written on the appearance of Dolet's *Commentarii* (vol. I) (*E*, 264; Visagier, 1537, p. 250) and is given in two versions: here one might think that Dolet is being flattered as well. The other rendering is of a dialogue between mind and body (*E*, 127-28); it is not addressed to the original dedicatee, Pierre Vuyard whom Visagier may not have known, but to Benoît Court, always remembered as the commentator of Martial d'Auvergne's *Arrêts d'Amour*. It may be of interest to place Visagier's version side by side with that published not so long after by Antoine de Gouvea:

Visagier, *Ex vernaculo Maroti, Ad B. Curtium*
Hoc corpus miserum petit salutem,
Frater chare mihi, sed hoc resolui, ut
Foedo a carcere, spiritus peroptat.
Mundum hoc somniat, his solutus esse.
Audire heu lachrymas graue est duorum.
Ah, sic (corpus ait) mori necesse est.
Ah, sic (spiritus) hic diu immorandum?
I, te suauius opto (corpus inquit).
I, nos (spiritus) error urget idem.
Ast fiat Domini voluntas. (p. 242)

Gouvea, *Epigrammata . . . 1540. Corpus et animi in morbo contentio*
Poscit opem Corpus medicam: Mens solvere terra
    Aestuat & medicas respuit usque manus.
Corpus humum, cognata leuis Mens suspicit astra.
    Quam dirum, O Superi, terrificumque fremunt.
Mene ita, Corpus ait, tristi succumbere morbo?
    Mens vero, invisas me trahere usque moras?
Caeca es, ait Corpus. Mene contra, erramus uterque
    Arbitrio summi stemus uterque Dei. (p. 23)

Visagier uses the hendecasyllable, whereas Gouvea contents himself with the elegiac couplet, which allows him to condense his version into eight lines. In spite of the quantitative difference in texture between Latin and French, quite a number of poets try to maintain the same number of lines in their renderings from the one language to the other. We shall find a sprinkling of translations in poets of this period, though not in the abundance to be found in the last third of the century (cf. Scévole de Sainte-Marthe, Jean de la Gessée, Florent Chrestien, etc.): by then certain principles were at hand in the Latin renderings, apart from virtuosity: Latin was still seen by some as more likely to last, for French was evolving it seemed almost too rapidly, and of course Latin was understood abroad: French had yet to acquire its diplomatic status as an international language. In the 1530s such considerations seem to have less force; one can understand renderings from Greek into Latin or French, because relatively few people were at home in the Greek language. Translations from French into Latin seem to be more a *divertissement*, involving technical skill, and also perhaps paying compliments to the author of the originals; there are in fact only a few vernacular poets who are overtly treated this way (Marot, Mellin de Saint-Gelais, Bouchet) and sometimes no clearer indication is given than *ex vernaculo*.

I am inclined to think that Visagier's example was not lost on Marot. The title *Epigrammes* (introduced by Marot in 1538) may owe something to him, but not exclusively so; he may nevertheless have encouraged Marot to exploit the Martialian formula more seriously. Visagier's own satiric epigrams are obviously indebted to Martial (though there are the complementary models of Ausonius and the *Greek Anthology*); and there are evident signs of his fondness for the Latin poet. He writes a poem to a friend from Arles, Veracius, originally penned on a copy of Martial (*Hendecasyllabi*, fol. 96 v); the satiric squibs against Dolet have a strong Martialian flavor; the *Inscriptiones* contain a trifle "Ex inverso carmine Martialis, ad Salm. Macrinum" (fol. 83 v). The 1537 edition of the *Epigrammata* includes an "imitatio Martialis, ad Gyr. Ruffum" (p. 214), and there is no need to look far for the source of "Quam nolit amicam" (p. 171). There is a further point: the 1537 *Epigrammata* were followed by a collection of *Xenia*, and the *Inscriptiones* likewise, though this collection was a different one. Could one not see a link between these collections and Marot's indulgence in *étrennes* c. 1541? The 1537 *Xenia* include two poems addressed to Marot, the first one of which reads: "Munere pro largo xeniorum nomine Musa / Mittet ad autorem carmina versa suum" (*Xenia, E*, p. 281). Given the closeness of relations between these poets, albeit over a short period, it is reasonable to suppose that Marot's *Epigrammes faictz à l'imitation de Martial* derive from this atmosphere and that the stimulus develops between Ducher, Bourbon, Visagier and Marot. In this context I doubt if Salmon Macrin and Dolet count for very much.

Other members or satellites of the *sodalitium* seem to me to have a very marginal importance for Marot's evolution, but they may interest us in other ways. A poet like Delaunay (*Alnetus*), whose Latin poems are published in this period[40] shows evidence of friendship for Marot, whom he probably knew in Paris earlier: he had c. 1520 published a text by Denys Fabre, but seems to have ended his career in the provinces. His *Epigrammata* refer to the Sagon controversy and include a poem against Nicolas Denisot, accused of being an "obtractor Maroti." Jean de Boyssonné also remains on the sidelines, though he keeps a watchful eye on Marot, whom he had met in Toulouse (*E*, 196).[41] He refers to the Sagon affair (*Poemata*, ms 835, B.M. Toulouse, fol. 70), talks disparagingly of the bickering that goes on among members of the *sodalitium* (*ibid.*, fol. 113); there are some allusions in the Correspondence, and he writes a poem on Marot's death (fol. 54), but none of this adds up to very much. Hubert Sussannée, sometimes mentioned in the context of Marot, and known as the author of a considerable body of Latin verse, seems to be even more marginal; I see no poem to Marot in his *Ludi*, though Sussannée addresses a good number of other Lyons friends. He is in both senses of the word an eccentric: Ciceronian and an erstwhile ally of Dolet, he writes epigrams that reveal a different pattern of friendships and acquaintances than other members of the *sodalitium*. Doubts have been expressed about his orthodoxy; my own impression is that, though he had a pretty unstable personality, at the end of the day, his attitude is essentially orthodox.[42] I do not see him as a friend of Marot. On the other hand, Antoine de Gouvea was an admirer and seems to have been in Lyons at the right moment. One of the most peripatetic of humanists, he came from Sainte-Barbe like other members of this Portuguese family, taught briefly at the Collège de Guyenne, was involved in the Ramus affair and finally made a considerable name for himself as a jurist.[43] He interests us here because of his poetic activity: he produced a volume of *Epigrammata* that came out in two rather different editions (1539 and 1540).[44] In the 1540 edition there is a short, admiring poem to Marot in which he talks of his own renderings (p. 23), of which there are two: one we have already mentioned, the other is rather intriguing because a different version had appeared in the 1539 edition:

> Ad Cath. Bof [fremontam] è gallicis Marotti
>
> Me nive candenti petiit Catharina: putabam
>   Igne carere nivem: nix tamen ignis erat.
> Non est vana fides, non experientia fallax:
>   Sensi etenim subitis corda cremata rogis.
> Ergo ubi tutus ero, nivibus si conditur ardor.
>   Effigiamque tuas, saeve Cupido, faces?
> Tu, Catharina, potes subitas extinguere flammas,
>   Non glacie, aut nivibus, marmoreis vel aquis,
> Sed si, quae patior, poenae quoque sentiat autor
>   Et nostrum flamma flagrat uterque pari.
>   (1540, p. 8)

The 1540 version is not only altered, but drastically shortened:

> Dum Catharina petis nive me candente, putabam
>   Igne carere niuem, nix tamen ignis erat.
> En, quid agam, fallax nivibus si conditur aqua?
>   Si latet adstricta frigus, & ignis aqua?
> An Catharina meo viuit quae in corde fauilla,
>   Crescit frigoribus uincitur igne pari?
>   (1540, p. 11)

The change of name from Anne (*E*, 115) follows Neo-Latin practice: sometimes metrical considerations must enter, frequently the poet tries to integrate a translation into a series of poems addressed to a lady of his own choice, here Catherine de Boffremont. Gouvea has moved from direct address to the monologue formula; but he may have changed the incipit because of its close similarity to a distich by Jean Visagier: "Me nive candenti petiit modo, Clinia, rebar / Igne carere niuem, tamen ignis erat?" (*Epigrammata*, 1537, p. 27). The theme of the poem goes back to Petronius,[45] but Marot may well have taken as his model a poem in G. Angeriano's Ἐρωτοπαίγνιον published in France more than once after c. 1520: of course, freedom in translation (which often overspills into paraphrase or "imitation") makes certain identification of source elusive.

For convenience I include two other poets here, although they are not directly associated with the Lyons group. The first is Jean Olivier for whom Marot wrote an epitaph based on a Latin original; Mayer is pretty certain that the poem is by Marot, though he does not know of any connection between the two men (*T*, 228-29). Olivier is not unknown: he is the author of a poem *Pandora*, which was published by Dolet[46] and which dwells on the allegorical significance of a relationship between Pandora and Prometheus, among other things. He was a nephew of François Olivier, Chancellor of France; I have wondered whether he harbored religious sentiments sympathetic to reform. Salmon Macrin wrote him a poem in his *Septem Psalmi . . .* (1538, fol. F r) and the bishop composed an Ode for the former's *Hymnorum selectorum libri tres* (Paris, 1540, p. 114). There are furthermore two poems to him from Nicolas Bourbon (*N*, 191 and 339), in the first of which he declares his ambition to be the finest poet of his time to sing Christ, and that he will write under the aegis of Olivier. In the second poem he stresses the quality of the bishop's faith.

The other poet is Théodore de Bèze, whose poem "Ad Marotum," first published in the *Poemata* of 1548, was retained until 1576 in subsequent editions: it contains a clear allusion to *rondeau* liv (*E*, 122). But the Orleans manuscript tells us a little more:[47] on the one hand, there is an unpublished poem of 19 hendecasyllables in which Bèze takes Marot's side in the Sagon affair (art. cit., p. 178). Now, at this time, Bèze was still in his teens and there is no evidence that he met Marot then; but he was closely associated with the Orleans group and especially with its chief Jean Dampierre, so that it is not surprising that several unpublished poems reflect the interest of that group and sometimes develop themes exploited by Marot and members of the Lyons *sodalitium* (e.g. no. 3 on the death of the dauphin; an epitaph on Longueil (no. 12), *icones* on a statue of Venus (nos. 14-16), and two on that offered to the King (nos. 29-30). Some of these were printed subsequently.

IV

We must now ask ourselves two questions: what was the overall value of these Neo-Latin connections for Marot's development? and what can we learn about Marot's importance in the eyes of his contemporaries?

We saw earlier the possible value Marot's contacts with humanist milieux in the 1520s had for his evolution. They probably made him more aware of the interest classical models transferred to the vernacular could have, and he would also see what the Neo-Latins, both at home and abroad, were able to make of these classical sources—in the field of the elegy, the eclogue, the epithalamium, the epitaph and the wider-ranging epigram; Neo-Latin writers may have stimulated his excursions into religious poetry, up to a point. But whereas we can be more precise about the importance of Neo-Latin exploitation of the epigram, the other genres are less easy to pin down. It is not only a matter of scant documentation about Marot in the 1520s, one must also recognize the fluidity of these genres, especially when they are transferred to French, where metrical differences hardly obtain. The range of the Neo-Latin eclogue is very considerable: it can move from the court and ceremonial to the personal, and even the formal, pastoral elements can fade into the background (Mantuan, Castellus). The elegy has important roots in Ovid, as we know, but even though practice tended to split it up into two branches, amatory and deplorative, I am not sure that thematically the genre remains so conveniently categorized; and in the Neo-Latins, there comes a point when so-called epigrams spill over into the autobiographical elegy or into more courtly *deploratio*. One cannot, in these circumstances, talk of clear lines of demarcation or evolution; on the other hand, all these examples so easily accessible may well have strenghtened Marot's resolve to acclimatize these genres in the vernacular (where some of course already had antecedents), but without constricting unduly the poet's originality within highly stylized conventions. At the same time, these humanist contacts did more than bring Marot's attention to rather specialized matters of genre and theme; I think that they helped to instill or fortify in him a sense of France's literary prestige (the humanists in particular were very sensitive to Italian superiority in this field); and equally important they played a part in forming Marot's *vision du monde*, and particularly in religious matters, however controversial the details of his attitudes must remain.

It may well be that these humanist milieux, in both their scholarly and literary manifestations, contributed to Marot's excursions into the psalm paraphrase. It is particularly during the 1530s, in an Erasmian climate, that the psalm paraphrase enjoys a *regain de jeunesse*: on the one hand, emphasis is laid on reading of the most personal of biblical texts, and on the other scholars are acutely aware of the linguistic problems posed by the psalms. The implications of such attitudes are well known and so is the opposition they raised in orthodox high quarters, and I shall not rehearse them here. But during these years, Hebrew studies gather impressive momentum (Vatable, Clénard for a time, and lesser figures teaching in Paris; the appearance of numerous commentaries on the psalms—Vatable, Bucer, Sanctes Pagninus, etc.); and towards the same time, the verse psalm paraphrase acquires increasing importance. A very successful set of paraphrases was published by Eobanus Hessus at Marburg in 1537;[48] it went through many editions and was also published in France. However, the genre was well under way in France slightly earlier: the first full series to appear in Latin was from the pen of François Bonade in 1531;[49] and during this decade poets try their hand at translations (or paraphrases) of individual psalms: Salmon Macrin, we saw, brought out his penitential psalms in 1538;[50] Bourbon, with his pronounced Erasmian bias, turned out a few (*N*, pp. 356, 361, 411); Gilbert Ducher published one such paraphrase. One may wonder whether Marot was not in some measure affected by these Neo-Latin exercises, especially as they were undertaken by friends and colleagues, and indeed by the current humanist ideas underlying these paraphrases. In the first place, let us recall the original title of Marot's sixth psalm paraphrase: "Le VI Pseaulme de David, qui est le premier Pseaulme des sept Pseaulmes translaté en françoys par Clement Marot varlet de chambre du Roy nostre sire au plus près de la verité Ebraicque"—a point retained in some subsequent editions. I shall not dwell on the problem whether Marot had any knowledge of Hebrew—he probably had none—nor which commentators he used (Bucer has been mentioned since Becker made the suggestion); what interests me here is that Marot's attitude is similar to that of some other poets, in that the psalm paraphrase is seen as a means of making the original text more accessible (but also more accurate) for the benefit of the reader. This leads on to a further point: the paraphrase should not only be underpinned by reliable scholarship, it should try to reproduce the tone as well as the content of the original. This point affects metrical considerations. Bonade—and later Hessus—rendered all their paraphrases in elegiac couplets, but this was not satisfactory in the eyes of everybody, because it produces a standardized, more homogeneous tone throughout. A different view was taken by Jean de Gagny, who felt that the paraphrase should be given the metrical correlative of the mood it expressed. Conveniently, this is a moment when Horace the lyric is coming into his own,[51] and is being exploited by the Neo-Latin poets: it does not take them long to adapt the meters of the *Carmina* to the psalm paraphrase. We can find examples in Bourbon and Macrin, particularly the latter who varies the meters of his *Septem Psalmi* in 1538. However, the theory of this practice is not made public till 1547 when Jean de Gagnay publishes his 75 psalm paraphrases accompanied by an illuminating preface on the genre as he sees it.[52] By then of course Marot was dead, but Gagnay had been a prominent theologian since the 1520s, well known in humanist circles frequented by Marot; he had studied Latin and Greek under Danès, he contributed to the *tombeau du dauphin* in 1536 (the Joannes Gagnius theologus of that collective volume is none other), he was a friend of Gilbert Ducher (*Epigrammata*, p. 51) and he became *aumônier du roi*. It is not unduly fanciful to suppose that Gagnay had been airing his views for some time among friends and colleagues, and many of his ideas are seen in Marot's practice, as they are also in George Buchanan's psalm paraphrases which, though not published in their entirety until the end of 1565, owe something to Parisian humanist circles active two or three decades earlier. Marot's and Buchanan's great success was due in part to their varying the meters of their paraphrases—Marot adapting what the vernacular *chanson* had to offer, Buchanan using Horatian meters among others.

What emerges very clearly in references to Neo-Latin writings of the 1530s is the genuine admiration expressed for Marot, once the *Adolescence* and the *Suite* had seen the light of day. Almost everyone contributes a note of praise and encouragement: a rare exception must be Hilaire Courtois who includes in his *Volantillae* a short poem that surely alludes to Marot: "De Clemente Poeta inclemente, demente & mordaci."[53] The epigram develops the wordplay so much in fashion, but even so it is hardly elogious, rather curiously from a respected humanist, who was a pupil of Geoffroy Tory and was on good terms with Danès and Toussaint; all other writers fall over one another to extol Marot, and it is worth looking at the reasons for this incense.

First of all, we frequently come across the inevitable wordplay *Maro/ Marot*—in Visagier, Bourbon, Dolet. Even allowing for friendly hyperbole and patriotic wishful thinking, the comparison hardly falls four-square: Marot wrote no epic, he had no interest in the "scientific" or technical poem, only in the eclogue can we discern a direct overlap. It is however important to remember what Vergil stood for in the Renaissance. He was naturally seen as an accomplished craftsman, he was endowed with great learning and he had exceptional range—Renaissance humanists credited him with texts now considered supposititious but which then seemed to make him even more universal in his achievement. One must add that he was valued as an exemplary national poet. Now, if we take the parallel

on these terms, we can understand that, *mutatis mutandis*, Marot's contemporaries were finding in him the answer to their patriotic and humanist
prayer. He was a highly talented master of technique, he had a wide range,
and he was learned. These claims will be found, not simply in the versified
comparisons between the two poets, but in other contexts as well. The
trait that occasions surprise is the claim that Marot was learned; after all,
had not an acquaintance, Boyssonné, remarked that "Marotus latinè nes-
civit"?[54] But he seems to be alone in saying this. No doubt at the highest
level, Marot could not and would not compete with contemporary scholars,
having neither Greek nor Hebrew at his command; and we know that it
took time for his knowledge of Latin to mature. His deficiencies were
plain for all scholarly men to see, but they did consider him to be *sufficiently* learned to write poetry of serious purpose. The old tradition that
the Muse is learned, which has echoes among the *rhétoriqueurs* and, as
we well know, with the Pléiade, finds its partisans among the humanists
of the 1520s and 1530s. In this context it is worth looking at some lines
from Dolet's epistle to the Cardinal de Tournon, in which he is writing on
the present state of culture, chiefly in France: he gives a roll-call from the
field of humanism, including one or two names from abroad, Melanchthon
and Erasmus: the familiar names, Budé, Bérault, Danès, Toussaint crop up,
and he continues:

> . . . . Macrinus, Apollo,
> Cui dedit omne genus versus: versu quoque dives
> Borbonius: Dampetrus: Vulteius non parvam
> De se spem praebens Doctis: Maro gallicus ille,
> Ille Marotus, habet diues qui in carmine vires:
> Franciscus Rabelaesus honos et gloria certa
> Artis Paeoniae: qui vel de limine Ditis
> Extinctos reuocare potest, & reddere luci.
> ("Ad Card. Turonium," *C*, p. 62-63)

This is a highly significant passage, even if we make allowance for the enthusiasm of a writer sometimes given to hyperbole, yet far from insensi-
tive to high standards of scholarship. The cultural distinction of France is
a pressing concern among humanists and poets, and let us remember that
Dolet was not yet won over to the vernacular cause. First, Marot appears
as "doctus" enough to be admitted to this company, thus confirming what
has been said of the *Maro/Marot* parallel. Secondly, no distinction is made
between Latin and vernacular in principle, though representatives of French
literature are naturally rather thin on the ground at that moment. Marot
emerges rapidly in the humanist fraternity as a poet fulfilling the best
aspirations of that generation. Elsewhere Dolet establishes a parallel be-

tween Marot's Anne and Bourbon's Rabella, so that these poets are seen to be on an equal footing in promoting something approaching a love cycle (*C*, p. 57). On another occasion Dolet compares himself and Marot:

> Peperere Musae sat beato, & optato
> Partu Marotum, & post Doletum: ac utrumque
> Iisdem fere instruxere moribus, & iisdem
> Probe artibus ornarunt: siquidem componendi
> Versus minime vulgari, at insigni, & rara
> Felicitate.
> ("Ad Franciscum Rabelaesum," *C*, p. 30)

What is valuable here is not the self-satisfied parallel, but the criteria used for judging excellence in poetry, criteria which certainly redound to Marot's credit. Nor is Dolet the only one to include Marot's name in a list of cultural celebrities: Visagier, in his *Inscriptiones*, includes a poem—"Ad ignarum poetam" (fol. 6 v), which brings together Macrin, Bezard, Delaunay, Visa, Rosset, Dampierre, Germain de Brie, the Scèves and Marot—the title is significant in this context. On the other hand, Macrin does not include him in his well-known poem "Ad poetas gallicos;[55] he mentions Germain de Brie, Dampierre, Bourbon, Dolet, Visagier "Queis & Gallia nostra gloriatur."

After 1540 references to Marot in the Neo-Latin world are few and far between: Marot soon goes into exile and will die in Turin. But, in any case, the Lyons *sodalitium* had broken up for a number of reasons: Dolet's personality did little to paste over the cracks in his relations with others; Visagier was to die in 1540; Bourbon retreated into silence until the end of Francis I's reign; Gouvea published no more volumes of poetry in his lifetime; Sussannée was never very close, Jean de Boyssonné's writings remained manuscript for centuries; of Ducher we hear nothing more, and Macrin remains at a distance. In any case, the last years of the reign were fallow in Neo-Latin annals, apart from Julius-Caesar Scaliger, never in the poetic mainstream in spite of his importance. In the fullness of time a few poets belatedly write epitaphs on Marot or translate from his verse: I can think of P. Fulvius whose poetry came out posthumously[56] or Nicolas Chesneau, active as a teacher in Paris in mid-century.[57] More interesting perhaps is Guy Coquille who made a name for himself as a jurist and published his *Poemata* in 1590:[58] this late appearance of his verse masks the fact that much of it belongs to the 1540s and that his tribute to Marot dates from 1541 and was probably written during a stay in Italy that lasted from March 1541 to August 1543. No doubt some other traces can be picked up, but they are hardly germane to our purpose, which has been to situate Marot in the humanist climate of his times, to show that his links with these circles were even closer than has been suggested and that his contemporary reputation depended up to a point on the fact that his poetry achieved some of the important goals on which the humanists had set their heart.

NOTES

1. Ph.A. Becker, *Clément Marot, sein Leben und seine Dichtung* (Munich, 1926); P. Villey, *Les Grands Ecrivains du seizième siècle, Marot et Rabelais* (Paris, 1923).

2. Some examples: F. Petrarch, *Bucolica*, with commentary by J. Bade (Paris: J. Petit, 1502); Mantuan's eclogues (*Bucolica*) went through a goodly number of editions of which the most important are that by Josse Bade, with commentary (Paris: J. Petit, 1503) reprinted more than once and that by Andreas Vaurentius (Lyons, 1519, 1523, and 1529); Faustus Andrelinus, *Livia*, printed several times as were his *Elegiae* (for full details, see the excellent edition recently published by Godelieve Tournoy-Thoen, *Publi Fausti Andrelini Amores sive Livia*, AWLSK, Klasse der Letteren, Jaargang 44, Nr. 100, Brussels, 1982); Salmon Macrin publishes one or two works by Pontano; Quintianus Stoa, for a while at the court of Anne of Brittany, had works published in France; A. Politian, *Opera omnia* (Paris: J. Bade and J. Petit, 1512; second ed. 1519); G. Angeriano, 'Ερωτοπάιγνιον (Paris: Vatel, c. 1520); M. Marullus, *Epigrammata . . .* (Paris: A. Wechel, 1529); the Strozzi's poems were published by Simon de Colines in 1530; Sannazar was first printed in France in 1536 (several further editions); H. Vida had several works published by Gryphius in 1536. Some Neo-Latin verse was to be found in the Royal Library (e.g. Petrarch's eclogues, a poem by Fr. Filippo, etc.), see H. Omont, *Anciens Inventaires et Catalogues de la Bibliothèque Nationale, Librairie Royale, Blois, Fontainebleau, Paris* (Paris, 1906) (see Inventory for 1518).

3. Apart from a flying visit to France in 1518, Longueil spent his last years in Italy; see Ph.A. Becker, *Christophe de Longueil, sein Leben und sein Briefwechsel* (Leipzig, 1924). His death was mourned by various poets (Dolet, Ducher, Bourbon, Bèze): this makes me think that here we have a humanist exercise, so that dates of composition cannot always be contemporary.

4. Marot addressed an early *rondeau* (*OD*, p. 82) to Theocreno. On this figure, see P. Jourda, "Un Humaniste italien en France, Theocrenus (1480-1536)," *Revue du Seizième Siècle*, 16 (1929), 40-58.

5. *Stephani Templari Aurelii in aduentum Domini Germani Ganeij Aurelie Episcopi Gratulatorie Elegie* (P. Asselineau, Orleans, s.d.—the colophon gives no year, c. 1515?); this work comprises three elegies. The *Concordia Galliae et Britanniae a Stephano Templario Aurelio edita* appeared without date or place of printing: the B.L. catalogue suggests ?1520.

6. See L. Delaruelle, *Etudes sur l'humanisme français, Nicole Bérault. Notes biographiques suivies d'un appendice sur plusieurs de ses publications, Musée Belge, Revue de Philologie Classique* (Louvain-Paris, 1909), pp. 253 ff.

7. Rosset's works include: *Laurentias* (Paris: Bade, 1515): *Stephanis . . .* (Paris: Bade, 1516); *Paulus* (Paris: Bade, 1522; also Paris: N. Buffet, 1537); *Pratum* (Bade, s.d.); *Christus* (Paris: S. de Colines, 1534 and 1543). Bourbon who had extracted

from Rosset a liminary distich for his *Ferraria*, written in his 14th year (*Nugarum libri octo*, p. 230), considered him the finest French poet of his youth (ibid., p. 455); Visagier wrote an epitaph on him (*Epigrammata*, 1536), p. 113; and H. Sussannée published his *Deploratio* in 1532 (through L. Cynaeus)—the Bodleian has two copies of this very rare *plaquette*.

8. There is no monograph on this attractive humanist; biographical notes may be found in lives of Thomas More and in P.S. Allen's edition of *Erasmi Epistolae*, I, 447-48. The *Chordigerae nauis conflagratio* first appeared in Paris (Bade, 1513) with a second edition at Strasburg in the following year. It has been reprinted with commentary by Donald Stone, Jr. in *Humanistica Lovaniensia*, 1980.

9. "Oraison contemplative devant le crucifix," *T*, p. 92. See R. Lebègue, "La Source d'un poème religieux de Marot," *Mélanges Abel Lefranc* (Paris, 1936), pp. 58 ff.; and by the same author, *La Tragédie religieuse en France. Les débuts (1514-1573)* (Paris, 1929), who devotes a chapter to Barthélemy. His works include: *Momiae* . . . (Paris: Bade, c. 1512-1513); *Epithalamium . . . Eiusdem Ennea ad sospitalem Christum dimetris iambicis. Eiusdem Epigrammata* (Paris: R. Chauldière, 1520); *Epigrammata, Momiae, Etdyllia* [*sic*], n.d.n.p.; *De vita activa et contemplativa* . . . (Paris: P. Vidoue, 1523) (includes two *Ennoeae*); *Christus Xylonicus* (Paris: G. Bozzozel, 1529); *Ennoeae* (Paris: S. de Colines, 1531); *Epigrammata* (Paris: L. Cynaeus, 1532).

10. See L. Delaruelle, *Guillaume Budé, les origines, les débuts, les idées maîtresses*, Bibliothèque de l'Ecole des Hautes Etudes, 162 (Paris, 1907) and his *Répertoire analytique de la correspondance de Guillaume Budé* (Paris-Toulouse, 1907); more recently D.O. McNeill, *Guillaume Budé and Humanism in the Age of Francis I*, Travaux d'Humanisme et Renaissance, 142 (Geneva: Droz, 1977); and various works by Marie-Madeleine de la Garanderie.

11. Charles Graf, *Essai sur la vie et les écrits de Jacques Lefèvre d'Etaples* (Strasburg, 1842). More recently a number of Lefèvre's key texts have been edited (by Eugene Rice, Jr. and others).

12. By Jean Visagier. It is not known if Jean du Bellay responded to this plea.

13. There were quite a number of now forgotten authors who were pointing the way forward, adapting classical models and trying their hand in various genres. In addition to Templier and Nicolas Barthélemy, one might mention: Michaelis Anglicus (from Hainault) whose *Varia opuscula* (Paris: Bade, 1507), include eclogues and elegies; Guy Chastel (*Castellus*) whose *Elegiae* (together with an eclogue and epigrams) appeared c. 1506 in Poitiers; Julius Pius (or Piellus), in whose *Epigrammata* published in 1509 is to be found a poem "Petro Maroto contubernali" (fol. 34 r)— the person mentioned by C.A. Mayer, *Clément Marot* (Paris, 1972), p. 13? One should also note the *Epigrammata*, published by N. Barbatus in Paris, later to become well-known in Germany: we find references to Bérault (fol. 18 r), Germanus Brixius (fol. 21 r), Danès (fol. 26 r) and Lefèvre d'Etaples (fol. 28 r). This list could be extended without any difficulty. Love cycles are not yet to be found among French Neo-Latin poets but two models are available: Faustus Andrelinus's *Livia*, already mentioned, and Remacle d'Ardennes's *Amorum libri tres* (Paris: Petit & Bade, 1513). Faustus Andrelinus, who was at the court of Louis XII and Anne of Brittany, became *poeta regius* and enjoyed considerable prestige; he worked in a wide range of genres. On the evolution of the eclogue see A. Hulubei, *L'Eglogue en France au XVIe siècle, époque des Valois (1515-1589)* (Paris, 1938); for the elegy, C.M. Scollen, *The Birth of the Elegy in France* (Geneva: Droz, 1967). There is no comparable monograph on the

development of the epigram; but information on those epigrammatists who were affected by the *Greek Anthology* will be found in J. Hutton, *The Greek Anthology in France and in the Latin Writers of the Netherlands to the Year 1800*, Cornell Studies in Classical Philology, 28 (Ithaca: Cornell Univ. Press, 1946). See also P.M. Smith and C.A. Mayer, "La Première Epigramme française: Clément Marot, Jean Bouchet et Michel d'Amboise. Définitions, sources, antériorité," *Bibliothèque d'Humanisme et Renaissance*, 32 (1970), 579-602.

14. *In Lodoicae Reginae Matris mortem Epitaphia Latina & Gallica. Epitaphes a la louenge de ma Dame Mere du Roy faictz par plusieurs recommendables Autheurs* (Geoffroy Tory, 1531). One week later a second edition appeared, *Epitaphes, a la louenge de ma Dame Mere du Roy, faictz par plusieurs recommendables Autheurs auec d'autres nouuellement adioutez. Et tous corrigez, & bien emendez.* Some of the new names were Jacques Toussaint, Nicolas Bourbon, G. de Verceil, German de Brie. Marot however published his funereal eclogue in the *Adolescence clementine*; a separate *plaquette* of this poem, mentioned by Brunet, has not yet been found.

15. Three contributors, designated by their initials (A.C., M.A., A. Gal.) have yet to be identified. The Latin meaning of *Adolescence*, as Mayer, *Clément Marot*, p. 18, has pointed out, refers to the age between 20 and 30. It is of course another sign of Marot's classical bent at that time. Was he perhaps thinking of Mantuan, whose eclogues appeared under the title *Bucolicon seu Adolescentiae Eglogae X*? Marot was following Neo-Latin practice in dividing up his volume according to genres.

16. The texts are reproduced in C.A. Mayer, *Clément Marot*, pp. 241-43.

17. Op. cit., pp. 243-44.

18. *Nugarum libri octo* (Lyons: Gryphius, 1538), p. 351.

19. See I.D. McFarlane, "Jean Salmon Macrin (1490-1557)," *Bibliothèque d'Humanisme et Renaissance*, 21 (1959), 55-84, 311-49; 22 (1960), 73-89; Georges Soubeille, *Jean Salmon Macrin, Le Livre des Epithalames (1528-31). Les Odes de 1530 (Livres I & II)* (Publications de l'Université de Toulouse—Le Mirail, Série A, tome 37, 1978).

20. The first edition of the *Nugae* was published by Gryphius in Lyons and Cratander in Basle in 1533. The second, augmented edition came out from Gryphius in 1538 and from Cratander in 1540, under the title *Nugarum libri octo*. We use the second edition (= *N*) except where otherwise indicated.

21. *Recueil de Vers Latins, et Vulgaires de plusieurs Poetes François, composés sur le trespas de feu Monsieur le Dauphin* (Lyons: F. Juste, 1536).

22. *Tabellae elementariae, Pueris ingenuis Pernecessariae*, Nicolao Borbonio Vandoperano Lingone Poeta autore . . . (Lyons: J. & F. Frellon, 1539), fol. 44 v. On Bourbon, see G. Carré, *De vita et operibus Nicolai Borbonii. Vandoperani* (Paris, 1888).

23. *Septum Psalmi in lyricos numeros . . . paraphrastiωs versi. Eiusdem Paeanum libri quatuor . . .* (Poitiers: Frères Marnef, 1538), fol. D v[v].

24. B.N. fonds Dupuy, 915, fol. 315 v "Epitaphium Gul. Bellaii Langaei, praefecti regii." Salmon Macrin wrote a number of translations from Greek, Italian (Petrarch) and French (St. Gelais, Francis I, and Marot).

25. The one in the Bodleian, the other in the William Drummond of Hawthornden Collection, Edinburgh Univ. Library. A third copy was sold by Sotheby's in 1917, presumably to a private collector.

26. See list in I.D. McFarlane, art. cit., *Bibliothèque d'Humanisme et Renaissance*, 22 (1960), 85-88.

27. On the Lyons *sodalitium* see F. Buisson, *Sebastien Castellion* (Paris, 1892), I, ch. 2; R. Copley Christie, *Etienne Dolet, The Martyr of the Renaissance* (London, 1899), ch. 4; V.-L. Saulnier, *Maurice Scève* (Paris, 1948-1949), I, chs. 5 and 6; J.-C. Margolin, "Le Cercle humaniste lyonnais d'après l'édition des *Epigrammata* (1537) de Jean Visagier," in *L'Humanisme lyonnais au XVIe siècle* (Grenoble, 1974), pp. 151-83. Lucien Febvre, *Le Problème de l'incroyance au XVIe siècle* (Paris, 1942), has an amusing, but slightly jaundiced view of what he calls "les Apollons de collège" (ch. 2).

28. A. du Verdier, *Les Bibliothèques de la Croix du Maine*, 6 vols. (1772-1773), IV, 514 recalls having seen some French epigrams by Salmon Macrin in the hands of a Poitiers bookseller.

29. See V.-L. Saulnier, "Recherches sur Nicolas Bourbon l'Ancien," *Bibliothèque d'Humanisme et Renaissance*, 16 (1954), 172-91.

30. Jean de Boyssonné's correspondence and poetry are to be found in two mss (nos. 834 and 835) of the Bibliothèque Municipale, Toulouse. See H. Jacoubet, *Les Poésies latines de Jehan de Boyssonnée* (Toulouse, 1931); *Les Trois Centuries de Me Jean de Boyssonné* (Toulouse, 1923); and summaries of the correspondence in *Les Annales du Midi*, 41 (1929), 168-79, 257-94, 383-408; 43 (1931), 40-76. The full text of some of the most important letters was printed by H. Buche, *Revue des Langues Romanes*, 8 (1895), 176-90, 269-78; 9 (1896), 138-43. On this humanist, see also F. Mugnier, *La Vie et les poésies de Jehan de Boyssonné, Mémoires et documents publiés par la Société savoisienne d'histoire et d'archéologie*, 1897.

31. See V.-L. Saulnier, "La Mort du dauphin Françoys et son tombeau poétique," *Bibliothèque d'Humanisme et Renaissance*, 6 (1945), 50-97.

32. See the aforementioned biography by Christie (note 27). The *Orationes . . . Epistolarum Libri II . . . Carminum Libri II*, appeared in 1534 from the house of S. Gryphius (though neither date nor place is indicated); the *Carminum libri quatuor* came out in 1538 (also from Gryphius). We use the 1538 edition (= *C*).

33. *Commentarium linguae latinae tomi duo* (Lyons: Gryphius, 1536-1538), II, col. 403 (reproduced by Christie, op. cit., p. 373).

34. This means that he is anti-Erasmian in certain respects, like Hubert Sussannée and Julius-Caesar Scaliger, though he protested later against the charge that he had underestimated Erasmus's achievement.

35. See note in *Revue d'Histoire Littéraire de la France*, 1 (1894), 350.

36. E. Gaullieur, *Histoire du Collège de Guyenne* (Bordeaux, 1874), p. 57.

37. The date is sometimes given as 1542, but see Richard Cooper, "Antoine Arlier à Turin, 1539-43," *Atti della Accademia delle Scienze di Torino*, 104 (1969-1970), 235-98 (especially p. 274, n. 3) for conclusive evidence that 1540 is the correct date.

38. V. Barral, *Chronologia Sanctorum et aliorum illustrium ac abbatum sacrae Insulae Lerinensis* (Lyons: B. Rigaud, 1613), II, 285.

39. Visagier's volumes of verse are as follows: *Epigrammatum libri duo* (Lyons: S. Gryphius, 1536); *Epigrammatum libri IV* (Lyons: J. Barbou, 1537); *Epigrammatum libri IV. Eiusdem xenia* (Lyons: Parmentier, 1537) (this is the edition we normally use and which we designate by *E*); *Inscriptionum libri II . . . Xeniorum libellus* (Paris: S. de Colines, 1538) (the Xenia included here are different from the 1537 collection); *Hendescayllaborum Libri IIII* (Paris: S. de Colines, 1538).

40. *Epigrammata ad Ioannem Bellaium*, 1539. Delaunay also edited an ode by F. Filelfo s.d.; Nicolas Bourbon (*N*, p. 294) refers to a volume of Delaunay's Elegies recently published, but these I have not seen.

41. See note 30.

42. On Sussannée (his name is spelled in various ways), see P. Renouard, "Hubertus Sussannaeus. Hubert de Suzanne," *Revue des Livres Anciens*, 2 (1917), 146-58, who gives a list of his many publications. His *Ludorum libri duo* (Paris: S. de Colines, 1538) is the volume most relevant to our subject. Jean Talpin, probably a biased witness, referred at the trial of João da Costa before the Inquisition at Lisbon, to Dolet as "ateista" and to Sussannée as "epicurea," see *O processo Inquisição de Mestre João da Costa*, ed. M. Brandão, vol. I (Coimbra, 1944).

43. See *The Latin Letters of Antoine de Gouvea*, ed. M.K. Zeeb (Philadelphia, 1932); F. Mugnier, *Antoine Gouvéan, professeur de droit, Mémoires et documents publiés par la Société savoisienne d'histoire et d'archéologie*, 40 (1901), 3-80; L. de Matos, *Sobre Antonio de Gouvea e a sua obra* (Lisbon, 1966).

44. *Epigrammaton libri duo* . . . (Lyons: S. Gryphius, 1539); *Epigrammata . . . Eiusdem Epistolae quatuor* (S. Gryphius, 1540). In the prefatory letter to Jacques de Beaune, Gouvea makes particular reference to Martial.

45. On the theme see P. Laurens, "Le 'dizain de neige': histoire d'un poème ou Des sources latines du pétrarquisme européen," *Acta Conventus Neo-latini Turonensis*, ed. J.-C. Margolin (Paris, 1979), pp. 557-69. Laurens however quotes only the 1539 version. Marot is thought to have written his version not later than 1530.

46. *Iani Oliverii Andium hierophantae* (Lyons: E. Dolet, 1541). French translations appeared in 1542 and 1548.

47. See F. Aubert, J. Boussard, H. Meylan, "Théodore de Bèze: un premier recueil de poésies latines de Théodore de Bèze," *Bibliothèque d'Humanisme et Renaissance*, 15 (1953), 164-91 (the second part is not relevant here).

48. Eobanus Hessus, *Psalterium Davidis carmine redditus* (Marburg, 1537); see Carl Krause, *Helius Eobanus Hessus: sein Leben und seine Werke*, 2 vols. (Gotha, 1879).

49. Franciscus Bonadus, *Eximii prophetarum antistitis regia Davidis oracula* (Paris, 1531). On this figure see R. Lebègue, *La Tragédie religieuse*, op. cit., pp. 123-28.

50. The title is given in n. 23.

51. Horace the lyric is appreciated earlier by the Neo-Latin than by the vernacular poets: see R. Lebègue, "Horace en France pendant la Renaissance," *Humanisme et Renaissance*, 3 (1936), 150 ff. and 289 ff.

52. J. Gagnaeus, *Psalmi Davidis septuaginta quinque* . . . (Paris: Le Riche, 1547). On Latin psalm paraphrases, see H. Vaganay, *Les Traductions du psautier en vers latins au XVIe siècle* (Fribourg, 1898); J.A. Gaertner, "Latin verse translations of the Psalms 1500-1620," *Harvard Theological Review*, 49 (1956), 271-305; W. Leonard Grant, "Neo-Latin Verse Translations of the Bible," ibid., 52 (1959), 205-11; I.D. McFarlane, *Buchanan* (London, 1981), ch. 7.

53. *Hilarii Cortaesii Volantillae* (Paris: S. de Colines, 1533), fol. 19 r.

54. In his letter to Jacques Delexius (De Lect), dated Cal. Mart. 1547, Bibliothèque Municipale, Toulouse, ms 834, fol. 98 r. A proper critical edition of these letters has yet to be undertaken.

55. *Hymnorum libri VI* (R. Stephanus, 1537), pp. 37-39.

56. P. Fulvius (Fauveau) wrote a "Cl. Maroti tumulus," included in his poems published posthumously together with those of Roland Bétolaud, *Hodoeporicum* . . . (1574), fol. 60 r.

57. N. Querculus, *Epigrammatum libri duo* (Paris: Richard, 1553), fol. 29 v

("Epitaphium cuiusdam ex Clemente Marotto . . .").

     58. Guy Coquille, *Poemata* (Nevers: Roussin, 1590) ("Ad Amicam claram ex Gallico Maroti [anno 1541]," p. 154). In 1592 Coquille published his psalm paraphrases.

Gianni Mombello

Notices sur un correspondant de Clément Marot:
Alexis Jure de Quiers

Lorsque Monsieur le professeur I.D. McFarlane nous a invité à collaborer aux mélanges en l'honneur du Professeur Claude-Albert Mayer, il nous a semblé que notre sujet était décidé d'avance: mener des recherches sur Alexis Jure. Quoi donc de plus naturel, pour un Piémontais, que d'essayer de fournir quelques lumières sur la personnalité de ce correspondant de Clément Marot, le poète dont la vie et l'œuvre ont trouvé chez le Professeur C.-A. Mayer un exégète savant et passionné!

Nous devons avouer tout de suite que, malgré de longues prospections dans les archives publiques et privées de Chieri et de Turin, cette recherche a abouti en partie seulement, à notre grand regret, du moins jusqu'à présent. Nous sommes partis à la recherche des œuvres de ce poète français né au Piémont et nous n'avons retrouvé que quelques renseignements documentaires sur sa famille et sa vie. Il nous est possible de nous expliquer, maintenant, les raisons de cet insuccès. Cela vient du fait qu'Alexis Jure n'a passé qu'une partie de sa vie à Chieri; probablement sa jeunesse et peut-être—mais cela est loin d'être sûr—ses derniers jours.

Nous sommes sur les traces d'Alexis Jure depuis un certain temps et nous ne sommes pas le seul, puisque le mystère lié à sa personne et à son œuvre a intrigué plus d'un chercheur. En effet, il est extrêmement rare de trouver des Piémontais qui se soient servis du français comme langue littéraire, au cours du XVIe siècle. Le problème que pose ce poète inconnu se rattache donc à un autre beaucoup plus vaste, qui concerne celui de l'étendue de l'influence linguistique française dans le Piémont, au début des temps modernes.

Il ne nous est pas possible de traiter un sujet aussi complexe dans ces pages, ni de faire état de tous les documents que nous avons trouvés sur Alexis Jure et sa famille. Cela demanderait beaucoup trop de place et, de surcroît, cela n'intéresserait que l'histoire de la culture locale, qui reste, hélas, en grande partie à écrire. Nous allons donc nous borner à exposer quelques données concernant notre poète et son ascendance et descendance immédiates, en espérant livrer, dans un mémoire à part, le résultat complet de nos recherches.

La première chose à faire était de retrouver sa famille. Cela nous a été aisé, grâce à l'admirable collection de documents conservés à l'Archivio Storico de la ville de Chieri.

On trouve, dans l'un des quartiers de Chieri, celui de Vairo, et cela dès le milieu du XIIIe siècle, une famille portant le patronyme "de Jula."[1] Cette famille semble s'être éteinte dès la fin de ce même siècle; par contre, les "Convocati del Maggior Consiglio"—recueils des procès-verbaux des corps constitués de cette ville—nous font savoir que, le 22 mai 1329, un certain Nicholonus Jula avait demandé d'être admis parmi les citoyens de Chieri avec ses enfants.[2] Nicholonus était donc un étranger.

Le cadastre de 1343 nous présente Oddinus Jula dit "de Butigleria" résidant dans le quartier d'Albussano.[3] Nous pensons qu'il s'agit d'un des enfants de Nicholonus, sans qu'il nous soit possible de prouver cette affirmation. Néanmoins, puisque Oddinus se dit "de Butigleria"—une petite ville sise aux frontières orientales de la ville-état de Chieri—nous pensons que cette hypothèse n'est pas à écarter. A partir de 1343, tous les cadastres de la ville attestent que, dans le quartier d'Albussano, vivaient une ou deux familles qui portaient ce patronyme, et cela jusqu'au milieu du XVIe siècle. Sous l'effet du rhotacisme—phénomène courant dans les territoires du Piémont placés au sud du Pô—ce nom de famille a été prononcé, par la suite, Jura et enfin Giura (XVIe siècle).

Les Jura étaient des cultivateurs nantis, au cours du XVe siècle. Deux descendants d'Oddinus: Guidetus et son neveu Johannes déclaraient posséder, en 1424, un patrimoine immobilier estimé à quatre-vingt-douze livres, cinq sols.[4] Outre trois maisons valant huit livres, quatre sols, Guidetus et Johannes déclaraient posséder trente parcelles de terre mesurant soixante-sept journaux et vingt-trois "tables,"[5] soit vingt-huit hectares et cinq ares et demie. Il s'agissait d'un fermage complet et fort bien diversifié, comprenant des terres labourables, du vignoble, des prés, des bois et un jardin potager. Encore aujourd'hui, une ferme de soixante-sept journaux est considérée comme supérieure à la moyenne, dans la région. Au Moyen Age elle devait exiger un outillage important, beaucoup de gros bétail et une main-d'œuvre qui devait dépasser le cadre familial, tout nombreux fût-il.

D'après les relèvements effectués par Claudio Rotelli, les familles de Chieri qui possédaient trente hectares de terre environ, au cours de la première moitié du XVe siècle, ne devaient pas dépasser la cinquantaine.[6] Nous pouvons donc penser que les Jura devaient compter parmi les propriétaires terriens d'origine bourgeoise les plus nantis, après les nobles. En outre, depuis le XIVe siècle, un certain nombre de membres de cette famille avait déployé une activité inlassable dans les différentes branches de l'administration de la ville-état de Chieri.

Il serait vraiment trop long de recenser toutes leurs fonctions. Il n'y a pratiquement pas de volume des "Convocati," avant 1476, qui ne signale un ou plusieurs membres de cette famille dans les listes des différents corps constitués. Dès 1347, Oddinus Jula est élu à la "Credentia Maior," l'organisme le plus représentatif de la commune; mais c'est avec Guidetus, et surtout avec Johannes que les Jura ont acquis le plus de poids dans l'administration de la ville. Ce dernier, tout en étant un bourgeois, avait été élu, en 1460 et en 1462,[7] parmi les vingt-quatre membres du conseil restreint chargé de choisir le nouveau vicaire ducal de la ville. Nous pensons pouvoir identifier dans ce document le témoignage du couronnement de toute l'activité politique de Johannes, activité qui avait été longue, puisque son nom paraît dans les documents administratifs depuis 1436-1437 jusqu'en 1476 et intense, puisqu'il a assumé, au cours de ce laps de temps, toute une série de fonctions qui n'étaient pas toujours modestes. Le cadastre de 1437 nous présente Guidetus et Johannes séparément.[8] Leurs biens sont encore importants, mais on assiste, à côté des achats, aussi à des ventes et à des partages.

Johannes a eu deux ou trois enfants: Beatrixina, Francischus et, peut-être, aussi Ludovicus. De Francischus est né Constantius (un contemporain d'Alexius) mort le 23 avril 1551.

Pour ce qui est de la descendance de Guidetus nous pouvons l'établir ainsi. Son fils Francischonus, actif, d'après les procès-verbaux des "Convocati del Maggior Consiglio," de 1441-1442 à 1471, a eu deux enfants mâles, Bartholomeus et Ludovicus. De Bartholomeus, actif d'après les cadastres et les "Convocati" de 1481 à 1533-1534, sont nés, à une date qu'il ne nous est pas possible de préciser, Alexius et Bartholomea.

Nous avons fait allusion ci-dessus à des ventes d'immeubles. La propriété de Johannes a été démembrée de 1447 à 1461, celle de Guidetus de 1442 à 1462. Les notes marginales du cadastre de 1466[9] nous attestent que les héritiers de ces deux personnages ont achevé de vendre ce qui restait de l'ancienne propriété des Jura, au cours des années 1480. Que s'était-il passé? Devons-nous supposer que les Jura de Buttigliera résidant à Albussano avaient pris eux aussi le chemin de la décadence comme les "de

Jula" du quartier Vairo? Nous ne le croyons pas. Nous pensons plutôt que cette famille fort active et engagée avait tout simplement reconverti ses activités.

En effet, dès la deuxième moitié du XVe siècle s'était implantée à Chieri la fabrication de la futaine.[10] Cette industrie était assez rentable et permettait, à ceux qui la pratiquaient, de se mettre à l'abri des vicissitudes économiques d'un duché aux finances peu brillantes. Rien d'étonnant donc si les Jura ont délaissé le labourage et s'ils se sont faits artisans ou marchands. En effet, la fabrication de la futaine exigeait l'importation du coton et la mise en place d'un réseau marchand pour l'écoulement du produit manufacturé.

On trouve des membres de cette famille (un Baptista, en 1482 et un Jacobus, en 1490) dans les plus anciens documents concernant cette industrie.[11] Il se peut donc que si Bartholomeus et Ludovicus, fils de Francischonus, ont vendu presque toutes les terres de leur père et surtout ses maisons, c'était parce qu'ils avaient pris le chemin de l'étranger.

Cette hypothèse est confirmée par le fait qu'après plus d'un siècle de présence active au sein des corps constitués de la ville, il faut attendre presque onze ans avant de rencontrer un Jura cité dans les procès-verbaux des "Convocati," après la dernière mention de Johannes remontant au 25 octobre 1476.[12] C'est en effet seulement après août 1487 que Ludovicus Jura est mentionné parmi les membres de la "Juncta" pour le quartier d'Albussano.[13] La "Juncta" était un organisme de constitution récente (début du XVe siècle) et ses fonctions étaient moins importantes que celles du "Consilium Maius," où avaient siégé les Jura, dès le XIVe siècle. Ludovicus a été actif jusqu'en 1518-1519[14] et il a été remplacé, dans les mêmes fonctions, par Bartholomeus, père d'Alexius, des 1521-1522[15] et ceci jusqu'en 1533-1534.[16] Le père et l'oncle de notre poète étaient probablement rentrés dans leur ville natale après un séjour à l'étranger.

Une fois rentré, Bartholomeus a essayé de reconstituer, petit à petit, son patrimoine immobilier. Il résidait toujours dans le quartier habité par ses ancêtres, non plus "in ruata podii Gayetorum," mais au Marché-aux-Bœufs, deux lieux-dits qu'on peut facilement identifier dans la topographie de la ville d'aujourd'hui. Ils sont situés sur deux coteaux qui s'étendent à partir de la butte Saint-Georges, dominant les quartiers bas de la ville, quartiers qui se sont développés à partir de l'emplacement de l'ancienne cité romaine. Au sommet de cette butte, s'élève l'église dédiée à saint Georges où avait son siège une puissante "Societas" du même nom[17] et qui a joué un rôle important dans la vie politique et administrative de Chieri durant tout le Moyen Age et bien après. Bartholomeus a été un membre actif de cette société de 1517 à 1533.[18]

Le cadastre de 1514[19] nous fait savoir que sa maison était modeste, puisqu'elle n'était estimée qu'une livre, quinze sols et qu'il ne possédait que trois parcelles de terre. Le cadastre de 1533[20] nous atteste que Bartholomeus avait acheté, entre temps, quatre autres parcelles de terre. Son patrimoine immobilier était estimé, alors, vingt-quatre livres, dix-huit sols, un denier. Cette propriété est passée à son fils Alexius, qui l'a encore augmentée, comme nous le documente le cadastre de 1551.[21]

Ce dernier document nous apprend qu'Alexius a fait sa déclaration "organo Constantii Jure," c'est-à-dire par l'intermédiaire de son cousin, ce qui nous porte à penser qu'il était absent de Chieri à ce moment-là.

Un document de tout autre nature nous certifie qu'Alexius ne résidait pas à Chieri au moins depuis 1540. Au mois de mars de cette année-là, Alexius et sa sœur Bartholomea avaient acheté, par procuration, à un de leurs voisins, Bartholomeus Calierij, une maison sise à côté de la leur au Marché-aux-Bœufs, pour la somme de cent vingt florins "parviponderis monete sabaudie." Cette maison devait être assez importante parce que "soleriata," c'est-à-dire qu'elle possédait un étage au-dessus du rez-de-chaussée. Le "solarium" était typique des demeures des nobles.[22]

Une clause de ce contrat, dressé par le notaire Giovanni Francesco Lucis,[23] nous fait savoir que les acheteurs permettaient au vendeur d'habiter cette maison encore pour la durée de quatre ans, à partir de la date de l'acte de vente. Evidemment Alexius et sa sœur n'étaient pas pressés de rentrer à Chieri. Cette maison à dû être vendue par la suite, puisqu'il n'en est plus question dans le cadastre de 1551.

Une note marginale à ce même cadastre nous apprend qu'Alexius avait acheté de Julianus Borgarelli une autre "domus" valant quatre livres, quatre sols. Cette mention semble être inexacte puisque ce même immeuble est décrit, dans ce même cadastre, au registre du vendeur, comme étant un "sedimen"[24] et donc une parcelle de terrain à bâtir. De toute manière, ce "sedimen" valait bien plus que la demeure qu'Alexius tenait de son père et qui n'était estimée que dix-huit sols, cinq deniers.

Comme on le voit, notre poète avait fait de nombreux achats dans sa ville natale, espérant peut-être y faire retour, mais une note, placée au pied de sa déclaration pour 1551, nous apprend que toute sa propriété avait été vendue à Johannes Anthonius Ferrerii, alias Brigha, le 11 novembre 1558. Alexius Jura avait donc abandonné tout espoir de réintégrer le berceau de ses ancêtres à cette date-là.

Le dernier document que nous avons retrouvé sur Alexius remonte à 1580. Il s'agit d'un "consegnamento" d'armoiries.[25] Ce document nous permet de savoir que notre poète était déjà mort et qu'il avait légué, à son enfant naturel nommé Francesco, une maison sise à Chieri. Il a dû acheter cette autre demeure après 1558, date à laquelle il avait vendu tous les biens qu'il possédait dans cette ville. Cette maison, échue à Francesco, portait des armoiries gravées sur la cheminée de la salle. Il ne nous est pas possible de savoir si ces armoiries, qui ne sont pas décrites dans le document de 1580, correspondaient à celles qui sont attribuées aux Jura dans un armorial de Chieri commencé en 1598.[26]

Il faut se demander maintenant pourquoi Alexius Jura n'a pas vécu à Chieri et où il a exercé son activité.

Pour ce qui est de la deuxième question, nous n'avons pas de réponse à donner, à l'état actuel de nos recherches. Nous avons fait des sondages sur les axes Chambéry-Lyon, Paris-Flandre et Avignon-Marseille, surtout grâce à la collaboration d'un certain nombre de collègues, auxquels nous exprimons toute notre gratitude, mais sans résultats jusqu'à présent. Cette recherche demande de nombreux et longs déplacements, qui risquent d'être inutiles aussi longtemps qu'on n'aura pas l'assurance de s'engager dans une direction qui pourrait être rentable. Il nous manque, en effet, et il nous manquera vraisemblablement encore pour longtemps, une étude sur le réseau commercial des marchands de Chieri au XVIe siècle, période qui n'est guère prospectée. Seule une trouvaille fortuite pourra nous signaler le ou les endroits où Alexius a exercé son activité.

En ce qui concerne la première question, nous ne pouvons formuler que des hypothèses.

Premièrement, Alexius aurait pu suivre ses aînés ou ses voisins (les de Villa et les Buschetti) à l'étranger pour exercer le commerce, en qualité de marchand ou de banquier, selon une consuétude bien établie dans la région, mais nettement en baisse au XVIe siècle.[27] Deuxièmement, ce correspondant de Marot aurait pu avoir été touché par les idées de la Réforme, dont Chieri avait été un foyer actif dès 1528.[28] Malheureusement, son nom ne figure pas parmi les étrangers vivant à Genève,[29] où résidaient de nombreux ressortissants de cette ville du Piémont.

A ce point nous pouvons évoquer un problème soulevé par l'édition Guiffrey-Yve-Plessis-Plattard des œuvres de Clément Marot.[30] S'appuyant sur une notice de La Croix du Maine, les éditeurs de Marot pensent qu'Alexius Jura aurait pu se cacher sous le pseudonyme de Alessio Piemontese, auteur d'un recueil de *Secreti*. C.-A. Mayer, plus prudent, ne souffle mot de cette identification.

On a fait récemment le point sur la question de l'identification de l'auteur possible des *Secreti* de Donno Alessio Piemontese.[31] La solution qui nous est proposée est finalement déjà ancienne et elle ne nous satisfait qu'à moitié, mais force nous est de constater que l'identification d'Alexius Jura avec Alessio Piemontese est plus que risquée. Il nous faut donc exclure, au moins provisoirement, que ce correspondant de Marot se soit intéressé aux simples et qu'il ait été apothicaire.

Nous arrivons enfin au poème que Clément Marot a adressé à Alexis Jure.

Le commentaire de ce texte pose de nombreux problèmes dûs non seulement au fait que le dédicataire est un inconnu, mais aussi parce que Marot le lui envoie "en France" (v. 59).

Les commentateurs de l'édition Guiffrey pensent que le destinataire de cette épître, "originaire de Quiers, en Piémont . . . faisait sa résidence habituelle dans cette ville située à peu de distance de Turin." Ce que nous venons de dire s'inscrit en faux contre cette interprétation.

Pour ce qui est du v. 59 plus particulièrement, nous pensons qu'il faut l'entendre dans son sens propre, puisque Alexius vivait déjà en France dès avant 1540, très probablement, et non plus dans le Piémont occupé par les milices françaises à partir de 1536.

Pourquoi en France? Parce qu'il est extrêmement rare de trouver des Piémontais capables de composer en français, au cours du XVIe siècle et aussi parce que Chieri n'était pas exactement une ville dans laquelle l'activité poétique ait été particulièrement appréciée.

Commençons par ce dernier point. Pouvait-on devenir poète, à Chieri, au cours du XVIe siècle? Les monuments littéraires qui nous sont parvenus[32] ne nous font pas pencher pour l'affirmative. D'ailleurs, un humaniste actif dans cette ville, vers 1430, en qualité de "magister scolarum," nous a brossé un tableau des habitants de Chieri, qui se passe de tout commentaire: "Haec gens prorsus hostilitatem virtutibus indicit, litteris praesertim immortale odium et clandestinas insidias agit."[33] Il faut dire que Bartholomeo Guasco, l'auteur de ces lignes, était un étranger et que les humanistes faisaient vite tourner à l'aigre leurs louanges faciles, surtout s'ils n'étaient pas bien payés. N'empêche que cette ville, peuplée surtout de cultivateurs, d'artisans et de commerçants, ne devait pas être trop favorable à l'éclosion de talents poétiques.

Peu favorable mais non hostile, puisque dès la fin du XVe siècle, nous trouvons, à la cour de Chambéry, un "poeta laureatus" natif de Chieri: un certain Gabriel de Ferrariis, dont l'œuvre a été complètement perdue.[34] Nous pensons que Gabriel de Ferrariis a été surtout poète en latin. Il serait du plus grand intérêt de retrouver quelques-unes de ses œuvres, parce que, malgré ce qu'ont dit les mauvaises langues, Chieri n'était pas habitée exclusivement par des bouviers illettrés. Bien des témoignages, qu'il ne nous est pas possible de rappeler ici, permettent de penser que les habitants de cette ville avaient quelque considération pour les œuvres de l'esprit, comme l'attestent les peintures et les livres qu'ils avaient accumulés dans leurs églises, dans leurs couvents et dans leurs maisons et dont quelques débris sont arrivés jusqu'à nous.

Il se peut aussi que les Jura aient compté des clercs parmi les leurs. Une pièce apographe des archives Bosio, conservées à la Biblioteca Civica de Turin,[35] nous permet de savoir qu'avant le 12 septembre 1520 était décédé un certain Martinus Jura, chanoine à Chieri. Il nous plaît d'imaginer que Martinus ait pu jouer le rôle de précepteur auprès du jeune Alexius.

Pouvait-on devenir poète français à Chieri au XVIe siècle? Voilà la deuxième question à laquelle nous essayons de répondre. La situation linguistique de Chieri ne devait être guère dissemblable de celle des autres territoires cismontains sujets au duc de Savoie, la Vallée d'Aoste exceptée. Les documents qui nous sont parvenus nous attestent que si, dans cette vallée, le français était la langue de la communication écrite, il en allait tout autrement dans le reste du pays. L'italianisation linguistique du Piémont, sensible au cours du règne d'Emmanuel Philibert (1553-1580), devait être chose faite ou sur le point de l'être, dès le règne de son père Charles II (ou III) (1504-1553), un prince qui ne se servait que du français,[36] au moins jusqu'en 1536. L'invasion française et la guerre semblent n'avoir nullement favorisé l'implantation de la langue de l'occupant, au contraire, il semble bien que cela ait agi en sens contraire.

Nous ne connaissons que deux écrivains originaires du Piémont qui se soient servis du français dans des œuvres littéraires: un au début du XVIe siècle et un autre à la fin.

On ignore presque tout de la vie de Giovan Giorgio Alione, poète et dramaturge d'Asti, actif au cours du premier quart du XVIe siècle, mais il se peut qu'il ait vécu en France, et, de toute manière, il a eu des contacts avec l'administration française.[37] Il a écrit de nombreux poèmes en français[38] et il a employé cette langue, avec une certaine aisance, aussi dans ses farces.[39]

Pour ce qui est du second, le duc Charles Emmanuel Ier, il a dû puiser ses connaissances du français à de bonnes sources. En effet, sa mère était Marguerite de France, fille de François Ier, protectrice des poètes. C'est d'elle, qui vécut jusqu'en 1574, que ce jeune prince a dû apprendre le français comme sa langue vraiment maternelle. Qu'on ajoute à cela que le français restait la langue de la cour de Turin, même au temps d'Emmanuel Philibert et on n'aura pas de difficulté à s'expliquer pourquoi Charles Emmanuel Ier a pu être poète tout aussi bien en français qu'en italien.[40] Mais les choses changent dès qu'on s'éloigne de la cour et elles changent de beaucoup. Si le duc correspond en français avec ses sujets Piémontais, ceux-ci ont quelque difficulté à se servir de cette langue, qui n'était certainement pas celle de la communication écrite. On connaît un petit nombre de textes rédigés en français, qui proviennent des communautés locales (Moncalieri, Chieri) et datés ou datables de la fin du XVe siècle ou du début du suivant. La langue de ces textes est fort incertaine et encombrée de barbarismes.[41] Ce n'est certainement pas avec de pareilles connaissances linguistiques qu'on pouvait aborder l'expression littéraire et surtout tenter la poésie.

Il faut donc prendre au pied de la lettre le témoignage de Claude de Seyssel, un savoyard qui a vécu longtemps au Piémont, au cours de la période qui nous intéresse. D'après lui, les habitants des territoires cismontains sujets du duc de Savoie comprenaient et parlaient le français.[42] Si les Piémontais comprenaient et parlaient le français ils avaient certainement du mal à l'écrire, à moins qu'ils aient eu des contacts fréquents avec la cour ou qu'ils aient fait des séjours en France ou dans des pays de langue française.

Il s'ensuit donc, à notre avis, qu'Alexius Jura a dû vivre en France, pour devenir poète français. Il ne nous est pas possible de prouver, en ce moment, ce postulat nécessaire, mais tous les documents qu'il nous a été possible de retrouver nous indiquent clairement que notre poète ne résidait pas habituellement dans sa ville d'origine. En attendant de pouvoir étayer par de nouveaux témoignages la solidité de l'hypothèse que nous proposons et surtout de retrouver, si possible, les œuvres françaises de ce poète piémontais, il nous est agréable de publier ces quelques renseignements sur lui dans ces Mélanges dédiés à Monsieur le Professeur C.A. Mayer.

NOTES

1. Maria Clotilde Daviso di Charvensod, *I più antichi catastii del comune di Chieri (1253)*, Biblioteca della Società Storica Subalpina, 161 (Turin: Ranotti, 1939), p. 335.

2. Paolo Brezzi, *Gli ordinati del comune di Chieri: 1328-1329*, Biblioteca della Società Storica Subalpina, 162 (Turin, Chieri: Tipografia M. Ghirardi, 1937), pp. 116-17.

3. Chieri, *Archivio Storico*, art. 143, vol. 21, fol. 7^v.

4. Chieri, ibid., art. 143, vol. 32, fol. 25^r-26^v.

5. Nous traduisons par "table" le mot latin "tabula." La "tabula" est la centième partie de la "jornata" (en français: journau). D'après une étude de Claudio Rotelli, que nous allons citer dans la note suivante, le journau de Chieri aurait mesuré, au Moyen Age, 0,4175 hectares. La "tabula" était divisée en douze "pedes."

6. Claudio Rotelli, *Una campagna medievale. Storia agraria del Piémonte fra il 1250 e il 1450*, Biblioteca di cultura storica, 120 (Turin: Einaudi, 1973), p. 335.

7. Chieri, *Archivio Storico*, art. 53, cart. 203 § 72, fol. 43^v (élection du 4 novembre 1460); ibid. § 74, fol. 42^r (élection du 22 décembre 1462).

8. Chieri, ibid., art. 143, vol. 35, fol. 17^v-18^r (pour Johannes) et fol. 26^r-27^r (pour Guidetus).

9. Chieri, ibid., art. 143, vol. 42, fol. 20ᵛ (pour Johannes et ses héritiers), fol. 21ᵛ (pour Francisc[h]onus, fils de Guidetus, et ses héritiers).

10. *Statuti dell'arte del fustagno di Chieri*, a cura di Vittorio Balbiano di Aramengo. Studio introduttivo di Anna Maria Nada Patrone, Studi e documenti di storia economica (Turin: Deputazione Subalpina di Storia Patria, 1966), vol. 1 *passim*.

11. Ibid., pp. 187* et 42.

12. Chieri, *Archivio Storico*, art. 53, cart. 205, ⸗ 83, fol. 45ᵛ.

13. Ibid. art. 53, cart. 206, ⸗ 90, fol. 21ᵛ.

14. Ibid. art. 53, cart. 210, ⸗ 108 (procès-verbaux du 27 septembre 1518 au 11 septembre 1519), fol. 11ʳ.

15. Ibid. art. 53, cart. 210, ⸗ 110 (procès-verbaux du premier juillet 1521 au 31 mars 1522), fol. 9ᵛ.

16. Ibid. art. 53, cart. 211, ⸗ 117 (procès-verbaux du 4 juin 1533 au 12 juin 1534, fol. 8ʳ.

17. Luigi Cibrario, *Delle storie di Chieri libri quattro con documenti* (Turin: Per l'Alliana, a spese di P.G. Pic, 1827), I, 220-54 et *passim*. Ouvrage à consulter dans la réédition de 1967 (Turin: Bottega d'Erasmo). Cf. aussi Gino Borghezio, Bartolomeo Valimberti, Mario Chiaudano, Carlo Dolza, *Statuta et Capitula Societatis Sancti Georgii seu Populi Chariensis*, Biblioteca della Società Storica Subalpina, 159-160, en 3 tomes [sic] (Turin-Chieri, 1936-1950).

18. Chieri, *Archivio Storico*, art. 52, cart. 188 contenant les procès-verbaux de la "Societas Sancti Georgii" du 22 juillet 1517 au 31 juin 1563. Bartholomeus est cité, parmi les conseillers, aux fols. 3ʳ, 7ʳ, 33ʳ, 36ʳ, 66ʳ et 121ʳ (pour l'année 1533).

19. Ibid. art. 143, vol. 47, fol. 62ᵛ.

20. Ibid. art. 143, vol. 52, fol. 55ʳ-56ʳ.

21. Ibid. art. 143, vol. 63, fol. 10ᵛ-11ʳ.

22. Luigi Cibrario, *Delle storie di Chieri*, II, 430.

23. Turin, *Archivio di Stato*. Sezioni Riunite (via Santa Chiara), *Notai di Chieri: Giovanni Francesco Lucis*, vol. I, fol. 17ᵛ-18ᵛ.

24. Chieri, *Archivio Storico*, art. 143, vol. 63, fol. 181ʳ.

25. Turin, Biblioteca Reale, ms. Storia Patria 452, fol. 16ᵛ.

26. Ibid. ms. Varia 656, fol. 28ʳ.

27. La bibliographie sur les "lombards" est considérable, nous nous bornons à citer trois ouvrages. Jean-François Bergier, "Marchands italiens à Genève au début du XVIᵉ siècle (1480-1540)," in *Studi in onore di Armando Sapori* (Milan: Istituto Editoriale Cisalpini, 1957), II, 883-96; Anna Maria Patrone, *Le Casane astigiane in Savoia*, Miscellanea di Storia Italiana, série IV, 4 (Turin: Deputazione Subalpina di Storia Patria, 1959); Richard Gascon, *Grand Commerce et vie urbaine au XVIᵉ siècle. Lyon et ses marchands (environs de 1502-environs de 1580)*, Civilisations et Sociétés, 22, en 2 tomes (Paris: SEVPEN, 1971).

28. Giovanni Jalla, *Storia della Riforma in Piemonte fino alla morte di Emanuele Filiberto, 1517-1580* (Florence: Libreria Claudiana, 1914), pp. 27-28 et *passim*.

29. *Livre des habitants de Genève*, t. I, 1549-1560; t. II, 1572-1574 et 1585-1587. Publié avec une introduction et des tables par Paul-F. Geisendorf, Travaux d'Humanisme et Renaissance, 26 et 56 (Genève: Droz, 1957-1963); Arturo Pascal, *La Colonia piemontese a Ginevra nel secolo XVI*, in *Ginevra e l'Italia*. Raccolta di studi promossa dalla Facoltà Valdese di Teologia di Roma, a cura di Delio Cantimori, Luigi Firpo, Giorgio Spini, Franco Venturi, Valdo Vinay, Biblioteca Storica Sansoni, nuova serie, 34 (Florence: Sansoni, 1959), pp. 65-133.

30. *Oeuvres de Clément Marot*, édition Georges Guiffrey mise au jour d'après les papiers posthumes de l'éditeur, avec des commentaires et des notes par Robert Yve-Plessis [et Jean Plattard], 5 vols. (Paris: Imprimerie Jules Claye, *deinde*, Damascène Morgand et Charles Fatout, *deinde*, Librairie de l'Art Français, Jean Schemit, 1875-1931), III, 381, n. 1 de la page 317.

31. Luigi Firpo, "Medici piemontesi del Cinquecento," in Leonardo Botallo, *I doveri del medico e del malato*, a cura di Leonardo Carerj e Anita Bogetti Fassone (Turin: Unione Tipografico-Editrice Torinese, 1981), pp. 17-22.

32. *Bibliografia ragionata della lingua regionale e dei dialetti del Piemonte e della Valle d'Aosta, e della letterature in Piemontese*, a cura di Amedeo Clivio e Gianrenzo P. Clivio (Turin: Centro Studi Piemontesi, 1971), pp. 7-12.

33. Ferdinando Gabotto, *Lo Stato sabaudo da Amedeo VIII ad Emanuele Filiberto* (Turin: Roux Frassati e C., 1892-1895), t. III: *(1496-1504) La Coltura e la vita in Piemonte nel Rinascimento*, p. 283 et n. 3.

34. Gustavo Vinay, *L'Umanesimo subalpino nel secolo XV (Studi e Ricerche)*, Biblioteca della Società Storica Subalpina, 148 (Turin: Tipografia Ed. M. Gabetta-Voghera, 1935), pp. 21-22 et *passim*.

35. Turin, Biblioteca Civica, Fondo Bosio, ms. 48, fol. 100^r.

36. Une très riche collection des lettres de ce duc est conservée dans trois séries de l'Archivio di Stato de Turin: *Casa Reale, lettere di principi: duchi e sovrani*, mazzi 3-6. *Registri lettere della corte*, reg. 4 (en deux vols.). *Minute lettere della corte*, mazzo 2.

37. Giovan Giorgio Alione, *L'Opera piacevole*, a cura di Enzo Bottasso, Collezione di opere inedite o rare, pubblicate a cura della Commissione per i Testi di Lingua, Nuova serie (Bologne: Libreria Antiquaria Palmaverde, 1953), p. viii et n. 3.

38. *Les Chansons françaises de Giovan Giorgio Alione, poète astesan du XV* [sic] *siècle, publiées à l'occasion du IV* [sic] *centenaire de sa mort*, avec introduction et notes littéraires et historiques par M. Maranzana (Milan: Charles Signorelli Editeur, 1929). Très mauvaise édition.

39. Giovan Giorgio Alione, *L'Opera piacevole*, éd. cit., pp. 79-95; *Farsa de la dona chi se credia havere una roba de veluto dal Franzoso alogiato in casa soa*, pp. 231-49: *Farsa del Franzoso alogiato a l'ostaria del Lombardo, a tre personagii*.

40. Maria Luisa Doglio, "Rime inedite di Carlo Emanuel I di Savoia," *Studi Piemontesi*, 8, 1 (mars 1979), 121-33. On trouvera, dans cet article, les renvois bibliographiques aux publications antérieures des poèmes de ce prince-poète.

41. Ferdinando Gabotto, *Lo Stato sabaudo da Amedeo VIII ad Emanuel Filiberto*, op. cit., II, 428, suite de la note 3 de la p. 427. Reproduction d'une lettre de la commune de Moncalieri à Charles VIII, roi de France, datée du 24 avril 1490. Gaudenzio Claretta, "Sulle antiche società dei nobili della repubblica di Chieri e sul suo patriziato sotto il dominio della R. casa di Savoia," in *Atti della R. Accademia delle Scienze di Torino*, 20 (1885), 589-90. G. Claretta publie un document non daté, mais qui remonte au début du XVIe siècle. Ce *Memorial des afferes de Quiers* est fort mal transcrit.

42. Gianni Mombello, *Claude de Seyssel: un esprit modéré au service de l'expansion française*, in *Culture et pouvoir au temps de l'Humanisme et de la Renaissance. Actes du Congrès Marguerite de Savoie*—Annecy, Chambéry, Turin 29 avril-4 mai 1974—publiés par Louis Terreaux (Genève-Paris: Slatkine-Champion, 1978), p. 85

R. Scheurer

Les Relations franco-anglaises pendant la négociation de la paix des Dames (juillet 1528-août 1529)

La défaite française devant Pavie et la capture du roi conduisirent rapidement à des trêves entre les belligérants; celle conclue le 13 août 1525 entre Louise de Savoie et Henry VIII à Moore[1] déboucha dès le 30 du même mois sur un traité de paix et d'alliance établi dans la même localité.[2] Dès lors les relations franco-britanniques évoluèrent rapidement de la neutralité réciproque à une alliance de caractère offensif avec la conclusion les 30 avril et 29 mai 1527 des deux traités de Westminster,[3] le second étant encore étendu et confirmé à Amiens le 18 août de cette même année.[4]

Pour des raisons qui sont bien connues, François Ier avait besoin de tout l'appui de Henry VIII pour obtenir, avec la libération de ses enfants détenus en otages, un traité de paix avec Charles Quint, puisque celui signé à Madrid était inexécutable dans la principale de ses clauses: la cession de la Bourgogne. Pour sa part, Henry VIII allait avoir un besoin croissant de l'alliance française à mesure qu'augmentaient les difficultés d'obtenir l'annulation de son mariage avec Catherine d'Aragon, tante de Charles Quint.

En bref, François Ier comme Henry VIII avaient intérêt à affaiblir Charles Quint sur le plan militaire ou diplomatique, et chacun d'eux était dans l'incapacité d'y réussir seul. Au fond, les deux souverains avaient en commun leur principal adversaire mais ils poursuivaient l'un et l'autre des buts particuliers: il importait à François Ier de sortir enfin de la mauvaise situation où il s'était mis devant Pavie, mais il n'avait aucune hâte de savoir Henry VIII hors d'affaire dans l'annulation de son mariage, tandis qu'il importait à Henry VIII de régler au plus tôt ses difficultés matrimoniales et qu'il lui fallait pour cela le maintien d'une pression française sur l'Empereur ainsi qu'un appui diplomatique en cour de Rome.

Dans la guerre ouverte comme dans l'effort diplomatique, Charles Quint avait l'avantage de l'unanimité de son entourage et du sûr appui, et très fidèle, de Marguerite de Savoie, régente des Pays-Bas. En France, malgré le peu d'amitié entre Antoine Duprat, le chancelier, et Anne de Montmorency, le Grand-Maître de l'Hôtel, il existait une véritable unité de vue, et François Ier pouvait compter encore sur les conseils avisés de sa mère, Louise de Savoie. Par contre Henry VIII, quels que fussent le pouvoir royal et son autorité personnelle, avait affaire à des factions: le cardinal Wolsey d'une part, Anne Boleyn et sa famille d'autre part, sans parler des ducs de Suffolk et de Norfolk qui cherchaient aussi à influencer la politique royale.

De toute évidence, François Ier compta d'abord sur la force des armes pour contraindre Charles Quint mais les efforts entrepris en Italie après la conclusion de la ligue de Cognac aboutirent à la prise de Rome par les Impériaux et à un échec français que Henry VIII ressentit durement puisque le pape Clément VII devenait prisonnier de l'Empereur. De même, la déclaration commune de guerre portée à l'Empereur par des hérauts de François Ier et de Henry VIII le 22 janvier 1528 aboutit bien à l'exaspération de l'inimitié entre Charles Quint et François Ier et à l'envoi réciproque de cartels surannés en ce temps de diplomatie froidement calculée mais la guerre qui devait être générale aboutit bientôt à la trève signée à Hampton Court le 15 juin 1528, avant même que n'éclatent les hostilités.[5] Il faut incontestablement voir dans ces trèves le résultat de la pression des marchands anglais que la guerre aurait durement touchés dans leurs intérêts aux Pays-Bas. En Italie, où la trève n'avait pas cours, Lautrec avait très bien inauguré une campagne qui tourna elle aussi au désastre après sa mort, dans la nuit du 15 au 16 août 1528.

Depuis 1525 François Ier n'avait donc connu face à Charles Quint que des revers militaires mais c'est à la poursuite de l'effort de guerre qu'il encourageait encore fortement Henry VIII durant toute l'année 1528 et pendant l'hiver et le printemps suivants, marqués par la préparation et le déploiement de l'opération conduite dans le Milanais par le comte de Saint-Pol. Pour sa part, Henry VIII optait pour une solution négociée et parlait de paix générale. Il est vrai que la guerre de François Ier lui coûtait cher puisqu'il s'était engagé à payer à titre de contribution quelque 30,000 francs par mois depuis la signature du second traité de Westminster, somme quelque peu augmentée encore à partir de la conclusion de la trève de Hampton Court. Plus encore Henry VIII recevait durant l'été 1528 de bonnes nouvelles de son ambassadeur à Rome Stephen Gardiner et le 29 septembre le légat pontifical Lorenzo Campeggio débarquait en Angleterre, de sorte que le roi pouvait espérer proches l'ouverture d'une cour légatine et l'annulation définitive et sans appel de son mariage avec Catherine d'Aragon. Volonté de paix qui s'explique encore par l'impopularité de l'alliance avec la France chez les Anglais et par la crainte de troubles intérieurs dont l'ambassadeur Jean du Bellay rend bien compte à Anne de Montmorency dans une lettre du 9 décembre 1528.[6]

Voilà pour le rappel des circonstances générales telles qu'elles étaient dans le courant de l'année 1528, à un moment où le roi d'Angleterre pouvait se croire en meilleure voie d'aboutir dans ses propres affaires et surtout plus rapidement que le roi de France, obstiné dans sa volonté de revanche militaire.

C'est dans le temps même où François Ier manifestait la volonté la plus belliqueuse et cherchait à convaincre Henry VIII de s'y rallier que Louise de Savoie amorça la négociation secrète qui aboutit au traité de Cambrai; et c'est cela qu'il s'agit maintenant de traiter, d'abord pour établir les faits et ensuite pour analyser certains aspects techniques d'une négociation diplomatique dans la première moitié du XVIe siècle.

La documentation pour l'histoire de la négociation du traité de Cambrai est constituée principalement d'un mémoire rédigé à l'intention de Charles Quint par Guillaume des Barres, secrétaire de l'Empereur, et par Pierre de Rosimboz, premier maître d'Hôtel de Marguerite d'Autriche;[7] des documents publiés dans la collection des *Letters and Papers*, en particulier les lettres de John Hackett, ambassadeur de Henry VIII auprès de Marguerite;[8] d'une lettre de Marguerite d'Autriche à Charles Quint, du 26 mai 1529[9] et de la correspondance de Jean du Bellay, ambassadeur de François Ier auprès de Henry VIII.[10]

La situation diplomatique au milieu de 1528 est marquée par la conclusion, sous la pression anglaise, de la trêve signée le 15 juin pour une durée de huit mois entre Charles Quint, François Ier, Henry VIII et Marguerite d'Autriche; l'abstinence de guerre ne s'étendait pas à l'Espagne ni à l'Italie où Lautrec conduisait au nom du roi une vaste opération militaire. Cette trêve ne préludait d'ailleurs pas à un retour à la paix puisque le 8 juin François Ier avait fait remettre à Charles Quint son cartel et l'appelait par l'intermédiaire du héraut Guyenne à régler leur différend en champ clos. Curieuse juxtaposition de relations internationales ramenées aux personnes des souverains et à un combat aussi théâtral que chevaleresque et de relations dictées par les intérêts économiques des marchands anglais.

C'est dans ces conditions que fut prise l'initiative d'une négociation dont il convient d'établir les phases.

1) L'amorce de la discussion semble être le fait de Louise de Savoie qui exprima une déclaration d'intention devant Guillaume des Barres lorsque celui-ci vint à la cour de France après la signature de la trêve de Hampton Court. Des Barres quitta l'Angleterre le jour même de la conclusion puisque le 19 juin il était déjà à Calais;[11] de là il se rendit auprès de Marguerite à Malines et fut envoyé en France, d'où il repartit avant le 8 juillet.[12] Sur ce point, le rapport de Rosimboz et de des Barres, tel qu'il a été publié par Le Glay, est confirmé.

2) Une autre ouverture fut faite directement à Marguerite d'Autriche par Marie de Luxembourg, duchesse de Vendôme, lorsqu'elle vint en Flandre prendre possession de la succession de Philippe de Clèves, son beau-frère, après le décès de Françoise, sa sœur. Nous savons par une lettre de John Hackett que la duchesse de Vendôme arriva à Malines le 16 septembre.[13]

3) Contrairement à ce que laisse entendre le rapport de Rosimboz et de des Barres, ce contact eut lieu avant la première mission de Gilbert Bayard[14] en Flandre qu'une lettre de John Hackett permet de situer à la mi-novembre.[15]

4) Une deuxième mission conduisit Gilbert Bayard en Flandre "environ cinq sepmaines après" selon le rapport de Rosimboz et de des Barres, indication confirmée par une lettre de John Hackett à Wolsey qui précise que l'arrivée du négociateur à Malines eut lieu le 8 décembre.[16] Il y resta une dizaine de jours.[17]

5) Du côté impérial, la première démarche consista en l'envoi de Rosimboz et des Barres à la cour de France où les ambassadeurs furent reçus le 30 janvier en audience officielle,[18] bien que leur voyage eût dû rester en principe secret. Sur ce point de la chronologie, il conviendrait donc de revoir le rapport publié sans justification par Le Glay à la date du 31 décembre.

Avec cette mission se termine la phase préparatoire de la négociation; celle qui, officiellement, appartient uniquement à Louise de Savoie et à Marguerite d'Autriche. La seconde phase, celle de la négociation ouvertement avouée, se situe durant le printemps de 1529, plus précisément avec le retour d'Espagne de Rosimboz et de des Barres qui avaient poursuivi leur voyage pour informer l'empereur.

Ces deux personnages passèrent à la cour de France au début de mai,[19] porteurs d'un pouvoir donné par Charles Quint à Marguerite d'Autriche et daté du 8 avril.[20] François Ier, pour des raisons qui ne touchent pas au fond, attendit jusqu'au 2 juin pour délivrer un pareil pouvoir à sa mère.[21]

C'est aussi vers la mi-mai que Henry VIII fut officiellement averti par François Ier de l'ouverture de négociations et invité à envoyer une délégation à Cambrai. Le porteur de la nouvelle fut Jean du Bellay, évêque de Bayonne, qui arriva à Londres le 13 mai et eut aussitôt une entrevue avec Wolsey.[22] De son côté, Marguerite d'Autriche, d'entente avec François Ier, envoya aussi un ambassadeur en Angleterre, Jean de La Sauch, secrétaire de Charles Quint, qui y résida du 21 au 30 mai.[23] Dans le même temps, Gilbert Bayard accompagna en Flandre Rosimboz et des Barres pour préparer la rencontre le plus tôt possible. La date arrêtée fut d'abord le 15 juin.[24] Divers obstacles la retardèrent mais sans qu'une nouvelle date fût décidée, ce qui donna beaucoup de fébrilité aux relations diplomatiques et permit finalement à Henry VIII de se faire représenter à Cambrai par Cuthbert Tunstall, évêque de Londres, et par Thomas More, chancelier de Lancaster, qui reçurent leurs lettres de créance le 2 juillet[25] et arrivèrent à Cambrai trop tard pour avoir une part active à la négociation et faire de Henry VIII l'une des principales parties contractantes au traité finalement conclu le 5 août par Marguerite d'Autriche et Louise de Savoie, et confirmé par Charles Quint et François Ier respectivement les 18 et 20 octobre 1529.

Il serait aisé, sur la base des documents existants, de faire le récit détaillé de la négociation, non pas de la discussion technique article par article, mais du procès général, mais ce n'est pas d'un chapitre à la Mignet sur la rivalité de François Ier et de Charles Quint qu'il s'agit car il paraît plus intéressant de connaître qui savait quoi des intentions des autres et comment: en France, en Flandre, en Angleterre et en Espagne pendant le déroulement des pourparlers; plus intéressant aussi de rechercher les intentions et de faire apparaître la manière de procéder de la diplomatie de cette époque.

Les premières ouvertures faites par Louise de Savoie puis par la duchesse de Vendôme aux messagers de Marguerite ou à la régente elle-même étaient très générales et trop imprécises pour que l'interlocuteur puisse en faire état. C'était une amorce en forme de déclaration d'intention. Ainsi, dans leur mémoire, postérieur de plusieurs mois à l'événement, Rosimboz et des Barres rapportent d'abord les plaintes exprimées par Louise de Savoie sur les conditions de détention infligées à ses petits-enfants et ses reproches envers l'empereur qui par ses propos a obligé le roi à lui adresser son cartel; cela malgré les conseils de sa mère qui voit bien tous les malheurs que cette haine réciproque peut engendrer. Et c'est cette perspective même qui la pousse à s'adresser à Marguerite d'Autriche "esperant que, si elle se vouloit employer en cest endroit d'aussi bonne affection que elle, il en sortiroit bon effect, et pourroit estre cause de mectre lesdits princes en paix.''[26] Il est vrai que c'est par un document du parti impérial que nous avons connaissance de la première amorce; nous pouvons d'autant mieux en retenir la pratique de Louise de Savoie qui, avant de se déclarer, prend soin de demander à des Barres s'il n'a pas des lettres ou un message pour elle. Dans tout cela, il n'y a rien qui dépasse une offre de bons offices et rien qui permette de savoir si elle fut faite au su ou à l'insu du roi.

Quant à la duchesse de Vendôme, ''elle tint plusieurs propoz de la paix, en termes generaulx et sans entrer en aucune chose particuliere touchant icelle.''[27]

Pour ce qui est de la première mission de Gilbert Bayard en Flandre, elle n'avait formellement aucun caractère officiel puisque le seul texte qui fut remis au messager était une simple lettre de recommandation de la part de Louise de Savoie à Marguerite: ''Madame ma bonne sœur, le porteur de cestes s'en va en Anvers pour aucun sien affaire particulier; je vous prie l'avoir pour recommandé.'' Gilbert Bayard eut soin de dire aussi que le roi ignorait la démarche. De plus, le diplomate n'avait pas Malines pour but de son voyage mais Anvers où, officiellement, l'appelaient des affaires privées. Reçu par Marguerite, il lui fut demandé s'il avait des moyens de parvenir à la paix. Il les exposa et reçut une réponse de non recevoir. Loin d'accepter la rupture, Gilbert Bayard demanda à son interlocutrice de bien vouloir réfléchir à la question pendant qu'il se rendrait à Anvers et de lui faire part de ses propositions à son retour. C'était, du côté français, la troisième ouverture mais cette fois la parole était à la partie adverse. De manière plus habile encore, Marguerite lui répondit à son retour que non seulement elle n'avait pensé à aucun moyen de paix mais encore ''qu'elle n'y avoit voulu penser'': le roi étant dans ses torts, c'était à lui d'y aviser. Mais Marguerite en même temps qu'elle semblait rompre ouvrait la voie à la négociation en ajoutant ''que si ladite dame d'Angosmois avoit si bonne affection qu'elle se meslast de cest affaire qu'elle lui avoit fait dire, convenoit qu'elle luy mist si bonne estoffe en main qu'elle ne s'en meslast a faulx.''[28]

En attendant, Marguerite tirait un avantage immédiat de la situation en informant John Hackett de l'envoi de l'élu Bayard afin de jeter quelque suspicion chez les Anglais,[29] qui dès le premier jour purent ainsi se méfier d'une volonté de paix séparée avec Charles Quint de la part de François Ier. C'est aussi un signe que Marguerite ne croyait pas à une possibilité d'accord.

Ainsi, alors que la France, en guerre, courait le risque de se voir abandonnée de ses alliés s'ils venaient à découvrir l'ouverture de négociations bilatérales, Marguerite exploitait immédiatement cette éventualité en avertissant Henry VIII. Il est vrai qu'à cet état de la négociation François Ier pouvait encore tout démentir.

C'est encore avec le souci de permettre à son fils de nier toute entreprise que Louise de Savoie dépêcha une deuxième fois Gilbert Bayard en Flandre. Ce fut toujours en son nom mais il est évident que désormais le roi était au courant. Cette manière d'entrer en matière et de discuter dans la plus grande méfiance réciproque mérite d'être rapportée avec quelque détail.

Bayard montre cette fois-ci de véritables lettres de créance. Usant de sa position de force, Marguerite somme alors l'ambassadeur de ne pas marchander mais de lui dire d'emblée "l'extreme de sa charge." Bayard s'exécute, "disant que c'estoit tout ce à quoi ladite dame d'Angosmois avoit seue faire condessendre le roy, son filz,"[30] et, si Bayard accepte finalement de mettre par écrit sa déclaration, il exige que ce ne soit pas de sa main.

Nouveau progrès, Marguerite, ayant lu la déclaration, accepte implicitement le principe de la médiation en posant des questions relatives aux modalités.

Pour Bayard, il convenait, dans un premier temps, que la régente persuadât l'empereur d'envisager le rétablissement de la paix et, si l'empereur acceptait de négocier sur la base des articles dictés par Bayard, qu'il autorisât Marguerite de Savoie à poursuivre la discussion. Cela obtenu, les deux dames pourraient, comme de leur propre initiative, préparer un traité de paix. Les raisons de leur démarche resteraient très générales: "les grans erreurs et troubles scismatiques qui croissent et pululent chacun jour," les invasions que le Turc fait et se prépare à faire contre la Chrétienté, les malheurs provoqués depuis environ huit ans par les guerres entre Charles Quint et François Ier. Le traité ainsi préparé, le roi, par respect pour sa mère, et l'empereur, par déférence pour sa tante, trouveraient bonne cette occasion de préférer à leur querelle le bien de toute la Chrétienté et désigneraient des ambassadeurs pour ratifier le traité.

Selon Bayard, les deux dames devaient seules arriver à cela, et pour trois raisons. Premièrement, depuis l'envoi du cartel et l'acceptation d'un combat singulier, il était évidemment impossible au roi et à l'empereur de négocier directement ou même de désigner officiellement des négociateurs. Deuxièmement, et la restriction prend tout son sens à l'égard de l'Angleterre comme à l'égard des alliés italiens "le Roy a plusieurs aliez et confederez sans lesquelz il ne pourroit traicter si lui-mesmes estoit traictant," alors que, sa mère étant négociatrice, il pourra prendre sur elle l'excuse des reproches qui lui seront faits "et lui en jecter le chat aux jambes, comme ayant traicté sans son sceu." Troisièmement, Louise de Savoie est la seule personne qui, traitant sans l'aveu du roi, puisse recevoir son accord et son approbation. A cet égard, la négociation de la paix de Cambrai est un bel exemple de l'indécision des limites entre l'exercice du pouvoir public et l'action découlant de l'autorité personnelle.

D'après le rapport de Rosimboz et de des Barres, la volonté française aurait expressément été d'exclure toute participation anglaise à la discussion car, selon les propos prêtés à Gilbert Bayard, Henry VIII et Wolsey "prendroient plus de plaisir d'entretenir la chose en longueur et pratique que de venir a l'effect pour laisser detruyre et affoler lesdits princes";[31] au mieux Henry VIII se ferait payer très cher. De même, il convenait de laisser le pape hors d'affaire.

Bayard était à Malines depuis le 8 décembre mais Jean du Bellay, ambassadeur de François Ier auprès de Henry VIII, se réjouissait trop tôt quand il écrivit le 20 décembre à Anne de Montmorency "Quant a Bayart, je n'en ay riens icy sentu; s'il s'en parle, j'en feray comme me mandez."[32]

En fait, le service de renseignements de l'ambassadeur John Hackett fonctionnait parfaitement puisque le 24 décembre ce dernier était en mesure d'avertir Londres que l'élu Bayard avait passé une dizaine de jours à Malines où il s'était secrètement entretenu avec Marguerite d'Autriche et Antoine de Lalaing, comte d'Hochstrate; d'avertir Londres aussi de l'envoi à la cour de France de Rosimboz et de des Barres pour obtenir confirmation des articles accordés et pour continuer ensuite leur route vers l'empereur en Espagne.[33] Hackett allait d'ailleurs écrire d'autres lettres bien embarrassantes pour l'ambassadeur de France à Londres.[34] Renseignements obtenus d'ailleurs sans grande astuce puisque c'est, semble-t-il, Marguerite d'Autriche elle-même qui faisait des révélations à l'ambassadeur de Henry VIII: ce fut le cas lors de la première mission de Bayard, et vraisemblablement lors de la deuxième. La qualité du renseignement est donc remarquable: dans la lettre du 25 janvier par exemple la seule erreur est la mention de lettres de créance du roi pour Bayard, mais la nature de la discussion est parfaitement rapportée—même si le doute subsiste sur l'offre française de verser 100,000 écus à ceux qui permettront l'accomplissement de la paix—et l'ambassadeur connaît l'exacte raison de l'envoi de Rosimboz et de des Barres à Paris.

Marguerite de Savoie, qui ne sait rien encore de la volonté impériale à propos des ouvertures françaises, continue de ménager toutes les possibilités en donnant suite aux propositions de Louise de Savoie et en alarmant l'Angleterre, terme vague ici mais commode car il n'est pas certain que Tuke et Wolsey, destinataires des lettres de Hackett, en aient fait part à Henry VIII.

Wolsey en tout cas ne tarda pas à convoquer Jean du Bellay pour lui faire part le 28 janvier de la lettre écrite, selon toute apparence, le 25 par John Hackett.

Après avoir insisté sur "la fermeté de l'amytié si franche et perpétuelle" entre François Ier et Henry VIII et après avoir protesté de "vouloir user envers madicte Dame de la mesmes sincérité et honneste façon de faire," dont elle use envers lui, Wolsey traduit en latin pour Jean du Bellay des passages d'une lettre écrite en anglais et faisant état des deux missions de Bayard, de la volonté de Louise de parvenir à la paix—fût-ce à l'exclusion des alliés du roi—et de l'envoi de Guillaume des Barres auprès de l'empereur pour la confirmation de l'accord.

Pendant que Wolsey traduit, du Bellay peut s'assurer que la substance de la lettre est bien telle. Il reconnaît aussi dans la lettre que tient Wolsey des passages dialogués en français comme "Ne vous diz-je pas, monsieur l'ambassadeur . . ." qui lui font deviner que c'est Marguerite d'Autriche qui s'adresse à John Hackett "car les dictz motz seulement de la lectre estoyent en françoys." Mais Wolsey refuse de nommer l'expéditeur.

Passons sur l'emploi des langues vernaculaires et du latin dans la langue diplomatique du milieu du XVIe siècle et examinons la réaction de l'ambassadeur de France au moment où il apprend que la négociation voulue secrète est découverte. Elle est d'abord de sang froid puisque du Bellay réussit à identifier à la fois l'auteur de la lettre que tient Wolsey et l'informateur, en l'occurrence Marguerite d'Autriche. Quant à la réponse, elle fut en quatre points et témoigne de beaucoup de métier:

1) remerciements à Wolsey pour sa sincérité et pour la confiance portée au roi et à Louise de Savoie.

2) rejet des soupçons sur les Flamands avec accusation d'intention de leur part de vouloir dissoudre le lien d'amitié entre la France et l'Angleterre, lien dont Wolsey est le meilleur témoin; ce qui est aussi une manière de rappeler au cardinal l'importance pour sa carrière et sa personne de l'alliance française.

3) explication de l'information reçue, mais fondée exclusivement sur le premier voyage de Bayard: désireux de troubler l'amitié franco-anglaise, les Flamands se seront "aydez d'une occasion dont il y a ung moys que je l'eusse adverty [Wolsey] si j'eusse pensé que la chose fust venue si avant." Cette explication permet aussi à Jean du Bellay de nommer à Wolsey des marchands anglais auprès desquels il s'était enquis d'un nommé Crocquet, marchand de Paris, débiteur de 10,000 écus envers Gilbert Bayard, que Bayard avait vainement recherché à Anvers lorsqu'il s'y était rendu pour se faire rembourser. Cela prouve accessoirement le soin mis du côté français à établir une couverture pour le cas où la négociation de Bayard serait éventée.

4) révélation à l'interlocuteur de ce qu'il sait déjà. Jean du Bellay avoue à Wolsey qu'un Flamand lui a appris voilà quelques jours que Guillaume des Barres était parti pour la France en habit dissimulé. Du Bellay en conclut ou qu'il sera pris au passage ou qu'il est muni d'un sauf-conduit pour demander une prolongation de la trêve à l'empereur.

En résumé, Jean du Bellay ne dément pas les faits mais il en réduit la portée et en change le sens. Le coup porté à l'amitié et à la confiance réciproque entre François Ier et Henry VIII par les révélations de Marguerite d'Autriche est atténué; et Wolsey, dont toute la politique est axée sur l'alliance française, sera aussi victime du *will to believe,* si souvent fatal aux hommes politiques, et particulièrement lorsqu'ils s'attendent à de la reconnaissance, comme Wolsey pouvait légitimement en espérer de Louise de Savoie.

Quant à la négociation de la paix, elle commença à prendre forme pendant ce même séjour que Gilbert Bayard fit à Malines au mois de décembre 1528. Une fois en possession des propositions dictées par l'envoyé de Louise de Savoie, Marguerite d'Autriche réunit en conseil les principaux personnages alors à Malines: Adolphe de Bourgogne, seigneur de Bèvres; Floris d'Egmont, comte de Buren; Antoine de Lalaing, comte d'Hochstrate, et Jean, seigneur de Berghes. En même temps, on passait de l'engagement politico-diplomatique à des aspects plus techniques et plus concrets de la négociation.

Les conseillers réunis par Marguerite d'Autriche constatèrent d'abord la disparate des propositions françaises: les unes faisaient référence au traité de Madrid, d'autres aux conclusions de Palencia, d'autres encore aux conclusions de Burgos, tandis que certaines enfin étaient nouvelles. L'imprécision qui en résultait leur semblait en elle-même dangereuse car dans la sommaire psychologie des peuples il était notoire chez les Flamands "que les François crestiennement interpretent ce qu'ilz dient, et mettent avant après cop autrement qu'ilz ne proferent au commencement."[35] Pour éviter de tomber dans le piège de l'habileté oratoire, il fut demandé à Bayard de rédiger la minute complète d'un projet de traité "depuis le commencement du préambule jusqu'a la date." Tout en se défendant qu'il n'était pas de sa compétence de le faire, Bayard s'exécuta, et le projet fut derechef soumis au conseil qui trouva la minute "bien maigrement et simplement couchee, et y avoit plusieurs articles captieux et ambiguz."[36] De toute évidence du côté français on cherchait à savoir ce que les Impériaux rabattraient du traité de Madrid avant d'en venir à des propositions fermes et solides. Cet entêtement fut fructueux car, plutôt que de demander à Bayard une nouvelle rédaction, Marguerite remit au secrétaire des Barres le soin d'établir une minute de traité au plus près possible des articles du traité de Madrid ainsi que des conclusions de Palencia et de Burgos. La qualité de l'organisation diplomatique de Charles Quint est attestée par l'existence des doubles de ces documents dans les archives de Marguerite.

Le projet rédigé par des Barres fut amendé par le conseil avant d'être soumis à Bayard qui obtint des corrections formelles: la suppression de termes désobligeants à l'égard de François Ier et hors de saison dans un traité de paix. Une fois mise au net, la minute fut encore envoyée au cardinal de Liège, lequel, moyennant quelques propositions d'amendements, estima qu'il y avait "bonne matiere et raison d'envoyer vers sadite Majesté ladite mynute pour sçavoir son bon vouloir et plaisir";[37] et il s'en expliquait.

Pour sa part, Gilbert Bayard quitta Malines en emportant un double du projet, précédant en France les messagers que Marguerite d'Autriche allait envoyer auprès de Charles Quint. Dans le souci de ne rien laisser transpirer des négociations, des mesures avaient été prises par Louise de Savoie pour que le passage de Rosimboz et de des Barres demeurât inaperçu et qu'elle ait avec eux une audience très secrète. Finalement, on jugea plus prudent que le roi les reçoive en audience publique, et l'on improvisa des demandes de réparations à la France pour des infractions à la trêve du 15 juin: demandes qui expliquaient la présence des deux hommes et servaient de manteau à la principale négociation. Mais dans l'entrevue secrète qu'elle eut avec Rosimboz et des Barres, Louise de Savoie ne put rien obtenir de plus favorable: les ambassadeurs jugèrent importants des amendements que Gilbert Bayard disait de détail et ils menacèrent de retourner à Malines pour consultation si l'on insistait. Finalement, après examen du texte par le chancelier Duprat, par l'amiral Chabot de Brion et par Anne de Montmorency, Grand-Maître de l'Hôtel, la minute fut à peu près remise en son premier état, à la satisfaction des Flamands. Mais ceux-ci ne parvinrent pas à arracher à Louise de Savoie sa signature ou celle de l'un de ses secrétaires pour l'apposer au pied du document.

Si l'ambassadeur de François Ier auprès de Henry VIII avait déjà préparé sur place une explication raisonnable à la présence de Gilbert Bayard à Anvers et s'il cherchait à jeter le doute sur les arrière-pensées de Marguerite de Savoie à propos des informations qu'elle donnait à John Hackett, il était aussi puissamment soutenu dans sa tâche par les lettres qui lui venaient de France. Ainsi, le 3 décembre, alors que Bayard était sur le point de se rendre à Malines, François Ier écrivit une longue lettre qui fut très vraisemblablement remise par du Bellay à Wolsey car cette lettre, comme toutes celles du roi à son ambassadeur pour cette période, se trouve aujourd'hui au British Museum. Dans cette missive—où le nom de Wolsey est toujours suivi de l'épithète "mon bon amy" et celui de Henry VIII de "mon bon frere et perpetuel allyé"—François Ier affirme que sa résolution est de ne rien faire "ny entreprendre jamais chose sans le sceu et consentement dudit roy, mon bon frere et perpetuel allyé, et de ne permettre, s'il est possible, que aulcune chose passe par aultres mains que par les syennes."[38]

Et plus loin, à propos d'une suggestion faite par Wolsey de paix séparée entre l'Angleterre et l'Espagne, le roi écrit à Jean du Bellay :

... je ne vous puis dire combien il seroit estrange et desplaisant a tous mes alliez et confederez de veoyr le Roy, mon bon frere et perpetuel allyé, que j'estime et aime comme mon meilleur et principal amy, et sy estroictement lié avec moy comme il est, prendre amytié, traicter et conclure sans moy avecques nostre commun ennemy, joinct en oultre qu'il seroit bien malaisé, encores que ce feust de mon sceu, de les garder qu'ilz ne pensassent que je feusse delaissé et habandonné de luy, chose que non seullement j'estime impossible de pouvoir advenir, mais de laquelle je ne vueil de ma part, en quelque sorte que ce soit, donner occasion a personne d'en riens doubter ny souspeçonner.[39]

Plus loin encore, évoquant la fin de la trêve de Hampton Court qui expirait à la mi-février, François Ier écrit qu'il va intensifier son effort de guerre et qu'il lui "semble de ceste heure estre besoin de parler de la deliberation en quoy vous trouverez ledict roy, mon bon frere, de se preparer a faire la guerre cest esté." Le roi termine en se disant ouvert malgré tout à une poursuite de la trêve, à condition qu'elle débouche sur une paix générale; qu'il a ordonné à ses ambassadeurs auprès du pape de tenir à Clément VII le même langage que les ambassadeurs de Henry VIII et il transmet encore des nouvelles très réjouissantes de la campagne d'Italie.

Ainsi, au moment où les Anglais pouvaient éprouver des doutes sur la loyauté de François Ier, du Bellay avait en main une lettre du roi très amicale et fraternelle dans le ton; exprimant le souci d'une action toujours étroitement commune entre François Ier et Henry VIII; manifestant un souci scrupuleux des alliances et des alliés et très réconfortante quant à ce qui se passait autour du pape.

A la fin de l'année 1528 et au début de 1529 il y a une froide duplicité dans la diplomatie du roi-chevalier; à tout le moins joue-t-il simultanément deux jeux; et le jeu secret est si dangereux par le risque d'isolement qu'il comporte (même si la plupart des alliés du roi ne pouvaient faire autrement que d'avaler la couleuvre) que François Ier exagère la manière de jouer cartes sur table l'autre partie.

Du point de vue français on pouvait, durant l'hiver 1528-1529, se réjouir de la sérieuse reprise des négociations avec les Habsbourg mais les indiscrétions volontaires de Marguerite d'Autriche étaient dangereuses et il avait fallu en faire beaucoup et pas du plus beau pour y remédier. Du point de vue impérial l'alternative n'était que positive: ou Louise de Savoie et son fils y allaient de bon pied et l'on marchait vers la paix, ou la négociation échouait et il était possible d'en tirer parti auprès des alliés du roi. Pour Wolsey l'avenir était plus sombre: si les informations venues de Flandre étaient vraies, la réconciliation laissait Henry III seul face au pape et à l'empereur dans l'affaire de l'annulation de son mariage; si ces informations étaient fausses ou si la négociation capotait, la fin de la trêve, suivie de la reprise de la guerre, le mettait dans une situation difficile devant l'opinion publique représentée par les puissants marchands londoniens beaucoup plus soucieux de privilèges à Anvers qu'à Rouen. La seule issue était d'obtenir l'annulation du mariage avant que François Ier n'ait signé la paix et de le mettre du même coup dans la dépendance de Henry VIII pour l'avenir.

C'est donc avec certaines espérances que Wolsey apprit la nouvelle de la mort de Clément VII; un faux bruit en vérité, mais qui avait été repris et diffusé simultanément par les agents français et impériaux à Rome,[40] car la fausse nouvelle n'avait pas été intentionnellement lancée, comme cela arrivait parfois. Sur le moment même, l'importance du fait provoqua le départ de Londres de Jean du Bellay qui avait besoin de nouvelles instructions pour faire face à la situation ainsi créée, d'autant que Wolsey était candidat à la succession pontificale. Pour la France, cette mort supposée pouvait bien faire oublier aux Anglais ce qui avait pu se passer à Malines, mais elle n'en était pas moins un mauvais coup du sort.

Jusqu'au printemps 1529, il ne se produisit rien de déterminant dans les relations franco-anglaises, et Guillaume du Bellay, successeur de son frère Jean en qualité d'ambassadeur, eut principalement pendant sa courte mission en mars et en avril à répéter à Henry VIII, afin d'obtenir son aide matérielle, la volonté de François Ier de reprendre durement la guerre contre Charles Quint.[41]

Dès le début de mai 1529 par contre, le retour d'Espagne de Rosimboz et de des Barres, munis du pouvoir de Charles Quint en faveur de Marguerite d'Autriche, provoqua une véritable course de vitesse entre, d'une part, la diplomatie de Henry VIII très pressée d'obtenir l'invalidation du mariage et, accessoirement, tentée d'intervenir pour ralentir la conclusion de la paix et, d'autre part, la diplomatie française très pressée d'aboutir à la paix comme bien décidée à tenir les Anglais hors des pourparlers, tout en les y invitant d'ailleurs maintenant que tout était sur le point d'aboutir.

Dans les premiers jours de mai, alors que François Ier n'avait momentanément plus d'ambassadeur en poste à Londres, Rosimboz et des Barres passèrent par la cour à leur retour d'Espagne. Leur venue n'échappa pas aux deux ambassadeurs que Henry VIII entretenait alors auprès de François Ier, John Taylor, son Maître des Rôles, et William Knight, son secrétaire, qui, rencontrant Jean du Bellay, lui demandèrent si ces messagers, qu'ils nommèrent, disaient rien de bon.[42] La réponse fut qu'ils disaient merveille de la volonté de l'empereur pour la paix mais que cela pouvait être "ung endormissement et art d'Espaignol" et que de toute façon, le roi était prêt à entrer en jeu en Allemagne dès que Henry VIII le voudrait: des troupes étaient même en Champagne, n'attendant que l'ordre de marche.

Le retour d'Espagne des serviteurs de Marguerite d'Autriche détermina aussitôt l'envoi une nouvelle fois en Flandre de Gilbert Bayard, chargé de préparer pour la date la plus proche les modalités de l'entrevue des deux dames ainsi que de solliciter l'envoi à Londres d'un ambassadeur dont les dires corroboreraient ceux de Jean du Bellay qui y retournait dans le même temps.

Du côté anglais, ce retour provoqua un revirement d'attitude: John Russell, dépêché auprès de François Ier pour lui faire savoir que son maître persistait dans sa volonté de paix, fut soudainement remplacé par le duc de Suffolk et le trésorier Fitzwilliam, chargés de pousser François Ier à la guerre et de lui offrir toute l'aide de Henry VIII. Ce fut aussi la seule réplique de la diplomatie anglaise, visiblement prise de court, jusqu'à la signature du traité de Cambrai.

En France, on estimait dans le même temps que les négociations étaient si bien engagées qu'il n'était plus nécessaire de maintenir le secret vis-à-vis de l'Angleterre, et l'on était bien déterminé à agir très vite. La lettre que Marguerite d'Autriche envoya à Charles Quint le 26 mai rend d'ailleurs bien compte du comportement français envers les Anglais, et elle est corroborée par les faits.

Monseigneur, au retour desdicts seigneur de Rosymboz et secretaire des Barres, et passant par la court de France, le roy et madame sa mere leur dirent entre autres choses que, a cause que les Anglois se doubtoient de ceste praticque de paix, et qu'ilz leur en avoient fait tenir quelque propos et ne les pouvoient mescontenter, pour ce qu'il convenoit qu'ilz s'aidassent d'eulx tant pour le fait de l'indempnité que des debtes, ilz estoient en vouloir de les en advertir; et estoient d'advis que deusse faire le pareil. Et a ceste fin firent convepvoir une mynute en forme de lectre, telle qu'ilz disoient vouloir escripre au roy d'Angleterre, dont ilz baillerent ung double ausdictz sᵣ de Rosymboz et secretaire pour me monstrer. Et depuis ledict Bayard m'a dict qu'ilz avoient changé propoz, et envoyeroient vers ledict sᵣ roy l'evesque de Bayonne avec seulement lectre de credence.[43]

C'est effectivement ce qui se passa mais non sans péripéties. Pour la netteté des relations franco-anglaises, il importait que la nouvelle de l'ouverture de négociations officielles fût annoncée par la France, et il fallait faire très vite puisque les ambassadeurs de Henry VIII à la cour de François Ier étaient déjà avertis du retour de Rosimboz et de des Barres.

La surprise fut donc mauvaise pour Jean du Bellay de rencontrer sur le chemin de Boulogne deux Anglais qui revenaient d'Espagne et qui, forts de ce qu'ils y avaient appris, se vantaient "de dire merveilles a leur roy . . . et qu'ilz luy compteront choses qui luy feront bien changer de voulenté envers nous."[44] Il fallait donc à tout prix précéder à Londres ces fâcheux, et l'ambassadeur s'entendit avec les gens des postes pour prendre sur eux une avance finalement inutile puisqu'il fut rejoint à Boulogne, où la tempête empêchait toute embarcation de prendre la mer. Voyant plus à loisir ces menaçants Anglais, et ne les reconnaissant pas comme serviteurs du roi ou de Wolsey, il en conclut à juste raison qu'ils étaient à la reine, et il prit définitivement les devants avec le premier bateau en partance, alors que les deux hommes attendaient que la mer fût meilleure.[45] Cette anecdote suggère des aspects très réels des dangers physiques d'une charge d'ambassadeur au XVIe siècle et l'importance, une nouvelle fois, du facteur temps dans la transmission des nouvelles, d'où les exploits, que nous dirions sportifs, de certains ambassadeurs ou de simples courriers.

A Londres, du Bellay avait à peine quitté ses bottes qu'il rencontra Wolsey. Le cardinal lui fit bon accueil, tomba d'accord qu'il fallait savoir ce que Marguerite d'Autriche avait à proposer (car c'est à elle que l'on imputait l'initiative) et que lui-même était prêt, avec l'accord de Henry VIII, de participer à la négociation en personne. C'était précisément ce que les diplomates français voulaient éviter mais l'essentiel était acquis: la négociation de paix entrait dans les faits admis.

Le 20 mai arrivait à son tour à Londres pour une brève mission Jean de La Sauch, ambassadeur de Marguerite d'Autriche, c'était donc que le plan élaboré à Paris avec Rosimboz et des Barres recevait son exécution. Le rapport d'ambassade de La Sauch est conservé[46] et il peut être complété par la lettre du 26 mai de Marguerite d'Autriche à Charles Quint. Les deux textes montrent que du côté impérial on facilitait maintenant la tâche de François Ier puisqu'à propos de la rencontre des Dames Henry VIII répondit à La Sauch qu'il en avait non seulement déjà été informé par Jean du Bellay mais encore de manière plus explicite. Quant à Marguerite d'Autriche, elle avait décidé d'oublier ses révélations de l'automne 1528; du moins La Sauch fit-il remonter l'amorce de discussion au passage de Rosimboz et de des Barres à Paris en janvier 1529.[47]

Si Henry VIII était invité à se faire représenter à la conférence de paix, l'intérêt des parties et surtout de la France restait qu'il n'y fût pas. Marguerite d'Autriche est ici très explicite dans sa lettre à Charles Quint:

Bien est vray, Monseigneur, que lesdicts seigneur roy de France et Dame sa mere m'ont fait dire que pour crainte que le cardinal [Wolsey] se y vueille trouver et qu'il empesche la conclusion des affaires, ilz desireroyent que la journee se prinst si briefve qu'il n'eust temps pour y estre: ce qui a esté fait.[48]

La date de la réunion fut ainsi initialement fixée au 15 juin d'entente entre Gilbert Bayard et Marguerite d'Autriche mais cette décision fut vraisemblablement prise après le 15 mai, date du départ de La Sauch pour Londres, car cet ambassadeur ne put ou ne voulut répondre lors de son audience à la question de Henry VIII qui lui demandait le jour retenu pour l'entrevue. Jean du Bellay fut tout aussi discret. Cette ignorance est l'une des raisons du désarroi que l'on constate autour de Henry VIII en mai et juin 1529. La paix ne fut finalement conclue que le 5 août mais la conviction persistante que l'accord était imminent paralysa l'entourage du roi.

Une autre cause de l'absence de réaction immédiate et vigoureuse est sans doute que l'on apprit à Londres la prochaine rencontre des Dames à peu près en même temps que l'on comprit que l'annulation du mariage demanderait beaucoup de temps encore et que, selon toute vraisemblance, François Ier en terminerait avec Charles Quint bien avant que Henry VIII ait obtenu satisfaction de Clément VII. Jean du Bellay fut très bien informé des difficultés rencontrées à Rome par les ambassadeurs de Henry VIII qui n'arrivaient pas à obtenir du pape une déclaration de fausseté pour le bref ampliatif, pièce maîtresse du dossier de Catherine d'Aragon; et l'envoi d'un nouvel ambassadeur à Rome le 20 mai ne lui échappa pas non plus. Enfin, la cour légatine, dont l'ouverture avait été tant retardée par Lorenzo Campeggio, ne devait se réunir pour connaître de l'annulation du mariage qu'à partir du 31 mai, et Jean du Bellay était bien persuadé que l'affaire prendrait non pas deux mois, comme le supposait Wolsey mais, au bas mot, quatre. Aussi l'ambassadeur ne voyait-il de risque que dans un décès inopiné de Catherine ou de sa fille Marie, mort qui abolirait toute cause de ressentiment entre Henry VIII et Charles Quint. De même, du Bellay n'envisageait rien de bon de l'éventualité d'un événement généralement réputé heureux: "Je me doubte fort que depuys quelque temps le Roy ait approché bien près de Anne Boleyn; pour ce ne vous esbahissiez si l'on vouldroyt expedition car si le ventre croist, tout sera bien guasté."[49]

La tâche de l'ambassadeur de François Ier à Londres était d'éviter que la délégation anglaise à Cambrai arrive tôt sur place et qu'elle empêche la conclusion rapide d'une paix bilatérale. La crainte française n'était plus tant maintenant que Henry VIII retarde le processus de paix en faveur de sa procédure de divorce mais surtout que ce délai permette au pape de se mettre en jeu et à sa suite les alliés italiens du roi. La rencontre voulue et organisée de manière quasi privée et préparatoire d'un traité à ratifier ensuite par les chefs des deux grandes puissances européennes ne devait pas finir en conférence générale de la paix. La volonté d'aboutir était donc sincère chez les Habsbourg comme chez les Valois. A cela, du Bellay fut aidé par les rivalités internes entre Wolsey, Anne Boleyn et les ducs.

Dès qu'il apprit l'imminence de la rencontre, Wolsey, nous l'avons vu, se déclara prêt à s'y rendre, quitte à remettre à plus tard le jugement du divorce en Angleterre. Le compte rendu que Jean du Bellay fait à Anne de Montmorency d'une entrevue avec Wolsey prouve qu'à la mi-mai ce dernier exprimait le risque où il était d'éprouver "une totale ruyne"[50] si le roi de France n'avait pas égard à lui. Convaincu que l'échec de l'annulation du mariage dans l'immédiat lui serait imputé, et après avoir imposé l'alliance française qui se révélait maintenant si décevante,[51] Wolsey ne pouvait espérer d'autre moyen de se sauver qu'en participant à l'entrevue au nom de Henry VIII et comme puissance contractante. Dès qu'il comprit qu'il n'en serait pas, il ne fit rien pour que quelqu'un y fût, et surtout pas le duc de Suffolk, alors à la cour de France, et que Jean du Bellay souhaitait aussi voir amusé à la chasse par le roi pendant que les Dames se rencontreraient.

Finalement, c'est le 2 juillet seulement que la délégation anglaise reçut ses instructions. Aux raisons déjà données de ce départ trop tardif, il convient d'ajouter l'absence de préparation: les traités passés entre l'Angleterre et la Bourgogne n'avaient pas été relus et il fallut les examiner tous afin d'établir les instructions aux ambassadeurs en vue d'une négociation générale.

Pour sa part, Jean du Bellay se montra actif et ne rechigna pas à l'emploi de petits moyens astucieux pour gagner encore un peu de temps. Ainsi, alors que les Anglais avaient obtenu un délai de dix jours pour une réponse, il fit offrir au porteur de celle-ci, déjà en route, des hacquenées, dans l'espoir que leur marche ralentirait la sienne et qu'il arriverait après l'expiration du délai. Et que penser d'un retard de courrier exprimé en ces termes: "Faites faire l'excuse de la longueur que mon courrier s'est rompu ung pied en chemin et a baillé le pacquet à ung aultre; ilz [les Anglais] le croiront car j'ay pourveu a cela."[52] De même, pour atténuer l'effet sur Henry VIII de l'annonce de la paix toute proche, du Bellay demande-t-il que celui qui viendra "soit bien embouché de honnestez propoz" et, se souvenant de l'heureux effet qu'avait eu au début de l'année l'annonce de la mort de Clément VII, il suggère aussi qu'on lui envoie "quelque advertissement de Fleurance [Florence] de la maladie du pape et que les médecins secretz tiennent qu'il est affollé."[53]

Ces ruses ne sont que des points de détails dans une conduite qui fut toute de duplicité pendant le printemps 1529 et dont le but évident était d'endormir Henry VIII et ses ministres.

La manœuvre générale fut à la fois simple et perfide. Dans un climat soigneusement entretenu d'amitié, réitérée et cultivée par tout ce que la parole peut avoir d'aimable, il fut surtout question dans les discussions entre Wolsey et Jean du Bellay de savoir ce que Marguerite d'Autriche avait à proposer car il était admis de part et d'autre qu'il convenait de saisir toute ouverture de paix même si du Bellay continuait à feindre de se méfier d'une tromperie ou de faux-semblants et à faire état de la volonté du roi en juillet encore, et alors que la capture du comte de Saint-Pol était connue, de se porter en Italie à la tête d'une armée si l'empereur s'y rendait. Jean du Bellay recourut pendant cette période à un double langage particulièrement cynique, ainsi qu'il apparaît par les couples de lettres qu'il écrivit à Montmorency ou à François Ier les 22 et 28 mai, et les 15 et 30 juin.[54] Dans tous ces cas, le procédé consiste à écrire, en clair, une première lettre dont la substance est communiquée à Wolsey ou même que Wolsey semble avoir eu la faculté de lire avant l'expédition. Il va sans dire que leur texte épouse les vues de l'allié. Mais simultanément Jean du Bellay en écrit une seconde, en chiffre, dans laquelle il explique et commente la première et exprime sa véritable pensée. Comme l'excellence de l'amitié et de la confiance entre François Ier et Henry VIII se serait mal accommodée de l'usage d'un chiffre dans la correspondance, ces lettres là furent sans doute acheminées en France par de ces hommes dont du Bellay disait que si on leur ouvrait le cœur on y trouverait une fleur de lys. Précaution d'autant plus nécessaire que Wolsey lui-même avait averti l'ambassadeur que le duc de Suffolk avait mis de ses gens à tous les relais de poste. Un paquet de lettres s'était d'ailleurs perdu, dont du Bellay était en peine.

Après des mois de mai et de juin très agités, Jean du Bellay passa juillet dans l'expectative de l'annonce de la signature du traité. Quant aux ambassadeurs de Henry VIII à Cambrai, il était trop tard pour eux d'intervenir efficacement et la paix fut signée beaucoup moins aux dépens de l'Angleterre que des alliés italiens de François Ier, à commencer par les Florentins, qui furent purement et simplement abandonnés à leur sort.

Quoi qu'il en fût, Henry VIII ne pouvait se passer de la pression de François Ier sur la Sorbonne et sur le pape et il fit bonne figure à mauvais jeu. Wolsey, qui avait été à l'origine de l'alliance avec la France, en fut aussi la victime. L'affaiblissement de l'influence de Wolsey sur son roi apparut déjà au mois de mai à Jean du Bellay qui s'en ouvrit à Anne de Montmorency en ces termes: "Il s'en faut beaucoup qu'il manye le roi d'Angleterre comme il a faict."[55] A la mi-juin, du Bellay, parlant de Wolsey, écrivait encore à Montmorency: "Il est vray, Monsr, que si par ceste heure voz affaires se concluent, eulx n'estant pas principaulx contrahens, le peuple criera bien sur lui 'Traistre!' et 'Françoys,' comme très bien desja ilz commencent" mais l'ambassadeur demeurait persuadé que le cardinal viendrait à bout de ceux qui voulaient sa ruine: "Il est trop fin pour eulx."[56] Dès la mi-septembre, c'en était fait, Wolsey était abandonné de la plupart: "je voy qu'il a fiance en aulcuns, faictz de sa main, lesquelz, je suis seur, luy ont tourné la robe, dont je suys fort esbahy car je n'eusse jamais pensé qu'il y eust eu si grande meschanceté en eulx. Et le pis est qu'il ne l'entend pas."[57] Un mois plus tard, du Bellay constatait ainsi la chute du personnage: "Quant a Wolsey, je le voy ruiné non seulement de credit mais en danger de ses estats et par adventure de sa personne."[58] A la mi-octobre, Jean du Bellay eut encore l'occasion de s'entretenir avec le jadis si puissant cardinal et il en rendit compte à Montmorency sur un ton où le froid réalisme, la référence quelque peu cynique à la *laesio ultra dimidium*, bien dans le style de l'humour que du Bellay mettait alors à la relation des choses graves, laisse apparaître tout de même de l'émotion:

J'ay esté veoir le cardinal d'York en ses ennuyz, ouquel j'ay trové le plus grant exemple de fortune qu'on sçauroyt veoir. Il m'a remonstré son cas en la plus mauvaise rhetorique que je viz jamais car cueur et parolle luy failloyent entierement. Il a bien pleuré et pryé que le Roy et Madame voulsissent avoir pitié de luy s'ilz avoyent trové qu'il leur eust guardé promesse de leur estre bon serviteur autant que son honneur et povoir se y est peu estendre. Mais il m'a a la fin laissé sans me povoir dire autre chose qui vallist myeulx que son visaige qui est bien descheu de la moictié de juste prix. Et vous promectz, Monsʳ, que sa fortune est telle que ses ennemys, encores qu'ilz soyent Angloys, ne se sçauroyent guarder d'en avoir pitié; ce nonobstant, ne laisseront de le poursuyvre jusques au bout et ne voyt plus de moyen de son salut.[59]

Après avoir établi la chronologie des événements et tenté de découvrir les intentions et l'évolution des intentions des parties en cause dans la négociation de la Paix des Dames, la richesse d'information des correspondances diplomatiques me semble bien plus grande qu'il n'y paraît d'abord et M. Jean-Daniel Pariset l'a bien exposé dans *Les Relations entre la France et l'Allemagne au milieu du XVIe siècle*.[60] Richesse bien plus grande si l'on veut tout simplement dépasser le récit de ce qui a abouti pour se replacer dans le temps des événements, en renonçant un peu au privilège que donne le recul pour mieux utiliser cet autre privilège de l'historien qui est de se trouver simultanément au conseil et dans les archives de tous. C'est la meilleure attitude pour ne pas se laisser abuser par des textes dont le sens réel est si souvent tellement éloigné du sens littéral parce qu'avant de devenir des témoignages ils ont été des armes. "Les Anglais, prévenus aussi par la France, firent tout leur possible pour entraver la marche des négociations," lit-on à propos de la paix de Cambrai dans la très classique *Histoire de France* de Lavisse. Pour écrire cela, il faut avoir pris au pied de la lettre les documents faisant état des appréhensions françaises et en avoir déduit une réalité qui n'est pas. Ma conclusion est que la France par crainte des entraves que l'Angleterre aurait pu mettre à la négociation a si bien manœuvré diplomatiquement que Henry VIII a été tenu hors de cause pendant de longs mois (et qui ont été très périlleux pour la mère et les serviteurs de François Ier) avant d'être averti de l'ouverture de pourparlers, et qu'au moment où il l'a été, il a cru qu'il était trop tard pour agir, été paralysé par les rivalités entre les grands du royaume et s'est fourvoyé dans la tentative d'obtention rapide d'une annulation de mariage qui le mettra pendant plusieurs années encore dans l'obligation de solliciter le roi de France.

NOTES

1. *Ordonnances des rois de France: règne de François Ier*, 9 vols. (Paris, 1902-1975), IV, 85-88.

2. Ibid., pp. 92-109.

3. Ibid., V, 41-56 et 69-75.

4. Ibid., pp. 87-89.

5. Ibid., pp. 155-68.

6. *Ambassades en Angleterre de Jean du Bellay. La première ambassade (sept. 1527-févr. 1529). Correspondance diplomatique*, p.p. V.-L. Bourrilly et P. de Vaissière (Paris, 1905), pp. 481-87.

7. *Négociations diplomatiques entre la France et l'Autriche durant les trente premières années du XVIe siècle*, 2 vols., p.p. A.J.C. Le Glay, Collection de documents inédits sur l'histoire de France (Paris, 1845), II, 676-91.

8. *Letters and Papers, Foreign and Domestic, of the Reign of Henry VIII*, p.p. J.S. Brewer (Londres, 1872), vol. IV, part II (1526-1528) et (Londres, 1876), vol. IV, part III (1529-1530).

9. *Correspondenz des Kaisers Karl V*, p.p. Karl Lanz (Leipzig, 1844), I, 300-08.

10. *Ambassades en Angleterre de Jean du Bellay*, et *Correspondance du cardinal Jean du Bellay*, 2 vols., p.p. R. Scheurer (Paris: Société de l'Histoire de France, 1969-1973), t. I.

11. *Letters and Papers*, vol. IV, part II, no. 4395, p. 1926.

12. *Ambassades en Angleterre*, p. 326.

13. *Letters and Papers*, vol. IV, part II, no. 4746, p. 2059.

14. Sur ce personnage voir A. Lapeyre et R. Scheurer, *Les Notaires et secrétaires du roi sous les règnes de Louis XI, Charles VIII et Louis XII*, Collection de documents inédits sur l'histoire de France (Paris, 1978), I, 23-24, et II, pl. XI.

15. *Letters and Papers*, vol. IV, part II, no. 4945, p. 2146.

16. *Letters and Papers*, vol. IV, part III, no. 5208, p. 2294.

17. Ibid., no. 5164, p. 2270.

18. *Ambassades en Angleterre*, p. 548.

19. *Correspondance du cardinal Jean du Bellay*, I, 8.

20. *Ordonnances . . . de François Ier*, V, 253-54.

21. Ibid., pp. 254-56.

22. *Correspondance du cardinal Jean du Bellay*, I, 11-12 et p. 15.

23. Ibid., p. 24 et p. 29.

24. *Correspondenz des Kaisers Karl V*, I, 301.

25. *Letters and Papers*, vol. IV, part III, no. 5753, p. 2563.

26. *Négociations diplomatiques*, II, 678.

27. Ibid., p. 680.

28. Ibid.

29. *Letters and Papers*, vol. IV, part II, no. 4945, pp. 2146-47.

30. *Négociations diplomatiques*, II, 680.

31. Ibid., p. 683.

32. *Ambassades en Angleterre*, p. 512.

33. *Letters and Papers*, vol. IV, part III, no. 5164, p. 2270.

34. Ibid., no. 5208, pp. 2294-2295 et *Ambassades en Angleterre*, pp. 544-47.

35. *Négociations diplomatiques*, II, 684.

36. Ibid.

37. Ibid., pp. 684-85.

38. *Ambassades en Angleterre*, p. 475.

39. Ibid., pp. 475-76.

40. Ibid., p. 548, n. 2.

41. V.-L. Bourrilly, *Guillaume du Bellay, sr de Langey, 1491-1543* (Paris, 1905), pp. 63-70.

42. *Correspondance du cardinal Jean du Bellay*, I, 8.

43. *Correspondenz des Kaisers Karl V*, I, 301.

44. *Correspondance du cardinal Jean du Bellay*, I, 12.

45. Ibid., p. 13 et p. 14, n. 2.

46. *Calendar of State Papers, Spanish*, 12 vols., p.p. G. Bergenroth, P. de Gayangos, M.A.S. Hume (Londres, 1862-1895), vol. IV, part I, no. 28, pp. 55-59.

47. *Correspondance du cardinal Jean du Bellay*, I, 28.

48. *Correspondenz des Kaisers Karl V*, I, 302.

49. *Correspondance du cardinal Jean du Bellay*, I, 40.

50. Ibid., p. 19.

51. Le 9 décembre 1528 Jean du Bellay écrivait à Anne de Montmorency: "Mondict sr le legat faict ce qu'il peult pour tourner ledict Empereur en hayne et le Roy en amour, mais c'est grant chose que de combattre contre nature," *Ambassades en Angleterre*, p. 482.

52. *Correspondance du cardinal Jean du Bellay*, I, 59.

53. Ibid., p. 49.

54. Ibid., pp. 18-40, pp. 51-60.

55. Ibid., p. 22.

56. Ibid., p. 39.

57. Ibid., p. 83.

58. Ibid., p. 106.

59. Ibid., p. 108.

60. Jean-Daniel Pariset, *Les Relations entre la France et l'Allemagne au milieu du XVIe siècle* (Strasbourg: Librairie Istra, 1981).

Pauline M. Smith

Clément Marot and the French Language

In spite of the undoubted revival of Marot studies initiated in this century by the work of Pierre Villey,[1] and further promoted by his successor in this field, Marot's most recent editor, C.A. Mayer, to whose labors the bibliography at the head of this present volume bears impressive witness, curiously little attention has so far been devoted to the poet's interest in questions of language.[2] True, Marot's pronouncements on the subject are scattered over a range of his *œuvre* (albeit chronologically largely concentrated within the period 1533 to 1538) and are disparate in nature, features which may partially explain their relative neglect by scholars. Yet, when taken in conjunction with the prose preface to his edition of Villon and the marginal annotations on the same text,[3] Marot's observations form a significant body of comment which both illuminates, and is itself illuminated by, 16th-century debates on the French language. In this context, our discussion may usefully be delimited by reference to two French Renaissance writers in particular, whose work on behalf of their national language has elicited critical attention, and in varying degrees, acclaim. Thus, interesting comparisons, some of which have been adumbrated but not previously developed in any detail, to my knowledge, may be made between Marot's activity in this respect and that of his close contemporary, the humanist printer Geofroy Tory, whose *Champ Fleury*,[4] published in 1529, has been hailed enthusiastically, although in the view of one critic extravagantly, as "the first manifesto to set out the claims to excellence of the French language."[5] Much later in the century, Marot's linguistic precepts, as well as his own practice, were to receive the accolade of endorsement from no less a figure than Henri II Estienne, whose achievements as a printer, classical scholar and philologist far outweigh those of Tory. Estienne's concern for, and nationalistic pride in, the French language led him to compose four major works in its service: *Le Traicté de la conformité du langage françois avec le grec* (1565), *Deux Dialogues du nouveau langage françois italianizé* (1578), *La Precellence du langage françois* (1579), and finally his *Hypomneses de lingua gallica* (1582).[6]

The evidence available concerning any relationship which may have existed between Tory the royal printer, and Marot the royal poet, is tantalizingly thin and suggests that the links between the two men were in the first instance of a purely professional nature. We know that Tory was the printer of the first, and three subsequent editions, of Marot's *L'Adolescence Clementine*, published in Paris by P. Roffet on 12 August 1532, again on 13 November of the same year, on 12 February 1533 NS and 7 June 1533.[7] To this extent he (and Roffet) enjoyed the confidence of the poet in a way which certain other French publishers and printers of the 1530s signally failed to do, when, partly through greed, partly through unscrupulousness and incompetence, they threatened the poet's livelihood, his reputation and even, in an age of repression, the safety of his person, with their unauthorized editions of inaccurate and sometimes falsely attributed texts.[8] Potentially more interesting for our investigation, although in this respect we cannot know how far the poet's approval was sought or gained, Tory proudly announced on the title page of the 7 June 1533 edition of *L'Adolescence Clementine* the introduction of certain spelling reforms, in particular the accentuation of final *e* and the use of the cedilla,[9] the desirability of which had been mooted by him some four years earlier in his *Champ Fleury*: "En nostre langage françois, n'avons point d'accent figuré en escripture, & ce pour le default que nostre langue n'est encores mise ne ordonnée à certaines reigles" (fo. LIIᴿ).[10] Finally and more tangibly, among the liminary tributes to the author of *L'Adolescence Clementine* was a Latin distich from the pen of Tory himself, an offering which suggests a degree of friendship and respect on his part for Marot,[11] and in which he recorded the poet's qualities thus: "Go. Torinus Biturigicus, In Eundem / Ad Lectorem / Vis lauros, cipryasque comas charitesque jocosque / Inde sales etiam nosse? Marotus habet."[12] Tory died before 14 October 1533. Strangely perhaps, Marot appears not to have written any poetic commemoration of his passing.

Whether or not these circumstantial points of contact between Tory the royal printer and Marot the royal poet allow one to infer any intellectual exchange between the two on matters of common interest, a striking parallel certainly exists in their treatment of the language of earlier French writers, even if they diverge again in their judgments of its quality. Tory extolls the "grande majesté de langage ancien" in the work of Jean de Nevelon and Pierre de Saint-Cloud (fo. III^v). At the same time, he was deeply conscious of the rapid change which had taken place, even over the last fifty years, in the French language, and recognized the barrier to comprehension and transmission which the passage of time threatened to erect between succeeding generations of the same linguistic and cultural heritage. His fervent hope was that this should be averted, that the language should be "mys & ordonné," otherwise "on trouvera que de cinquante ans en cinquante ans la langue françoise, pour la plus grande part, sera changée & pervertie" (Aux lecteurs, sig. A viii^r). From the list of obsolescent words, expressions and verbal forms which he quotes from the *Livre des Eschecqtz* [13] in illustration of such changes, and which he accompanies by their current equivalents, it is clear, although incompletely formulated, that one of the remedies he has in mind to counter the increasing opacity of the older language for his contemporaries and indeed subsequent generations, is a dictionary or glossary: "On porroit trouver dix milliers de telz motz & vocables laissez & changez desquelz cent aultres autheurs usoient au temps passé . . . & desquelz on porroit faire ung grant & juste volume" (ibid. sig. A viii^{r-v}). Marot was no less aware from an early stage in his poetic career, of linguistic change. But, far from regretting it, he associated such change with progressive refinement and improvement. Accordingly, in a *rondeau* addressed to a contemporary poetess, Dame Jeanne Gaillarde de Lyon, [14] and written before 1527, Marot esteems her "plume dorée" above that of Christine de Pisan: "Car, tout ainsi que le Feu l'Or affine, / Le Temps a faict nostre langue plus fine" (*OD*, Rondeau XVIII, 85). The same notion is present in the preface to the edition of the works of Villon which Marot published in 1533. Although clearly less appreciative than Tory of the language of his predecessors, he speaks for instance of the "langaige mal lymé" of Villon's day (sig. A v^r), Marot nevertheless feels it incumbent upon him to preserve "l'antiquité de son parler" (sig. A iiij^r) and to explain any difficulties it might cause for his own contemporaries by a system of marginal glosses: "Et pour ce (comme j'ay dit) que je n'ay touché à son antique façon de parler, je vous ay exposé sur la marge avecques les annotacions, ce qui m'a semblé le plus dur à entendre" (sig. A v^r). Only Villon's *jargon* is exempted from such treatment: "Touchant le jargon, je le laisse à corriger & exposer aux successeurs de Villon en l'art de la pinse & du croq" (sig. A v^v). To what extent was Marot's reluctance to tackle this thieves' jargon due quite simply to the knowledge that the task was beyond him? Or to some other scruple? Was he influenced perhaps by the attitude of Tory who refused on moral grounds to quote even a sample of it in his *Champ Fleury*? Villon may well have shown himself "grandement ingenieux" in its use, Tory concedes, but "toutesfois eust-il myeulx faict d'avoir entendu à faire aultre plus bonne chouse . . . J'alleguerois quelque peu du dict jargon, mais pour en eviter la meschante cognoissance, je passeray oultre" (sig. A viii[r]). With his marginal annotations, Marot is undoubtedly the first in a long line of 16th-century French writers to gloss the language of a fellow poet,[15] and certainly unique in undertaking this task for a late medieval one. Was this pioneering work inspired perhaps by the sample glosses contained in Tory's *Champ Fleury*? It would be unwise to exclude the possibility.

Critical reaction to Marot's commentary has been mixed and, on balance, hostile. Thuasne, in the notes to his 1923 edition of Villon, declared himself unimpressed, dismissing Marot's work as "presque toujours insignifiant quand il n'est pas erroné,"[16] a judgment which clearly fails to take account of the dual standpoint from which the commentary may, indeed *should*, be assessed, for even Marot's errors are significant and interesting for the linguistic historian. Madeleine Lazard, largely concerned with textual matters in her recent study on "Marot éditeur et lecteur de Villon," devotes one page only to this aspect of Marot's editorial practice before dismissing the glosses thus: "Nous ne tenterons pas de réhabiliter cette partie de son travail. La faiblesse en est évidente," a criticism mitigated somewhat by the recognition that "Marot fait œuvre de précurseur."[17] Only Mayer, in his biography of the poet, gives some indication of the potential interest of the work: "Il est regrettable que cette édition si intéressante du point de vue philologique n'ait jamais été étudiée."[18] It is our hope in the following pages to make good this omission as far as possible.

Leaving aside the historical, topographical and literary annotations which, while undoubtedly interesting, are peripheral to our particular enquiry,[19] we find that Marot's philological glosses may be classified under four main headings: lexis, morphology and syntax, pronunciation and, closely related to this last, versification. They are inspired, as the preface makes clear, partly by a desire to remove obstacles to comprehension, partly by a desire to elucidate "plusieurs autres incongruitez" (sig. A v[r]), these last relating mainly to accidence and pronunciation. Our aim has been to establish wherever possible how successfully or otherwise Marot performed his self-appointed task; how far he respected and satisfied his own terms of reference, since this is an essential preliminary to discovering the evidential value of Marot's commentary to the modern linguistic historian.

As we have seen, Marot's policy in his commentary assumes a close and not unreasonable correlation between linguistic archaism, that is, Villon's "antique façon de parler" as it was transmitted to Marot by various intermediaries, namely the texts of whichever early printed editions, or other sources, including oral ones, were available to him in the establishment of his text,[20] and difficulty of comprehension. In the operation of this policy Marot is, of necessity, confronted by the problems posed by his criteria. Much has been written on the problematic nature of the linguistic archaism[21] and it is clear that in the absence of total command by an individual of the resources of his own language, and their development at a given time, only the most approximate and subjective judgments of what constitutes an archaism will be possible; scarcely less subjective will be Marot's estimation of what his contemporaries will find difficult to understand. However, Marot's subsequent editorial comments suggest an intelligent appreciation of the complexities involved, and a pragmatic attempt to delimit them. For instance, both notions are perceived as relative. Therefore some features of Villon's language are felt to be more easily apprehended by the "promptes intelligences" of 16th-century readers of Villon than others. Examples cited by Marot from this category, and which he says he will, for this reason, abstain from glossing (a promise he sometimes fails to keep) are: "ly Roys, pour le Roy: homs pour homme, compaing pour compaignon: aussi force pluriers pour singuliers, & plusieurs autres incongruitez" (ibid.). Marot also reveals in this passage an awareness of *kinds* of archaism (*formal*, in the case of *ly Roys* and *homs*, even though this does not extend to an *understanding* of the morphology involved) as well as an awareness of *degrees* of archaism, of the stages in the life and death of words, of words *passing out of*, as well as no longer *being in*, current usage. The word *compaing* for instance is perceived as archaic but not unfathomably so; it is not seen as presenting an obstacle to comprehension. In fact, Marot was to use the word himself in 1539 in his third Eclogue (*OL*, LXXXIX, 32) in a passage relating the exploits of his childhood where it may possibly be construed as a conscious archaism, the more so since his literary source on this occasion, Jean Lemaire de Belges, had at this point employed the more current *compaignons*.[22] Ronsard too used *compaings* only to replace it in 1560 by *amis* as if aware of its, by then, too archaic savor.[23] What is perhaps even more instructive though, in this particular instance cited by Marot, is the absence of recognition, and hence of comment on his part, that, on the formal level, *compaing* is simply the old nominative case, derived from *companio*, of the word of which *compaignon*, derived from *companionem*, is the accusative. Marot's ignorance of this fact, which parallels his ignorance of the function of flexional *s* here in the preface ("force pluriers pour singuliers" being mentioned in the same breath as "plusieurs autres incongruitez") and in individual glosses, was no more profound that that displayed by Villon himself in his *Ballade en vieil langage françois*[24] or by later 16th-century writers, even such as Henri Estienne who took a special interest in, and probably had a wider knowledge of, the older language, than Marot. For instance, while discussing old French proverbs in his *Precellence du langage françois* (1579), Estienne appended the following comment to the example *Povre homs n'ha point d'ami*: ". . . vaut mieux suivre ceste escriture d'un vieil exemplaire (estant *homs* dict à la façon ancienne pour homme)," while in the case of *Qui de ses subjects est hays, n'est pas seigneur de son pays*, he commented: "Mais il faut noter en ce dernier proverbe que *hays* est dict pour *hay*, la lettre *S* estant superflue: comme elle est souvent au langage ancien."[25] Similarly, the precise relationship between *compaing* and *compaignon*, to say nothing of the word's etymology, excited speculation throughout the century, although much of it stemmed from a single source, namely the following entry in Robert Estienne's *Dictionnaire françois-latin* of 1549: "*Compaignon*. Apud Picardos *Compain & Compaignon* synonyma sunt: nisi quòd Compaignon forma dicitur diminutiva," repeated verbatim by Thierry in 1572, and so on.[26] Rather than lamenting Marot's ignorance, as Thuasne did, we should therefore accept it as one more confirmation among others of linguistic change which, inevitably, affected cultural transmission and even colored value judgments, in the case of those of Tory and Marot, as we have seen, in sometimes diametrically opposed ways.[27]

In our review and classification of Marot's marginal glosses, we must examine to what extent his perception of archaism, difficulty of comprehension, and *incongruité*,[28] receives independent confirmation in the works of his fellow writers; to what extent his testimony is open to verification in more formal sources, 16th-century lexicographers, grammarians and other commentators, as well as modern authorities in these fields. Although we start with the advantage of the hindsight denied to Marot, and a greater range of written source material available at any one time, the *caveat* must be entered that the present state of lexicographical research has its own limitations (not the least of them being the loss of the spoken language of Marot's day) and inadequacies, which make our knowledge patchy and the control we may exercise far from total. The pattern of entries, in alphabetical order under the four main headings, will be as follows: the item in question, its gloss, its location in Marot's 1533 Villon by work and page number (there are unfortunately no line numbers) followed, for the convenience of readers, by reference to the corresponding work and line of text in the most recent critical edition of Villon's work, that of Rychner and Henry; a note of the attestation of the item in 16th-century or modern authorities; finally, further comment as available.[29]

Lexis

1. The following items glossed by Marot are *not* attested in the sense and usage indicated (even when this appears to have been correctly established and is confirmed by modern commentators such as Thuasne, Burger, Rychner and Henry) by any 16th-century lexicographer quoted or by Huguet. In the absence of more complete or reliable criteria, this may be taken as provisional confirmation of Marot's judgment of their desuetude at the time he prepared his edition of Villon. (Italics, and square brackets isolating a headword where the marginal gloss itself contains more than one word, are mine.)

chevaucheur d'escouvettes, chevaucheur de balays, sorcier (*GT*, p. 43; RH, *T*, 668).

combien, toutesfoys (*GT*, p. 16, p. 95; RH, *T*, 97, 1825).

[*deffaçon*], *à ma deffaçon*, à ma deffaicte, à ma mort (*PT*, p. 2; RH, *L*, 19); also *de ma deffaçon seur*, parente de ma ruyne & deffaicte (*GT*, p. 55; RH, *T*, 945). H has only the verb *desfaçonner*, défaire, abattre, détruire. Brunot lists the noun as one of the words "qui existaient encore au XVe siècle, et que la Pléiade n'a point employés, les laissant mourir obscurément" (*HLF*, II, 188).

desprins, dessaisiz, desnuez (*PT*, p. 7; RH, *L*, 203). G records only this example; *FEW*, IX, 348 also suggests that the word was already passing out of current usage in the 15th century.

engeaultre, trompe, deçoyt (*GT*, p. 44; RH, *T*, 695). Unknown elsewhere, this verb may be related to *engaudrer*, 3e Ballade en jargon (Stockholm ms).

escourgeon, fouet (*PT*, p. 5; RH, *L*, 143, *escourgon*). 16th-century lexicographers know only *escourgée* in this sense.

extrace, origine (*GT*, p. 24; RH, *T*, 274).

feautre [chapeau de], fustre (*GT*, p. 44; RH, *T*, 692); also *feautres*, feustres (*GT*, p. 62; RH, *T*, 1091).

flou, flouet, delicat (*GT*, p. 63; RH, *T*, 1112).

[*foys*], *pour à la foys*, pour une foy (*PT*, p. 6: "Pour à la foys laisse ung canart"; RH, *L*, 186: "Je laisse à la foys ung canart," glossed as "en même temps, aux deux ensemble" with reference to Loup and Cholet, the legatees of the preceding line (*Com*, *L*, p. 156).

huy & hier, tousjours (*GT*, p. 32; RH, *T*, 439).

lectry, lectrain (*PT*, p. 8; RH, *L*, 220). Very rare in 15th-century French in this form, but not aberrant (*FEW*, V, 236).

[*maillon*], *de maillon*, de maillot (*GT*, p. 51; RH, *T*, 852).

mathon, laict caillé (*GT*, p. 81; RH, *T*, 1487).

[*mousche à masché*], *estront de mousche à masché*, estront de mousche de la cire (*GT*, p. 67; RH, *T*, 1199; *Com*, *T*, p. 173, "mouche à miel . . . abeille").

[*papaliste*], *le papaliste*, le siege papal (*GT*, p. 28; RH, *T*, 359; *Com*, *T*, p. 57: "liste, . . . registre des papes et par conséquent, la papauté"). H has only the sense of *papiste, catholique* in the 16th century.

poirre, peter, & fault prononcer poarre à la parisienne (*GT*, p. 62; RH, *T*, 1100). See also below, p. 184.

[*pres*], *pres voysin*, prochain voysin (*GT*, p. 88; RH, *T*, 1654).

Scotiste, d'Escosse (*GT*, p. 28; RH, *T*, 365).

[*senez*], *ly senez*, le vieil ou ancien, Et est extraict de Senex, vocable latin (*GT*, p. 30; RH, *T*, 402). The word means "sage, prudent." Marot's gloss is also etymologically incorrect. See below, p. 179.

sume, preigne, trop tiré du latin (*GT*, p. 76: "Dieu m'ordonne que je le face & sume"; cf. RH, *T*, 1400, "Dieu m'ordonne que le fouysse et fume"). See also below, p. 179.

In only two of the cases listed above is there any measurable discrepancy between Marot's interpretation of a term glossed (*à la foys; senez*) and that of Villon's most recent editors. In the first instance, the difference of interpretation may be partly accounted for by the slightly different reading adopted by Marot and RH for the line in question. In the second, Marot has been led into error by a false etymology.

2. The words in the following list *are* attested in the sense given by Marot (errors excepted) in the 16th-century and modern lexicographers indicated. It would however be wrong to assume from this that such words were not in the process of passing out of current usage, or were not *felt* to be in some way archaic, and even, in some cases, specifically recommended for retention on that account, as conscious or stylistic archaisms. Indeed, in some instances Marot's judgment is corroborated from other sources. Nevertheless, it is not always possible for us to appreciate why a particular term glossed should have been thought by Marot to be "dur à entendre" for his contemporaries. But changes to the form of a word or idiom, alternative and perhaps less familiar spellings (although certainly not an uncommon feature of the language of the period) are other factors which may have prompted a gloss in some of the instances given below (see for example *estant en bonne, mau, oystres, telles*). But whatever Marot's criteria may have been in specific cases, it is scarcely to be wondered at that his glosses should sometimes include items not as *désuets* in fact as in appear-

ance. The problem was to perplex more erudite commentators. Thus, Henri Estienne, in the course of a discussion on linguistic change in the *Deux Dialogues*, makes Philausone say: "Il me faiset voir aussi des changemens en quelques mots non pas quant à leurs significations, mais quant à eux-mesmes. Et vous confesseray que je me trouvay bien loing de mon conte touchant quelques-uns, quant à estre modernes ou anciens" (ed. Smith, p. 155).

aherdre, prendre (*GT*, p. 50, "Ne eau au bout de ses doiz aherdre"; RH, *T*, 819, "N'au bout d'icelluy doiz aerdre" and *Com*, *T*, p. 121). Marot's reading of the text involves the transitive use of the verb *aherdre*, attested in R. Est, T; C; H and B-Wart in the senses, respectively, of "arripere, corripere; to snatch, or plucke; to catch, gripe, or take by violence; s'attacher; saisir." The intransitive use is also recorded (H). In his *Art poëtique*, Peletier du Mans cites the word as an example of an archaism which could well be reinstated in a stylistically appropriate context: "Il nę sęra defandù dę ramęner quelquefoęs les moz anciens. Comme adęrdrę pour aderer, dont use souvant Jan Dęmeun."[30] A marginal note, probably by Ronsard himself, in the *Septiesme livre des Poëmes* of 1569 (p. 27[r]) likewise confirms the word's status as an archaism: "tenant bien fort: vieil mot François, qui vient du latin adhaerens."[31]

m'apastela, me repeut (*GT*, p. 65; RH, *T*, 1156). Well attested up to the early 17th century (R. Est, T, C, H). Listed by M.-L, I, 222 as an archaism (but on what grounds?).

[*bel*], *s'il luy est bel*, s'il luy semble beau (*GT*, p. 100: "S'il luy plaist, & il luy est bel"; RH, *T*, 1932). Cf. "Bel me seroit," Michel d'Amboise (H).

[*bonne*], *estant en bonne*, estant deliberé (*PT*, p. 10; RH, *L*, 274). While the expression *estre en ses bonnes* is well attested in the 16th century in the sense of to be of good humor, well disposed (cf. Rabelais, *Quart Livre*, XII, XLVI; Henri Estienne, *Deux Dialogues*, ed. Smith, p. 220), there is no other known example at present of *bonne* in the singular.

[*bouffez*], *suys bouffez*, suys fasché (*GT*, p. 30; RH, *T*, 391 reads *buffez* and glosses "emporté comme par un souffle, soufflé," *Com*, *T*, p. 60). The form and meaning given by Marot are both confirmed by B-Wart, the latter as a development from " 'souffler en gonflant ses joues,' d'où 'gonfler' en général et 'être fâché,' XVe, encore au XVIIe." R. Est, T, and C likewise indicate the notion of anger with "bouffer de couroux & de maltalent" and "to swell with anger" respectively; but H, under *buffer*, gives "souffler, souffleter."

[*bourde*], *bourde ius mise*, toute raillerie laissée (*GT*, p. 50; RH, *T*, 824 gives a completely different reading). Attested in this sense, among others, by T, C and H; M.-L, I, 233, archaism. *Mettre ius* is presumably not considered by Marot to pose any major difficulty in this line, since he uses the expression himself (*OL*, VI, 377). But cf. *doubtans* below.

branc d'acier, braquemard ou espée (*PT*, p. 2; RH, *L*, 83); also *mon branc*, mon espee ou braquemart (*GT*, p. 57, p. 59; RH, *T*, 971, 1025). *Branc* or *brand* is very well attested in T, C, G and H, but the bulk of examples given by the latter suggest that the word was most often employed in an archaizing context. Rabelais uses it twice, in the *Tiers Livre* in describing the weapons of the Corinthians (Prologue), in the *Quart Livre*, XXXIV in an anecdote relating to Alexander the Great. Des Essars, noted for his use of archaisms drawn from the *rommans* (see Brunot, *HLF*, II, 183) employs it in his translation of the *Amadis*, V, 4 (H). It is listed by Silver as an archaism used by Ronsard (*Ronsard's General Theory of Poetry*, p. 108).

ceps, maniere de prison (*PT*, p. 5; RH, *L*, 144). Well attested in the literal (stocks, shackles, fetters, prison) and figurative senses. R. Est, T, C, G, H. The word was also thought to require a gloss by Muret in his commentary on Ronsard's *Amours* of 1553, pp. 242-43. The line "Si hors du cep où je suis arrêté" elicited the following: "Si hors du cep, S'il peut echapper de la servitude en laquelle il est. *Du cep*, du lien."

chastoy, chastiement (*GT*, p. 87; RH, *T*, 1640). Well attested (H).

doubtans, craignans (*GT*, p. 100; RH, *T*, 1947). Well attested (R. Est, T, C, H). Used twice by Marot himself in this sense (*OL*, II, 115; LIII, 14), the word can hardly be considered incomprehensible for his contemporaries.

[*doulouse*], *ne te doulouse*, ne te plains (*GT*, p. 24; RH, *T*, 283). Well attested not only by lexicographers but throughout Marot's own work. Nevertheless, the word is listed as an archaism by M.-L, I, 254, a verdict endorsed on this occasion, at least, by Brunot, with only one reservation: "on peut . . . considérer comme ayant vraiment été recherché dans 'les romans'—mais on sait qu'il faut entendre sous ce mot des écrits du XVe siècle aussi bien que des textes du moyen âge—ceux qui suivent: . . . *se doulouser* = se désoler" (*HLF*, II, 185).

embeu, emboyté, yvre (*GT*, p. 69; RH, *T*, 1254 reads *beu*). C; H, one example.

enfermes, malades (*GT*, p. 94; RH, *T*, 1804). Well attested, C, G, H.

enfonduz, creux & descharnez (*PT*, p. 9: "Gelez, meurdriz & enfonduz"; RH, *L*, 240, glossed "trempés"). Marot seems to be in error here. The adjective is well attested throughout the 16th century, but predominantly in the sense indicated by RH. See C, G, H (the latter also gives "répandu").

engigne, deçoyt (*GT,* p. 69; RH, *T,* 1240). Well attested, R. Est, T, C, H.

eschevez le, evitez le (*GT,* p. 91; RH, *T,* 1724). Well attested, R. Est, T, C, H). However, there is some evidence that it was increasingly felt to be archaic. On two separate occasions, those responsible for preparing the 1557 edition of Claude de Seyssel's *Monarchie de France* (1515) replaced the ms *eschiver* by the synonym *eviter.*[32] Nor is this an isolated example of modernizing tendencies in this edition. See also *remanant* below. *Eschever* is listed as an archaism by M.-L, I, 257.

[*escry*], *sans escry,* sans bruyt (*PT,* p. 8; RH, *L,* 221 reads *estry*). Well attested, R. Est, T, C, H.

establis, estaulx (*PT,* p. 6; RH, *L,* 148). R. Est, T, C, but H only *establie* in the theatrical sense of "échafaudage."

faitard, paresseux; qui tard faict sa besongne (*GT,* p. 13; also p. 69; RH, *T,* 36, 1251). Very well attested throughout the 16th, and up to the mid-17th, centuries, R. Est, T, C, G, H; M.-L, I, 279, archaism.

[*fenestre*], *une fenestre, &c* ["aupres sainct Jacques"], une des petites boutiques d'escrivain pres. S. Jaques de la boucherie (*PT,* p. 4; RH, *L,* 120). Unrecorded by 16th-century lexicographers but *FEW,* III, 452, quoting Gay, regards the word as still current.

fiert, frappe (*GT,* p. 72; RH, *T,* 1320). Very well attested, T, C, H. M.-L, I, 278, noting that Baïf replaced the form *tu fiers* in his *Amours de Meline* (1552) by *tu mors* in a later version, gives the word as an archaism. But the reason for Marot's gloss may well owe as much to morphology as to lexis. See below, p. 181.

foleur, follie (*GT,* p. 56 and *AO,* p. 110; RH, *T,* 961 and *PV,* p. 70, v. 13). Absent from T, C, and attested only in the early part of the century in H, this word would seem to be passing out of current usage.

[*forfaictz*], *trouble forfaictz,* larrecins cachez (*PT,* p. 6; RH, *L,* 164 reads *troubles, forfaiz*). Both terms are attested, T, C. The purpose of the gloss may be to support the reading of adjective and noun, rather than the more plausible possibility of two nouns separated by a comma.

[*greigneur*], *le greigneur,* le plus grant (*GT,* p. 56; RH, *T,* 966). Very well attested, R. Est, T, C, H, but nevertheless widely felt to be distinctly archaic. The term is used in a pastiche of the "brave gergon de la table ronde" by René Macé in his *Voyage de Charles Quint par la France*[33] and as a conscious archaism by Scève, *Délie,* XIX, 8 who uses a parenthetical "comme on dit" to highlight its archaic savor.[34] Glossed by Muret in Ronsard's *Amours,* 1553 (p. 152), the term was replaced by *gouverneur* in 1578 (Terreaux, *Ronsard correcteur,* p. 98, 243-44). Pasquier also comments on the antiquity of the term and its replacement by "plus grande, & meilleure part" in his *Recherches de la France.*[35]

[*grief d'amours*], *du grief d'amours*, du mal d'amours (*PT*, p. 2; RH, *L*, 24). C, G, H.

[*guementant*], *me guementant*, me complaignant, me souciant (*GT*, p. 24; RH, *T*, 281 reads *me grementant*). R. Est, T, C, H. Brunot quotes *guermenter* in this sense as a word which the Pléiade allowed to die (*HLF*, II, 188).

[*Jacopin*], *Emmailloté d'ung Jacopin*, tousjours empesché d'ung flegme, ne pouvant cracher (*PT*, p. 6; RH, *L*, 159). *Jacopin* in the sense of "crachat" appears elsewhere in Villon (*GT*, p. 46; RH, *T*, 731) without attracting a gloss from Marot, although the existence of a prior gloss does not normally inhibit repetition on his part. The expression *cracher un Jacobin*, "to spit out a collop, or dol of flegme" is recorded in C, the noun in H. This sense has led Marot here into an erroneous gloss for the participle *emmailloté* which would presumably not otherwise have presented any difficulty (attested by T, C), and *d'ung Jacobin*, understand, "in the manner of, a Jacobin," with its allusion to the white woollen robe of the Dominicans or white Friars, Jacobins so called from the Church of Saint Jacques in Paris.

jus ne sure, soubz ne sus (*GT*, p. 77; RH, *T*, 1417). *Jus, sur/sus* are separately attested in R. Est, C, H; *jus ne sus*, up to 15th century, G.

[*jusques*], *jusques mort*, tant que mort (*GT*, p. 76; RH, *T*, 1387). R. Est, T, C, H.

[*lame*], *soubz lame*, soubz tumbe (*GT*, p. 25; RH, *T*, 301). Well attested, C, H.

ledanger, blasmer (*GT*, p. 38; RH, *T*, 571). Many examples, R. Est, T, C, H.

loirs, l'outre (*GT*, p. 73; RH, *T*, 107). Marot's forte does not appear to be natural history! Even if one takes into account the fact that *glir* and *gliron* were the more commonly used terms for dormouse in the 16th century,[36] the word *loir* nevertheless merits an entry in Charles de Bovelles's *Liber de differentia vulgarium linguarum, et Gallici sermonis varietate* (Paris, 1533), p. 65, and is attested in R. Est, T, C and Littré (Desportes), but not H.

mailler, martteller (*AO*, p. 113; RH, *PV*, p. 52, v. 4). H records only one example in this specific sense (Cretin), but gives some early examples of the more general one of "frapper," "battre."

[*mais*], ne moins ne mais, ne moins ne plus (*GT*, p. 21; RH, *T*, 215); also *mais*, plus (*GT*, p. 25; RH, *T*, 290). Although *mais* in the sense of "plus" will persist for some time yet (R. Est, T, C, H), its gradual disappearance, except in the expression *n'en pouvoir mais*, is already under way according to Brunot (*HLF*, II, 378).

mande, envoye (*GT*, p. 79; RH, *T*, 1458). Common, R. Est, T, C, H.

[*mate*], *mate chere*, pouvre & piteuse chere (*GT*, p. 50; RH, *T*, 821). Although not in R. Est or C, well attested in the above sense by H.

[*mau*], *de ce mau hasles*, de ce mauvays hasle (*GT*, p. 91; RH, *T*, 1722). R. Est, only in the proverb *mau chat, mau rat*; C, only as noun; H, only with *temps*, in *mautemps* (only two examples, as opposed to the very many of the now prevailing form *mal*, adjective).

[*mauffez*], *ly mauffez*, le dyable (*GT*, p. 30; RH, *T*, 388). One example in H. Recognized as an archaism by Henri Estienne, *Precellence*: "nos ancestres . . . appeloyent *mauffaits* ceux que nous appelons *diables*" (ed. Huguet, p. 197). C also identifies the word as an archaism (possibly on Estienne's authority): "*Mauffait/mauffé*, A Bug, Fairie, the Spirit, old words."

[*merit*], *ne merit*, ne merite (*GT*, p. 49; RH, *T*, 799); also *merir*, meriter (*GT*, p. 52; RH, *T*, 880). Clearly in the process of being eclipsed by the synonymous -*ER* verb (a not uncommon phenomenon), *merir* is not recorded by R. Est, T or C, while H's three examples are all early century ones.

[*meshaing*], *sans meshaing*, à l'aise (*GT*, p. 102; RH, *T*, 1974). *Mehaing*, although well attested in T, C, G, H, was considered archaic. Ronsard defiantly defends his use of the term: "Nos critiques se moqueront de ce vieil mot François: mais il les faut laisser caqueter" which he nevertheless deletes from the 1584 edition (M.-L., I, 307; Silver, *Ronsard's General Theory*, p. 65). Comment on its antiquity also comes from Henri Estienne, *Precellence*: "Il y-a un autre ancien mot, *meshain*, au second vers, selon les vieux registres: où nous lisons, *Qui veut la guarison du mire, Il luy convient son mehain dire*" (ed. Huguet, p. 251).

miches de sainct Estienne, des pierres (*GT*, p. 99; RH, *T*, 1912, 1915). C, H (one example).

[*miege*], *bon miege*, bon mire, mon medecin (*GT*, p. 64; RH, *T*, 1140). Rare in the 16th century; one example, *mege*, in H. *Mège* however survived as a pejorative (quack) in Swiss particularly, from which it re-entered literary French in the 18th century (*FEW*).

moulier, femme (*GT*, p. 42; RH, *T*, 643). H has only one example, *mulier* (*Anc. Poes. fr*, V, 312), apart from the Gascon form *moulhé* (Monluc) which is the only form known to C.

[*mouse*], *sa mouse*, sa moue, son museau (*GT*, p. 61; RH, *T*, 1074). One example, H.

[*oystres*], *d'oystres*, d'huystres (*GT*, p. 22; RH, *T*, 239). An entry in R. Est suggests that *huitres* was the more common spelling, but *ouystres* the preferred one, presumably on etymological grounds: "*Huitres*, ou mieulx *Ouystres*, ostrea ostreorum." C has both; H, *oystre*, two examples.

parit, enfante (*GT*, p. 48; RH, *T*, 794). H only, three examples.

peaussues, qui ne sont plus que peaulx (*GT*, p. 36; RH, *T*, 516). C, H.

perit, pour perdit, mais il ne se peut dire (*GT*, p. 49; RH, *T*, 797). See below, p. 182.

[*recullet*], *tappy en recullet*, caché honteux en derriere (*AO*, p. 109; RH, *PV*, p. 70, v. 5). One example, H. For *tappy*, see below.

[*remains*], *je remains*, je demeure (*GT*, p. 34; RH, *T*, 486). Well attested, T, C, H. Henri Estienne quotes a proverb containing this verb as having more authority by virtue of the archaic flavor of its language: "les proverbes ont plus d'autorité en leur ancien langage, qu'en l'autre . . . Pour exemple, si nous disons, *Moult remaint de ce que fol pense*, ce langage ha plus d'autorité que si nous parlons ainsi, *De ce que fol pense, souvent en demeure*" (ed. Huguet, p. 251).

[*remenant*], *le remenant*, le demourant (*GT*, p. 22; RH, *T*, 232); also *du remenant*, du residu (*GT*, p. 46; RH, *T*, 749). Well attested, T, C, H. An interesting clue to the word's status, however, is to be found in the variants to successive "modernized" editions of Claude de Seyssel's *Monarchie de France*. Where the base ms (c. 1510) has *remanant*, this is revised in subsequent editions in all but three instances (ed. Poujol, p. 100, p. 115, p. 148) to *reste* or *demeurant* (1544 and 1560 editions, p. 82, p. 83; 1557 edition, pp. 145, 158, 161, 172, 185, 217, 219 in Poujol). Brunot lists it as a term not revived by the Pléiade poets (*HLF*, II, 188).

[*ru*], *comme a ru telles*, comme toilles à ung ruisseau (*GT*, p. 42; RH, *T*, 658); also *ru*, ruisseau (*GT*, p. 56; RH, *T*, 963). Well attested, R. Est, T, C, H. *Telles* for *toilles* is not a difference of lexis so much as of pronunciation, the substitution of *è* for *oi* (wè) being considered a feature of Parisian speech from the 15th century onwards.[37] In any case, the phenomenon was sufficiently well known in Marot's day to provide Rabelais with an easy pun in *Gargantua*, LII.

[*sommet*], *le sommet*, le hault de la teste (*GT*, p. 86; RH, *T*, 1613). R. Est, T, C.

sume, seme (*GT*, p. 76; RH, *T*, 1398). One example, H.

[*tant que*], *tant que je suys*, tandis que je suys (*GT*, p. 15; RH, *T*, 75). R. Est, T, H (this sense but + subjunctive). In Seyssel's *Prohème d'Appien* (ed. Poujol, p. 84) the ms *tant que* + indicative is modernized in 1544 and 1560 editions to *tandis que*, thus confirming Marot's gloss and its purpose.

[*tant que*], *tant qu'il mourra*, jusques à ce qu'il mourra (*GT*, p. 15; RH, *T*, 87). T, H (with subjunctive or indicative). The construction appears in Marot (*Ep*, XIII, 10; *OS*, I, 215; *OL*, LXVII, 41).

tappy en recullet, caché honteux en derriere (*AO*, p. 109; RH, *PV*, p. 70, v. 5). R. Est: "aussi disons-nous tapi pour caché"; T, C.

[*telles*], *comme a ru telles*, comme toilles à ung ruisseau (*GT*, p. 42; RH, *T*, 658). See above, *ru*.

[*tends*], *je leur tends,* je leur presente (*GT*, p. 85; RH, *T*, 1597). R. Est, T, C.

In only three of the instances cited in our second list has Marot erred in his interpretation of a word or phrase (*enfonduz, emmailloté d'ung Jacopin* and *loir*).

3. Terms which relate to objects (mainly items of attire) more or less specific to Villon's own period may be considered archaic by virtue of this fact. In some cases, to judge from the form of words employed, it seems that Marot was able to furnish only a vague historical note, rather than a lexical gloss in his annotations, whether it be for the ensemble invoked in "Dames à rebrassez colletz/ . . . / Portans attours & bourreletz" (*GT*, p. 25; RH, *T*, 309, 311) and perfunctorily glossed as "l'habit des dames du temps de Villon," or the following individual items:

[*bottes*], *fauves bottes,* la belle chausseure d'alors (*GT*, p. 102; RH, *T*, 1974). *Porter botte fauve* was not only a love token but also a mark of elegance in Villon's day, as we may gather from another text, Martial d'Auvergne's *Arrêts d'Amour,* but in spite of frequent reprintings of this popular text throughout the 16th century, [38] lexicographers of the period do not record the term.

chauses semellées, brodequins (*PT*, p. 6; RH, *L*, 166). *Chausses* alone, same sense, H.

hucque, habit du temps (*PT*, p. 4; RH, *L*, 122). C, H (one example).

tabart, manteau (*PT*, p. 7; RH, *L*, 189); also, quelque sorte de manteau (*GT*, p. 63; RH, *T*, 1116) and, une manteline de alors (*GT*, p. 71; RH, *T*, 1294). C, *tabarre,* and H.

4. Marot has also glossed set, or figurative, expressions, difficult and/or archaic, for which it was not always possible to find direct, word for word equivalents. In the first category are oaths which may simply be characterized as such:

[*Enné*], Enné est ung juron de fillez (*GT*, p. 85; RH, *T*, 1580), a gloss not entirely supported by the few early 16th-century examples available which suggest an exclamation of affirmation (G; Roger de Collerye, H). Alternatively, an oath may be paraphrased, as in the line "*Ce jura il, sur son chaignon,* Serment antique, comme par son chef" (*GT*, p. 103; RH, *T*, 2002, reads *couillon*). In the second category, Marot may gloss an expression used figuratively by making explicit the metaphor involved, as in the line

Le frain aux dents, franc au collier (PT, p. 1; RH, *L*, 4) which attracts the comment

Franc au collier, Travaillant voulentiers comme les chevaulx qui franche-ment tirent au collier. This metaphor, cultivated in the 15th century by Alain Chartier,[39] as well as by Villon, survived at least to the end of the 16th, T, C; Pasquier, D'Aubigné, G. Similarly, a line which has the lapidary, as well as the archaic, formulation of a proverb is an obvious choice for amplification, so that

Que charreterie se boyt toute (GT, p. 90; RH, *T* 1686) is paraphrased: Quelque vin que l'on charroye (soit bon, soit mauvays) se boit tout. How-ever, it is clearly not within the scope of the present essay, nor would space allow it, to provide exhaustive treatment of all the glosses which elaborate expressions in varying degrees, and for various reasons—more often literary than linguistic (such as metonymy, euphemism, word play, allusion)—elliptical rather than simply archaic.

5. Marot's interest in lexis extends beyond archaism to certain categories of specialized vocabulary, peculiar to regions or classes of individuals, etc. Thus, the following glosses draw the reader's attention to alleged or actual

(a) Criminal argot

joncherie, joncherie est ung mot jargon (*AO,* p. 106; RH, *PV,* p. 74, v. 13). The sense of the word, which Marot was either unable or unwilling to give (see above, p. 165), is "plaisanterie, finesse." Far from being restricted to jargon, although confirmed as such by its presence in the *Cinquieme Ballade en jargon* (RH, *Com, PV,* p. 129), the term was not unknown in literature ranging from classical literary comedy (*Therence en François*) to farce (G), and from poetry to translations into French by Le Blond of Valerius Maximus and More's *Utopia* (H).

pigeons, prisonniers (*PT,* p. 8; RH, *L*, 229). Cf. T's entry: "les pigeons de la Conciergerie, ou autre prison."

trappe volliere, une prison (ibid.; RH, *L*, 230).

(b) Regionalisms

ung tantinet, un peu & ne se dit gueres hors Paris (*GT,* p. 63; RH, *T*, 1109). Recorded without comment by T, C.

tayon, pere grant en langage picard duquel Paris tenoyt plus lors que à present (*GT,* p. 29; RH, *T*, 379). Recorded, without note of origin, as *avus* by T; C lists as a Picardism and translates "a great grand father."

(c) Foreign expressions

Brelare Bigod, en Angloys, Dieu et nostre Dame, & appert icy que du temps de Villon restoit encore à Paris quelque mot des Angloys qui avoient passé par là (*GT*, p. 85; RH, *T*, 1585 reads *brulare bigot*). Marot's translation is somewhat approximate since *Brelare* was in fact a corruption of *by'r Lord* and *Bigod* of *By God!* Marot's attempt to account for the presence of this foreign element in Villon's poetry reveals a better grasp of history than of the English language. It is perhaps worth noting that this linguistic relic of the English presence during the Hundred Years War still had enough currency in 1489 to be recalled and quoted in a poem by Robert Gaguin: "Jamais Françoys bien ne saura / Jurer *by God*, ni *brelaré*."[40]

Que bien stat, que tout est bien, & est tiré de l'italien (*GT*, p. 86; RH, *T*, 1598 reads *Bene stat*). A symptom of the increasing influx into French of italianisms in the second half of the 15th century? The form *stat* is Latin however; the rhyme is with *estat*.

(d) Latinisms

Two further items are deemed latinisms: *ly senez* incorrectly, as it derives from the Germanic *sinno* (*FEW*, XVII, 72) and *sume*, preigne, correctly, from *sumere* (for the full text of these glosses, see above, p. 000).

Morphology and Syntax

A foretaste of Marot's work in this field is provided in his editorial remarks where, as we have seen, what are actually remnants of the old French case system and, as such, historical forms of the language in themselves neither good nor bad, are described as "force pluriers pour singuliers" and dismissed along with "plusieurs autres incongruitez" which Marot regarded as an unfortunate concomitant of the unpolished language of Villon's day. In fact, as we now know, chaos set in in the French case system long before Villon's time even, and given the haphazard way the latter distributed his -s endings in a fanciful attempt to archaize his language in the *Ballade en vieil langage français*, it is hardly surprising that Marot could neither deduce nor intuit any grammatical system of which they might be the vestiges.

1. Flexional *s*

Ainsi maid dieux, ainsi m'aide Dieu (*GT*, p. 17; RH, *T*, 124).

ly sainctz Apostolles, Le pape. Et se trouve tousjours icy le plurier pour le singuler, à l'antique (*GT*, p. 30; RH, *T*, 385).

[*Le beau nez ne grant ne petiz*], plurier pour singulier (*GT*, p. 35; RH, *T*, 497).

[*Le vis pally, mort & destaincts*], plurier pour singulier (ibid.; RH, *T*, 515).

[*S'aucunement tu n'est lettrez*[*Assez auras, si tu prens en grez*], pluriers pour singuliers, à la mode antique (*GT*, p. 91; RH, *T*, 1711-12).

2. Pronouns

(a) Personal Pronouns

The confusion frequently to be found in the 15th century between *ilz/elles* is resolved by Marot for his readers in the following instance: "Les sonneurs auront quatres [sic] miches / . . . / Mais ilz seront de sainct Estienne" by the gloss: *Ilz pour elles* (*GT*, p. 99; RH, *T*, 1912, 1915) although since previous examples were allowed to pass without comment (*GT*, p. 32, twice), it might better be described as an afterthought. This in itself should not surprise us since the confusion persisted into the 16th century. Indeed, Brunot cites an instance in Marot's own *4e Coq à l'Ane*, v. 75 but this is confined to the less authoritative text preserved in BN MS 1718 as Mayer's variants make clear (*OS*, X, p. 148). Moreover, the confusion is still to be observed in Ronsard (Brunot, *HLF*, I, 439; II, 313).

(b) Relative Pronoun

Similarly, to avoid confusion, Marot resolves the elision of nominative *que*

qu'est hom', qui est homme (*GT*, p. 51; RH, *T*, 860), although this was by no means unusual in the 16th century (cf. Du Bellay, *Regrets*, XXI, 6).

3. Possessive Adjective

Par m'ame, par mon ame (*GT*, p. 14, 34, 84; RH, *T*, 60, 474, 1569). This set expression exemplifies perhaps the most tenacious survival of the old feminine possessive adjective elided before a vowel which, from the 14th century onwards, had been progressively replaced by the masculine *mon, ton, son*.[41] By the 16th century its use, outside of this expression, seems to be restricted almost entirely to the words *amye, amour*. Notwithstanding these survivals, contemporary comment, as well as Marot's gloss, leaves us in no doubt whatever that the form was considered archaic. Thus Sebillet, commenting on Marot's own usage, writes: "trouveras souvent en Marot m'amour, t'amour, s'amour pour m'amour, ton amour, son amour, ce que je pense attribueras avec moy plus tost à la liberté de noz majeurs, que Marot en cest endroit comme en d'autres a quelque fois suivie."[42] Ronsard's practice was gradually to eliminate this archaic possessive, *m'amye* being replaced by Marie in the 1567, 1578, 1584 editions (Terreaux, *Ronsard correcteur*, p. 115). As a result of his study of the older language Henri Estienne observed that: "ce *mon* n'a pas esté si commun à nos ancestres qu'à nous, et mesmes il semble qu'ils l'ayent evité tant qu'ils ont peu devant un mot de genre feminin. Qu'ainsi soit, vous lisez en Villon, qui a esté du temps de nos ayeuls, *m'ame* pour mon ame" (*Deux Dialogues du nouveau langage françois*, ed. Smith, p. 135).

4. Verbs

(a) Present Indicative

Two present indicative forms attract glosses. They are:

fiert, frappe (*GT*, p. 72; RH, *T*, 1320). Felt to be archaic (see above, p. 173), this verb may also have been glossed as difficult to identify, and hence to interpret, by reason of its defective and irregular conjugation. See *ferir* (Brunot, *HLF*, II, 346).

[*ot*], *qui m'ot*, qui me oyt (*GT*, p. 48; RH, *T*, 779). Old and middle French *ot (oïr, ouir)*, although still attested in the early 16th century in Jean Lemaire de Belges and Gringore (H), is finally superseded by its alternative form *oit*, analogous rather than phonetic, generalized on *voit*.[43]

(b) Past Participles

Marot's glosses in this category largely reflect the continuing evolution of certain conjugations. This is most marked in the case of past participles of *-IR* and *-RE* verbs where, for a time, usage hesitated between two forms. In every case, Marot's gloss confirms the emergence, and his acceptance, of the form which was to become the dominant one. Thus:

abolus, aboliz (*GT*, p. 53; RH, *T*, 884). We may note in corroboration of Marot's gloss that T and C quote only *aboli* for the past participle of this verb.

absolus, aboliz, absoulz (*GT*, ibid.; RH, *T*, 887). While the first gloss is lexical, the second is morphological. Cf. *absouls* for Latin *absolutus* in T; *absous, absouls* likewise in C, although in the appended *Briefve Directions to learne the French Tongue*, p. 6, we find the alternatives: *j'ay absouls* or *abselu* [sic] for *absolu*.

boulluz, boilliz est le vray françoys (*GT*, ibid.; RH, *T*, 897). Here Marot is more explicitly prescriptive. Although the form in *-u* continues to be attested throughout the 16th century as the examples in H testify, and the coexistence of the two forms is apparent in R. Est, T and C, 17th-century grammarians considered it rare or popular.[44]

(c) Miscellaneous

Again in prescriptive vein, Marot turns his attention to *revencher*:

revencher, revenger est le vray terme (*GT*, p. 20; RH, *T*, 191). What reasons, if any beyond personal conviction, prompted this gloss, we can only speculate. Both *revencher* and *revenger* are well attested throughout the century (*FEW*, *vindicare*; H) and appear side by side in Lanoue's *Dictionnaire des rimes françoises* (1596). Marot's own texts, including a later, non-linguistic gloss in his Villon (*GT*, p. 66), consistently respect his declared preference for *revenger* (*Ep*, XX, 70; *OS*, VI, 225).

5. Government of verbs

Only two glosses appear to fall under this heading. In the first case, against the solemn affirmation represented by the formula

[*foy que doy mon baptesme*], à mon baptesme (*GT*, p. 13; RH, *T*, 42), the gloss makes explicit the indirect nature of the complement *baptesme*. In a note on this line of Villon, Rickard observes of the construction that: "le complément indirect de *doy* variait selon les besoins de la cause—et de la rime."[45] Marot's note repairs the licence.

The second case is more problematic. The line *Qui saulva ce qu'Adam perit* attracts the comment:

perit, pour perdit, mais il ne se peut dire (*GT*, p. 49; RH, *T*, 797). Is Marot objecting to the transitive use of *perir* in the sense indicated? *Perir* transitive, for *faire périr*, is not unknown however according to H. But in an exactly similar context, Calvin used the following construction: ". . . les merites humains . . . lesquelz sont periz en Adam," *Instit.*, VI, 392 (H).

Pronunciation/Versification[46]

1. Vowels

(a) *A/E* before *R*

Marot's commentary offers abundant evidence of the hesitation between *a/e* before *r* in a pronunciation which he, and many others after him, regarded as typically Parisian (Thurot, I, 4 ff.). We list below the pairs of rhyming words followed by the marginal annotations they prompted:

haubert/part: Haubert rymé contre part monstre que Villon estoit de Paris & qu'il prononçoit Haubart & Robart (*PT*, p. 4; RH, *L*, 116-117).

appert/part: Fault dire appart & non appert à l'usaige de Paris (*GT*, p. 40; RH, *T*, 602, 604).

Robert/Lombart: Fault prononcer Robart, & non Robert au dict usaige (*GT*, p. 46; RH, *T*, 750, 752).

terre/serre: Fault prononcer tarre pour terre, & sarre pour serre, à cause du terrouer (*GT*, p. 47; RH, *T*, 762, 764 reads *terre/Barre*).

barre/erre: Ce qui se ryme en erre se doit prononcer en arre, comme dessus (*GT*, p. 55; RH, *T*, 937-38).

Garde/perde: Le Parisien dit parde, & non perde (*GT*, p. 74; RH, *T*, 1354, 1356).

There is no attempt on Marot's part to condemn this pronunciation. He merely records the fact of its existence. It would have been surprising had he done otherwise. Had he not himself exploited this phonetic confusion to make a pun on the name of a Paris diocese, *St. Méry/St. Marry* (*marry* = affligé) as a burlesque euphemism for the prison in which he was held (*Ep.* XI, 5)? Ronsard himself justified such rhymes not on regional or dialectal grounds but on phonetic ones: the two sounds were so close that not to recognize this fact was to demonstrate ignorance of one's own language.[47] Henri Estienne, however, although mindful of Villon's example in this respect, and notwithstanding that he considered him "un des plus éloquens de ce temps-là," was to condemn this pronunciation on the one hand as vulgar and on the other as an aberration perpetrated by the court.[48]

(b) *A/E* before *M*

The two vowels were similarly confused before other consonants, notably *m* (Brunot, *HLF*, II, 251). Hence Marot's observation on the rhyme *dyademe/lame*: Dyademe, fault prononcer diadame à l'antique ou à la Parisienne (*GT*, p. 25; RH, *T*, 298, 300).

2. Diphthongs, etc.

(a) *OI/OA* before *R*

The substitution of *oa* for *oi* before *r* is another feature of Parisian speech to draw comment from Marot. Of the verb *poirre* (see above p. 170), he says: "fault prononcer poarre à la Parisienne" (*GT*, p. 62; RH, *T*, 1100). Noted in 1530 by Palsgrave, this pronunciation was to be roundly condemned by Robert Estienne and Théodore de Bèze, and parodied by Henri Estienne and D'Aubigné among others (Thurot, I, 356; Estienne, *Deux Dialogues*, p. 46, n. 9).

(b) *OE/OEU* before *F*

Noted as archaic rather than Parisian (although as we have seen above the two descriptions are sometimes used as if interchangeable), is the pronunciation of *œf* for *œuf*, to rhyme with *soif*:

soif/œf: Les anciens disoient oef, pour oeuf (*GT*, p. 46; RH, *T*, 731 reads *estuef*).

(c) *OU/OUE* and *QUI/QUIE*

An observation on the Parisian pronunciation of *où* and *qui* is prompted by the rhyme *Culdoue/Prins oue?* Marot notes: "La commune de Paris ne dit ou, ne qui, mais oue & quie" (*GT*, p. 73; RH, *T*, 1338, 1340). Thuasne, normally critical of Marot's commentary, regards this gloss as substantiated by a document published in Du Cange's edition of Joinville (Thuasne, III, 351-52).

3. Final *C*

Marot's observation on the rhyme *comment don?/quelque don* in which *don* for *donq* is seen as explicable, if not excusable, in terms of poetic licence

don, pour donq, par trop grand licence poetique (*GT*, p. 19; RH, *T*, 174)

does not, however, command the same assent, especially as the form *don* is to be found in contemporary prose as well as verse (Thuasne, II, 121). Secondly, and the point is not without interest for a controversy which was to deepen as the 16th century progressed, the gloss suggests that *donq* with full value given to the final consonant was either the norm, or the preferred pronunciation, in Marot's view. A statement from Henri Estienne in 1565 puts the position in reverse: "*Don*, pour lequel on escrit *donc*."[49] At the close of the century Tabourot des Accords's acceptance of *don* as a poetic convenience is opposed by Lanoue (Thurot, II, 126-33; Brunot, *HLF*, II, 269).

Overall, there is little in Marot's linguistic commentary on Villon which would support the adverse judgments which have been passed upon it, and certainly not the categorical "presque toujours erroné quand il n'est pas insignifiant" of Thuasne. Against the infrequent *contresens*, and the ignorance of morphology, instructive in its own right, must be set the undoubted value of Marot's commentary to lexicographers and linguistic historians for new items or corroborative evidence. How different in this respect from the "commentary" to another medieval text which Marot is alleged to have edited, and which had been published only seven years previously, namely the *Roman de la Rose* (1526). The marginal annotations to this text, little more than summary analyses of narrative and moral content, are totally devoid of philological comment and interest.[50] This disparity in the conceptions and execution of two commentaries supposedly by the same editor is all the more striking since the texts in question, the modernized *Rose* and the Marot-Villon, offer countless items of identical lexical and morphological interest, glossed in the one and not in the other, although the declared editorial policy in each case was to make the text more comprehensible to a 16th-century readership.[51] Thus, to take a few examples culled at random (the list could without difficulty be extended), although the words *engigner, eschever, greigneur, ledanger, mau, mauffé, merir, moulier, remanant, senez* are glossed in the Marot-Villon as archaic and difficult to understand, in the alleged Marot version of the *Rose* (ed. Baridon, vv. 3939, 7202; 4363, 6829, 16222, 16321; 5936; 3128, 3584, 3675, 5916, 7123, 7197, 7404; 7530; 6523; 5244; 4697; 1578, 3424, 5195; 7846 respectively) they apparently present no problem to comprehension at all; similarly, the gratuitous use of flexional *s* (ibid., v. 3039) and a rhyme in Villon regarded as excessively lax (ibid., *ce don/dictes-le don*, vv. 3405, 3406) pass unremarked. If we have stressed this disparity, it is because it has so far, regrettably, found no place in any discussion of the attribution to Marot of the 1526 *Roman de la Rose*.[52] Taken in conjunction with the absence of any claim whatsoever by Marot himself to have edited this text, an absence never more conspicuous than in the potentially apposite preface to the Villon edition, and the lack, on all but one[53] of many possible occasions, of what might otherwise be described as retrospective cross-references by Marot to the language and poetics of the *Rose* in the Villon marginalia, it is a disparity which must surely make less, rather than more, plausible, the case for Marot's editorship of this text.

If Marot's Villon then fails to corroborate the attribution to him of the modernized *Rose*, it does, however, corroborate certain tendencies within his own poetic *œuvre*. For, while there is no integral *doctrine de Marot* as such, he shows a willingness in his editorial capacity, as well as in some of his poetic pronouncements, to assume the role of *chef d'école* in matters of language, as elsewhere in matters literary. It is precisely as an arbiter of usage and a custodian of correctness that Marot's memory is cherished and his words quoted by Henri Estienne in his campaign against the "gastefrançois" of later years, whether they be Pléiade poets or the linguistically corrupt at the court of Henri III.

Marot's claim in his editorial remarks that Villon's language lacked the polish which the court of kings and princes would have conferred (sig. Aiiij[v]) is prompted no doubt by his own experience, recounted in *L'Enfer* (*OS*, I, 402-404) and enshrined in subsequent metaphorial tributes to the court as his "maistresse d'escolle" (*Ep*, XLV, 34) and, a recurrent motif, the "Lyme et rabot des hommes mal polys" (*OL*, LXXVIII, 38). In identifying the French of the court of François Ier as the model of usage and refinement, Marot was propagating a view endorsed by numerous contemporaries, including Tory in his *Champ Fleury* (sig. Bi[v]) and repeated enthusiastically in subsequent decades by writers unwilling in the main to accord the same authority to later French courts. Of these writers Henri Estienne is not unrepresentative: "la cour a eu cest honneur autrefois (et principalement au temps de ce tant admirable roy François premier) de donner loy à la France universelle touchant le bon langage" (*Deux Dialogues*, p. 119).[54]

On matters of lexis, there is again convergence between Marot the editor and Marot the poet. The preference for words "receuz communement," although expressed in advice given not later than 1527 to another (unidentified) poet in the context of the *rondeau* (*OD*, I, 10), underlies both precept and practice in later years. It may explain that, while respecting Villon's archaic language sufficiently to reproduce it, Marot does not recommend to young poets that they should imitate it, any more than Villon's irregular prosody: ". . . & ne suys d'advis que en cela les jeunes poetes l'ensuyvent" (sig. Aiiij[v]); and further that Marot himself did not consciously affect archaisms except where their use was stylistically appropriate to an older person or remoter period, thereby anticipating in his practice a concept later formulated by Peletier du Mans.[55] Marot's modest stricture on Villon's use of the word *sume* in the sense of *preigne* as "trop tiré du latin" (see above, p. 170) may be seen in the same light. It is a muted echo of the chorus of concern led by Tory in his *Champ Fleury* (Aux lecteurs) against heavily Latinized French, and explains the efforts made by Marot in his maturity to expunge such excesses from the texts of his youth.[56] Much amplified, the echo returns in the abuse and counter abuse exchanged with his enemy Sagon.[57] On the other hand, Villon's two brief excursions into English and Italian (?) (see above, p. 179) provoke no adverse comment from Marot, unless the very existence of a gloss implies one. Marot did not exclude foreign borrowings from his own verse where they are used with apparent restraint, considerable skill and often specific intent. Skill, in the pivotal pun on the words *Angloys/creancier* and *bye, bye/baille, baille* in the *rondeau A ung creancier* (*OD*, II, 3-4); specific intent in the use of Italianisms with pejorative force (*Ep*, XLV, 58; *OL*, LXXVI, 57) in a manner later to be approved, with biting satire, by Henri Estienne (*Deux Dialogues*, p. 93). The critical faculty exercised by Marot on Villon's use of language was turned to positive account in defense of his own. Challenged by no less a person than Jacques Colin, *lecteur du roi*,[58] that the word *viser* was not "bon langage" and would be better replaced by *regarder*, Marot had no difficulty in justifying his choice of *viser* by reference to both its literal and figurative applications (*E*, XLV).

In his poetry Marot evinced as much concern at the linguistic *incongruités* of his contemporaries as at those of Villon. In fact, the occasional infringement ascribed by Marot to Villon in the matter of past participles (see above, p. 181) is minor indeed when compared to the degree of confusion which commonly prevailed in Marot's day in the conjugation of French verbs, even among the highest in the realm (the king himself, as his correspondence reveals, was not immune from it, in spite of tributes paid to him and his court as the ultimate linguistic authority in the land!).[59] As if to second an earlier attack from Tory on such barbarisms (*Champ Fleury*, sig. Biij^v), Marot administered this poetic rebuke to his readership: "Je dy qu'il n'est poinct question / De dire j'allion, j'estion; / Ny se renda, ny je frappy / Tesmoing le Conte de Carpy" (*OS*, VIII, 155-58), which was later quoted with evident approval by Henri Estienne (*Deux Dialogues*, p. 45; p. 164). Confusion was not limited, however, to the plural and singular endings of the preterite tense. "Ce vilain mot de concluer" (*OS*, VI, 63) allegedly used by Sagon, no doubt in mistake for *conclure*, is further evidence that verbs were liable to be assigned to the wrong conjugation.

Doubtless, though, Marot's most positive contribution to the ordering of the French language, and the one for which he is best remembered, is his formulation in an epigram *A ses disciples* of the rule of the agreement of the preceding direct object with a past participle conjugated with *avoir* (*E*, LXXVI). Although the tendency for this to happen had been noted by Palsgrave in 1530, Marot was the first, in 1538, to formulate a rule which usage, if not all grammarians, found elegant, and which gained increasing acceptance as the century progressed.[60]

By reconciling the claims of current usage, the virtues of correctness, and the need for rules, Marot displayed a sense of what was fitting to the language of his day. Despite their polemical context, Estienne's words: "Marot . . . ne desplaise à messieurs les poetes de la Pleïade, congnoissét bien le naturel de la langue francese" (*Deux Dialogues*, p. 340) are an apt and deserved tribute.

NOTES

1. See P. Villey, "Tableau chronologique des publications de Marot," *Revue du Seizième Siècle*, 7 (1920), 46-97 and 206-34; 8 (1921), 80-110 and 157-211; also published in book form (Paris: Champion, 1921); *Recherches sur la chronologie des œuvres de Marot* (Paris: Leclerc, 1921) and in *Bulletin du Bibliophile* (1920-1923); *Les Grands Ecrivains du seizième siècle, Marot et Rabelais*, Bibliothèque Littéraire de la Renaissance, Nouv. Série, 11 (Paris: Champion, 1923) for the major part of this scholar's contribution to Marot studies.

2. Passing reference is made by R. Griffin, *Clément Marot and the Inflections of Poetic Voice* (Berkeley: Univ. of California Press, 1974), pp. 193 ff.; P. Rickard, *La Langue française au XVIe siècle* (Cambridge: Cambridge Univ. Press, 1968), pp. 95-96 and 278-79, reproduces and annotates Marot's epigram "A ses disciples" on the agreement of the past participle. See also S.G. Nichols, Jr., "Marot, Villon and the *Roman de la Rose*. A Study in the Language of Creation and Recreation," *Studies in Philology*, 63 (1966), pp. 140 ff.

3. *Les Oeuvres de Françoys Villon de Paris, reveues & remises en leur entier par Clement Marot, valet de chambre du Roy* (Paris: Galiot du Pré, 1533). All subsequent references will be to this edition.

4. Geofroy Tory, *Champ Fleury* (Paris: Geofroy Tory and Gilles Gourmont, 1529). There have been two modern reproductions of this edition, the first with introduction, notes, index and glossary by G. Cohen (Paris: Ch. Bosse, 1931), the second with a brief foreword and bibliography by J. Jolliffe in the series French Renaissance Classics (East Ardsley, Yorkshire: S.R. Publishers; New York: Johnson Reprint Corporation; Paris-The Hague: Mouton, 1970). We quote from this last. On Tory see A. Bernard, *Geofroy Tory, peintre et graveur, premier imprimeur royal* (Paris: Tross, 1857; 2nd ed. 1865); G. Cohen, "Un Grand Imprimeur humaniste au XVIe siècle. Geofroy Tory de Bourges et son *Champ Fleury*," *Annales de l'Université de Paris*, 7 (1932), 209-22; finally, as a self-styled corrective to the two items above,

B. Bowen, "Geofroy Tory's *Champ Fleury* and Its Major Sources," *Studies in Philology*, 76 (1979), 13-27. For parallels, briefly touched upon, between Tory and Marot, see A. François, "Une Préfiguration de la langue classique au XVIe siècle," in *Mélanges Abel Lefranc* (Paris: Droz, 1936), pp. 91-100; S.G. Nichols, art. cit., p. 140; G. Cohen, *Champ Fleury*, ed. cit., *Notes*, p. 3.

     5. G. Castor, *Pléiade Poetics* (Cambridge: Cambridge Univ. Press, 1964), p. 8. The countervailing view is that of I. Silver, *Ronsard's General Theory of Poetry*, vol. II of *The Intellectual Evolution of Ronsard* (St. Louis: Washington Univ. Press, 1973), p. 49, n. 78.

     6. On Estienne see L. Clément, *Henri Estienne et son œuvre française* (Paris: Picard, 1899).

     7. For details of these editions see C.A. Mayer, *Bibliographie des œuvres de Clément Marot. II. Editions*, Travaux d'Humanisme et Renaissance, 13 (Geneva: Droz, 1954), Nos. 9, 11, 12, 14 (hereinafter abbreviated to *Bibliographie*, II and item number).

     8. A complaint Marot was to make on no fewer than three occasions: in the preface to the first edition of *L'Adolescence Clementine*, he speaks of "le desplaisir que j'ay eu d'en ouyr cryer & publier par les rues une grande partie [de ses œuvres], toute incorrecte, mal imprimée, & plus au proffit du Libraire qu'à l'honneur de l'Autheur." C.A. Mayer, *Clément Marot* (Paris: Nizet, 1972), p. 230. On the poet's return from his first exile, the danger to his own person is a consideration which weighs still more heavily with him as we see from the prefatory prose letter to Dolet in *Oeuvres* (Lyons: Dolet, 1538) and that which he addressed to "ceulx qui par cy devant ont imprimé ses œuvres" in the almost contemporaneous *Oeuvres* (Lyons: S. Gryphius, n.d. [1538]). Both these texts are discussed and quoted in full by Mayer, ibid., pp. 423-27.

     9. *Bibliographie*, II, No. 14: "Avec certains Accens notez, Cest assavoir sur le e Masculin different du Feminim. Sur les dictions joinctes ensemble par sinalephes, Et soubz le c quant il tient de la prononciation de le s. Ce qui par cy devant par faulte dadvis, n'a este faict au langaige françoys, combien q'uil y fust & soyt tres-necessaire." On the reforms introduced by Tory in this edition see N. Catach, *L'Orthographe française à l'époque de la Renaissance*, Publications Romanes et Françaises, 101 (Geneva: Droz, 1968), pp. 44-47. However, there is no documentary evidence whatsoever to support the highly suppositious assertion made later in the book: "Aux alentours du 7 juin 1533, Tory, ayant convaincu Marot de ses propres idées orthotypographiques . . . ," p. 57. There is equally no hard evidence to support the thesis canvassed on pp. 53-60, of Marot's participation in the anonymous *Briefve Doctrine pour deuement escripre selon la propriete du langaige* (Paris: A. Augereau, 1533).

     10. The accents in this quotation have been added according to the customary rules for the transcription of non-bibliographical material. In keeping with Tory's statement, there are *no* accents in his text.

     11. This point has been made by Mayer, *Clément Marot*, p. 167. See also I.D. McFarlane, "Clément Marot and the World of Neo-Latin Poetry," above.

     12. *L'Adolescence Clementine*, 12 August 1532. Quoted from P. Villey, "Tableau chronologique des publications de Marot," *Revue du Seizième Siècle*, 7 (1920), 59.

     13. Cohen, in the introduction to his edition of *Champ Fleury*, fo. XVII, identifies this work as the *Livre des Eschecqtz* (Paris: Vérard, 1507). In the notes, however, he refers to "*Le Jeu des Eschez moralisé*, achevé d'imprimer le 6 septembre

1504 à Paris pour A. Vérard" (p. 3), a French translation by Jean de Vignay of the *Libellus de Ludo Schaccorum* by Jac. Cessoli (1476).

14. On Jeanne Gaillarde see Marot, *OD*, p. 85, n. 1.

15. Such a list would include, among others, the commentaries of Barthélemy Aneau on Du Bellay, the unpublished marginalia of Henri Estienne on the same poet (see L. Clément, *Henri Estienne*, op. cit., pp. 153-62), of Muret, Belleau and Jean Martin on Ronsard, and of Malherbe on Desportes. But in every case contemporary, or near contemporary authors were involved and the emphasis of the commentator was slightly different.

16. L. Thuasne, *François Villon. Oeuvres*, édition critique avec notices et glossaire, 3 vols. (Paris: Picard, 1923), III, 421.

17. Madeleine Lazard, "Clément Marot éditeur et lecteur de Villon," *Cahiers de l'Association Internationale des Etudes Françaises*, No. 32 (1980), 7-20 and particularly p. 18.

18. Mayer, *Clément Marot*, p. 239, n. 256.

19. Interested readers will find the complete text of Marot's glosses reproduced by two 18th-century editors of Villon: Urbain Coustelier (1723) and Adrien Moetjens (1742).

20. On this point see the excellent review article by M. Speer, "The Editorial Tradition of Villon's *Testament*: From Marot to Rychner and Henry," *Romance Philology*, 31 (1977), 346: "A thorough study of Marot's editorial practices has yet to be done, and the question of his sources remains open."

21. On the problems associated with the discussion and definition of archaism see Paul Zumthor, "Introduction aux problèmes de l'archaïsme," *Cahiers de l'Association Internationale des Etudes Françaises*, No. 19 (1967), 11-26.

22. Cf. Jean Lemaire de Belges, *Illustrations de Gaule et singularitez de Troye*, I, xxi: "en esmouvant ses freres et compaignons ou à aller cueillir les houx piquans en la forest . . . Aucunesfois luy et eux grimpoient sur les hauts arbres pour desnicher les pies, les chauuettes, les jays et les coquus" and Marot, Eglogue III, 29-32: "O quantes fois aux arbres grimpé j'ay / Pour desnicher ou la pie ou le geay, / Ou pour gecter des fruitz ja meurs & beaulx / A mes compaings, qui tendoient leurs chappeaulx" (*OL*, p. 344 and n. 1, pp. 344-45).

23. On this point see L. Terreaux, *Ronsard correcteur de ses œuvres*, Publications Romanes et Françaises, 102 (Geneva: Droz, 1968), p. 268.

24. See Jean Rychner et Albert Henry, eds, *Le Testament Villon, I, Texte*, Textes Littéraires Français, 207 (Geneva: Droz, 1974), pp. 48-49 and, *II, Commentaire*, Textes Littéraires Français, 208 (Geneva: Droz, 1974), p. 59. See above, p. 179.

25. Henri Estienne, *La Precellence du langage françois*, ed. E. Huguet (Paris: A. Colin, 1896), pp. 208-209.

26. See Henri Estienne, *Deux Dialogues du nouveau langage françois*, ed. P.M. Smith (Geneva: Slatkine, 1980), p. 233 and n. 682.

27. See p. 165. The relationship between *literary* history and value judgments was studied by C.A. Mayer, "Clément Marot and Literary History," in *Essays in French Literature Presented to H.W. Lawton*, ed. J.C. Ireson, I.D. McFarlane and G. Rees (Manchester: Manchester Univ. Press, 1968), pp. 247-60. Less attention has been devoted to the relationship between linguistic history and literary judgments. C. Camproux, however, has shown how failure sufficiently to appreciate and to take into account linguistic changes can lead to distortions in literary history and critical judgment in an interesting article on "Langue et métrique: à propos du décasyllabe des *Epîtres* de Marot," *Le Français Moderne*, 32 (1964), 194-205.

28. Cotgrave translates the term thus: "Incongruitie; unfitnesse, illfavourednesse; absurditie, irregularitie."

29. The following abbreviations will be used. 1, *Texts*: Marot's Villon, ed. cit., *PT* (*Petit Testament*); *GT* (*Grant Testament*); *AO* (*Autres Oeuvres*); Rychner and Henry, RH, *T* (*Le Testament Villon*, ed. cit.); *Com, T* (*Commentaire*, ed. cit.); *L*, *PV* (*Le Lais* suivi des *Poèmes variés*, Textes Littéraires Français, 239, Geneva: Droz, 1977); *Com, L* or *PV* (*Commentaire*, Textes Littéraires Français, 240, Geneva: Droz, 1977). 2, *Dictionaries and glossaries, etc.*: R. Est (Robert Estienne, *Dictionnaire françois-latin*, Paris, 1549); T (Thierry, *Dictionnaire françois-latin*, Paris, 1572); C (Cotgrave, *A Dictionarie of the French and English Tongues*, London, 1611); G (Godefroy, *Dictionnaire de l'ancienne langue française*, Paris, 1881-1902); H (Huguet, *Dictionnaire de la langue française du seizième siècle*, Paris, 1925-1967); *FEW* (Wartburg, W. von, *Französisches Etymologisches Wörterbuch*, Tübingen and Basle, 1948-75); B-Wart (Bloch, O., and Wartburg, W. von, *Dictionnaire étymologique de la langue française*, Paris, 1968); Burger (Burger, A., *Lexique complet de la langue de Villon*, 2nd ed., Publications Romanes et Françaises, 127, Geneva: Droz, 1974); M.-L (Marty-Laveaux, Ch., *La Langue de la Pléiade*, Paris, 1896-1898); *HLF* (Brunot, F., *Histoire de la langue française*, vols. 1 and 2, reprinted Paris, 1966-1967).

30. *L'Art poëtique de Jacques Peletier du Mans (1555)*, ed. A. Boulanger (Paris: Les Belles Lettres, 1930), pp. 121-22.

31. Ronsard, *Oeuvres complètes*, ed. P. Laumonier, completed by R. Lebègue and I. Silver, 20 vols. (Paris: STFM, 1914-1975), XV, 241, 175 quoted in I. Silver, *Ronsard's General Theory of Poetry*, p. 103.

32. Claude de Seyssel, *La Monarchie de France et deux autres fragments politiques*, ed. J. Poujol (Paris: Librairie d'Argences, 1961), ch. 2, pp. 131-32, n. 10 and n. 5 respectively.

33. R. Macé, *Voyage de Charles Quint par la France*, ed. G. Raynaud (Paris, 1879), v. 1156 quoted by Terreaux, *Ronsard correcteur*, p. 98.

34. M. Scève, *Délie*, ed. I.D. McFarlane (Cambridge: Cambridge Univ. Press, 1966), p. 52.

35. Estienne Pasquier, *Recherches de la France* in *Oeuvres* (Amsterdam, 1723), I, VIII, 762-63.

36. See H. Naïs, *Les Animaux dans la poésie française de la Renaissance* (Paris: Didier, 1961), p. 242.

37. See Ch. Thurot, *Histoire de la prononciation française*, 2 vols. (Paris: Imprimerie Nationale, 1881-1882), I, 374-76.

38. Martial d'Auvergne, *Arrêts d'Amour*, ed. Rychner (Paris: SATF, 1951), V, 94; XLIII, 15 (and glossary). On the popularity of this text in the Renaissance see I.D. McFarlane, *A Literary History of France: Renaissance France (1470-1589)* (London and Tonbridge: Ernest Benn Ltd, 1974), p. 236.

39. A. Chartier, *Le Quadrilogue invectif*, ed. Droz (Paris: Champion, 1923), p. 40.

40. R. Gaguin, *Le Passetemps d'oysiveté* quoted by Thuasne, III, 421.

41. On this point see P. Rickard, "The Rivalry of *m(a), t)a), s(a)*, and *mon, ton, son* before Feminine Nouns in Old and Middle French," *Archivum Linguisticum*, 11 (1959), 21-47, 114-47.

42. T. Sebillet, *Art poétique françoys*, ed. F. Gaiffe (Paris: STFM, 1910), p. 57.

43. See P. Fouché, *Le Verbe français. Etude morphologique*, Publications de

la Faculté des Lettres de l'Université de Strasbourg, Fasc. 56 (Paris: Les Belles Lettres, 1931), p. 363.

44. P. Fouché, ibid., p. 86.

45. P. Rickard, *Chrestomathie de la langue française au quinzième siècle* (Cambridge: Cambridge Univ. Press, 1976), p. 336.

46. We shall confine our remarks to rhyme. Marot's glosses on syllable count, in which factors other than pronunciation alone are involved, are few in number and offer little of specific interest to the present enquiry. Some indeed are problematic and the precise cases at issue are the subject of continuing debate among scholars.

47. Ronsard, ed. cit., I, 54.

48. Henri Estienne, *Apologie pour Herodote*, ed. P. Ristelhuber, 2 vols. (Paris: Liseux, 1879), II, 135-36; *Deux Dialogues*, ed. Smith, p. 47, n. 10; pp. 404-405, n. 407; pp. 420-21; *Hypomneses de gallica lingua* (Geneva, 1582), p. 10.

49. Henri Estienne, *Traicté de la conformité du langage françois avec le grec*, ed. L. Feugère (Paris: Delalain, 1853), p. 157.

50. *Cy est le Rommant de la Roze* (Paris: Galliot du Pré, n.d.). Privilege dated 1526. The marginal annotations to which we refer are unique to the Marot version so-called. See F. Bourdillon, *The Early Editions of the Roman de la Rose* (London, 1906; rpt. Geneva: Slatkine, 1974), pp. 57-64.

51. Guillaume de Lorris, *Le Roman de la Rose. Dans la version attribuée à Clément Marot*, ed. S.F. Baridon, 2 vols., Testi e Documenti di Letteratura Moderna, 1 (Milan: Istituto Editoriale Cisalpino, 1954), p. 89. The editor's intention was "pour laquelle chose restituer en meilleur estat et plus expédiente forme pour l'intelligence des lecteurs et auditeurs" at the instigation of Galiot du Pré "qui nouvellement l'a faict imprimer apres avoir veu sa correction tant du mauvais et trop ancien langaige sentant son invétéré commencement et origine de parler." For Marot's policy in this regard in his Villon, see discussion above.

52. The arguments for and against the case for Marot's editorship, which is based partly on the request for a *privilège d'imprimer* made by Galiot du Pré in 1533 in which he specifically names Marot as editor, and partly on the authority of Estienne Pasquier, are summarized and evaluated by Baridon in the introduction to his edition, pp. 56-80.

53. Marot-Villon: "Il faict eage trissilabe comme Peage, si faict le Romant de la Rose" (*GT*, p. 12; RH, *T*, 1).

54. The same sentiments are expressed by Du Bellay, *Deffense*, I, IV. For further opinions on the subject see Henri Estienne, *Deux Dialogues*, ed. Smith, p. 79, n. 80.

55. For Marot's practice with regard to archaisms see R. Griffin, *Clément Marot*, p. 194 (examples from *Ep*, XIII, XVII; *OL*, I). But more work is needed on Marot's language: very little has yet been done. Peletier formulates his proposal for conscious archaisms in his *Art poëtique*, ed. Boulanger, pp. 121-22: "Il nø søra defandù dø ramøner quelquefoøs les moz anciens . . . E principalømen søront bien apliquèz, quand nous føron parler quelquø pørsonnage du vieus tans Françoøs."

56. An analysis of the variants of *Le Temple de Cupido* is particularly instructive in this context (*OL*, I). See P.M. Smith, *Clément Marot, Poet of the French Renaissance* (London: The Athlone Press, 1970), p. 70.

57. For the relevant parts of this polemic see Brunot, *HLF*, II, 224.

58. See V.-L. Bourrilly, *Jacques Colin, abbé de Saint-Ambroise (14 ?-1547)*. *Contribution à l'histoire de l'humanisme sous le règne de François Ier*, Bibliothèque

d'Histoire Moderne, vol. I, fasc. 5 (Paris: Société Nouvelle de Librairie et d'Edition, 1905), ch. 2 in particular. A Latin source speaks of Colin's expertise in language matters, and describes him as "in lingua populari mirabiliter facundo" (Sleidan, quoted by Bourrilly, p. 41, n. 1).

59. See F. Génin, *Lettres de Marguerite d'Angoulême* (Paris, 1841), I, 467.

60. See P. Rickard, *La Langue française au seizième siècle*, pp. 278-79.

Lionello Sozzi

Come ride il mercante. Astuzia premiata e ignoranza punita nei racconti di Philippe de Vigneulles

La "forma semplice," lo schema narrativo che consiste nel ribaltare una situazione iniziale iniqua e nel premiare l'attesa dell'eroe diseredato, la cui astuzia è data come vincente, costituisce, dice Jolles, una costante, ovunque riscontrabile nella narrativa popolare.[1] Nel racconto francese, esclusi i *fabliaux* che probabilmente si rivolgono, secondo quanto ha scritto Nykrog correggendo Bédier, ad un pubblico cortese e feudale, quella "forma" riaffiora in quasi tutte le raccolte, si tratti degli *exempla* di Jacques de Vitry o di Etienne de Bourbon, o dei *Contes moralizés* di Bozon, o della raccolta di Sens, o delle *Cent Nouvelles Nouvelles*, le quali per altro alternano a schemi popolari strutture più complesse di forte ispirazione umanistica; la *forme simple* troverà poi nelle novelle di Nicolas de Troyes la sua formulazione forse più limpida e convincente.[2]

E' naturale, quindi, che anche un autore come Philippe de Vigneulles, di estrazione popolare ma giunto, per tenace sforzo, a far parte della borghesia alsaziana più facoltosa grazie alla sua attività di *chaussetier* e di avveduto mercante, sia indotto si direbbe per acritica consuetudine a dar spazio nelle sue *Cent Nouvelles Nouvelles*, redatte tra il 1505 e il 1515, allo schema della *morale naïve* che premia lo sprovveduto e l'ingenuo, ai danni dell'astuto prevaricatore.[3]

Il racconto del prete e della mucca (VIII) sembra avviato inizialmente sul binario della satira dell'ignoranza: un *pauvre bon simple homme* dà ascolta in chiese alla predica del prete il quale assicura che ai parrocchiani che gli daranno *aumosne* verrà dispensato *double des biens* da Dio misericordioso. L'effetto comico è assicurato dall' artificio che Plattard chiamava

"réalisation de la métaphore": il pover'uomo crede infatti che il prete
abbia alluso a beni terreni anzichè a beni spirituali, e collabora quindi a
quel fraintendimento della massima evangelica del *centuplum accipies*
(Matteo, XIX, 29) che già era presente, ci ricorda Livingston, in un noto
fabliau di Bodel, negli *exempla* di Etienne de Bourbon e di John Bromyard,
in Boccaccio ed in Poggio, prima di esser ripreso da Rabelais.[4] E' una
comicità, quindi, nello stesse tempo di degradazione (una massima alta-
mente spirituale è intesa in un senso grossolanamente materiale) e di auto-
matismo (mette in risalto, cioè, il torpido meccanismo mentale di uno
sprovveduto). Tale intento però è nettamente sopravanzato da quello che
consiste nel render nota e nel punire l'ingordigia, l'ipocrisia e la malizia
di un esponente del clero. Così il congegno si capovolge: del *bon homme* si
finisce col mettere in luce non la pochezza ma, in un primo tempo, la fidu-
cia in Dio, la pazienza nei confronti della moglie iraconda, la disposizione
bonaria all'attesa (ceduta al prete la sua mucca, spera di vederne arrivare
due):

> Et le povre homme avec sa femme atandoient tousjours . . . Mais tant atendirent
> qu'ils en avoient perdu toutes esperances; et s'en prenoit la femme à son maryt, disant
> qu'il estoit bien fol d'avoir donné leur vaiche au curé . . . Mais le bon homme la
> reconfortoit au mieulx qu'il pouvoit et luy disoit: "Ne te chaille, non, ma femme,
> encor Dieu nous aidera. Or atendons, belle dame . . .

Poi, in secondo tempo, la pazienza diventa astuzia, capacità di giocare la
cupidigia ed i piani vendicativi del prete antagonista, grazie al ricorso a un
adjuvant rappresentato dallo stesso figlioletto che il prete intendeva uti-
lizzare a suo danno. Chiamato, infatti, l'*enfant* sul pulpito perchè confessi
pubblicamente il furto della mucca (furto involontario, del resto, poichè
il contadino, in buona fede, ha finalmente accolto nella sua stalla la mucca
che aveva data in elemosina, accompagnata da quella del prete, che ha
seguìto la prima e di cui lui ignora il proprietario), l'*enfant*, avvedutamente
preparato dal padre, dirà dal pulpito non la verità che il prete ha annun-
ciato ("tout vray et aussi vray comme l'Evangille") ma un'altra che concerne la sua lussaria. Per evitare la *fureur du peuple*, il prete dovrà fuggire
e così, alla fine, l'equità compromessa sarà ristabilita. Lo schema usuale
del *trompeur trompé* si carica, con ogni evidenza, di connotazioni sociali:
il diseredato ribalta una situazione di svantaggio e mette in difficoltà chi
approfittava dontro di lui del suo privilegio. Il rovesciamento è nelle stesse
scelte lessicali: se il prete ha escogitato un piano di vendetta (*se advisa d'un
bon tour*), la stessa formula si trasferisce successivamente sul suo avversario;
se prima *marry et encor plus esbahis* è il *pauvre homme* di cui Philippe
sottolinea anche la sbigottita imperizia (*et ne sçavoit comment qu'il en
deust faire*), successivamente lo stesso termine *esbahis* definisce lo smarri-

mento del prete. Direi che lo stesso riferimento evangelico, inizialmente utilizzato per evidenziare il torpore mentale dell'ignorante, assume infine un significato del tutto opposto: la verità che l'*enfant* dirà dal pulpito sarà *aussi vray comme l'Evangille* ma questa volta il testo sacro avrà la funzione di evidenziare l'ipocrisia e le magagne del sacerdote. Nella tradizione medievale, lo sviluppo della diffusissima trama si fermava all'arrivo delle due mucche: l'avarizia del prete era già punita da questo esito non previsto e certo non preordinato da un "eroe" di cui si sottolineava la sprovvedutezza e la cui vittoria, aveva detto Bodel, era solo il frutto della buona fortuna (*Par grant eür*).[5] In Boccaccio, è con piena lucidità che il protagonista, beffato da un prete, utilizza la massima del *centuplum accipies* per smascherare le "pestilenziose avarizie de' chierici" (*Decameron*, I, 6). In Rabelais, come già (in parte) in Nicolas de Troyes, la massima è deliberamente utilizzata per realizzare una spregiudicata e ridanciana *escroquerie*: non un intento di denuncia, ma solo il piacere di compiere un gesto truffaldino e dissacrante è all'origine del comportamento di Panurge (*Pantagruel*, XVII). Philippe si pone a mezza strada fra la tradizione e Boccaccio, segue la prima sino all'episodio del ritorno delle mucche, poi sovrappone a quell' implicita vendetta un' iterazione di più esplicito sapore polemico e di più aspro respiro conflittuale. Traccia un percorso, cioè, che va dai confini dell' ingenuità a quelli dell'astuzia disincantata, dalla passività sprovveduta all'attivo e lucido attacco, da Bodel, si potrebbe dire, a Boccaccio.

Nella novella XXXI, il personaggio-vittima, *ung homme lequel n'estoit mie fort riche*, viene definito anch'egli, ripetutamente, *pouvre homme*. Angustiato per la scomparsa di un suo unico bene e *reconfort*, una capra che un lupo ha divorata, si trovo nella tipica situazione iniziale di privazione:

> laquelle [chievre] estoit tout son reconfort pour aidier à nourir ses petis enfans . . . Il advint que . . . le loup vint qui estrangla la chievre de ce pouvre homme, dont il en fut fort mal content, comme chascun peut penser, car c'estoit tout son bien et son reconfort.

Alla privazione si aggiunge l'esoso tranello teso all'eroe da un vicino *plus riche que lui*, un personaggio che con tipica esplicitazione è definito come *cault et malicieux*, dotato di *fallace et malengin*: rimasto anch'egli privo di una mucca, anch'essa divorata da un lupo, pretende un rimborso dal *pouvre homme* sol perchè questi, un giorno, all'osteria, ascoltando il racconto del ricco, ha esclamato, inavvertitamente, e dinanzi a tutti: "c'est mon loup!" La privazione, aggiunta al sopruso, si traduce nello stato già noto di sgomento e disarmato stupore (*fut si espoventez . . . et le pouvre homme demeura avec les autres bien esbahis*), di abbandono (*mais nulz ne luy donnoit conseil*), di impotenza (*il ne savoit que repondre . . . il ne luy sçavoit donner aultre responce . . . le pouvre homme ne savoit sur ce que respondre*). Si inseriscono a questo punto le funzioni "allontanamento" (*si s'en alla le pouvre homme*) e "intervento del protettore": nella fattispecie, il *bon defenseur* è Jean Gerard, sindaco di Vigneulles, il quale assume l'impegno di resolvere la difficile situazione, liberando l'eroe dall'ambascia che non gli dà pace e pronunziando la tipica frase che traduce la funzione protettiva e che, in contesti analoghi, diventa quasi rituale: *Mon amy, ne te soucie de rien*. Escogiterà, quindi, lo stratagemma che consentirà una "comicità d'inversione" e l'affermarsi della *morale naïve*: chiamato a dirimere il conflitto, fingerà di ammettere che il brav'uomo debba restituire la mucca divorata dal *suo* lupo, ma in cambio esigerà che il ricco restituisca il lupo da lui, per sua stessa confessione, inseguito fino ai limiti del bosco. Lo sgomento e l'impotenza si trasferiranno allora all'antagonista: *Le riche fut bien esbahi et ne sçavoit que respondre*. Se il tranello teso alla vittima era stato possibile sfruttando l'uso anomalo e pleonastico (tipico per altro della lingua francese) dell' aggettivo possessivo ("*mon* loup"), la punizione del sopruso si opera utilizzando, a suo danno, le parole stesse dell'antagonista: un tipo di soluzione e rovesciamento che ricorda, da un lato, la storiella del profumo dell' arrosto pagato a suon di monete, dall'altro la rivalsa su Shylock, in *The Merchant of Venice*.

In altre novelle si sviluppa un'interessante duplicità: avviate su temi scontati, esse si risolvono nel rovesciamento del tutto insolito di norme etiche correnti o gettano su di esse, per lo meno, i bagliori fluttuanti di un' ambiguità. Nella novella XLV, apparentemente siamo in presenza di un caso tipico di narrativa misogina: in assenza del marito, ricco mercante sempre in giro per i suoi affari, la moglie, definita con scontate antifrasi (*bonne femme, preude femme*) o con gustose similitudini (*chaude comme une caille; aussi lealle qu'ung Lombard*), lo tradisce ripetutamente e allegramente. Il consueto binomio, quindi, marito mercante/moglie infedele (cfr. la prima facezia di Poggio), sfruttato, si direbbe, per dimostrare "la finesse et la malice des femmes." In realtà, il racconto segue poi un percorso insolito: invitata dal prete a cui ha confessato le sue colpe a rivelarle al marito, e soprattutto a dirgli che uno dei figli non è suo ma è *avoultre* e *bastard*, la donna riesce a fare al marito una sorta di confessione, ma formulata in modo tale (ha picchiato il bambino in modo da farlo piangere, poi ha invitato il marito a nascondersi dietro la porta e a fingere l'ululato del lupo, in modo da potergli dire: "Allés, allés! mauvais loup . . . tu ne l'auras pas, car ce n'est pas à toy l'enfant," da non far nascere in lui alcun sospetto. Il prete, ligio alle norme, aveva invitato la donna all'*aveu* per evitare che l'*enfant qui est bastard* fosse nutrito, calzato e vestito da chi non era suo padre, e soprattutto perchè venisse diseredato, perchè non accadesse cioè che "possedera ses biens aussi biens comme les leaulx enfans." Il comportamento della donna mira così, più che a nascondere la sua colpa, ad assicurare al *bastard* una confortevole condizione futura, e la novella si configura, così, come scrittura narrativa tra le piè tipiche se è vero, come vuole Marthe Robert, che ogni racconto è all'origine la storia del riscatto di un eroe da una condizione di *bâtardise*.[6] L'autore stesso, dinanzi allo scopo liberatorio dell'astuzia escogitata dalla donna, sospende il suo giudizio, cioè implicitamente ne riconosce la legittimità: "Aussi ne sçay je se le prebtre faisoit bien ou non de luy faire dire à son mary et reveler le pechiez qui estoit secret et le faire publique. Je m'en rapporte à ce qui en est et n'en vueil pas juger." Un tema tradizionale, improntato al più usuale antifemminismo, si arricchisce pertanto, di sfumature nuove e recupera, grazie all'innesto della *morale naïve*, una sua dimensione umana.

Anche in altri racconti la degradazione dello sprovveduto, dell'insi- piente, del diseredato è solo apparente. *Ung pouvre fol ygnorant* è l'eroe della novella LXXXIV. La sua testarda stoltezza è, apparentemente, risi- bile: arrestato e condannato a morte per un furto che in realtà non ha commesso, continua a dichiararsi colpevole sia per assicurare al suo padrone (è il *fol* dell'arcivescovo di Treviri) una ricca ammenda, sia per un suo inespresso e ostinato orgoglio. Anche quando, sul punto di morire, è rico- nosciuto da un *gentil homme* che assiste tra il pubblico e che, dichiaran- done l'identità, lo fa liberare, manifesta una sorta di dispettosa collera, quasi che intenda rendere esplicita, col suo sacrificio, l'assurdità del duro castigo voluto dai suoi avversari: "Et le povre folz, qui estoit sur l'eschielle qui n'attendoit que la mort, oyant ce gentil homme qui disoit qu'on le laissa, luy faisoit signe de la teste et des yeulx qu'il se taisist et avoit grant despit de ce que ledit gentil homme le congnoissoit." Siamo in presenza, così, di un altro topos narrativo, quello del riscatto e, si potrebbe dire, dell'elogio della follia. All'eroe apparentemente risibile va, in realtà, l'aiuto di Dio: "A qui Dieu vuelt aidier, nulz hommes ne le peuvent nuyre." L'os- tinatezza del *fol* suscita il riso della gente comune ("congneurent aucune- ment à ces parolles que se n'estoit que ung folz"), in realtà ha una sua logica, serve a smascherare l'assurdità dei procedimenti di una dubbia e sbrigativa giustizia:

Moult de pouvres gens et ygnorantes personnes sont desfaiz par justice en divers lieux parmey le monde à tort et sans cause et portent la peine des mauvais, lesquels eschap- pent, les ungs par leurs finesses et les autres par argent, et les pouvres ygnorans sont mis à mort et destruits aucunesfois par force de gehynes ou par faulte de juge et au- cunesfois par leurs ygnorances et qu'ilz ne se scevent excuser."

La novella, pertanto, va ricondotta allo schema della *morale naïve* rinvigorito, per di più, da un'indubbia carica polemica e contestatrice, cosa che non può affatto dirsi, invece, per la novelletta di Des Périers che Hassell e Livingston mensionano come affine, centrata non sull'ambiguità della follia ma, in termini quasi antitetici, sulla goffaggine dell'altezzosa presunzione (*Nouvelles Récréations*, XLIV).[7]

Un analogo atteggiamento, vagamente anarchico, sembra cogliersi anche nella parte introduttivo della novella XCI, centrata sul personaggio dell' *ivrogne*, più precisamente di un Tedesco, Hannes, *lequel estoit l'un des grans yvrognes de quoy l'on sceut parler*. Anch'egli presenta un'interessante ambivalenza: degno di riso, agli occhi dell'autore, per l'ingenuità dello stratagemma da lui inventato per poter coltivare tranquillamente la sua unica passione—gli è stato chiesto di non comprar puì vino se non col reddito di un' effettiva mercatanzia, ed egli compra dalla moglie e le rivende quotidianamente una capra, suo unico bene—egli à tratteggiato in termino negativi anche per la sua testarda dissipazione ("il gastoit et fondoit tout à la taverne . . . il estoit incorrigible et obstinez"), e tuttavia il suo comportamento traduce anche l'anarchia libertà del diseredato: "ilz ne se lessoient rien que tout ne fut vendus ou engaigez pour boire et yvrongner, et n'y avoit en leur maison guiere aultre chose que les quatre murs . . . s'en alloit tout son gaing par le val de gorge." Angustiato dal divieto di un potere che mira solo a strappare ai suoi sudditi imposte e gabelle, egli ha a tutta prima la consueta reazione dell'umile ingiustamente oppresso: *lequel se trouva de ce bien esbahis*. Lo stratagemma che Hannes escogita con la moglie corrisponde, quindi, a una sorta di gratificante rivalsa contro la macchina autoritaria e tributaria che vorrebbe impedirgli di sfuggire a imposizioni esose:

Quant il estoit question de paier taille au prince ou les feux ou aultres empruntes ou gabelles, le maire et les maimbours du villaige ou ceulx qui estoient ordonnez à ce faire pourtoient au prevost de Briey ou a aultres officiers le nombre des feu et des mesnaiges que audit villages estoient, mais quant se venoit au payer, lesdits officiers trouvoient tousjours moins ung mesnage qu'ilz n'avoient eu rappourtez.

Di fronte a questo aggiramento della lege, l'atteggiamento di Philippe rimane ambiguo, in bilico tra il dileggio e la simpatia. L'intreccio, già presente in Jacques de Vitry e in altri predicatori, si carica nel narratore cinquecentesco, ancora una volta, dei positivi risvolti della *morale naïve*.

Il povero diavolo, il *fol*, il *bâtard*, l'*ivrogne*: sono questi dunque gli eroi di un tipo di narrativa che preferiace il volto umano del reietto a quello duro e impietoso del suo antagonista. L'assunzione della *morale naïve* non costituisce, però, l'unica scelta di Philippe: si direbbe, anzi, che lo schema narrativo da lui preferito sia quello di segno in certo senso opposto, centrato non sul riscatto e la rivalsa del misero, dell'emarginato e del diseredato ma, al contraio, sulla risibile sprovvedutezza dell'ignorante, dello sciocco, del disadattato. Il contrasto fra astuzia e stoltezza costituisce, ben inteso, un vecchio filone tematico della narrativa sia letteraria, sia orale. In età umanistico-rinascimentale, da Boccaccio a Poggio ai narratori del Cinquecento, un simile tema conosce, senza dubbio, uno sviluppo nuovo e più ampio, probabilmente perchè motivato dalla nuova valutazione della sagacia intellettuale e pratico-mondana, riscontrabile nel pensiero umanistico. Ma l'ironia ai danni dello stolto costituisce, ripetiamo, una costante narrativa di tutti i tempi e di tutti i paesi, ed invade largamente anche la letteratura orale. "Le storie degli sciocchi," dice il Thompson, "pur essendo entrate in buon numero nella tradizione sia come aneddoti sia come canzoni, fioriscono soprattutto nelle raccolte di facezie."[8] La facezia umanistica sfrutta quindi un filone popolare di universale fortuna dando ad esso il suggello di una nuova vivacità intellettuale. L'effetto comico nasce dalla lentezza impacciata e mecanica di comportamenti umani privi della *souplesse* della mente e del corpo che richiede il vario e il mutevole della vita. "Ce qu'il y a de risible," scrive Bergson in un noto brano di *Le Rire*, "c'est une certaine raideur de mécanique là où l'on voudrait trouver la souplesse attentive et la vivante flexibilité d'une personne."[9]

Il tema, per altro, assume di volta in volta connotazioni diverse e va quindi concretamente storicizzato e ricondotto alla diversità dei temperamenti e delle culture. Nella tradizione della facezia, esso si risolve o nel trionfo della burla e della beffa, vittoria di menti lucide su animi ottusi, o nel gusto di evidenziare un torpore mentale, una sprovvedutezza incolmabile, un'ingenuità disperante: in ogni caso, è il risultato divertito e gratuito di un gioco intellettuale puro. Non così nel commerciante di Metz, il quale lega la sprovvedutezza al tema dell'inerzia improduttiva. Il borghese arricchito trasporta in questi casi nel racconto la sua etica mercantile, trasforma il gioco ironico in sprezzante commiserazione e giudica i suoi personaggi con la tipica ideologia del *parvenu*.

Naturalmente tale impressione di lettura andrà verificata caso per caso. In taluni racconti, Philippe riprende vecchi schemi narrativi relativi, ad esempio, all'ignoranza di personaggi che fraintendono il senso di parole poco usuali. Nella novella IV, *un bon simple prebtre*, costretto a trattenere a colazione degli alti prelati, fraintende le parole dell'arciprete, che l'ha invitato ad offrire un pasto *modicum et bonum*. Poichè ha un asino che si chiama appunto *Modicum*, tra pianti e lamenti lo fa squartare e mettere in pentola: "Et en grant regretz fust tuée ladite asne, puis escorchiez et mis en pieces." Il racconto, in questo caso, non tradisce connotazioni particolari: Livingston ricorda la sua presenza nel patrimonio esemplare, in un *fabliau*, in una novelletta del folklore veronese e, soprattutto, nella *Mensa philosophica*, che è del 1470 c.[10] Se mai, è da notare che nella tradizione medievale ed orale l'equivoco era attribuito a personaggi generici, mentre solo Philippe e la *Mensa* fanno, ci pare, del protagonista un prete: segno indubbio della nuova, vistosa presenza del tema dell'ignoranza dei sacerdoti in una narrativa ormai largamente aperta all'influsso della cultura umanistica ed ai suoi umori polemici e preriformati. Philippe intende sorridere, evidentemente, di un *clerc* che è *despourveu de toute clergie*: il *pouvre homme* e *sa pouvre asne* sono l'oggetto della stessa, ironica commiserazione, anche se nell' evidenziare il ridicolo di un prete che non capisce il latino ("car il ne sçavoit et n'entendoit comme point de latin") egli non sembra far suoi in ingente misura i sottinte si polemici che si riscontrano in un umanista come Poggio o nella narrativa colta di Bonaventure des Périers et di Henri Estienne, oltre che dell'autore dei *Comptes du monde adventureux*, e sembra assumere piuttosto l'atteggiamento del borghese che si compiace di far sua l'opinione di *gens clercs et dignes de foi*: la *clergie* è per lui la condizione privilegiata che consente di ridere (*et puis chacun se print à rire; vous ne veistes jamais tant rire*) con soddisfatta superiorità della sprovvedutezza e dell'imbarazzo dell'incolto: "Il luy sembloit qu'il ne seroit pas l'homme pour bien servir ses seigneurs ... Il s'embaissoit tant du service qu'il lui falloit faire."[11]

La novella dei *Trois Allemans* (LX) è anch'essa centrata sulla *raideur* intellettuale di chi non conosce, nè si sforza di comprendere, il senso esatto delle parole che ascolta o che adopera: vi si parla della dabbenaggine di chi ai reca in un paese senza conoscerne la lingua, e usando a casaccio le poche frasi apprese e incomprese. La storiella, di larga diffusione popolare, è nota in un gran numero di varianti. Ai fini del nostro discorso, è assai più ricca di connotazioni la novella XXVIII: *D'ung de noz josnes enffans de Mets lequel à la requeste de son pere volt devenir merchampz*. Al centro, è la figura del figlio sciocco e ignorante, sullo sfondo di una società in mutamento in cui si assiste all'ascesa di "gente nova," ai suoi "subiti guadagni," al declino dei vecchi ceti dominanti:

En la noble cité de Mets, comme j'ay desja dit, sont et demeurent beaucoup de manieres de gens. Les ungs ont eu leur pere et leur mere, aussi leurs aultres parens et amys, grant riches gens lesquelz par leur mauvais gouvernement, après ce qu'ilz ont eu leurs biens, ont tout disciplés et gaistés et les ont exposez en jeuz, en tavernes et en oisivetez et . . . ance de rien faire. Et les aultres sont venu de petits . . . de petit estat extraict, qui par leurs beaux services et . . . en grant estat et honneurs. Et aucuns ont . . . et richesses à la sueur de leur corps et . . . à leur mestier et practicques.

In un simile contesto, l'etica imperante è quella produttiva e mercantile cara, come già sappiamo, al nostro *chaussetier*. Per affermarsi e progredire socialmente, occorre combattere l'ozio, sapersi sagacemente adeguare alla norma della *grande diligence*, evitare che i beni si disperdano, assicurarne la trasmissione ad eredi che sappiano mantenerli ad accrescerli. Occorre, anche—e qui si scopre l'intento parenetico di Philippe—che i genitori divenuti ricchi ("Devint riche homme et de grante puissance selon l'estat dont il estoit venu") si rendano conto della necessità di non adagiarsi in un benessere che potrebbe essere effimero; che intendano, quindi, l'opportunità di educare avvedutamente i loro figli perchà apprendano un sapere che sia nelle loro mani strumento di stabilità ed anzi di ulteriore ascesa sociale: "se vous voullés avoir des enfans plaisant et saiges, faictes les apprendre en leur jeunesse, ou aultrement ne vauldront rien." La sprovvedutezza del figlio è dunque il frutto dell'errore di genitori *parvenus*, troppo teneri, troppo indulgenti, propensi a risparmiare ai loro figli, per un malinteso riguardo, le dure esperienze di vita da loro patite:

Or avoit il ung fils qui estoit encor jeune et l'avoit cest homme nourris moult delicieusement et mignottement et ne luy avoit rien fait apprendre .... et luy sembloit que ce fut ung dieu assis sur une paelle, tant l'aymoit. Car communement il n'y a enfans gasté ny amignoté que de pouvres gens quand il viengnent à quelque peu de richesse, et leur semble que le roy garde leurs oyes.

Il figlio, così, cresce inetto e ignorante: "Or creut cest enfans et devint grand et . . . ne sçavoit rien ne ne vouloit rien apprendre." Troppo tardi il padre decide di dargli un lavoro, di farne uno dei tanti "qui praticquoient et merchandoient." Gli espone, quindi, i suoi progetti e la sua etica:

Mon filz, je vois que tu es grant et gros et ne fait rien chascun jour que truander le temps par ce que je ne t'ay rien fait apprendre, dont je m'en repens. Ores je considere que je deviens vieu et caduc et se tu ne vueil aultrement penser à toy, du temps venant je doubte que les bien et le grant avoir que j'ay gaingnez en grant peine et à la sueur de mon corps ne soient tous disciplés et gastez, car, dez que l'on prent tousjours en ung lieu et y rien mettre, il n'y a si grant puix que on n'en trouva le fon. Pour ce, mon filz, j'ay deliberez de toy faire marchans et de toy mectre porcion de mes richesses entre les mains affin que tu praticque pour ta vie à gaigner, comme les aultres font. Mais voie bien que tu y soie prudent et saige et que tu ne face folle marchandise, car aujourd'huy l'on trouve tant de tromperie parmey le monde, et se tu n'est sur ta garde, tu y seroie tantost deceu. Aussi voye bien que la marchandise que tu acheteras soit marchandise convoitée et requise, car en cela tu ne pourras faillir, et jaçoit ce que je ne soie point marchans ne jamais ne l'apprins, si te vueil je enseigner affin que tu ne soies trompez ne deceu.

Invito all'incremento dei beni, a una prudente diffidenza nei confronti di ogni *folle marchandise*, a un'attenta valutazione dell'andamento del mercato. Il figlio imprime meccanicamente queste norme nel suo ottuso cervello e parte, con la borsa colma di danaro, lasciando padre e madre tra pianti e gemiti. Dura, per l'ingenua recluta, l'esperienza del viaggio: Philippe sa narrare una vicenda così poco libresca, così autentica, rifuggendo da ogni formula ormai consunta a ricorrendo, come già si è visto nelle precedenti citazioni, a un "parlato" colorito e realistico:

Dieu sceit se le pouvre homme eust le cul escorchez, et fut quasi mort de doleur pour ce que jamais n'avoit esté à cheval ne jamais hors de Mets à plus d'une lieue loing; ne n'avoit, comme j'ay dit, rien appris, par quoy les aultres marchans se moquoient de luy, et cuidoit ce pouvre homme estre au bout du monde.

Lo vediamo mentre gira per le vie ed i mercati di Parigi "en levant la teste en hault et en regardant deçà et delà où il verroit la plus grant presse de gens." Il padre gli ha raccomandato di acquistare merce assai richiesta e assai venduta ed egli attende, di giorno in giorno, finchè non s'imbatta nell'occasione buona, e intanto se ne sta solo, chiuso nella sua presunzione e nella sua diffidenza: "et ne volt jamais dire aux aultres marchans sen qu'il avoit fait." Poi, vedendo gran folla presso le botteghe dei trippai, intesi a vendere a viandanti e mercanti la trippa che servirà a una sbrigativa colazione, ne acquista una quantità inverosimile, e ne riempie barili e barili, e poi porta a casa, soddisfatto, "selle belle et precieuse marchandise." Il padre vede arrivare con gioia i carri carichi di merce, poi ne scopre esterreffatto il contenuto:

Pour tant incontinent fist desfoncer l'ung des tonneaux, duquel sortit si grant puanteur comme se fut esté toutes les punaises du monde, et furent quasi tous enpunasiez. Puis en estouppant le nez se approcherent près du tonneau et veirent tant de piedz, tant de testes et de mullettes de chastrons, avecques grosses pence de beuf et pis de vaiche, que c'estoit une horreur de veoir tout cela ensemble, infectz et à demys pourris pour les grandes challeurs qu'il avoit faict. Et y estoient les groz vers, de quoy c'estoit hideux à veoir ce piteux mesnage.

Il tema della dabbenaggine dello sciocco è pertanto utilizzato da Philippe sul terreno dell'etica mercantile. La miopia di un padre arricchito, incapace di intendere i pratici vantaggi di un'adeguata preparazione del figlio in vista del mantenimento e dell'incremento della posizione sociale da lui raggiunta è all'origine della stolta *méprise* compiuta dal figlio ignorante: *ces dames de trippes* ripagano adeguatamente la sua improvvidenza, *folle marchandise* dimostra i suoi catastrofici effetti, rispetto alla norma prudente di *grande diligence*. L'intento del narratore non è più puramente ludico: si tratta di dimostrare, sullo sfondo vivace della Parigi dei negozianti e dei mercanti, delle botteghe del Pont Notre Dame o della folla che gremisce il Petit Pont, che l'arte della mercatanzia richiede impegno e lungimiranza. Al di là della stoltezza del figlio, il racconto di Philippe mette in risalto l'imprevidenza del padre, vero obiettivo della storia.

Ma il racconto più significativo è quello che si collega al noto aneddoto del *pot au lait*: nella novella LXXVIII (*D'une femme de village qui avoit allez querir du let pour l'amour de Dieu et de ce qu'il en advint*) si parla di due poveri diavoli, marito e moglie, che fantasticano sulla loro futura richezza finchè il marito con un calcio inavvertitamente rovescia il bricco di latte che costituiva, di quei castelli in aria, il risibile fondamento. Hassell ha raccolto tutte le numerose varianti di questa diffusissima storia;[12] una nota allusione di Rabelais alla "farce du pot au lait" ci fa del resto capire che esistevano varianti del racconto oggi perdute. Rispetto alla versione presente in Jacques de Vitry, Etienne de Bourbon, il *Dialogus creaturarum* ecc., quella di Philippe sembra risalire ad un archetipo diverso, in cui non è un singolo personaggio ad abbandonarsi ai suoi sogni e a dar prova di allegra sventatezza, ma una coppia di coniugi, come pare si verifichi anche in nvellette di folklore tedesco ed asiatico, per altro assai diverse secondo quanto afferma il Livingston.[13] Ma a noi il racconto interessa soprattutto per l'etica mercantile che ne costituisce il più vero nucleo ispiratore. Il "sognatore" è tutt'altro che l'oggetto di quella scherzosa e bonaria indulgenza con cui sapranno guardare alla loro *laitière* Des Périers e, più tardi, soprattutto La Fontaine: in lui nessun ironico idoleggiamento, nessun invito a capire l'umanissima evasione dalla grigia insufficienza del reale. *Chacun songe en veillant . . .* Per Philippe, appunto il sogno è da mettere sotto accusa. Dell'eroe della storia inizia col darci un profilo tutto in negativo:

Ores advint que audit village demeuroit ung pouvre malheureux qui y estoit nouvellement venu et estoit ung vacabonde nommez Jehan de Toutes Villes, car il faisoit plus de maison que tous les massons du pays. Celuy pouvre malfortunez de quoy je parle estoit tant pouvre et avec cela, tant orgueilleux, glout et truant et mal devot qu'il n'estoit rien plus.

I termini negativi si affastellano in tal quantità da impedire che si ritagli nella pagina un qualsiasi margine di umana simpatia e di connivenza; essi coprono un arco larghissimo di significati che vanno dall' assoluta indigenza alla scioperataggine, alla furfanteria, allo spirito irreligioso. Ma soprattutto, l'esplicito segno della negatività è nel fatto che la domenica mattina, mentre in chiesa già si cantava la messa grande, *ce truant estoit encor au lit*: a letto, cioè appunto nel luogo in cui si poltrisce e si sogna. La moglie tornata a casa dal suo giro che le ha fruttato un po' di latte in elemosina, scopre con irritazione "son groz paillart de maryt au lict qui dormoit." Ne nasce uno scambio vivace di insulti e di biasimi finchè, gradatamente, l'alterco si muta in una catena di progetti e di sogni. Il *truand*, infatti, promette di riscattarsi dedicandosi all'attività mercantile: "Car par ma foid, je me vueil de ces jours en avant mesler de quelque pratique et deviendrez marchant." Il suo parlare è tutto intessuto di formule che rinviano ad una sana economia domestica e ad un'impegnata professionalità: *faire ung bon mesnage, tenir bon mesnage, avoir tant de bel mesnaige, devenir marchant*, questi gli obiettivi che il dormiglione si propone di raggiungere. La moglie, inizialmente assai critica, a poco a poco è coinvolta nel facile gioco immaginativo, ed anzi enuncia la regola che dovrà presiedere al loro progetto: bisogna, lei dice, iniziare dal poco, "encommencer à ung bout, car par ainsi sont venus les riches gens petit à petit à voir leur chevance." Philippe dovrebbe apprezzare una così laboriosa prudenza, non racchiude essa forse la norma di tutti i *parvenus* come lui? In realtà, il suo giudizio è duro e sprezzante, e non perchè egli orgogliosamente non sia propenso a spartire con altri il suo successo e le sue fortune, ma perchè non ammette che il mercante ami pascersi di parole e di sogni: Così, i due eroi fanno a gara nell'immaginare, come Perrette, profitti e fortune sempre più alte, tutti però formulati con connotazioni negative, prospettati cioè come meschina rivincita, come sfogo di aggressivi rancori ("Pense tu poinct que le maire aura bien grant despit et bien grant dueil quant il me verront ainsi? . . . J'en ferez des bien camuz se je vis ung an"), come spietato egoismo, indifferente alla mala sorte dei diseredati loro simili ("Et au moins, dit elle, aie pitié des pouvres gens. —Et je aurés, dit-il, le deable. Je n'en aurés pitié ne pitesse"), come manifestazione di una gretta rivalità e competitività ("desirant fort à estre riche affin qu'ilz puissent sormarcher leurs voisins"), di una presuntuosa alterigia ("Cer je leur monstrerez qui que je suis et se je suis maistre ou nom"), di una volontà di vendicativa rivalsa ("Car je ferez ainsi comme on m'a faict"), di una ridicola ambizione a cariche di troppo alto prestigio ("Et par Dieu, je serez encor eschevin. —Eschevin? dit elle. Vouldroie tu estre d'office? —Pourquoy non, dit il, nes [sic] q'un aultrez? Si ferez bien, dea, et yrés bien des premier à l'offrande et si me soiras au cueur ou au chancel de l'eglise comme ilz font"). Così, la conclusione della vicenda giunge come punizione di un miraggio evasivo che è, appunto, non costruito su dati reali ma su facili, gratuite chimere, comodo alibi alla vuota inerzia del presente. Alla rigida scala gerarchica non è facile, ormai, portare correzioni e modifiche: "Qui ne doit avoir que deux blancz jamais n'aura V sous en son vivant." Philippe, forse, vuole anche dirci che la situazione è ormai bloccata. Ma soprattutto, vuole distinguere il rude impegno del suo ceto dalla *follie* di chi fa sogni troppo facili, di chi aspira alla ricchezza e al successo senza pagarne duramente il prezzo. Di tali sogni ci vuol far ridere senza indulgenza, senza l'ombra di alcuna connivenza.[14]

NOTE

1. Cfr. A Jolles, *Formes simples* (Paris: Seuil, 1972).

2. Cfr. L. Sozzi, "Le *forme semplici* di Nicolas de Troyes," in *La Nouvelle française à la Renaissance*, études réunies et présentées par V.-L. Saulnier, Bibliothèque Franco Simone, 2 (Genève: Slatkine, 1981).

3. Rinviamo, per tutte le nostre citazioni, all'ed. curata de Charles H. Livingstone, Philippe de Vigneulles, *Les Cent Nouvelles Nouvelles*, Travaux d'Humanisme et Renaissance, 120 (Genève: Droz, 1972). Non daremo, di volta in volta, l'indicazione della pagina, avendo fornito il numero di ogni singola novella.

4. Ibid., p. 79.

5. *Fabliaux*, racconti comici medievali a cura di G.C. Belletti (Ivrea: Herodote, 1982), p. 68.

6. M. Robert, *Roman des origines et origines du roman* (Paris: Grasset, 1972).

7. Cfr. J.W. Hassell, *Sources and Analogues of the "Nouvelles Récréations et Joyeux Devis" of Bonaventure des Périers* (Chapel Hill: Univ. of North Carolina Press, 1957), pp. 163-67, e Ch. Livingston ed. cit., p. 330 (ma prima, dello stesso, un articolo nella *Revue du Seizième Siècle*, X [1923], 159-203).

8. S. Thompson, *La Fiaba nella tradizione popolare* (Milano: Il Saggiatore, 1967), p. 278.

9. H. Bergson, *Le Rire* (Paris: PUF, 1969), p. 22.

10. Cfr. Ch. Livingston, ed. cit., p. 68.

11. Inserita nella vicenda è la storia del contadino che non intende la domanda che gli viene rivolta: "Mon amy, a bu l'aine à guet?" e risponde: "Je ne sçay point de latin, sire." Qui, la *moquerie* è ancora più radicale, non nasce dal conflitto tra latino e volgare, ma da quello tra lingua e dialetto (*gué* e *wez*): si ride, cioè, di un'umanità dialettale, che non sa ascendere a livelli linguistici non provinciali e che vede dovunque l'ombra inquietante del latino, strumento di oscuri privilegi.

12. J.W. Hassell, pp. 64-71.

13. Cfr. Ch. Livingston, p. 302.

14. Segnaliamo, su Philippe de Vigneulles, scrittore sul quale manca per altro, sinora, un esauriente lavoro d'insieme, il bel capitolo che gli dedica G.-A. Perouse, *Nouvelles françaises du XVIe siècle. Images de la vie tu temps*, Travaux d'Humanisme et Renaissance, 154 (Genève: Droz, 1977), pp. 29-68, e gli studi di A.A. Kotin, *The Narrative Imagination. Comic Tales by Philippe de Vigneulles* (Lexington: Univ. Press of Kentucky, 1977) e "Le Comique et les moralités dans les *Nouvelles* de Philippe de Vigneulles: leur sens ultime," in *La Nouvelle française*, pp. 171-82. In questa stessa raccolta, pp. 167-70, un saggio di M. Cavalli, "Boccaccio e Philippe de Vigneulles."

Annette H. Tomarken

The Lucianic Blason:
A Study of an Edition by Jean de Tournes

In 1547, Jean de Tournes published in Lyons a collection of three anonymous poems entitled *Blasons, de la Goutte, de Honneur, et de la Quarte*.[1] The works represent an important stage in the development of that popular Renaissance genre, the blason. For whereas most earlier blasons had been short descriptive poems of straightforward praise or blame, the Lyons works all adopted a markedly ironic attitude towards their subject-matter. The present study seeks to explain the sources and significance of this startling change of tone. It will be shown that the author's attitude towards his topic was not the only new aspect of the three works; the topics themselves were unusual material for blasons. The origins of both these innovations will be found in two different but related forms, the satirical eulogy and the Bernesque "capitolo." In addition to being an historical investigation into the evolution of a genre, the article will, by discussing the details of the three works, attempt to analyze their originality and literary qualities.

With the exception of D.B. Wilson's *Descriptive Poetry in France from Blason to Baroque* of 1967, the blason, despite its popularity in the 16th century, has not yet been the object of a full-length critical study.[2] Wilson, like the authors of articles and sections of books devoted to the genre, takes as the basis of his definition of the genre Thomas Sebillet's description, contained in his *Art Poétique françois* of 1548:

Le Blason est une perpétuéle louenge ou continu vitupére de ce qu'on s'est proposé blasonner. Pource serviront bien a celuy qui le voudra faire, tous lés lieus de demonstration escris par lés rhéteurs Grecz et Latins. Je dy en l'une et en l'autre partie de louenge et de vitupére. Car autant bien se blasonne le laid comme le beau, et le mauvais comme le bon. . . . De quelconque coin soit-il sorty, le plus bref est le meilleur, mesque il soit agu en conclusion: et est plus dous en ryme platte, et vers de huit syllabes: encores que ceus de dis n'en soient pas regrettés comme ineptes.[3]

That Sebillet's definition was indeed the standard one of the day is attested to by Claude de Boissière, who in 1554 wrote that "Blason est composition invective, contenant la louenge ou vitupére d'autruy."[4] However, Sebillet's criteria, although formulated well after the form had become established, prove difficult to apply consistently, since many blasons, including those published by de Tournes, do not manifest one or more of the characteristics he selected.

Two solutions to this problem of identification and classification have been proposed. On the one hand, critics have invented names for what are perceived as sub-categories of the blason, the "blason médaillon," the "blason symbolique," the "hymne-blason," and the "blason satirique," titles not used in the 16th century.[5] On the other hand, attempts have been made to simplify and thus render more inclusive Sebillet's formulation. Enzo Giudici, for example, characterized the form as one seeking to "cogliere la segreta essenza" of a theme or object.[6] The result of these efforts has been either an excess of critical hair-splitting—is a given work best read as a "blason satirique" or an "hymne-blason"?—or recourse to generalizations too broad to be of much help in elucidating the texts.

One source of this confusion probably lies in the fact that a combination of continuity and discontinuity, repetition and innovation, has been characteristic of the genre throughout its history. Although generally recognizable as a short poem praising or blaming a single theme, the blason was at the same time regularly influenced by related genres.[7] These external elements, whether of style, topic, or tone, seem on occasion to have been significant or useful enough to have been retained by subsequent "blasonneurs." Such is the case with the introduction of an ironic perspective, a change most apparent in the three Lyons poems and later found in most of the Pléiade "hymnes-blasons." Sebillet's models for the genre in 1548 were Marot and Scève, both of whose blasons, although sometimes playful, were not sustainedly ironic. It remains nonetheless an odd quirk in the history of the form that a year *before* Sebillet (and, after him, most subsequent critics) posited direct praise or blame as the chief characteristic of the blason, a collection had appeared in which the praise was bestowed ironically.

As was noted above, the two genres which exerted the greatest influence on the three Lyons blasons were the Lucianic satirical eulogy and Bernesque "capitolo." Indeed, de Tournes's collection is notable for being the first in French to contain clear elements of both the classical and the Italian forms. The Renaissance vogue for Lucian has been widely discussed, in particular by C.A. Mayer.[8] Like the blason, the satirical eulogy appears to have been readily recognizable to Renaissance readers despite its flexibility of form.[9] The most obvious features common to all blasons were their monographic, descriptive nature and relative brevity. The constant aspect of the satirical eulogy, or paradoxical encomium, was the playful, ironic or satiric praise it conferred on seemingly trivial or unworthy objects, from insects, diseases, and villains to false or amoral ways of life. Since the majority of blasons were eulogistic rather than vituperative, the common ground between the two genres is apparent; both contain description and praise of a given, usually a single phenomenon. The difference in attitude, however, between the directly expressed admiration or scorn found in most blasons prior to 1547 and the mocking compliments contained in the Lyons poems is striking and is the chief source of the latter works' originality.

The other genre to have influenced the development of the blason, the Bernesque "capitolo," was a relatively short verse form. As such, it bore a more obvious surface resemblance to the blason than did the satirical eulogy, which was generally composed in prose. In the 1530s Berni, Mauro, Bino, Molza and others composed a remarkable series of "capitoli" which, when eventually published, enjoyed widespread popularity.[10] Earlier Italian poets had composed satiric poetry on traditional burlesque themes such as uncomfortable inns, difficult journeys, decrepit donkeys, and so on. The Bernesque writers, often seeking to parody the excesses of Petrarchan poetry and familiar with the mock encomia of antiquity, introduced many literary elements into their "capitoli." The attacks, now more veiled, abounded in sophisticated word games and literary references. As we shall see, these innovations were a fruitful source of ideas for the anonymous French "blasonneur."

In fact, the Bernesque writers' choice of theme was frequently determined by their familiarity with Lucian. Like most Renaissance mock encomia, their works tend to deal with one of the three groups of topics praised by their Greek predecessor. Thus Lucian's *Podagra*, a parody of classical tragedy in which gout was deified and glorified, gave rise to numerous encomia on disease. His *Muscae Encomium* (often in conjunction with the equally popular sparrow epitaph by Catullus) served as a source of much 16th-century prose and poetry praising small animals and insects.[11] His *De Parasito* and *Rhetorum Praeceptor* provided material for those wanting to criticize ironically certain human vices and failings.[12] Amongst the Bernesque writings, we find "capitoli" on gout, the cough and the plague, on eels, the mosquito, and the crow, and, lastly, on debt, lying, and on luxury-loving monks. Lucian thus exerts a dual influence on the development of the ironic blason, directly, by way of the editions of his works available in France, and indirectly, by way of the Bernesque poems.

Nowhere is this influence more apparent than in the de Tournes edition, in which Lucian is mentioned by name and certain lines are almost direct translations of lines in Italian "capitoli." So popular was Lucian's *Podagra* that the titles alone of the gout and quartan fever blasons would have suggested to an alert Renaissance reader the possibility, even the probability of a Lucianic, i.e. ironic work. A famous 16th-century imitation of the *Podagra*, sometimes printed with the Greek work, was Pirckheymer's *Podagrae Encomium*.[13] Other Neo-Latin gout encomia prior to 1547 were those by Girolamo Cardano, the Italian scholar-philosopher, H. Eobanus Hessus, and Christophe Arbaleste, a Frenchman.[14] Quartan fever had been praised in antiquity by the first-century A.D. rhetorician, Favorinus of Arles, whose work survived only in an abbreviated version discussed by Aulus Gellius in the *Noctes Atticae*. In the 16th century, the theme had been treated by Guilielmus Menapius Insulanus, the German scholar.

Any reader unaware of these likely sources for the Lyons blasons or other mock encomia of the period would soon have his doubts removed. For most composers of such works seem to have felt it part of their autho-rial duty, almost an integral part of the form, to provide, either as a preface or as a part of their text, a list of illustrious practitioners of the genre. Erasmus, in his preface to the *Moriae Encomium*, lists several predecessors, who were to become standard authorities in later encomia.[15] The Lyons "blasonneur" adopts the same formula, mentioning Lucian, Favorinus, and Menapius. The paradoxical nature of the two poems becomes further apparent in the full titles of the works. That on gout reads as follows: "Louange de la tresfroide, treschaude, inexorable, trespuissante, & tres-redoutable Dame, la Goutte." The playful use of lists of adjectives was a technique used by Lucian in the *Podagra*, when he called the goddess (to quote Filbert Bretin's 1583 translation) "Podagrie rebandee, / Empes-che course, Enlitee / March'-à peine, trembles-tos, / Gambe-route, surveil-lante, / Plye-genoux, bourrelante."[16] As D.B. Wilson has demonstrated, series of adjectives were also popular with writers of blasons.[17]

The second disease blason presents its attack on received opinion more directly: "Louanges de la tres medicinable et salubre Quarte, *à tort dite* Fievre, & incurable" (italics mine). Since the expression "à tort dite" occurs in the other disease blason, it is worth noting here that the numer-ous editions of *Paradoxes* in France, all imitations or translations of the original *Paradossi* of Ortensio Lando, were also usually introduced as being "contre la commune opinion."[18] We can begin to see another instance of the satirical eulogy's tendency to overlap with or be subsumed by other genres, such as the paradox, the allegory, and the blason.

The third Lyons blason poses a different problem, in that it is an attack, an ironic attack, not an encomium. Most earlier blasons had adopted a positive attitude towards their subject-matter, with the result that the title "blason" seems to have become associated with such a stance. Even a blason such as Eustorg de Beaulieu's "Le Pet," for example, was in general favorable to its odd subject. This tendency to praise rather than blame may have convinced other writers to adopt the more obviously negative title of "contre-blason."[19] Thus Jean Rus, a Bordeaux poet, composed in about 1540 a "Contre-blason du nez" describing in revolting detail, with no attempt at mock praise, an unattractive nose.[20] The Lyons "blasonneur," however, uses a play on words, rather than the term "contre-blason," to clarify his satiric intentions: "Blason Declamatoire au Deshonneur de Honneur."

Turning now to a more detailed study of the three poems, we find that the gout blason shares several arguments with earlier encomia on gout. In particular, it borrows from Matteo Francesi's "Capitolo delle Gotte," a Bernesque work which mockingly eulogizes what Sebastian Brant, in the popular *Narrenschiff*, had called "the rich man's malady."[21] The originality of the French poem will be more apparent if we first recall the arguments advanced by Francesi, to whose encomium it bears the closest resemblance.[22] The Italian writer's central thesis was that gout is a benevolent, not an evil force. Doctors claim, he explains, that gout is caused by the body's inability to absorb more than a certain amount of wine and meat. Francesi maintains that it is hereditary, sent from God, and therefore not to be resisted.[23] Fostered by wine, leisure, and lechery, the affliction is particularly common in the well-appointed homes of abbots and priors. Poor working monks, those who fast on more days than those marked for abstinence in the calendar, are spared. Gout is attentive to our spirit, our body, and even our fortune; the spirit is elevated by enforced bedrest and contemplation, the body cleansed by the necessity of observing a simple diet, and wealth is of course the universal concomitant of the disease. Perhaps, continues Francesi, gout is not in fact a disease at all, for sufferers are never sent to hospital and no chemist stocks cures for the afflicted.

This brief résumé is sufficient for us to notice Francesi's use of certain traditional mock-encomiastic techniques—the modification or distortion of some facts, the omission of others, and the clever expansion of selected characteristics into admirable and desirable qualities.[24] It also shows how wide was the range of arguments used in favor of gout, religious—since God sends the malady, we must not rebel against it, moral—gout affords men time to read and meditate, and social—gout cannot be so terrible, since we do not have to go to hospital with it and our friends are not afraid to visit us. Although he refers to the lack of medical cures for the illness and thereby implies some Lucianic criticism of doctors' false claims, Francesi concentrates on satirizing gouty members of religious orders.[25] By combining a moral interpretation of gout as God's punishment for dissolute living with the traditional attribution of gout to self-indulgence, he is able to make a dramatic satiric point.[26] The wealthy friars ignore both the teaching of God and their own unfortunate social spectacle; a gouty monk, according to the then current understanding of the disease's causes, showed himself to even the most ignorant of laymen to be an unworthy monk.

In the French poem, the mention of Lucian, the most famous of gout-praisers, occurs early on. The poet declares that his admiration for the enforced continence of gouty people has inspired him

> De reciter plus de louange d'elle,
> Que Lucian en ce beau dialogue,
> Ou il la met au ranc, & catalogue
> Des Dieux trescraintz, recitant plusieurs preux
> N'estre famés, que pour estre goutteux. (p. 3)

The presentation of a disease as a powerful goddess was first undertaken by Lucian in the *Podagra*. Although personification was a standard rhetorical device, it was peculiarly appropriate for conveying the sense in which the attacks of a disease seemed at times to the afflicted to be controlled and directed by an external power bent on vengeance or punishment. Accordingly, the tone adopted by authors eulogizing a disease would frequently be one of more or less mocking awe and respect. Presenting themselves as humble admirers of their (usually female) deity, they would profess themselves eager to defend her against the attacks of the unbelievers. Another favorite device of mock encomia was to "reinterpret" historical events. Thus, Lucian had claimed that Gout, not Paris, had laid Achilles low. Other "preux" whose fate could be presented as a triumph of the goddess Gout were Bellerophon, Oedipus, and Philoctetes.[27] After a passing mention of gout's selectivity, for she spares women and the virtuous, the French poet goes on to remind the reader of the disease's incurability. This notion, found in almost all the gout encomia, was based on Ovid's much-quoted statement that "tollere nodosam nescit medicina podagram."[28]

The next passage in the blason is one for which I have found no precedent in previous gout eulogies. The source of the malady is traced back to the circumcision of Abraham, Gout marking her elect as indelibly as does the ancient rite or as did the angel who, in struggling with Jacob, marked "the hollow of his thigh" (Gen: XXXII, 24-32). The idea that gout is a kind of external brand making visible to others that the bearer belongs to a particular group of people was implicit in Francesi's portrait of the gouty monks. But whereas the Italian suggested that gout betrayed something the monk would have preferred to hide, his fondness for luxurious living, the "blasonneur" treats the "signe" of gout as a matter for an almost religious form of pride. Only in this manner can the sufferer prove himself one of the "vrays esleuz," the "vrays Israëlites" whose selection by God is marked upon them by the angels. By comparing gout to circumcision the poet suggests that man may come to accept certain forms of pain as a way of raising himself above ordinary mortals.

The religious imagery and presentation of the gouty man as a kind of priest figure continue as the poet addresses the goddess directly:

> O caractere indelebile & cher!
> O *sainte* Goutte indigne d'attoucher
> Fors delicatz, & qu'on doit dorlotter
> Sus coussinetz, & en douceur frotter,
> Et dyaprer comme un *reliquiaire*:
> Ou autrement elle peult grand mal faire.
> Car c'est (pour vray) un *sacrement* tresdigne.
> (p. 4, italics mine)

The traditional claim made on behalf of gout, that she does not attack women, takes on a different dimension in this religious context. Instead of being a sign of the goddess' merciful nature, as was usually asserted, it becomes proof that she seeks a band of strong men who, once converted to her cause, can become loyal priests. Indignantly, the poet explains that true gout has nothing to do with the "raige enragee," the illness that attacks the "impudicz." We may see here a reference to some form of venereal disease, perhaps syphilis, which can eventually attack the joints. The name "Goutte," on the other hand, is related to "Artique" and "Sciatique," "Noms derivans de tous biens & sçavoirs." The reader will presumably perceive the similarity between the words "Art" and "Artique," "Science" and "Sciatique." This section of the poem concludes with another declaration that gout is "tresssainte & Angelique," seeking only her disciples' "ayse, & proffit." The link between the material world of pain and swollen joints and the spiritual realm of religion and meditation has thus been carried through into the very etymology of the words describing the various types of gout.

The "blasonneur" next explains, as had Francesi before him, that gout does no harm to man's chief blessings, "de l'esprit, de fortune, & du corps." Like Francesi's sufferers, or like the happy debtors in Berni's "capitolo" in praise of debt, the gouty man is always surrounded by well-wishers.[29] This statement is another instance of reinterpretation of the truth. The debtor is surrounded by well-wishers only because no creditor wants harm to befall him before he has repaid his debt. The gouty man's visitors are happy to visit him because his affliction is what might be termed a sociable, not a contagious one. No one would visit him if he had the plague; indeed, Berni, in his first "capitolo" on the plague, recommended complaining of plague symptoms precisely because this was such an effective way to be rid of creditors.[30]

As if in recognition of the gouty man's superiority, people make way for him in the streets;

> . . . quand dans la chaire à bras
> Portés en Ducz, faisans des Fierabras,
> Il fault qu'honneur chacun aux goutteux face,
> Soit en l'Eglise, en maison, ou en place. (p. 6)

Those making way for the patient may even, suggests the poet, credit him with as much intellectual as physical weight. This passage serves as a humorous reminder that gout is a very visible, but also a "safe" disease. The sufferer does not have to retreat from his fellow men, but can remain in their midst, showing them how he copes with pain. As for the patients' enforced avoidance of the excesses of "Venus, & de table / Cela leur est (peult estre) profitable." The "peult estre" may seem an odd interjection, but it underlines the fact that not all react courageously to their trials, despite the noble birth and powerful social position of most victims. The "blasonneur" passes over the opportunity for social satire which Francesi had grasped at this point. Instead, he details the different kinds and levels of benefits conferred by his new divinity. First among these is a purely physical one, the freedom to take life easily:

> O comme au lict ses possesseurs esgaye,
> Tresexcusés pour affaire, qu'on aye,
> De n'en bouger: ou le sain malheureux,
> Dormant à l'ayse, encor tout sommeilleux
> Sort de son lict pour courir & baller. (p. 7)[31]

The next advantage of gout concerns a more significant realm of activity: the varying degrees of pain in his joints enable a gout victim to foretell changes in the weather "mieux, qu'un grand Astrologue." Again, the almost religious nature of the affliction is stressed. Furthermore, gout forces her elect to lead a sober life, thereby encouraging them to cultivate "bon corps, & bonne ame." Surely, therefore, she must be viewed as a "tresadmirable dame," raising our thoughts "au Ciel." There follows a description of famous gout-sufferers, the first of whom is not a classical or mythological figure, but a Spanish contemporary, "feu Antoine de Leve,"

> Assis en chaire, & ne bougeant d'un lieu,
> Craint des Soudars, plus obey, qu'un Dieu:
> Qui aux assaux, & mirables victoires
> Ha plus acquis à son Cesar de gloires,
> Que maintz Ducz sains. Car en sa providence
> Plus de force eut, qu'en son Ost de puissance.
>
> (p. 7)

Leyva (1480-1536), one of Charles V's most successful generals, helped defeat the French at the battle of Pavia (1525) and was therefore well known in France. Brantôme, in discussing his career, mentions Leyva's gout, while Rabelais, by entitling a book in the library of Saint Victor the *Entrée . . . es terres du Bresil*, mocks the general's desire to invade Provence.[32] The most hostile presentation of Leyva, however, is perhaps the epitaph on him by Mellin de Saint-Gelais, which includes the following lines:

> Sous ce tombeau gist une sepulture,
> J'entens un corps servant de monument;
> Car il n'avoit d'humaine creature
> Proportion, chaleur, ne mouvement.[33]

The unusually favorable portrait of Leyva found in the Lyons blason can be explained by the poet's desire to continue his presentation of the beneficial transformations brought about by gout. For instead of gout being a divininity, it is now her famous disciple, Leyva, who is "plus obey, qu'un Dieu." Having accepted the necessity of being carried ignominiously into battle, he has turned a disability into an advantage. As the rhyme makes plain, his thoughtful "providence" has become a more powerful force than the solely physical "puissance" of the "Ost."

An even more effective illustration of the transforming power of gout is provided, according to the "blasonneur," by the Roman emperor Severus, who is reported to have remarked, when pardoning a group of conspirators, that the head, not the feet, rules a man.[34] This statement might seem to call into question the importance of gout, but the poet interprets it as a reflection of the goddess' worth, "Dont dire fault, que sa suave oppresse / Mere est (pour vray) de toute gentillesse" (p. 8). By first understanding and learning to control his own baser emotions and feelings, the

LITERATURE AND THE ARTS

emperor has found that the best way to govern others is to temper firmness with compassion. Gout now becomes a mother figure, whose "suave oppresse" teaches men the way to "toute gentillesse."

Her compassionate nature even extends to her treatment of the sufferer's body; gout lessens the force of other diseases, such as the quartan fever, does not affect "cœur, langue, ou chef," the "membres hautains," but renders the rest of the body incapable of such vain activities as running and dancing. The disciple can devote all his mental energies to religious and philosophical meditation. Moreover, this change of direction is brought about not merely by the blocking of other paths, such as those leading to the ballroom or the tavern, but by a more positive impetus:

> . . . elle rend les espritz plus adroitz
> Pour artz apprendre, & justice, & tous droitz:
> Foy observer, exercer charité:
> Dompter la chair, despriser vanité. (p. 8)

These improvements are of course those traditionally associated with the effects of religious faith.

So great a degree of moral and religious transcendence of pain has now been achieved by the ennobled sufferer that the poem might seem to have moved beyond the need to discuss disease at all. In a sudden twist typical of paradoxical writers, the poet returns to a consideration of gout as a disease, a disease which we all at first hope to cure completely by medical means. He notes that if the gouty man observes a sufficiently "povre" regimen, he may well free himself entirely from his "gouttiques douleurs." Like most other gout-praisers, from Lucian to Arbaleste, the "blasonneur" recommends patience and abstinence as the best weapons against the tyrant.[35] He cites a case mentioned by Pliny of a man cured of gout by a fall into a bin of "froment," but does not go so far as to suggest, as did one later poem, that this recovery was due to divine intervention.[36] Great men are exhorted not to complain of their afflictions: Domitian's baldness, Caesar's nightmares, and Severus' gout should serve as reminders of shared humanity, not as pretexts for self-pity:

> Telz feroyent mieux de remettre es memoires
> Leurs grandz honneurs, triumphes, & victoires,
> Sans estre ingratz de ce bien, qu'ilz sont hommes
> Subjetz aux maux, ainsi que tous nous sommes.
> (pp. 9-10)

No longer a divinity, the gouty man must view as a "bien" his inevitable human weakness. Since we can never know perfect happiness or freedom from adversity, it is foolish to make "tant d'Agios pour la Goutte."

This passage differs from that concerning Leyva and Severus in being a defense by negatives, not positives. The moment of controlling the flesh and despising worldly vanity has passed, to be replaced by renewed anxiety about the ability even of great men to sustain such a lofty state of mind and body. We are now urged to accept our gout not as a good, but as a relatively bearable instance of life's many and necessary ills.

The poet's conclusion, adapted from Francesi, is at first presented firmly: "Je vous dis d'abondant, / Qu'en Goutte n'ha ne mal, ne maladie: / Mais dons divins, quoy qu'on mumure, ou die" (p. 10). This assertion is said to be borne out by the fact that neither "Medecins," "Drogueurs," "Charmeurs," or "saccageurs de vie & de santé" stock a cure for gout. Such a statement, claiming that if there is no antidote there is no disease, too obviously flouts known experience to be taken at face value. The absence of a cure proves only the inadequacy of medical knowledge, not the non-existence of the disease. But the poet, pushing his argument *ad absurdum*, tells the sufferer: "Garde la donc, & guerir n'en demande / Celuy, à qui par grace Dieu la mande" (p. 10). The favorable presentation of gout has moved from a defense back to a panegyric. Pain has once again been so distanced that the reader is placed in the ridiculous position of being exhorted to long for gout's continuance rather than its alleviation or cure. Even the most fervent of the goddess' disciples might hesitate to beg for such a boon.

The last four lines of the blason are set in larger type than the remainder of the poem. The fact that they contain a series of puns on the word "goutte" is thus made doubly prominent. The lines run as follows:

> Fin des goustz goustés de la Goutte,
> Qui, quand en degouttant degoutte,
> De gouste un trop meilleur gouster,
> Que Goutte au vin me fait gouster. (p. 10)

The various words based on "goutte" can mean to drip, to disgust, to taste, or to enjoy. The chief source of the joke, medically speaking, is that some Renaissance physicians believed that the word "goutte," from the Latin "gutta," a drop, had been used to designate the disease because gout was caused by liquid gradually dripping into and irritating the joints.[37] The reader of the blason is struck both visually and linguistically by the forms of the word "goutte," repeated nine times in these concluding lines. Gout, at first presented by the "blasonneur" as an external sign conferred upon a group of "esleuz," was gradually transcended as the poem continued. Now we are reminded in a most obvious manner of the persistence of this most public disease. The pleasure of playing with words, with the "goustz" of "Goutte," may indeed have replaced the now forbidden pleasures of wine. But the gout-laden foot of this page provides a salutary and humorous corrective to anyone naive enough to suppose that the source of all this clever paradoxy is anything other than a painful and incurable disease. The blason has proposed various ways of coping with pain, even of achieving moments of resignation and contentment. But Gout's priests cannot for long elude her power. The verbal drunkenness, like that of wine, will pass, leaving the sufferer yet more acutely aware of his vulnerability.

The Lyons blason on gout thus offers an interesting and original presentation of earlier arguments in favor of the malady. The choice of gout as a disease to be eulogized owes much to the Renaissance interest in Lucian and in the satirical eulogy in general. It is also an appropriate topic because it permits consideration of so many different aspects of disease, from the religious and the moral to the social and even the selfish. The "blasonneur" concentrates chiefly on the gouty man's function in society. As one marked for life by his goddess, he can become an honorable and respected disciple, like Antonio de Leyva or Severus, or a weak and complaining victim, forever making "tant d'Agios pour la Goutte."

The Renaissance mock encomiasts' predilection for non-fatal diseases reappears in the second disease blason, which concerns a malady of uncertain, but usually limited duration, the quartan fever. As we found in discussing the gout poem, the originality of the French treatment of these themes becomes plain if earlier works on the same topic are considered first. Indeed, such a comparison is invited by the "blasonneur," who begins by referring to his predecessors, Favorinus and Menapius. He does not mention or make use of Aretino's "Capitolo della Quartana," a largely autobiographical poem having little in common with the French work.[38] The earlier of the two works cited is Favorinus' brief encomium on the fever. According to Aulus Gellius, Favorinus had asserted that sufferers from this fever became stronger after than before they were ill. He had added that since man's fortunes are inevitably variable, he is well advised to be content with an affliction from which he can be sure of having certain days of respite. To illustrate this point, Favorinus cited an ancient saying that "Sometimes a day is like a stepmother, / And sometimes like a mother."[39]

Menapius' *Encomium febris quartanae* was published in 1542 in Basle and had been preceded by a *Ratio curandi febrim quartanam*.[40] This strange, at least to the modern reader, phenomenon of a writer first explaining how to cure and then eulogizing the disease he had tried to treat was not uncommon at the time. A regular part of training in rhetoric had always consisted of learning to defend either side of a given question or even both sides successively. Indeed, precisely this skill had been responsible for much of the mistrust in which orators were often held from classical times on.[41] Satirical encomia frequently ran the risk of being taken seriously, although most writers contrived to insert enough signals to the reader to leave their true feelings in no doubt. If the text itself was too ambiguous, the author alerted his readers in a preface, as did Erasmus. In the early days of the Renaissance satirical eulogy, such prefaces were particularly common.[42] One anxious German, Christoph Hegendorff, even went so far as to publish, first, a *Carmen in vituperium ebrietatis* to counteract any misleading impressions left by the *Encomium ebrietatis* which preceded it, and then a separate work, the *Encomium sobrietatis*, refuting again everything he had said in favor of drunkenness.[43]

In this, the best known Renaissance encomium on quartan fever, Menapius displays considerable learning and great prolixity. Upon the slight foundation of Favorinus' arguments as reported by Aulus Gellius he erects a complex scaffolding of medical discussion, quotations from authorities such as Galen and Hippocrates, fervent pleas for patients to obey their doctors' advice, suggestions as to diet and behavior, and the customary recommendation to accept the fever as a relatively mild form of the suffering inherent in man's mortal state. The Lyons blason, although making use of some of Menapius' medical learning, adopts in general a more light-hearted tone. The introductory lines are of interest in that they refer to the author's own earlier blasons. He becomes, in a sense, his own authority:

> Pour avoir fait au deshõneur d'Hõneur
> Blasonnements, aussi en la faveur
> De la grand' Goutte, *à tort dite* incurable,
> Je veux aussi à l'exemple notable
> Des plus sçavans Modernes, & antiques,
> Canonizer par raisons autentiques
> La Quarte icy, l'engin exercitant.
> Car Phavorin jadis en feit autant:
> Puis Menapie, Encomiaste exquis,
> En dit maints loz: & duquel ay enquis
> Maints argumens pour former sa louange.
>   (p. 18, italics mine)

Addressing all "febricitans," the poet criticizes their belief in the severity of their affliction:

> A telz propos je vous peux contredire,
> Qu'il n'y ha mal (au vray) pour mal receu,
> Si ainsi n'est par opinion creu,
> Au dire au moins d'aucuns philosophans.
>   (p. 19)[44]

The line of attack here is slightly different from that followed in the gout blason. In the earlier work, gout was admitted to involve suffering, but such publicly endured and visible pain could be rendered more tolerable if the individual could achieve and sustain the right attitude towards his "calling." Quartan fever, on the other hand, was not usually a lifelong or a fatal illness. Its defense will be based primarily on its most striking characteristic, that of being absent for more days than it is present (at four day intervals in the ancient, and three in the modern system of reckoning).

But first the poet questions the very name of the malady. It should never have been called a fever, for it has nothing to do with "ferite" or "ferveur," terms commonly related to it.[45] Not even meriting the epithet of "fiere," it is the mildest of fevers, a "gratieux tourment," a "douce langueur," and a "purge salutaire." Turning next to his own historical situation, the "blasonneur" remarks that in recent times people have observed an increase in the severity of the disease. This change he attributes to "aucune insolence / Faite au manger, ou en quelque autre affaire." If not prolonged by the patient's intemperance, the fever will gradually subside. All other fevers are more dangerous than the quartan, particularly since it strikes in winter, the safest season for such diseases. A fever caught in the summer will be aggravated by the heat, whereas we are happy to remain indoors when it is cold outside. A cosy picture of the patient tucked up by a warm fire, "demenans pres du feu chere lie," impresses this point upon the reader. The illness is beginning to resemble a state of health, in which "à toute heure est loysible / De s'esventer, manger, boire, & courir" (p. 20). In a sense it is even superior to normal health, for it can drive off other fevers from which the patient was suffering previously. Doctors, continues the poet, may wish their patients to catch the "Quarte," hoping to drive off a greater with a lesser ill. The "Quarte," a disease, now becomes not a goddess, as had been the case with gout, but a force having "puissance / Plus grande assez, que l'hautaine science / Des Medecins" (p. 21). This paradoxical idea of a disease as a kind of doctor is the second recurrent theme of the blason.

We are blessed also in the fact that the "Quarte," because of its characteristic pattern of attacks at regular intervals, can never be wrongly diagnosed and treated. Indeed, on the days between bouts of fever, "on joue, on rit, on s'esbat," whereas with most illnesses the suffering is so constant that "rien, que mort, on n'attend, ou demande." Repeating his claim that the "Quarte" immunizes its victims against other infections, the poet recalls the advantages of the fever's regular but relatively mild attacks. Surely, he suggests, it is better to contend with a known but intermittent ill than face one of life's countless disagreeable surprises. That the "Quarte" is not a very severe disease is proved by the fact that, even if he is "enquartene," a man summoned before a judge is still expected to appear. In short, we can lead much the same life with the fever as without. Even exercise is deemed beneficial to it, whereas sufferers from other diseases are forced to modify and restrict their activities drastically.

Despite their professed admiration and desire for the disease they were eulogizing, most disease-praisers included in their encomia either a section discussing the cure for the illness or some recommendations as to how best to cope with its attacks. The French poet follows this trend but introduces a slightly ambiguous note into his description of the process:

> Car simple peur, leger ou grand exces,
> Maints ont gueriz, & guerissent assez,
> Voire à simple eau d'un simple distillee
> Souventesfois elle s'en est allee. (p. 23)[46]

Continuing this seemingly scientific discussion of how to cure a disease whose very reality he had previously questioned, the poet inserts a passage describing personal experience. He states that in 1545, the year of the composition of the blason, he, although not a physician, cured several cases of quartan fever in patients for whom qualified doctors were too expensive. The cure was achieved by administering "de ladite eau," that said earlier to have been distilled from a "simple." Since the promise the "blasonneur" makes to describe this brew is never fulfilled, we must look elsewhere for what he may mean by a "cure."

The answer will be found in the gradually unfolding procedure of the blason, which continues as the poet explains that the "humeur melancolique," cause of the fever, makes a patient "Docte, & prudent, en tout ingenieux." The fever strikes only those strong enough to withstand it; the very old, like the very young, usually escape. A similar claim had been made for gout. Only if he refuses to behave sensibly while suffering from the "Quarte" will a man be anything other than stronger after than he was before contracting the disease. We have been maneuvered into the now familiar paradoxical situation of asking to have the "quarte": "tresjoyeux ilz sont un peu l'avoir, / Comme à purger faisant meilleur devoir, / Que nul bolus, ou pillule, ou breuvage" (p. 26). And yet health still remains the ideal; the fever is to be welcomed only as a means of attaining this ultimate goal:

> Donc pour un peu, qu'elle peult tourmenter,
> Ne vault il mieux la Quarte supporter
> Pour puis avoir santé perpetuelle,
> Qu'estre en danger d'un grand meschef sans elle?
>   (p. 26)

Not only does the fever eventually strengthen the body, it also transforms the personality:

> Tristes espritz fait devenir joyeux,
> Vivre en espoir, rejouvenir gens vieux,
> Extenuant humeurs melancoliques,
> Qui rendent gens bien souvent fantastiques.
>
> (p. 27)

Once again a disease is portrayed as a kind of healer, a cure for other maladies. "Gens enquartenes" are therefore urged to accept their sufferings with "joye, & patience," secure in the knowledge that, if careful, they will enjoy

> . . . une convalescence
> Trop plus utile, & salubre, & durable,
> Que si n'eussiez eu la Quarte louable.
> Et plus facile à guerir, qu'on ne dit,
> Si lon sçait bien ce, qu'à sa cure duit.
>
> (p. 27)

Thus ends the second disease blason. Where the gout poem had sought to investigate the best way of living with what was almost always an incurable illness, the poem on the "Quarte" continually stresses that the fever is both curable and physically beneficial. The goddess Gout, after branding her followers with the external signs of fleshly overindulgence and weakness, then gave them the chance to achieve moral and spiritual superiority and strength. Severus and Leyva typified this process. The quartan fever functioned and was presented differently. A serious but not necessarily incurable illness, it was characterized by the intermittence of its attacks and by the fact that it was commonly held to strengthen and cleanse the body of the survivor. The idea of a disease whose presence is identified by the number of days on which it is absent is at first sight as strange as that of a disease being a kind of cure. Yet each of these propositions contains an element of truth, presented playfully by the French poet in the form of interlocking paradoxes. The allegedly effective "simple" is of course never supplied, for the writer is a paradoxist, not a doctor. His claim to have cured some sufferers is not the main point made in his poem, but a short section in a wide-ranging investigation into the positive and negative aspects of this peculiar type of fever. The "Quarte" can be neither eliminated nor disregarded: the conclusion cautiously suggests that by pondering "ce, qu'à sa cure duit" a fever-sufferer may learn what might be termed a healthy way of coping with what nonetheless remains a disease. This changed state of mind and body, a combination of mental agility and physical moderation, has been described in and illustrated by the very procedure of the blason. A kind of intellectual "simple," the poem encourages reflection and broadens our understanding of the mysterious and two-sided nature of disease.

The third blason follows in the tradition of the "vitupére," but instead of inveighing against a known ill or an evil person or way of life, it seeks to denigrate a concept generally venerated, that of honor. This type of attack on something usually seen as praiseworthy had always been an accepted form of paradoxical encomium, but had not hitherto been found in the blason.[47] Since the Italians, however, had already imitated such pieces in their "capitoli," it is not surprising that the blason against honor is the one which owes most to an Italian source, Mauro's "Capitolo in dishonor dell' Honore al Prior di Iesi" and "Del Dishonore al medesimo." These appeared in the 1542 edition of the Bernesque writers' works, *Tutte le opere del Bernia*, and may also, according to O. Trtnik-Rossettini, have influenced the famous passage in Marot's third "Epître du coq à l'âne," that on the disadvantages of honor on the battlefield.[48]

Consideration of honor was a popular theme at the time. Whereas the blasons on gout and quartan fever seem to have been the only full-length mock encomia in verse on these two diseases to have been composed in France in the 16th century, the satirical treatment of honor, bane or glory of the courtier's existence, was frequent. Marot, Amadis Jamyn, and Regnier all condemned the restrictions imposed upon man by that elusive ideal.[49] Later on, the same arguments are repeated, in a vividly dramatic setting, by Falstaff, who, on the battlefield of Shrewsbury, reflects ruefully on the inability of Honor to mend the physical injuries suffered in its defense, and on the ease with which it is irretrievably lost:

Well, 'tis no matter, honour pricks me on. Yea, but how if honour prick me off when I come on, how then? Can honour set to a leg? No. Or an arm? No. Or take away the grief of a wound? No. Honour hath no skill in surgery then? No. What is honour? A word. What is in that word honour? What is that honour? Air. A trim reckoning! Who hath it? He that died a-Wednesday. Doth he feel it? No. Doth he hear it? No. 'Tis insensible, then? Yea, to the dead. But will it not live with the living? No. Why? Detraction will not suffer it. Therefore I'll none of it. Honour is a mere scutcheon— and so ends my catechism. (I *Henry IV*, V, i)[50]

O. Trtnik-Rossettini compares the Lyons blason in some detail to Mauro's two "capitoli." Unlike P. Toldo, she believes that the French poem imitates Mauro more closely than Jamyn was to do in his "Contre l'Honneur": "Car l'anonyme n'a imité plus ou moins directement que douze tercets du premier capitolo et un seul du deuxième. . . . [Jamyn] s'éloigne surtout du paradoxe burlesque et satirique. L'anonyme français, tout en voyant, comme Mauro, dans l'honneur la cause des différents maux qui affligent l'humanité, ajoute cependant des détails originaux et conserve l'allure du paradoxe bernesque."[51]

In beginning his first "capitolo" against honor, Mauro had asserted that the topic had never before been treated. Although most men revere honor, he would prefer to banish it from the world. It forbids us to enjoy the sexual pleasures so natural to man and even seeks to convince us "che'l morir di lancia é bello." Surely it is far better to lead a peaceful life than die in battle. Mauro sees himself as the defender in particular of women, whose right to sensual enjoyment he seeks to champion. Every pleasure is, unfortunately, marred by the thought of honor. Indeed, his beloved is so hardheaded to him only because she follows honor as a blind person does his dog. Like an invisible disease, honor gradually destroys us, making us prepared even to die for its sake. The first "capitolo" ends with a renewed plea for support from the ladies. The second "capitolo" considers the primitive golden age, when the concept of honor was unknown. All human laws making men work, fight battles, and restrict their love-making can be traced back to their origins in some rule of honor's endless code. As O. Trtnik-Rossettini puts it, "Mauro fait ainsi apparaître la décadence des mœurs dans l'Italie du seizième siècle, l'absence de principes moraux, le cynisme, l'indifférence envers la patrie et l'avidité de jouissances" (p. 170). The poet's chief scorn is reserved for the knightly "point d'honneur," cause of so much useless bloodshed at the time. It should be pointed out at this stage that Mauro, like the French "blasonneur," undercuts his own indifferent stance by confessing at the end of his "capitolo" that despite his professed scorn he remains terrified by honor. As we shall see, the French poet extends this notion considerably, thereby altering the balance of the entire poem.

The full title of the French poem is "Blason Declamatoire au Deshonneur de Honneur," a close copy of Mauro's "In Dishonor dell'Honore." The poem is presented as an intellectual exercise leading us to appreciate the unchangeable, but mysterious nature of God's wisdom. The poet proposes to demonstrate that we can question everything, "fors divine science" (p. 11). The intangibility of honor is first stressed; it is but a word, "et pour autant chose plus que frivole" (p. 11). Honor is portrayed as a kind of malady, blighting our lives in much the same way as does a physical disease. The "blasonneur" here inserts a clever reference to two familiar afflictions, fever and gout. Although the immediate source for these lines is Mauro, the passage gains added force from the fact that these are precisely the topics of the two other blasons in the collection. The ironic assertion that honor is a form of disease is reinforced by the poem's position between two mock encomia on physical illnesses.

The French writer's first departure from Mauro's arguments concerns the origins and gradually increasing power of honor. First introduced when Adam and Eve sought to conceal their nakedness with the "Figuier," honor in the "beaux siecles dorés" did not prevent men from enjoying the pleasures of love:

> Alors Amans avecques leurs Amyes
> Sans d'Honneur crainte, ou d'aucune infamie
> Par champs, par boys, par montaigne, ou valee
> S'entredonnoyent l'un l'autre l'accollee. (p. 13)[52]

As time passed, the "blasonneur" explains, honor grew from a "Gars" to a tyrant, "le pire des pires" (p. 14). Using the customary mock-encomiastic technique, the poet rewrites history. Honor, he explains, was the reason for the death of Abel, the fame of Nimrod as a hunter, the building of the tower of Babel, and the creation of countless false gods and idols. It even led to the invention of the various arts and to the divisions amongst "escoles." These sweeping assertions are not explained, but the lines in general seem to equate honor with ambition or personal pride. Even noble souls, this passage concludes, are often corrupted by honor, led to commit deeds of oppression. Cain, presumably, is to be viewed as such a man.

Returning briefly to the sexual barriers raised by honor, the author wonders how many abortions have been performed in order to maintain an honorable facade. Heresy, treachery, theft, and conspiracy frequently result from our attachment to honor. We can even be tricked by it into believing that an honorable death in battle is glorious. The following section seems to be an attack on Machiavellian-type politics:

> Mais n'ha il pas une plus grande erreur?
> Disant qu'on doit, & peult sa foy faucer
> L'homme, qui veult regner, ou s'avancer?
> (p. 15)

The suggestion here is that for different people there are different rules concerning what is honorable. Most men are taught that it is dishonorable to betray their "foy." The "blasonneur" states, however, that an ambitious monarch or leader may be permitted to break his word, presumably because he has in mind some more important consideration, such as his own political future or the good of his realm. This ambiguous, even self-contradictory notion of a non-absolute honor is at first surprising, but seems to be part of the author's presentation of the gradual evolution of honor through the ages.

Its distinctive nature is further illuminated when the poet dismisses in three lines the "inhumains" Greeks and Romans, capable of destroying themselves or members of their own families to preserve their honor. The danger to families had been noted earlier in the reference to the murder of Abel, although the biblical murder was that of an honorable man by a dishonorable one. The famous Greek and Roman murders, on the other hand, were generally of family members believed by their killers to have disgraced the shared family name. In the case of suicide, the action was undertaken by honorable men who felt that only in death could their integrity be preserved.

After a brief mention of Lucifer's fall, also to be blamed on honor, the "blasonneur" develops once again Mauro's theme of unnecessary sexual restrictions:

> Bref il leur fait si honteuses molestes, [aux femmes]
> Que plusieurs ont regret de n'estre bestes
> Pour prendre, ainsi qu'elles, sans deshonneur
> Leurs appetitz, desirantes qu'Honneur,
> Et ses respectz, vraye gehenne mortelle,
> Fut forbanny de l'humaine cervelle. (p. 15)

Demanding absolute marital fidelity and refusing recognition to illegitimate children, honor may eventually make marriage almost impossible. It is the thorn in every rose of pleasure, laments the poet, echoing Mauro; "on ne sçauroit à rien faire, ou entendre, / Aller, venir, manger, dormir, & boire, / Ou damp Honneur ne survienne en barboire" (p. 16). In short, it demands more love and respect even than God: "Et plus, que Dieu, veult qu'on l'adore, ou prise" (p. 16). This startling line, not found in the Italian poem, completes in a dramatic manner the portrait of honor's evolution, from its beginning with Eve's figleaf to a superhuman, omnipresent force. The conclusion drawn by the poet is that this new religion, rather than elevating man, has degraded him. The cuckold's horns, legendary signs of dishonor, are but one of a series of far more serious metamorphoses "Horribles plus, que celles la d'Ovide."[53] Men become foxes, pigs, wolves, and dogs at the false god's bidding. This passage is presumably to be understood in the light of those relating the deceptions, duels, murders, and other crimes performed in honor's name. At this stage of the poem, the reader must feel that the treacherous idol should be overturned, its powers destroyed. In debasing and animalizing its followers, honor has achieved precisely the opposite effect of that sought by traditional religions.

Yet all this chaos is brought about by no more than a "vent mobile," swiftly lost and rarely regained. The choice of the term "vent" here serves to emphasize honor's elusiveness and also the sense that it is but a word, a breath of wind, like Falstaff's "air." But despite this seven-page tirade the poet reaches a conclusion recalling that of Mauro:

Quoy que ce soit tant la finesse, & ruse
De cest Honneur me fait craindre & m'amuse,
Que toutesfois, qu'il vient au devant moy,
Tremble de peur, & suis en tel esmoy,
Que tous plaisirs je laisse pour le suyvre,
Aymant plus tost mourir, que sans luy vivre.

(p. 17)

We may view these lines as a final, albeit reluctant acceptance of the need
for social hypocrisy. Such a view would seem to be borne out by Mauro's
conclusion, but does not, I believe, do justice to the tone of the last couplet
of the French poem. Mauro had emphasized that he obeyed the god out of
fear ("mi trema ogni membro, & nerva, & ossa"), but the "blasonneur" goes
further, stating that he prefers death to life without honor. In so doing, he
makes more apparent the logical impasse to which his paradoxical reason-
ing has brought him. For he implies that, despite all, there remains some
positive motivation behind the return to honor. The poem encouraged the
reader to recognize as snares many false forms of honor, but these debased
forms never seemed to efface all of honor, even as the word "honneur"
remains visible within the word "deshonneur." The "blasonneur" is still
haunted by the word he seeks to efface. Indeed, each new attack on the
concept seems but to elevate it yet further, until it finally achieves the
status of a divinity, beyond the reach of mere words. Behind Falstaff's
battlefield tricks lay his desire that his prince should believe him an honorable warrior, capable of slaying Hotspur in a fair fight. While the manifestations of honor in the blason's post-lapsarian world may fall so far short
of the ideal as almost to contradict it, the would-be rebel retains an un-
easy sense of the loftier purpose behind the irksome, seemingly unnecessary
restraints and rules.

The fact that the very terms of many attacks tend to be borrowed from
the domain of the concept or object attacked was of constant interest to
paradoxists. When Synesius of Cyrene, in another famous mock encomium
familiar to Renaissance readers, sought to eulogize baldness, he made this
dependence quite apparent. Including in his own text one by Dio Chrysostom in praise of hair, he attempted to refute point by point his predece-
sors' arguments.[54] But for all his rhetorical skill, Synesius' baldness nonetheless remains the absence of hair, not a positive attribute; he finally
voices regret at his own hairless state. Similarly, the "blasonneur" can
never escape his fascination with honor, despite his attempts at denigrat-
ing it. This eventual return to "the fold" and departure from paradoxical
investigation and hesitation are completed in the short "Chanson Sus"
which closes the de Tournes collection. Also anonymous, the poem is a
lament over the "grande guerre, qu'un chacun ha contre soymesmes."

After seven stanzas of seven lines each, the concluding stanza cites Job and St. Paul as having also longed for an end to man's eternal struggle against his baser passions and instincts. The poet begs God, "qui seul les deffaitz reffait" (p. 30), for deliverance from this long battle in which, as his introductory stanza had put it, "mon grand ennemy, las, c'est moy" (p. 28).

The three Lyons blasons, as we have seen, are alike in being paradoxical presentations of familiar phenomena. In the same year, 1547, de Tournes published two other works related to the paradoxical tradition—Philibert de Vienne's *Philosophe de Court*, one of the most interesting French imitations of Lucian's *Rhetorum Praeceptor*, and the *Opuscules d'Amour*, containing La Borderie's *Amye de Court*, another work of ironic advice (first published in 1541). In 1546 and 1547 respectively, he published works by the two best-known exponents of the blason, Marot and Scève. His Italian preface to his 1547 edition of Petrarch, dedicated to Scève, indicates de Tournes's familiarity with that language.[55] He might easily have known the Bernesque "capitoli" well enough to be interested in publishing imitations of them in his native tongue. He thus combined in himself, as the reader of his collection of blasons needed to do, an awareness of the classical mock encomiastic tradition, of its Italian revival, and of earlier examples of the French blason. As the above analysis has sought to demonstrate, only with such an awareness does the reader not risk being more puzzled than pleased by the three poems. A reader unfamiliar with Lucian and expecting a traditional blason of praise or blame would be jarred by the ironic tone of the Lyons poems. One unacquainted with the Bernesque "capitoli" but familiar with classical satirical eulogies would be surprised by the use of a verse form for what had usually been a prose genre. And yet only a reader with some knowledge of the "typical" blason could adequately savor the Lyons works' highly original use of the form.

The reasons for the Renaissance fondness for paradoxical argumentation are numerous, but derive chiefly from the desire to explore new ways of investigating philosophic, moral, and even physical problems. The three anonymous blasons focus on two medical problems and one moral one. With humor and ingenuity they lead us step by step to reconsider certain preconceptions about disease, to reevaluate the importance of honor and to appreciate better the subtle possibilities of descriptive poetry. It is of course impossible to determine the influence of this obscure collection on the subsequent history of the blason. However, two observations may be made, one general, one specific. In an article on the blason, K. Kupisz notes that one reason the blason disappears as a form in the late 16th century is that its subjectivity, always inherent in the seemingly objective descriptions of phenomena, increased so much as the century went by that the blason frequently became indistinguishable from lyric poetry.[56] The Lyons poems are early examples of blasons in which the subtle fluctuations of the author's *attitude* to his subject are as important to our understanding of what he is describing as is the accuracy of the description. The more specific point concerns the well-known "hymnes-blasons" of the Pléiade. Most of these poems, on insects, the frog, the mule, and so on end with a half-joking, half-serious invocation to the poem's subject, begging it to be merciful to the poet or to his friends. Such invocations naturally tend to contradict the attitude of approval expressed in the remainder of the poem. Thus Ronsard begs the much-lauded "freslon" and ant not to bite his friend Belleau, and asks the equally praiseworthy frog not to keep Belleau awake at night, while Du Bellay, in concluding the "Hymne de la Surdité," expressed for the first time some reservations about the advantages of deafness.[57] This type of last-minute reversal of attitude was precisely that noted both in Mauro's and in the Lyons poet's treatment of honor. We can say, therefore, in conclusion, that in the thirty pages of his slim volume, the great Lyons publisher managed to print (a) the first verse mock encomium on gout in French, b) the only such work on the quartan fever, and c) one of the most original and daring ironic treatments of a topic often discussed in Renaissance France, that of honor.

NOTES

1. Copies of the edition are in the Arsenal, the Bibliothèque Mazarine, the Bibliothèque Nationale, and the libraries of Chantilly and Besançon, see Alfred Cartier, *Bibliographie des éditions des de Tournes, imprimeurs lyonnais* (Paris: Editions des Bibliothèques Nationales de France, 1937), I, 222.

2. Dudley B. Wilson, *Descriptive Poetry in France from Blason to Baroque* (Manchester: Manchester Univ. Press; New York: Barnes and Noble, Inc., 1967). For other studies of the genre, see Bertrand Guégan, *Blasons anatomiques du corps féminin* (Chartres: Duraud, 1931); Enzo Giudici, ed., *Le Opere minori di Maurice Scève* (Parma: Guanda, 1953); Henri Guy, "Les Sources françaises de Ronsard," *Revue d'Histoire Littéraire de la France*, 9 (1902), 217-56; Charles d'Héricault, *Les Oeuvres de Guillaume Coquillart* (Paris: Bibliothèque Elzévirienne, 1857), 2 vols.; Hélène Harvitt, *Eustorg de Beaulieu, A Disciple of Marot (1495(?)-1552)* (Lancaster, Pa.: New Era Printing Co., 1918), pp. 79-83; C.E. Kinch, *La Poésie satirique de Clément Marot* (Paris: Boivin, 1940); Kazimierz Kupisz, "Des Recherches sur l'évolution du blason au XVIe siècle," *Zagadnienia Rodzajow Literackich*, 9 (1966), 67-81; Robert Pike, "The *Blason* in French Literature of the Sixteenth Century," *Romanic Review*, 27 (1936), 223-42; Verdun L. Saulnier, *Maurice Scève* (Paris: Klincksieck, 1948-1949), I, 72-87; Alison Saunders, "Jean de Vauzelles—Moralist and *Blasonneur*," *Studi Francesi*, 24 (1980), 277-88 and "Sixteenth-Century Collected Editions of *Blasons Anatomiques*," *The Library*, 31 (1976), 351-68; Annette

and Edward Tomarken, "The Rise and Fall of the Sixteenth-Century French Blason," *Symposium*, 29 (1975), 139-63; A. Tomarken (listed under the name Porter), *The Satirical Eulogy in the Literature of the French Renaissance*, unpublished Ph.D. thesis, London, 1965; Dudley Wilson, "Le Blason," *Lumières de la Pléiade* (Paris: Vrin, 1966), pp. 97-112; Albert-Marie Schmidt, ed., *Poètes du XVIe siècle* (Paris: Gallimard, 1953), pp. 293-364.

3. Thomas Sebillet, *Art Poétique françoys*, ed. Félix Gaiffe (Paris: E. Cornély, 1910), pp. 169-70.

4. Claude de Boissière, *Art Poétique réduict* (Paris: Annet Brière, 1554), p. 255. As Giudici puts it, "il 'blason' tipico resta sempre quello individuato all'epoca di Scève" (*Le Opere minori*, p. 75). Saulnier (*Maurice Scève*, I, 73) notes that the same definition was later echoed by Delaudun d'Aigaliers in his *Art Poétique françois* (Paris: A. Du Brueil, 1598). Saulnier adds that this definition is "trop étroite," but explains that it came into vogue because of the popularity of the anatomical blasons inspired by Clément Marot.

5. Saulnier (I, 74) perceives two distinct genres within the so-called blason. The first, which he calls the "blason satirique," is typified by Guillaume Alexis's "Blason de faulses amours" (1486), and by Pierre Gringore's "Blason de l'heretique" and "Blason de Pratique" (1505). The second type is the "blason médaillon," similar to Scève's "Blason du sourcil" and Marot's poem on the "Beau Tétin." Saulnier notes that 15th-century blasons are of the satirical type, and believes them to be distantly related to Latin satires. The "blason médaillon" is a short descriptive poem that can be part of a series of blasons on related topics, for example parts of the body, wines, towns, and so on. This relatively clearcut distinction has to be further subdivided as the 16th century progresses, for then we find the "médaillon satirique et symbolique" (I, 76) and the Pléiade "hymnes-blasons," not to mention the "contre-blason" and the "blason marotique." Being a direct attack, Saulnier's "blason satirique" is not a mock encomium, and therefore cannot include the Lyons blasons. For further discussion of these complex problems of nomenclature, see Giudici, *Le Opere minori*, pp. 73-85.

6. Giudici, p. 80. This phrase echoes Sebillet's explanation of the "Definition": such a poem, he states, "exprime la sustance de la chose definie, et le naturel fond d'elle" (*Art Poétique*, p. 170). For Sebillet, the element of praise or blame essential to a blason seems to have served to distinguish it from the "definition." Giudici's formulation lays less emphasis on this laudatory or vituperative aspect.

7. Wilson, for instance, notes the relationship between early blasons and the medieval "débat" and "dit" (*Descriptive Poetry*, pp. 9-10), and excludes certain blasons from his discussion on the grounds that they are not really blasons (p. 9, for the exclusion of Gringore's "Description de Procès et de sa figure").

8. See G. Manacorda, "Notizie intorno alle fonti di alcuni motivi satirici," *Romanische Forschungen*, Band. 22, H. 3 (1908), 733-60; Claude-Albert Mayer, *Satire in French Literature from 1525 to 1560 with Special Reference to Sources and Technique*, unpublished Ph.D. thesis, London, 1949; C.A. Mayer, "Lucien et la Renaissance," *Revue de Littérature Comparée*, 47 (1973), 5-22; Robert V. Merrill, "Lucian and Du Bellay's 'Poète Courtisan,'" *Modern Philology*, 29 (1931-1932), 11-20; Christopher Robinson, *Lucian and His Influence in Europe* (London: Duckworth, 1979); C. Robinson, "The Reputation of Lucian in Sixteenth-Century France," *French Studies*, 29 (1975), 385-97; Craig R. Thompson, *The Translations of Lucian by Erasmus and Sir Thomas More* (Ithaca, N.Y.: Chicago Univ. Press, 1940); Pauline

M. Smith, *The Anti-Courtier Trend in Sixteenth-Century French Literature* (Geneva: Droz, 1966), Part I, "Sources and Models," and the articles by Miller, Malloch, and Pease described below, n. 9.

9. See A.H. Porter, thesis cit., p. 6. On the genre as a whole, see Theodore C. Burgess, *Epideictic Literature*, Univ. of Chicago Studies in Classical Philology, 3 (1902); Adolf Hauffen, "Zur Litteratur der ironischen Enkomien," *Vierteljahrschrift für Litteraturegeschichte*, 6 (1893), 160-85; A.E. Malloch, "The Techniques and Function of the Renaissance Paradox," *Studies in Philology*, 53 (1956), 191-203; Rosalie Colie, *Paradoxia Epidemica* (Princeton, N.J.: Princeton Univ. Press, 1966); Sister Mary Geraldine, "Erasmus and the Tradition of Paradox," *Studies in Philology*, 61 (1964), 41-63; Walter Kaiser, *Praisers of Folly* (Cambridge, Ma.: Harvard Univ. Press, 1963); Henry Knight Miller, "The Paradoxical Encomium with Special Reference to Its Vogue in England, 1600-1800," *Modern Philology*, 53 (1956), 145-78; Arthur Stanley Pease, "Things without Honor," *Classical Philology*, 21 (1926), 27-42; Brian Vickers, "'King Lear' and Renaissance Paradoxes," *Modern Language Review*, 63 (1968), 305-14. See also below, n. 23. In her study, Colie states that "The rhetorical paradox as a literary form has duplicity built into it. As an ancient form—like tragedy or pastoral, like epic or satire—it set traditional models to be imitated and improved upon; unlike those mentioned, however, the rhetorical paradox had no set style, no steady, reliable, fixed decorum" (p. 5).

10. On the various editions of Berni, see Giorgio Bárberi Squarotti, ed., Francesco Berni, *Rime* (Turin: Einaudi, 1969), pp. xxix-xxxii. Berni's "capitoli" were first published in 1537 and 1538 in Venice by Curtio Navo, then in a longer edition by Grazzini, Il Lasca, in 1548, by I. Giunti. All the publications were posthumous, Berni having died, probably from poison, in 1535 (b. 1497).

11. On the animal poetry of the Renaissance, see Hélène Naïs, *Les Animaux dans la poésie française de la Renaissance* (Paris: Didier, 1969). See p. 8 for mention of the popularity of Catullus. See also Mary Morrison, "Catullus in the Neo-Latin Poetry of France before 1550," *Bibliothèque d'Humanisme et Renaissance*, 17 (1955), 25-56, and A.H. Porter, thesis cit., ch. VII.

12. Best known amongst the French Renaissance works of ironic advice are La Borderie's *Amye de Court* (1541), Philibert de Vienne's *Philosophe de Court* (1547) and Du Bellay's *Poète Courtisan* (1559).

13. Bilibaldus Pirckheymer, *Apologia seu Laus Podagrae* (Nuremberg: F. Peypus, 1522); published with Lucian's *Podagra* in 1529 (Strasburg: H. Sybold) and in 1570 with the addition of C. Ballista's work (see below, n. 14). Pirckheymer's encomium was translated into English as *The Praise of the Gout* (London, 1617).

14. Composed around 1546, Cardano's encomium was not published until later on (it appears in the best-known collection of Renaissance encomia, that by Caspar Dornavius, the *Amphitheatrum sapientiae socraticae iocoseriae* (Hanover, 1619). On Cardano, see Henry Morley, *Jerome Cardan* (London: Chapman and Hall, 1854); Oystein Ore, *Cardano the Gambling Scholar* (Princeton: Princeton Univ. Press, 1953); and A. Wykes, *Doctor Cardano, Physician Extraordinary* (London: Muller, 1969). Of Arbaleste (Ballista) little is known. His *In Podagram Concertatio* (s.l. n.d. [Zurich?] 1525 or 1528) was in fact designed to give a suffering friend (the bishop of Sion, cf. Mauro on gouty clerics) ways of combating the disease. The work was reprinted in 1570 with Lucian's and Pirckheymer's encomia (Strasburg: apud haeredes Christian Milii). In 1571 it was translated into English by B.G. (probably Barnaby Googe) and entitled *The Overthrow of the Gout* (London: A. Veale). Hessus' *Ludus de Podagra* appeared in 1537 (Mainz: I. Schoeffer).

15. Erasmus, *Praise of Folly*, trans. Betty Radice, ed. A.H.T. Levi (Middlesex: Penguin Books, 1971). This edition is based on the 1898 J.B. Kan one, supplemented when necessary from the 1515 Froben edition. Erasmus' prefatory letter cites thirteen authors of mock encomia and similarly playful works. For our purposes, the most important amongst these are Synesius, Lucian, and Favorinus.

16. *Les Oeuvres de Lucian de Samosate*, trans. Filbert Bretin (Paris: Abel l'Angelier, 1583), p. 691.

17. *Descriptive Poetry*, p. 14: "The *blasonneur* uses a great number of adjectives in particular (as one would expect in a descriptive genre) and adds variety to his pattern of repetition mainly by the use of subtle rhythms and combinations of parts of speech repeated with various shiftings of emphasis and in different feet in successive lines."

18. In Italian, "fuori del comun parere." On Lando, see Paul F. Grendler, *Critics of the Italian World, 1530-1560* (Madison: Univ. of Wisconsin Press, 1969). The *Paradossi* were first published in Lyons by Pullon de Trino in 1543. They were soon translated into French by Charles Estienne and published by de Tournes in 1545. We begin to see the printer's interest in paradoxical writing in the 1540s. Estienne's translation was an extremely popular one, see A.H. Porter, thesis cit., pp. 393-94. For the same type of questioning of received opinion with regard to the quartan fever, see below, n. 44. Colie (p. 10) expresses a similar view: "The subject of a rhetorical paradox is one officially disapproved in received opinion."

19. A. and E. Tomarken, "The Rise and Fall," p. 141.

20. Jean de Rus, *Oeuvres*, ed. Philippe Tamizey de Larroque (Paris: A. Claudin, 1875), pp. 23-26. Schmidt (ed. cit., p. 300) notes that the poet "reçoit l'Eglantine aux Jeux floraux en 1540," Eustorg de Beaulieu composed a blason praising the nose (see Schmidt, pp. 315-18).

21. See Sebastian Brant, *The Ship of Fools*, trans. Edwin H. Zeydel (New York: Columbia Univ. Press, 1944), p. 229. (Part of ch. 67, "not wishing to be a fool.")

22. In defense of this comparative method, to be employed in discussing all three of the Lyons blasons, I cite Colie (p. 33): "When the rhetorical paradox moved out of the classical languages into the vernacular literatures, it remained a sophisticated form, written for a learned and experienced audience, an audience of men and women in the know, who could be expected to understand the paradoxists' learned wit and to admire the rhetorical skills demonstrated in the paradoxes themselves." Further on in the same study (p. 35), Colie remarks that "since paradoxes are so traditional, in both their form and their subject matter known to sophisticated audiences, they present their composers with terrible difficulties in finding the surprise." To discover some of these surprises is of course the aim of the present essay.

23. On the history of gout, see W.S.C. Copeman, *A Short History of Gout and the Rheumatic Diseases* (Berkeley: Univ. of California Press, 1964), and Ralph H. Major, *A History of Medicine* (Springfield, Ill.: Charles C. Thomas, 1954), 2 vols. On the Italian "capitoli," in general, see N. Condeescu, "Le Paradoxe bernesque dans la littérature française de la Renaissance," *Beiträge zur Romanischen Philologie*, 2 (1963), 27-51, and Paolo Cherchi, "L'Encomio paradossale nel manierismo," *Forum Italicum*, 9 (1975), 368-84. On the disease "capitoli" see A. Tomarken, "'Let us laugh our pains away': The Italian Bernesque Poets' Encomia on Disease," *Fifteenth-Century Studies*, 3 (1980), 211-17.

24. On these techniques as used in straightforward encomia, see Aristotle, *Rhetoric to Alexander* (Loeb Classical Library), p. 307.

25. Lucian's criticism of doctors had been quite overt. In the *Podagra*, the goddess Gout rapidly subdued two quack physicians who claimed to be able to cure sufferers. From the example of the two limping doctors, she bade all men learn "que je suis / Invincible & qui seule aux drogues n'obeis" (*Les Oeuvres de Lucian*, trans. Bretin, p. 695).

26. Pirckheymer, Cardano, Ballista, and other gout-praisers all repeated this notion. Eustache Deschamps had made the same point much earlier, see his *Oeuvres complètes*, ed. Le Marquis de Queux de Saint-Hilaire (Paris: Firmin-Didot, 1878), VIII, mccccviii, a letter addressed "a un nouvel marié gouteux."

27. The legend of Bellerophon could be used in connection with gout because of the lameness caused by his fall from Pegasus when he tried to fly the magic horse up to heaven. Philoctetes, the slayer of Paris in the Trojan war, was wounded by the bite of a water-snake. Sophocles' *Philoctetes* portrays him as a man triumphing over pain. Oedipus was called "Swell-foot" because he had been bound by the feet and left to die as a baby. The same unfortunate trio reappears in most Renaissance gout encomia. The *Ocypus* ("Swift-foot"), a short play sometimes attributed to Lucian, was also known in the 16th century. Bretin (ed. cit., p. 696) calls it a "tragedie manque, imparfaite & pleine de fautes infinies."

28. Ovid, *Epistulae ex Ponto*, trans. Henry T. Riley (London: George Bell, 1885), Epistle III to Rufinus, p. 377.

29. Berni, *Rime*, ed. Squarotti, p. 147, "Capitolo del debito," ll. 94-96, 102-105, and 109-11.

30. Berni, *Rime*, ed. Squarotti, p. 129, "Capitolo primo della peste," ll. 102-105: "Non è creditor che ti molesti: / se pur ne vien qualch'un, di'che tu hai / doglia di testa, e che ti senti al braccio; / colui va via senza voltarsi mai." On the plague in literature and art, see Sir Raymond Henry Payne Crawfurd, *Plague and Pestilence in Literature and Art* (Oxford: Clarendon Press, 1914).

31. Compare these lines with the poems on similar topics by Berni, "Capitolo del caldo del letto" and Mauro, "Capitolo del letto," both in the 1538 Venice edition (see above, n. 10), I, 50^r-51^v and II, 51^v-54^v respectively.

32. Rabelais, *Pantagruel*, ch. VII, in *Oeuvres complètes*, ed. Jacques Boulenger (Paris: Gallimard, 1955), p. 198. The title invented by Rabelais is "L'entrée de Anthoine de Leive es terres du Bresil"; Boulenger's footnote explains that Leyva helped launch a fruitless invasion of Provence for Charles V: "Rabelais considère comme aussi possible ou avantageuse son entrée dans le Brésil" (p. 198, n. 6). For Brantôme's description, see Pierre de Bourdeille, seigneur de Brantôme, *Mémoires*, "Les Vies des hommes illustres & grands capitaines estrangers de son temps" (Leyden: Jean Sambix, 1699), pp. 125-37. Despite some criticism, Brantôme praises Leyva's military prowess, courage in the face of illness (gout), and capacity for leadership. On the same invasion as referred to both by Rabelais and Montaigne, see Marcel Françon, "Sur l'Invasion de la Provence, en 1536, et Montaigne," *Bulletin de la Société des Amis de Montaigne*, 23 (1976), 113-14 and "L'Invasion de la Provence et l'allusion au Brésil," ibid., 24 (1977), 51.

33. Mellin de Saint-Gelais, *Oeuvres complètes*, ed. Prosper Blanchemain (Paris: Paul Daffis, 1873), I, 119: "Epitaphe d'Antoine de Leve." Leyva died of the fever.

34. Severus and Leyva were also used by Cardano as examples of correct behavior when suffering from gout.

35. As the English translation of Lucian's *Podagra* by Thomas Francklin puts it: "Hard is the lot of mortals here below; / But we some intervals of comfort know, /

For use and patience lessen ev'ry woe." *The Works of Lucian*, trans. T. Francklin (London: for T. Cadell, 1780), II, 588.

36. Pliny, *Natural History*, trans. W.H.S. Jones (Loeb Classical Library), VI, 381 (Bk. XXII, lvii, 119-21): "Sextus Pomponius, father of a man who was praetor, himself the most distinguished man in nearer Spain, was superintending the winnowing in his barns when he was seized with the pains of gout. Burying himself above his knees into the wheat he was relieved of the pain, and the water in his feet dried up in a wonderful way, so that afterwards he adopted this procedure as a remedy." René Bretonnayau, a doctor who composed poems on gout and on haemorrhoids, stated that Sextus Pomponius' cure must have been due to divine intervention, see *La Génération de l'homme* (Paris: Abel l'Angelier, 1583), p. 155ᵛ.

37. See, for instance, Guillaume Rondelet (1507-1566), *Methodus curandorum omnium morborum corporis humani* (Geneva: J. Stoer, 1609), ch. 81, p. 601: "Arthritis, articularis morbus ab articulis dicitur, à Barbaris gutta, quod existiment esse defluxionem guttatim factam."

38. Aretino, "Capitolo della Quartana," in *Il Secondo libro dell'Opere burlesche* (Florence: I Giunti, 1555), pp. 119ᵛ-22ᵛ. See also Olga Trtnik-Rossettini, *Les Influences anciennes & italiennes sur la satire en France au XVIᵉ siècle*, Publications de l'Institut Français de Florence, Iᵉʳᵉ série, 13 (Florence, 1958), p. 175.

39. For Aulus Gellius' résumé of Favorinus' encomium, see *The Attic Nights* (Loeb Classical Library), III, 251-53.

40. Menapius died in 1561. His *Encomium febris quartanae* (Basle: J. Oporinus, 1542) contains also the *Ratio curandi febrim quartanam*.

41. See H.K. Miller, "The Paradoxical Encomium," p. 172, and Philodemus of Gadara: "the sophists by their praise of Busiris and similar characters persuade men to become villains. Not only do they fail at times to praise anything useful, but they frequently praise bad things, and by lavishing praise on matters of small account they incline us to treat all subjects lightly." *The Rhetoric of Philodemus*, trans. H.M. Hubbell, Transactions of the Connecticut Academy of Arts and Sciences, 23 (1920), p. 304.

42. Pirckheymer and Cardano are but two of the many panegyrists to have provided such lists.

43. *Encomium Ebrietatis* (Leipzig: V. Schumann, 1519); *Encomium Sobrietatis* (s.l.n.d.). The text makes clear that the encomium on drunkenness preceded that on sobriety.

44. For the same type of attack on received opinion, and the same expression "à tort dite," see the gout blason, above, n. 18.

45. "Ferite" derives from the Italian "ferita," a wound, according to Edmond Huguet, *Dictionnaire de la langue française au seizième siècle* (Paris: Librairie Ancienne Edouard Champion, 1925). Huguet quotes Henri Estienne's satirical *Dialogues du nouveau français italianisé* of 1578 as an instance of the use of the word. The early use of the term in a series of blasons inspired by Italian works is therefore interesting.

46. A somewhat more mocking reference to the healing power of fear was made by Cardano in his encomium on gout: "multi in incendiis distenti acerbissimis doloribus Podagrae, fuga tanquam sani essent, se propripuerunt" (in Dornavius, *Amphitheatrum*, p. 219).

47. See Pease, "Things without Honor," p. 36, for a description of Libanius' vituperation of Achilles and Hector, and mention of Polybius' reference to a vitu-

peration of the faithful Penelope. As Alison Saunders shows in her article "Sixteenth-Century Collected Editions" (see n. 2 above), p. 359, a blason on honor appeared in the various collections of *blasons anatomiques* from 1537 onwards. Attributed to Lancelot Carle in the 1550 Charles l'Angelier edition published in Paris (and printed in the text immediately after Carle's other poems in l'Angelier's 1543 edition), the poem bears little resemblance to the Lyons blason. Both the attitude of the narrator and the focus of the two poems are entirely different. The Lyons narrator is hostile to honor, which he treats with mocking scorn, whereas the composer of the poem in the l'Angelier collection is cautious and respectful in his presentation. While the Lyons poet deals with political and family as well as social honor, the Paris poem, like most of the *blasons anatomiques*, concentrates on the feminine point of view. The blason dwells on the need for woman to be beautiful, virtuous, loved and loving. If she falls from this lofty state, she may be consoled by the knowledge that many others have been similarly weak, and that God pardons all offenses but ingratitude. The lady should however not cease striving for self-control, for love without "jouis-sance," since such behavior will earn her the title of "femme de bien." As this brief résumé indicates, the l'Angelier poem is in no way a Lucianic blason.

48. See O. Trtnik-Rossettini, *Les Influences anciennes*, p. 172, n. 3. Marot's third *coq à l'âne*, composed by 1536, appears in the *Oeuvres satiriques*: "Fy, fy, de mourir pour la gloire, / Ou, pour se faire grant seigneur, / D'aller mourir au lict d'honneur, / D'un gros canon parmy le corps, / Qui passe tout oultre dehors" (IX, 143, ll. 204-208). Jacques Tahureau, in his *Dialogues*, ed. Max Gauna, Textes Litté-raires Français, 291 (Geneva: Droz, 1981), pp. 186-88, comments with similar sar-casm on the vanity of honor. The *Dialogues* were first published in Paris in 1565 by Gabriel Buon. Speaking of the "homme de guerre," Tahureau notes scornfully that such a man thinks he cannot join the "bien-heureus" unless he dies "à une breche," trampled under foot by men and horses. He is ready to fight over the "couleur d'un bonnet" or some other trifle.

49. O. Trtnik-Rossettini, *Les Influences anciennes*, pp. 181-93.

50. Shakespeare, *King Henry IV Part I*, ed. A.R. Humphreys (Arden edition, London: Methuen & Co. Ltd., 1959), pp. 125-26. The play was printed by 1598, and reprinted five more times before the first folio of 1623.

51. O. Trtnik-Rossettini, *Les Influences anciennes*, p. 174, referring to Pietro Toldo, "Etudes sur la poésie burlesque française de la Renaissance," *Zeitschrift für Romanische Philologie*, 25 (1901), p. 263.

52. These lines recall those by Marot in his *rondeau* LX, "De l'Amour du Siecle Antique," first published in 1538, and composed by the middle of the same year: "Au bon vieulx temps ung train d'amour regnoit / Qui sans grand art & dons se demenoit, / Si qu'un boucquet donné d'Amour profonde / S'estoit donné toute la Terre ronde; / Car seulement au cueur on se prenoit" (*OD, Rondeau* LX, 129). Victor Brodeau's reply, published with Marot's *rondeau* in all the editions appearing in Marot's lifetime, contained a more cynical view of ancient courtship procedures: "Au bon vieulx temps que l'amour par bouquetz / Se demenoit et par joieux caquetz, / La femme estoit trop sotte ou trop peu fine. / Le temps depuis qui tout fine & affine / Luy a monstré à faire ces acquets" (*OD*, p. 129, n. 1).

53. The cuckhold's horns were to be the subject of two Renaissance mock encomia, by Remy Belleau in 1557 and by Caye Jules de Guersens, prior to 1583.

54. Synesius of Cyrene, *The Essays and Hymns of Synesius of Cyrene*, trans. and ed. Augustine Fitzgerald (London: Oxford Univ. Press, 1930), II, 243-74, "A

Eulogy of Baldness." In the Renaissance the work was usually entitled *De laudibus calvitii oratio*. A popular translation was that by John Free for Froben in Basle. It was reprinted many times between 1515 and the 1550s. Badius produced editions in Paris in 1519 and 1524. Adrien Turnèbe's Paris edition of Synesius' works dates from 1553. The Bibliothèque Nationale has a copy of this edition with manuscript notes by Théodore de Bèze and the signature of Montaigne. We can begin to understand why the encomium on baldness (often printed with Erasmus' *Moriae Encomium*) was one of those most widely cited in prefaces to Renaissance mock encomia. When translated into English, by Abraham Fleming in 1579, it was entitled *A Paradoxe, Proving by reason and example that Baldness is much better than bushie haire* (London: H. Denham).

55. This information is derived from A. Cartier, *Bibliographie des éditions*, see above, n. 1.

56. K. Kupisz, "Des Recherches," p. 80. D.B. Wilson, *Descriptive Poetry*, ch. II, also describes the more personal elements introduced into the post-Marot blasons.

57. Pierre de Ronsard, *Oeuvres complètes*, ed. Paul Laumonier (Paris: M. Didier, 1965), VI, *Le Bocage* (1554). "La Grenouille" is on p. 88, ll. 117-19: "C'est que ta vois un petit rude / N'aproche jamais de l'estude, / Ni du lit, de mon cher Belleau." For similar endings to "Le Freslon" and "Le Fourmi," see the same vol., pp. 92 and 97. Du Bellay ends the "Hymne de la Surdité" with the following ambiguous wish: "Si quelqu'un enrage / De vouloir par envie à ton nom faire oultrage / Qu'il puisse un jour sentir ta grande deité, / Pour sçavoir, comme moy, que c'est de Surdité." *Divers Jeux Rustiques*, ed. Verdun L. Saulnier, Textes Littéraires Français, 12 (Geneva: Droz, 1947), p. 188. The *Divers Jeux Rustiques* were first published in 1558.

Henri Weber

Etienne Dolet: l'énigme d'une pensée et le sens d'un combat

Etienne Dolet est mort sur le bûcher de la place Maubert le 3 août 1546 après avoir été préalablement pendu. Les livres écrits dans sa prison furent consumés avec son corps. Il était accusé "de blasphèmes et sedition et exposition de livres prohibés."[1] Le principal motif de sa condamnation paraît avoir été l'impression de livres de propagande évangélique et la saisie d'un ballot de livres plus compromettants encore, imprimés à Genève, qui lui étaient adressés. Le Parlement voyait aussi en lui un récidiviste qui avait obtenu de la part du roi des lettres de rémission pour le meurtre inexpliqué du peintre Compaing et qui avait trompé la justice en s'échappant à ses mains, lors de son transfert de la prison de Lyon vers Paris.

Cependant Dolet a aussi la réputation d'être athée et de ne pas croire en l'immortalité de l'âme. Les défenseurs d'Erasme qu'il a violemment attaqués dans son *De Imitatione ciceroniana adversus Desiderium Erasmum*, Francesco Florido et Jean Michel Odon l'affirment, l'un dans son pamphlet contre Dolet, l'autre dans une lettre.[2] Calvin en fera de même quelques années plus tard dans le *Traité des Scandales* de 1550, en associant le nom de Dolet à celui de Rabelais et de Des Périers.

Lucien Febvre nous a appris à attacher peu d'importance à ces accusations d'athéisme que les hommes de la Renaissance se lancent facilement à la tête à propos d'une querelle religieuse ou littéraire. Dolet lui-même n'accuse-t-il pas Erasme d'être secrètement luthérien, bien qu'il ait attaqué Luther?

Mais si l'on étudie soigneusement les deux volumes de ce gros dictionnaire raisonné de la langue latine que constituent les *Commentarii* publiés en 1536 et 1538, on y perçoit, sans d'ailleurs aucune trace d'athéisme, une mise en question de l'immortalité de l'âme et un ensemble d'idées voisines de celles de Pomponazzi, l'averroïste padouan mort en 1523. Dolet avait précisément étudié à Padoue, dans les années 1526-1528. L'influence de Pomponazzi y devait être encore considérable.

Comment expliquer la contradiction qui oppose ces idées à l'évangélisme modéré, certainement très distinct de la réforme luthérienne ou calviniste, qui est la principale cause de la mort de Dolet? Y a-t-il eu, comme l'a pensé O. Douen,[3] une conversion de Dolet à l'évangélisme qui se situerait autour de l'année 1539, après la publication des *Commentarii*? Dolet en choisissant l'évangélisme, n'aurait-il fait que choisir le moindre mal, comme Rabelais et Des Périers? C'est ce que suggère C.A. Mayer[4] en rappelant l'opinion de Richard Copley Christie, pour qui la cause des réformateurs est apparue à Dolet comme la cause du progrès intellectuel?

Dolet ne s'est-il fait éditeur de livres évangélistes que par intérêt commercial? Ils se vendaient bien et le bailleur de fonds de son imprimerie, Hellouin Dulin est un sympathisant de la Réforme, homme de confiance de Guillaume du Bellay.[5]

Que nous offrent les écrits de Dolet pour tenter d'apporter une réponse à cette question?

Leur interprétation reste d'autant plus difficile qu'au XVIe siècle toute affirmation religieuse dissidente, lorsqu'elle n'est pas publiée clandestinement ou à l'étranger, doit s'envelopper de prudence et de dissimulation. D'autre part, les querelles littéraires, les querelles personnelles, conduisent à faire flèche de tout bois, à utiliser des arguments qui n'expriment pas toujours les convictions de l'auteur. Il y a cependant, dans certains morceaux d'éloquence de Dolet, une flamme qui paraît témoigner de sa sincérité. Mais il est aussi prudent de se méfier de cette appréciation subjective.

Les idées exposées dans les *Commentarii* sont quelquefois l'expression directe de la pensée de Dolet, quelquefois de simples citations de Cicéron utilisées pour montrer l'emploi correct d'un mot. Il nous paraît que, même dans le second cas, le choix de la citation peut nous donner une indication sur la pensée de Dolet lui-même. En tout cas, c'est très directement que Dolet exprimant son angoisse devant la mort, ne voit pour la vaincre que l'activité qui fera vivre son nom pour la postérité: "De me sane, quod verum est, testari hic non verebor. Ne vivam, si re ulla, quam assidua mortis commentatione, et recordatione, alacrior animosiorque vel ad arma, vel ad literas reddar."[6] Il n'y a pas d'immortalité pour tous les hommes:

Gradibus vitae demonstratis, nunc ad mortem labimur, vitae extremam lineam, morituris terribilem, immortalibus vero ridiculam: id est, vel armorum gloria, vel literarum laude celebribus. Etenim animae a corpore dissolutione se ne in perpetuum interiturum putet, cui certa est post mortem in omne tempus vita, virtutis celebritate quaesita?[7]

Le mot vertu se retrouvera fréquemment sous la plume de Dolet; comme ici, il désigne l'effort et l'activité qui conduit à une juste réputation. Cette vertu qui rend immortel, elle confère par là, aux hommes qui y consacrent leurs efforts, la qualité de dieux: "Otium vero, et ignaviam complexii, quid a beluis distant? . . . At quos ad virtutis studium impellit posteritatis honos, num magis diis similes?"[8] Le caractère extrême de Dolet détruit en quelque sorte la notion traditionnelle de l'homme qui n'est ni ange ni bête, pour lui l'homme ne peut être que bête ou dieu.

Cette accession possible de certains hommes à la divinité, nous la retrouvons développée à l'article *Homo* (II, 326).

Si l'homme a la tête levée vers le ciel, c'est sans doute pour qu'il puisse connaître les dieux, mais aussi "pour accéder à la divinité." On ne peut nier qu'il y ait eu chez les Grecs des hommes de la nature des dieux comme Aristote, Platon, Démosthène en Grèce, comme Bembo et Sadolet, etc. en Italie: ". . . nihil fere diis proprium videris quod cum tantis talibusque viris maiori ex parte non commune sit."[9]

A l'article *Adscriptitius* (I, 790), Dolet utilise encore une citation du *De Natura deorum* évoquant les hommes comme Hercule, Esculape, Romulus qui ont été élevés au rang des dieux. Faut-il en conclure, comme Lucien Febvre, que Dolet est "évhémériste," juge que les dieux sont d'origine humaine et par là admire le Christ en tant qu'homme, donc participe volontiers à la diffusion de son enseignement?[10] Il y a là une hypothèse bien aventureuse; pour nous, si Dolet rapproche les hommes des dieux, c'est parce qu'ils peuvent acquérir l'immortalité par leurs travaux.

Dolet partage aussi l'opinion de Pomponazzi sur un déterminisme qui réduit le monde à un enchaînement de causes et exclut le miracle:

Fatum id appellant Latini, quod Graeci εἱμαρμένην: id est, ordinem seriemque causarum, cum causa, causae nexa, rem ex se gignat. Ea est ex omni aeternitate fluens veritas sempiterna. Quod cum ita sit, nihil est factum, quod non futurum fuerit: eodemque modo nihil est futurum cuius non causas idipsum efficientes natura contineat. Ex quo intelligitur ut fatum sit non id, quod superstitiose sed id, quod Phisice dicitur causa aeterna rerum, cur et ea quae praeterierunt facta sint et, quae instant, fiant, et quae sequuntur futura sint.[11]

A l'article *Necessitas* une citation du *De Fato* de Cicéron précise que l'enchaînement causal du destin exclut toute idée de hasard. Comme pour Pomponazzi, pour Dolet le déterminisme exclut la possiblité du miracle. A l'article *Portentum*, il se contente de citer ce passage du *De Divinatione* de Cicéron:

Nihil enim fieri sine causa potest: nec quicquam fit, quod fieri non potest: nec si id factum est, quo fieri potuit, portentum debet videri. Nulla igitur portenta sunt. Nam si, quod raro fit, id portentum putandum est, sapientem esse, portentum est.[12]

L'article *Miratio* va dans le même sens: "Causarum ignoratio in re nova mirationem facit: eadem ignoratio si in rebus usitatis est, non miramur."[13] L'article *Miraculum* se borne à une remarque purement sémantique, mais quelque peu méprisante pour le christianisme: "Quae vero Christiani digna admiratione miracula nunc dicunt, antiqui in rebus turpibus utebantur."[14]

Cependant, chez les Stoïciens partisans de ce déterminisme,[15] l'ordre de l'univers n'excluait pas mais impliquait l'idée de providence, permettait la prédiction de l'avenir et justifiait toute forme de divination. Les citations utilisées dans les articles *providus, providere, providentia*, ne permettent guère de nous éclairer sur ce point. Elles rappellent que la nature ne fait rien au hasard et pourvoit à tout ce qui peut être utile à chacun, mais évoque aussi l'opinion de philosophes parmi les plus réputés pour qui les dieux ne veillent pas seulement à l'administration de l'univers, mais aussi à la vie de chaque homme. Il y a donc place pour une vue chrétienne de la providence, sans que Dolet se prononce à ce sujet.

De même, Dolet ne suit pas Pomponazzi jusqu'à soutenir que l'enchaînement naturel des causes exclut le libre arbitre. Tout en contestant la bonne latinité de l'expression *liberum arbitrium* et en lui préférant *libera voluntas*, Dolet emprunte au *De fato* de Cicéron, deux citations qui contestent le déterminisme psychologique:

Non enim si alii ad alia propensiores sint propter causas naturales et antecedentes, idcirco etiam nostrarum voluntatum atque appetitionum sunt causae naturales et antecedentes.

Qui introducunt causarum seriem sempiternam, ij mentem hominis voluntate libera spoliatum necessitate fati devinciunt.[16]

A l'article *Fortuna*, Dolet semble partagé, même déchiré, entre son volontarisme moral et sa logique déterministe; il s'indigne qu'on ait pu faire de la Fortune une déesse:

Quasi vero non suae quisque fortunae sibi artifex sit: quanquam non negabo, praeter voluntatem nostram vel vitae nostrae institutionem, quaedam nobis persaepe accidere, quae fortunae et sorti tribuere possumus.[17]

C'est sans aucun doute à l'accident qui lui a fait tuer le peintre Compaing que songe ici Dolet, puisqu'il renvoie à l'article *Fatum* dont le développement philosophique est brusquement interrompu par l'évocation de ce meurtre (II, 1107).

On saisit ici l'interférence entre la philosophie des livres et l'expérience dramatique de la vie.

En tout cas, Dolet n'a pas, même à l'époque des *Commentarii*, partagé totalement la doctrine de Pomponazzi. C'est sur la question de l'immortalité de l'âme qu'il en est le plus proche, bien que le projet qu'il nous révèle à l'article *Pulmones* reste énigmatique. Après avoir rappelé que *anima* désigne d'abord le souffle contenu dans les poumons, il ajoute:

Praeter hanc significationem anima est nescio quid vis coelestis, qua vivimus, movemur, et rationis participes sumus. Quam nonnulli sanguinem interpretantur: nonnulli ad alias corporis partes referunt. Quam praeterea mortalem nonnulli arbitrantur, et simul cum corpore extingui: nonnulli immortalem asseverant et post extinctum corpus (ut recta, et integra: vel flagitiosa vita viventis fuerit) vel in coelum evolare, vel ad orcum deprimi. Has de animae mortalitate vel immortalitate sententias . . . discutimus iis libris qui de opinione posteritati a nobis relinquentur, ut nos plane viros vixisse intelligat, non ineptiis cruciatos elanguisse.[18]

La postérité n'a pas eu ce livre qui aurait sans doute donné réponse à nos questions. Rapprochés des articles *Mors* et *Posteritas* ou des vers de Lucrèce évoquant les vaines terreurs de châtiments après la mort, ces lignes peuvent faire penser que Dolet aurait conclu à la mortalité de l'âme, et que les inepties sont les vaines croyances.

Inversement on peut penser en opposant, suivant Platon, l'opinion à la vérité intellectuelle, estimer que les "inepties" sont les vaines discussions philosophiques, opposées à la fermeté d'une foi évangélique.

N'oublions pas que, à l'origine, l'averroïsme repose sur la distinction radicale de la raison philosophique et de la foi. Chez Pomponazzi, ceci ne paraît qu'une couverture pour développer librement des idées philosophiques contraires à la foi; il n'en est peut-être pas de même chez Dolet, si l'évangélisme est vraiment chez lui une conviction profonde.

L'*Erasmianus* publié un an avant le premier volume des *Commentarii*, en 1535, mais rédigé à peu près en même temps, contient des affirmations religieuses très nettes, mais il est difficile d'en mesurer la sincérité. En accusant Erasme d'être luthérien, c'est toute la secte luthérienne qu'il accuse: ". . . universam Lutheranorum sectam . . . accusem, qui suis commentariis et discrepantibus inter sese scriptis, Christi disciplinam vel illustrare et patefacere vel ornare ad eamque nos rapere arbitrantur."[19]

C'est vanité de croire que des commentaires humains peuvent plus que la volonté et la puissance divine. Faut-il croire que les divins auteurs nous ont laissé des écrits dont le sens est obscur et caché! Faut-il croire que sans l'*Enchiridion*, et les paraphrases des épîtres de Paul nous ne pourrions connaître le Christ? "Religionem omnem ingenua animi inductione, metu et reverentia contineri, non verbis induci, sapientibus exploratum est."[20] Qu'ont apporté à la religion les commentaires de Bucer, d'Erasme, de Melanchton, de Lambert, de Farel? Il s'ensuit

. . . ut introspectis mysteriis, quae reverebantur antea, multi iam multa negligant, vanaque et commentitia opinentur, Christi institutionem despiciant, Deum humana curare negent, animam corpori non superstitem praedicent, credantque omnia morte deleri nec ullum sensum manere.[21]

Remarquons qu'on trouve dans le *Cymbalum Mundi* de Des Périers une idée analogue: les réformateurs, par leurs discussions, ont brisé la pierre philosophale que constituait l'Evangile et, aujourd'hui, il n'est plus possible d'en retrouver le sens. Mais, il reste à interpréter les paroles mêmes de Dolet; peut-être, Dolet, rendu circonspect par son récent emprisonnement à Toulouse, feint-il de s'indigner de ce qui a été la conclusion qu'il a tirée lui-même des discussions entre réformateurs: une certaine incrédulité qui correspondait précisément aux idées des *Commentarii*? Inversement, on peut penser que, repoussant tout commentaire et toute discussion théologique, Dolet veut s'en tenir à la lettre même des *Evangiles* et des *Psaumes*, qui constituent l'essentiel de ses publications religieuses à Lyon. C'est dans ce sens qu'il serait évangélique, et même biblien. Il reste tout de même qu'il va éditer pendant cette même période une traduction de l'*Enchiridion* d'Erasme, qu'il avait attaqué dans son *Erasmianus* et un autre petit traité d'Erasme sur *Le Vray Moyen de se confesser*.

Chacun de ces petits livrets sera accompagné d'une préface d'Etienne Dolet, le premier vise les censeurs de la Sorbonne qui ont attaqué l'*Enchiridion* et proclame "que touts livres non contrevenantz à l'honneur et gloire de Dieu doibvent plus tost estre repceus que rejectés."[22] Dans le second il remarque que la confession ne doit pas se faire "seulement deux ou trois foys l'an, mais touts les jours et à toutes heures devant celluy qui congnoist et peult relever nostre infirmité. Et ce non tant par cerimonie mondaine, que pour ung vray recours que debvons avoir au consolateur des affligés, et contrits d'esperit."[23] Il s'agit donc bien de la confession directe à Dieu et non pas de la confession à un prêtre.

Ce qui est commun à l'*Erasmianus* et aux préfaces de Dolet, malgré certaines contradictions, c'est la revendication de la liberté de l'esprit, contre toute censure, d'origine religieuse ou morale. Dolet s'élève dans l'*Erasmianus* contre les moines qui jugent que dans l'étude des lettres le souci de la beauté de l'expression détourne de la pureté et de la religion: "ego literas non cultu probitatis quaeri, nec probitatis studio quemquam impediri quin literas discat et in omni doctrinae genere excellat, asserere non verebor."[24] E.V. Telle a bien montré la nouveauté de cette idée au sein du courant humaniste qui tend le plus souvent au contraire à justifier l'étude des lettres ou de l'éloquence par le service qu'elle peut rendre à la morale ou à la religion.

Lorsqu'en 1538 Dolet a obtenu, de François Ier, un privilège de 10 ans pour éditer ses propres ouvrages et donner des éditions amendées et corrigées d'autres auteurs, il expose ainsi dans la préface latine des *Catonis disticha* une sorte de programme d'édition:

sic aliquid perpetuo conandum est, quod nos literis unice inservire testetur, et in publicum Iuventutis usum non sine utilitate redundet. Id quod dum praestare laboramus, modo sermoni ornando necessaria, conscribimus (ut nostros Dictionarii Latini Tomos) modo delectationis plena fundimus (ut quatuor Epigrammatum libros) modo ad religionem informantia commentamur (ut Catonem Christianum proxime a nobis in lucem editum) modo vitae communis institutioni conducentia edolamus, integritati suae restituimus, verbosius quibusdam in locis explicamus, ut Catonis disticha.[25]

La religion entre dans ce programme, au même titre que la morale, l'agrément, ou la formation rhétorique. Il correspond à une volonté pédagogique de l'humanisme. Elle n'a pas une place privilégiée et, comme le fait remarquer Claude Longeon, l'année 1542 où Dolet multiplie les opuscules évangéliques est aussi celle où il publie *L'Amye de Court* de Lefèvre de La Borderie et *La Parfaicte Amye* d'Héroët, *L'Enfer* de Clément Marot et sa propre traduction des *Epîtres familières* de Cicéron. Constamment, dans ses préfaces, Etienne Dolet se réfère à l'utilité publique. Le changement, c'est que la gloire qu'il cherchait à obtenir par de savants ouvrages latins, il la cherche maintenant par la publication d'ouvrages français ou de traductions françaises. Aux *Commentarii linguae latinae* succède un projet d'*Orateur françois* dont il ne réalise qu'une partie.

Les humanistes ont d'abord le souci de la langue en tant qu'elle est le véhicule de la pensée comme le rappelle si justement E.V. Telle. De là, chez eux, la recherche d'un latin pur, clair, élégant, cicéronien en un mot. De là, chez Dolet l'entreprise des *Commentarii* et le combat contre Erasme qui a attaqué les cicéroniens. Mais très vite Dolet, comme d'autres, a compris qu'une véritable diffusion des connaissances passait par la langue nationale. Avant la Pléiade, il sent qu'elle peut être développée, perfectionnée, mais, en bon grammairien, ce qui lui paraît essentiel, ce sont des règles précises qui fixent sa structure encore flottante.

Le sentiment national ne sépare pas le progrès de la culture et de la langue de la personne du roi. François Ier l'a fort bien compris en se voulant protecteur des lettres. Les humanistes ne cessent de lui répéter l'importance de ce qui sera plus tard le budget de la culture et qui se résume alors en des pensions ou des bénéfices accordés aux lettrés. Un vieux lieu commun l'illustre: les exploits militaires les plus éclatants seront oubliés s'ils ne trouvent pour les transmettre à la postérité des poètes et des historiens dignes de ce nom. Dolet le répète inlassablement dans ses épîtres dédicatoires. Et il donne lui-même l'exemple en composant, d'abord en latin, puis en traduisant en français, *Les Gestes de Françoys de Valois*. Mais sa fonction d'éditeur lui confère une situation très particulière, il ne sollicite pas de pensions, mais la liberté d'imprimer; la protection du roi devrait le mettre à l'abri des censures de la Sorbonne. De là, l'importance du privilège obtenu pour dix ans, en 1538. Privilège qui n'excluait pas l'accord préalable des autorités pour l'impression. Dolet ne l'a pas entendu ainsi. Il a payé d'audace, imprimant et préfaçant des traités religieux d'Erasme censurés par la Sorbonne et l'*Enfer* de Marot qui ne pouvait que déplaire aux gens de Justice. C'est que l'édition était moins pour lui une source de profits, qu'un moyen de combat, un jeu risqué où devaient s'unir la ruse et l'audace.

Sans doute n'a-t-il pas su mesurer exactement les dangers, dans le jeu complexe des pouvoirs qui s'opposaient; Sorbonne et parlement d'un côté, le roi et ses conseillers de l'autre, avec parmi ces conseillers des influences contraires. Sans doute a-t-il cru qu'un personnage aussi puissant que Guillaume du Bellay, gouverneur du Piémont, dont le protégé Hellouin Dullin était le bailleur de fonds de l'imprimeur Dolet, pourrait garantir sa sécurité. Mais Guillaume du Bellay mourut l'année même de la dernière arrestation de Dolet, en 1543.

Comment pourtant ne pas penser qu'il fallait certaines convictions religieuses pour assumer tant de risques, même sans en connaître toute l'étendue? Un dernier élément nous éclairera-t-il sur la pensée religieuse de Dolet? Ce fameux cantique imprimé après sa mort dont on peut difficilement contester l'authenticité, bien qu'il ne soit pas non plus possible de la démontrer avec une totale certitude. Ce cantique ne confirmerait-il pas l'opinion d'un témoin de son supplice, Michel Bâris, qui écrit à Amerbach que Dolet est mort "propter Christum"?[26] Le nom du Christ n'y figure pas expressément, il est vrai, mais la philosophie suffit-elle à expliquer des strophes telles que celle-ci:

> Sus donc, esprit, laisses la chair à part
> Et devers Dieu qui tout bien nous depart
> Retirez-vous comme à vostre rempart
>   Vostre forteresse
>
> .   .   .   .
> Mais vous, esprit, qui savez la parolle
> De l'Eternel, ne suivez la chair folle
> Et en celuy qui tant nous consolle
>   Soit vostre espoir.

L'image du Dieu rempart et forteresse est fréquente dans les *Psaumes*,[27] elle est aussi dans le célèbre cantique de Luther "Ein feste Burg ist unser Gott"; "la parole de l'Eternel," c'est bien la Bible. Si, dans l'ensemble du cantique, l'opposition de la chair et de l'esprit reste essentiellement platonicienne, si la réunion de l'esprit à Dieu peut encore être considérée comme un thème néoplatonicien, même plotinien, on ne peut nier l'évangélisme de ces deux strophes.

Les épreuves de la prison, la perspective de la mort prochaine ont-elles amené Dolet à une perception plus vive du sentiment religieux, à la conviction d'une survie bien différente de celle du nom laissé à la postérité? Etait-ce vers 1538-1540 un sentiment déjà assez fort pour l'amener à la publication d'ouvrages religieux?

En tout cas, l'accent qui domine le cantique est celui d'une victoire sur soi-même, la chair, c'est ce qui inclinerait à se plaindre ou à gémir, c'est ce qui le fait entrer en rage "Destre captif sans rien avoir mesfaictz." Dieu lui donne le courage de supporter et d'être digne.

Selon une lettre de Belloni à Myconius: "Is ergo tantus vir . . . . qui mane eo quo combustus est, die contra duodecim doctores Sorbonicos disputavit nec vinci potuit."[28] N'oublions pas que parmi les livres saisis dans la maison de Dolet, après son arrestation à Lyon, il y a l'*Institution chrétienne* de Calvin en latin. La possédait-il par simple curiosité? Cette lecture avait-elle entraîné sa conviction?

Ce qui nous paraît en fin de compte dominer la vie de Dolet, c'est le sens du combat, combat qu'il inaugure dans ses discours de Toulouse en attaquant imprudemment l'intolérance des magistrats qui ont condamné Caturce au supplice et imposé à Boysonné une humiliante rétractation, combat pour Cicéron contre Erasme, combat de l'éditeur contre toutes formes de la censure, combat de l'exilé pour reconquérir la faveur du roi, combat du prisonnier contre lui-même et ses tentations de faiblesse. Ce combat a pu changer d'objectif, passer de la défense du latin cicéronien, à celle de la langue française. Il en a probablement été ainsi de la question religieuse. Si à Padoue Dolet a pu être gagné par les idées de Pomponazzi, en France il se trouve peu à peu amené à prendre parti dans le combat de l'évangélisme contre le catholicisme traditionnel; il ne peut rester indifférent, la question religieuse apparaît comme la question clef de l'époque. Presque tous les humanistes français sont partisans de l'évangélisme dans les années trente du siècle. La religion a pris ainsi peu à peu une place importante dans sa vie; jusqu'où est-il allé dans cette voie? Le cantique écrit en prison nous apporte un élément de réponse, mais il aurait fallu assister aux discussions qu'il eut avec ses juges pour en avoir une idée plus exacte.

NOTES

1. *Documents d'archives*, pp. Claude Longeon (Saint-Etienne: Publications de l'Université de Saint-Etienne, 1977), p. 75.

2. Sur tous les problèmes concernant la querelle de Dolet contre Erasme, nous utilisons l'excellente introduction d'E.V. Telle à l'*Erasmianus* de Dolet, Travaux d'Humanisme et Renaissance, 138 (Genève: Droz, 1974).

3. "Etienne Dolet, ses opinions religieuses," *Bulletin de la Société de l'Histoire du Protestantisme Français*, 30 (1881), 337.

4. "The Problem of Dolet's Evangelical Publications," *Bibliothèque d'Humanisme et Renaissance*, 17 (1955), 401.

5.Voir Cl. Longeon, *Documents d'archives*, p. 9.

6. "Certes, je ne craindrai pas d'en témoigner moi-même; que je meure, si rien ne m'aiguillonne et ne me stimule d'avantage aux armes ou aux lettres que la pensée et la méditation assidue de la mort" (Art. *Mors*, II, 1163).

7. "Les étapes de la vie tracées, nous glissons maintenant vers la mort, l'extrême limite de la vie, terrible pour ceux qui sont destinés à mourir, risible pour ceux qui sont immmortels, c'est-à-dire pour ceux que la gloire des armes ou des lettres a rendus célèbres. Car qu'il ne pense pas qu'il doive périr à jamais par la dissolution de l'âme du corps, celui à qui la certitude de la vie éternelle est assurée par la renommée qui provient de la vertu" (ibid., 1162-63).

8. "Ceux qui s'adonnent à l'oisiveté et à la paresse, en quoi diffèrent-ils des bêtes? . . . Mais ceux que la gloire posthume a conduits à l'amour de la vertu ne doivent-ils pas être estimés plus semblables à des dieux qu'à des hommes?" (Art. *Posteritas*, I, 1310). On peut rapprocher ceci d'une remarque de Pomponazzi concernant non pas la vertu ou l'activité mais l'intelligence. "Un nombre infini d'hommes semble avoir moins d'intelligence que beaucoup d'animaux" (*De Immortalitate animi*, ch. IX).

9. "Il n'y a rien de si propre aux dieux qui ne leur soit en grande partie commun avec de si grands hommes" (Art. *Homo*, II, 326).

10. "Dolet propagateur de l'Evangile," *Bibliothèque d'Humanisme et Renaissance*, 6 (1946), 98.

11. "Les Latins appellent destin ce que les Grecs appellent εἰμαρμένην: c'est-à-dire un certain enchaînement de causes liées entre elles de telle sorte que l'une produit nécessairement l'autre. C'est là qu'est contenue cette vérité éternelle qui coule de toute éternité. De sorte que rien ne s'est produit que ce qui devait se produire, de plus rien ne se produira sans que la nature en contienne dès maintenant les causes efficientes. On comprend donc que le destin c'est bien, non pas selon une formule superstitieuse, mais selon la raison physique, la cause de toute chose" (Art. *Fatum*, II, 1106-1107). Ce passage est emprunté au *De Divinatione* de Cicéron, I, LV; on le retrouve à peu près identique dans le *De Natura Deorum*.

12. "Rien ne se produit sans cause, il ne se fait rien qui ne puisse se faire. Et l'on ne peut considérer comme un prodige qu'il se soit produit ce qui devait se produire. Il n'y a donc point de prodiges car, si l'on veut considérer comme un prodige ce qui se produit rarement, un homme sage en sera un . . ." (Art. *Portentum*, I, 663).

13. "C'est l'ignorance des causes qui dans un fait nouveau provoque notre étonnement; si la même ignorance se produit dans des faits connus, alors nous ne sommes pas étonnés" (Art. *Miratio*, II, 1300).

14. "Les chrétiens appellent aujourd'hui miracles des événements qui provoquent l'admiration, les anciens utilisaient seulement ce mot dans des cas honteux" (Art. *Miraculum*, ibid.).

15. Pour expliquer "rationem reddere" (I, 683), Dolet cite un passage du *De Divinatione* de Cicéron qui se réfère à Chrysippe pour soutenir que ni les tremblements de terre, ni une pluie de sang, ni le passage d'une comète ne doivent nous effrayer, puis qu'ils ont des causes naturelles.

16. "Ce n'est pas une raison, si la diversité des inclinations provient de causes naturelles et antérieurement données, pour que nos volontés et nos désirs aussi aient

des causes naturelles et antérieurement données." "Ceux qui nous représentent une série éternelle de causes, ceux-ci enchaînent par la nécessité du destin l'esprit éternel de l'homme" (Art. *Arbitrium*, I, 806).

17. "Comme si chacun, à vrai dire, n'était pas l'artisan de sa propre fortune; je ne nierai pas pourtant qu'il nous arrive des accidents contraires à notre vie et à la direction que nous lui avons fixés, accidents que nous pouvons attribuer à la Fortune et au sort" (Art. *Fortuna*, II, 1095).

18. "Outre cette signification, *anima* est aussi je ne sais quelle force céleste qui assure en nous la vie et le mouvement, et nous fait participer à la raison. Pour certains, elle est le sang; d'autres l'assignent à d'autres parties du corps. En plus, les uns croient qu'elle est mortelle et périt avec le corps; les autres assurent qu'elle est immortelle et qu'après la destruction du corps, selon qu'elle a vécu dans la justice ou le crime, elle vole au ciel ou est plongée dans les Enfers. Nous discutons de ces idées concernant la mortalité ou l'immortalité de l'âme . . . dans un livre intitulé *De l'Opinion* que nous laissons à la postérité pour montrer que nous avons vécu en hommes véritables et que nous ne nous sommes pas laissés affaiblir et tourmenter par des inepties" (Art. *Pulmonum functionis verba*, II, 413-14).

19. "J'accuserai toute la secte luthérienne qui par ses commentaires et ses écrits en désaccord les uns avec les autres s'imagine éclaircir et illuminer ou orner la discipline chrétienne et ainsi emporter notre adhésion" (*Erasmianus*, éd. E.V. Telle, p. 35).

20. "Les sages savent que toute religion repose sur une adhésion spontanée de l'esprit, sur la crainte et la révérence, qu'on n'y est point conduit par des mots" (ibid., p. 36).

21. ". . . [qu']à partir de leurs discussions, bien des gens sont maintenant amenés à ne tenir aucun compte de beaucoup de mystères divins qu'auparavant ils respectaient, qu'ils sont amenés à les juger vains et imaginaires, à mépriser l'institution du Christ, à nier que Dieu s'occupe des choses humaines, à soutenir que l'âme ne survit pas au corps, à croire que tout est détruit par la mort et qu'aucune conscience ne nous demeure" (ibid., p. 37).

22. Etienne Dolet, *Préfaces françaises*, textes et commentaires de Claude Longeon, Textes Littéraires Français, 272 (Genève: Droz, 1979), p. 141.

23. Ibid., p. 137.

24. "Ce n'est pas par la recherche de l'intégrité morale que l'on acquiert une culture littéraire, et ce n'est pas non plus le souci de cette intégrité qui peut empêcher d'apprendre les lettres et d'exceller dans tout genre de connaissance, je ne craindrai pas de l'affirmer" (*Erasmianus*, p. 112).

25. Cité par Claude Longeon dans l'introduction aux *Préfaces françaises* de Dolet. En voici la traduction: "ainsi il nous faut toujours nous efforcer de produire ce qui témoigne que nous servons uniquement la cause des lettres, à ce qui profite abondamment à l'usage de la jeunesse non sans utilité pour tous. En travaillant à ce but, tantôt nous rédigeons ce qui est utile à l'ornement du discours (comme les tomes de notre dictionnaire latin) tantôt nous produisons des œuvres d'agrément (comme les quatre livres de nos Epigrammes), tantôt nous nous appliquons à ce qui forme la religion (comme le Caton Chrestien que nous éditons), tantôt nous façonnons ce qui est avantageux pour l'institution de la vie commune, nous le restituons dans sa forme originale ou nous l'expliquons plus en détail par quelque commentaire, comme les distiques de Caton."

26. Lettre du 5 août, 1546. *Die Amerbach Korrespondenz*, t. 6 (1967), No. 2844.

27. Cf. Ps. XVIII, 3: "Dieu, c'est mon roc, mon rempar hault & seur"; Ps. XCI, 2: "Je dis à Yaveh, tu es mon refuge et ma forteresse"; cf. aussi Ps. CXLIV, 1-2; XXI, 3-4.

28. *Die Amerbach Korrespondenz*, ibid., No. 2623 cité par Cl. Longeon, *Documents d'archives sur Etienne Dolet*, p. 79, n. 10.

TABULA GRATULATORIA

Dr. Peter Amelung
Professor Robert Aulotte
Professor William Barber
D. Bentley-Cranch
Mrs. Jean H. Bloch
Professor Guy Bourquin
Professor Barbara C. Bowen
Professor George William Brandt
Professor Frieda S. Brown
Professor Howard M. Brown
Mrs. Rozel H. Burn
Professor C.A. Burns
Miss J. Carol Chapman
Mrs. Aline Mary Clark
Dr. J.E. Clark
Professor H. Peter Clive
Dr. and Mrs. C.H. Clough
Dr. R.A. Cooper
Professor C. Dionisotti
Dr. Frank Dobbins
Miss P. Drinnan
Professor Alison Fairlie
Mr. John Farquhar
Mr. C.R. Frankish
Professor P.F. Ganz
Professor Paul Ginestier
Professor Robert Griffin

Professor Francis Higman
Miss C.M. Hill
Mr. Alan Howe
Mr. Roger Jacob
Mrs. S. Bentley-Cranch Jarvis
Mr. W.L. Jarvis
Professor P.D. and Mrs. C. Jimack
Dr. G. Jondorf
Professor Howard K. Kalwies
Dr. June E. Kane
Professor Wallace Kirsop
Mr. B. Kite
Mr. R.J. Knecht
Professor Raymond C. La Charité
Professor Annette Lavers
Madame Madeleine Lazard
Monsieur Alain Leduc
Professor Wolfgang Leiner
Monsieur François Lesure
Professor Klaus Ley
Dr. J. Linskill
Professor K. Lloyd-Jones
Professor Claude Longeon
Professor Deborah Losse
Dr. Harry Lucas
Mrs. Amelda Helen Lynch
Mr. and Mrs. Harry Lynford
Mr. Michael McCarthy
Professor I.D. McFarlane
Mr. Robert Mahoney
Dr. Sheila Mason
Mrs. D. Mayer
Mr. and Mrs. E.B. Mayer
Dr. J.D. Mills-Pont
Professor G. Mombello
Mr. Alan Morgan
Professor Kenneth Muir
Professor Glyn P. Norton

Dr. Yon Oria
Myra D. Orth
Dr. Trevor Peach
Mr. W.E. Pobjoy
Miss Jane Pratt
Dr. Malcolm Quainton
Professor David B. Quinn
Monsieur Bruno Radius
Mrs. Margarita Reeve
Dr. Catherine Reuben
Penelope Richards
Professor Hugh Richmond
Professor D.J.A. Ross
Miss E.M. Rutson
Mr. Stephen Ryle
Mrs. B.M. Sanderson
Professor R. Scheurer
Professor Isidore Silver
Dr. C.N. Smith
Dr. Pauline M. Smith
Professor L. Sozzi
Dr. J.J. Supple
Professor Marcel Tetel
Dr. Annette H. Tomarken
Dr. Hilary M. Tomlinson
Dr. Philip Tomlinson
Dr. J. Trethewey
Mrs. Heather Vose
Dr. David H. Walker
Professor Henri Weber
Annwyl Williams
Professor Mary Beth Winn
Miss L.A. Zaina
Mrs. C.M. Zsuppan

Libraries, Institutions, Booksellers

Bibliothèque de l'Université de Reims, France
Bibliothèque Nationale, Paris, France
Brotherton Library, University of Leeds, England
Brynmor Jones Library, University of Hull, England
Centre for Reformation and Renaissance Studies, Victoria University Library, Toronto, Ontario, Canada
Diffusione Edizioni Anglo-Americane, Milan, Italy
Editions Ophrys, Paris, France
Fondren Library, Rice University, USA
Grant & Cutler Ltd, London, England
John Rylands University Library of Manchester, England
Library, Chester College, Chester, England
Library, College of St. Paul and St. Mary, Cheltenham, Glos., England
Library, Gonville and Caius College, Cambridge, England
Library, King's College, London, England
Library, Miami University, USA
Library, Pennsylvania State University, USA
Library, Princeton University, USA
Library, Queen Mary College, London, England
Library, Royal Holloway College, London, England
Library, St. David's University College, Lampeter, Wales
Library, Trinity College, Hartford, CT, USA
Library, University College, London, England
Library, University College of Swansea, Wales
Library, University of Waterloo, Canada
Library, University of Winnipeg, Canada
Library, Wake Forest University, USA
Library, Westfield College, London, England
Musée Historique de la Réformation, Geneva, Switzerland
Musée National des Thermes et de l'Hôtel de Cluny, Paris, France
Museo Civico, Piacenza, Italy
Museum Slaskie, Wroclaw, Poland
Queen Mother Library, University of Aberdeen, Scotland
Seminarium Philologiae Humanisticae, Katholieke Universiteit, Leuven, Belgium

John Smith & Son (Glasgow) Ltd, Scotland
Starkmann Library Services Ltd, London, England
Stephen Chan Library of Fine Arts, New York University, USA
Sydney Jones Library, University of Liverpool, England
University of Birmingham Library, Birmingham 15, England
University of Dundee Library, Scotland
University of Durham Library, England
University of East Anglia Library, England
University of Exeter Library, England
University of Glasgow Library, Scotland
University of Lancaster Library, England
University of Leicester Library, England
University of Nottingham Library, England
University of St. Andrews Library, Scotland
University of Southampton Library, England
University of Sussex Library, England
University of Waikato Library, Hamilton, New Zealand
University of Warwick Library, England
Vrije Universiteit, Amsterdam, Holland

INDEX

(Excluded from this index are personifications, place names, and names occurring in minor references in the notes.)

FRENCH FORUM MONOGRAPHS

27. Donald M. Frame and Mary B. McKinley, eds. *Columbia Montaigne Conference Papers.* 1981.
28. Jean-Pierre Dens. *L'Honnête Homme et la critique du goût: Esthétique et société au XVIIe siècle.* 1981.
29. Vivian Kogan. *The Flowers of Fiction: Time and Space in Raymond Queneau's* Les Fleurs bleues. 1982.
30. Michael Issacharcff et Jean-Claude Vilquin, éds. *Sartre et la mise en signe.* 1982.
31. James W. Mileham. *The Conspiracy Novel: Structure and Metaphor in Balzac's* Comédie humaine. 1982.
32. Andrew G. Suozzo, Jr. *The Comic Novels of Charles Sorel: A Study of Structure, Characterization and Disguise.* 1982.
33. Margaret Whitford. *Merleau-Ponty's Critique of Sartre's Philosophy.* 1982.
34. Gérard Defaux. *Le Curieux, le glorieux et la sagesse du monde dans la première moitié du XVIe siècle: L'exemple de Panurge (Ulysse, Démosthène, Empédocle).* 1982.
35. Doranne Fenoaltea. *"Si haulte Architecture." The Design of Scève's* Délie. 1982.
36. Peter Bayley and Dorothy Gabe Coleman, eds. *The Equilibrium of Wit: Essays for Odette de Mourgues.* 1982.
37. Carol J. Murphy. *Alienation and Absence in the Novels of Marguerite Duras.* 1982.
38. Mary Ellen Birkett. *Lamartine and the Poetics of Landscape.* 1982.
39. Jules Brody. *Lectures de Montaigne.* 1982.
40. John D. Lyons. *The Listening Voice: An Essay on the Rhetoric of Saint-Amant.* 1982.
41. Edward C. Knox. *Patterns of Person: Studies in Style and Form from Corneille to Laclos.* 1983.
42. Marshall C. Olds. *Desire Seeking Expression: Mallarmé's "Prose pour des Esseintes."* 1983.
43. Ceri Crossley. *Edgar Quinet (1803-1875): A Study in Romantic Thought.* 1983.
44. Rupert T. Pickens, ed. *The Sower and His Seed: Essays on Chrétien de Troyes.* 1983.
45. Barbara C. Bowen. *Words and the Man in French Renaissance Literature.* 1983.
46. Clifton Cherpack. *Logos in Mythos. Ideas and Early French Narrative.* 1983.
47. Donald Stone, Jr. *Mellin de Saint-Gelais and Literary History.* 1983.
48. Louisa E. Jones. *Sad Clowns and Pale Pierrots: Literature and the Popular Comic Arts in 19th-Century France.* 1984.
49. JoAnn DellaNeva. *Song and Counter-Song: Scève's* Délie *and Petrarch's* Rime. 1983.
50. John D. Lyons and Nancy J. Vickers, eds. *The Dialectic of Discovery: Essays on the Teaching and Interpretation of Literature Presented to Lawrence E. Harvey.* 1984.
51. Warren F. Motte, Jr. *The Poetics of Experiment: A Study of the Work of Georges Perec.* 1984.
52. Jean R. Joseph. *Crébillon fils. Economie érotique et narrative.* 1984.
53. Carol A. Mossman. *The Narrative Matrix: Stendhal's* Le Rouge et le Noir. 1984.
54. Ora Avni. *Tics, tics et tics. Figures, syllogismes, récit dans* Les Chants de Maldoror. 1984.
55. Robert J. Morrissey. *La Rêverie jusqu'à Rousseau. Recherches sur un topos littéraire.* 1984.
56. Pauline M. Smith and I.D. McFarlane, eds. *Literature and the Arts in the Reign of Francis I. Essays Presented to C.A. Mayer.* 1985.